Gender and Power in Affluent Asia

The modernising and globalising of East and Southeast Asia have been systematically gendered processes. In this book detailed case studies of China, Indonesia, Thailand, Malaysia, Singapore and the Philippines explore such changes in depth.

The contributors to this study argue for a focus on the reworkings of the 'public' and 'private' in order to understand the development of new affluence, middle-class values and indeed modernity in the region. The volume is especially concerned with the links between femininities, public and private spheres and the changing shapes of class and nation in the countries examined.

Gender and Power in Affluent Asia shows the importance of women's agency in transforming economies and ideologies. It also reveals the costs of authoritarianism and development borne by women, and the contradictory searches for new forms of autonomy through political action, intimacy and the juggling of 'work' and 'home'.

Krishna Sen is Senior Lecturer in Communication Studies at Murdoch University. **Maila Stivens** is Associate Professor and Director of Women's Studies at the University of Melbourne.

The New Rich in Asia Series
Edited by Richard Robison

The New Rich in Asia: Mobile Phones, McDonalds and Middle-class Revolution
Edited by Richard Robison and David S.G. Goodman

Political Oppositions in Industrialising Asia
Edited by Gary Rodan

Gender and Power in Affluent Asia

Edited by
Krishna Sen and Maila Stivens

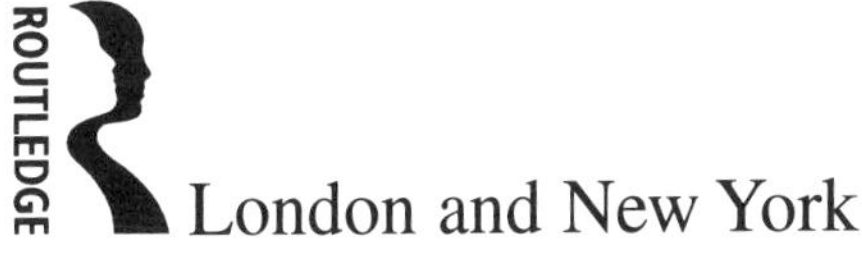

London and New York

This book is a project of the Asia Research Centre, Murdoch University, Western Australia

First published 1998 by Routledge
11 New Fetter Lane, London EC4P 4EE

Simultaneously published in the USA and Canada
by Routledge
29 West 35th Street, New York, NY 10001

Typeset in Times by
J&L Composition Ltd, Filey, North Yorkshire
Printed in Great Britain by T.J. International Ltd, Padstow, Cornwall

British Library Cataloguing in Publication Data
A catalogue record for this book is available from the British Library

Library of Congress Cataloging in Publication Data

Gender and power in affluent Asia/Krishna Sen and Maila Stivens.
p. cm. — (The new rich in Asia)
Includes bibliographical references and index.
ISBN 0–415–16471–0 (hb : alk. paper). — ISBN 0–415–16472–9 (pb : alk. paper)
1. Women—Asia, Southeast—Social conditions. 2. Women—Asia, Southeast—Economic conditions. 3. Women in development—Asia, Southeast. 4. Middle class—Asia, Southeast. 5. Middle class women—Asia, Southeast. 6. Sex role—Asia, Southeast.
I. Sen, Krishna. II. Stivens, Maila. III. Series.
HQ1745.8.G45 1998
305.42′0959—dc21 97–27163
CIP

Contents

Figures

Tables

Notes on contributors

Nerida Cook lectures in the department of Sociology and Social Work at the University of Tasmania, having previously taught at Monash University. She has researched extensively in Thailand, with her most recent project looking at changes in sexual and gender identities among women in the country.

Stephanie Fahey is Professor and head of the department of Asian Studies and Languages at Victoria University of Technology in Melbourne. Since 1990 she has been engaged in research on contemporary socio-economic change in Vietnam, focussing on the 'hidden economy', changes in labour relations, and the history of trade unions, with specific emphasis on women.

Beverley Hooper is Professor of Asian Studies at the University of Western Australia. She is the author of *Youth in China* and *China Stands Up: Ending the Western Presence, 1948–1950* and joint editor, with David Goodman, of *China's Quiet Revolution: New Interactions between State and Society*. She is currently researching the gender implications of the growth of consumerism in China on a grant from the Australia Research Council.

Anne E. McLaren is Senior Lecturer and co-ordinator of the Chinese programme, Department of Asian Studies, La Trobe University, Melbourne, Australia. She is the author of *The Chinese Femme-fatale, Chinese Popular Culture and Chantefables of the Ming Period* and co-editor of *Female Matters: the Construction of the Chinese Woman.*

Nirmala PuruShotam is Lecturer in the Department of Sociology at the National University of Singapore. She holds a Masters degree from the Tata Institute of Social Sciences, Bombay, India and a PhD from the National University of Singapore. She is currently finalising a book, *Language Negotiations and Ethnic Constructions: The Case of Singapore*.

Kathryn Robinson is a Senior Fellow in Anthropology at the Research School of Pacific and Asian Studies, Australian National University. She is the author of *Stepchildren of Progress: The Political Economy of Development in an Indonesian Mining Town* as well as many articles. Her most recent research is looking at authorised models of femininity, women migrant workers and regional identity expression in architecture in Indonesia.

Mina Roces is Senior Lecturer in History at Central Queensland University. Her doctoral research was on *Kinship Politics in Post-War Philippines: The Lopez Family 1945–1989* (Michigan). She is the author of *Woman, Power and Kinship Politics in Post-War Philippines* (forthcoming) and has published articles in *Modern Asian Studies, Asian Studies Review and LILA: Asia Pacific Women's Studies Journal*.

Krishna Sen is Senior Lecturer in Communication Studies and Women's Studies at Murdoch University. She is the author of *Indonesian Cinema: Framing the New Order*. Her research on Indonesian media, drawing on feminist perspectives, has been published extensively in edited volumes and journals.

Maila Stivens is Director of Women's Studies at the University of Melbourne. Her main publications include *Why Gender Matters in Southeast Asian Politics* (editor), *Malay Peasant Women and the Land* (with Jomo Sundaram and Cecilia Ng), and *Matriliny and Modernity: Sexual Politics and Social Change in Rural Malaysia*. Her most recent research has explored public, private and modernities in Southeast Asia.

Preface

This book was conceived in 1994 – in a period when the Asian Dragons, Tigers and NICs were growing faster than ever. The phenomenal rise of East and Southeast Asian economic power was frequently presented as the panacea for the ills of the West and East alike. But the picture always appeared a little cloudier to those of us who saw the process as a gendered one and who did not want to forget that citizens everywhere – even in a period of 9 per cent growth – remain divided by class and sex.

We were therefore always cautious about Asia's enthusiastic embrace of capitalist modernity. For sure, modernisations and globalisations had opened up certain kinds of options for women in many of the nations we were looking at – more designer and 'high-street' middle-class clothes and cosmetics, more well-paid jobs and more language within which to lay claims for women's rights. But the same clothes and cosmetics that liberated the Chinese woman's body from the drab communist uniform also reshaped that body as an object of display, selling everything from calendars to computers. The business opportunities that have allowed the Vietnamese woman to earn more than her husband are the other face of the policies undermining free health care, child care and access to education. The vocabulary of gender equality mobilised by Thai and Indonesian women also reinvented class contradictions between middle-class urban women and their working-class and rural sisters.

These ambivalences, which run through the volume, do not, however, align us with the nationalist discourses espoused by Asian political leaders: these discourses construct women as the repository of national–traditional values, underscore 'Asian' women's domesticity and asexuality and ultimately privilege the male as the national subject. Indeed, we have seen this posing of an opposition between tradition and modernity as both pervasive and problematic. On the one hand, we find 'traditions' fabricated within national discourses as an antidote to the perceived excesses of 'outside' westoxifying influences, as in Malaysia. On the other hand, Chinese and Vietnamese women are reviving, rediscovering and recomposing past cultural forms and performance practices even as their countries open their economies, media and culture to global modernities.

What, then, are the symbols, codes and icons of affluent, powerful, global, and modern, if not post-modern, femininity in Asia? We might call this the cover story, since the problem of 'representing' contemporary Asian women came to the fore as we sorted through images for the cover of this book. Could we have an Asian woman on the cover without objectifying the feminine, and feminising the Asian? And what in any case would mark the intersections between Asia and the world, between class and gender, between power, affluence and femininity with which we were concerned?

We were comfortable with the image suggested by our Routledge editor Vicky Smith of a female hand holding a mobile phone. It spoke to metaphors of many kinds: the hand that rocks the cradle talks to the world! To us, with our knowledges of some (but not all) Asian societies, that image invoked mobility, global connections, affluence, even power – telephony as the quintessential signifier of modern communications in the hands of an Asian woman.

When we showed the cover to a China Studies colleague, however, she pointed out that in urban mainland China the cover would most likely be interpreted as picturing a prostitute. Only successful business**men**, and women who sell sex, carry such devices – or at least that is the popular belief. The icon of power and affluence in Southeast Asia becomes in the hands of a woman in China the site of contravention of law, morality and authority. This is emblematic of the double-edged relationship between femininity and modernity that we have been trying to tease out here. And it points to an issue of which we were only too aware throughout the course of working on this volume: all symbols, even signifiers, however global their circulation, make sense differently in different contexts. In other words, though the message or image may be global, most of its consumers live in a specific place at a specific historical moment. Global modernities do not mean the same thing in the same way to all women and men in Asia. We hope we have been able to understand some of these contradictory interpellations of East and Southeast women into transnational economies, cultures and communications.

This book was written at a critical distance from the high optimism about Asian economies in the early 1990s. It is going to press at a time of serious doubt about Asia's economic and hence political future. The

Thai financial crisis has spread to neighbouring countries and on to South Korea; Indonesian forests have been burning out of control for months; Indonesian President Suharto has requested more repressive powers from the Legislative Assembly; and Malaysian Prime Minister Mahathir is resorting to increasingly nationalist rhetoric about global markets. It is too early to predict what the fall-out will be from these recent events and to say what share of the burden of change will fall on women. One thing is certain, however: men and women will fare differently. If feminism is to have a global face and future, it will need to ensure that Asia is not marginalised yet again from theory and practice, as the malestream multinationals, governments and academics associated with them lose interest in an Asia that no longer appeals so strongly to the market.

Krishna Sen

Acknowledgments

This book is the third in the New Rich Series arising out of the project on emerging social forces in Asia based in the Asia Research Centre at Murdoch University. The major focus of the series is the analysis of the newly emerging classes of East and Southeast Asia (South Asia is not included in the brief of the project).

We wish to thank the Asia Research Centre at Murdoch University for its financial and administrative support. We are grateful to Professor Richard Robison for his encouragement and suggestions in formulating this project, and to Del Blakeway for helping organise the conference in February 1995 which brought together the contributors to this volume. Thanks especially to Helen Bradbury, Mandy Miller and Ruth Stone for creating a readable manuscript out of computer disks, printouts and anxious editorial notes! Thanks are also due to Doug Steley of the Educational and Media Section, Central Queensland University, who photographed the magazines for Figures 10.1 and 10.2. We also wish to thank Victoria Smith, our editor at Routledge, for all her help and support.

Finally, this book is dedicated to all those women who enriched our view of the world by letting us into their worlds, theories and their juggles and struggles.

NOTE ON THE ILLUSTRATIONS

While every effort has been made to trace the copyright holders of the illustrations used in this book, this has not been possible in every case. The publisher would be pleased to hear from anyone with information regarding the original copyright holders of these illustrations.

1 Theorising gender, power and modernity in affluent Asia

Maila Stivens

This book is about women, new money and power in East and Southeast Asia. We do not aim simply to analyse the 'effects' on women of the dramatic economic and social changes sweeping the region, or to add women to the many mainstream accounts of these changes that so persistently exclude them. Instead, we hope to show that the modernising and globalising of Asia have been systematically gendered processes. The collection of articles presented here aims to document and analyse some of the relationships between gender and the shifts of power accompanying Asia's new affluence[1] by concentrating on the reworkings of 'public' and 'private'. We are particularly interested in the contests around the links between femininities, public and private spheres and the changing shapes of class and nation in the countries examined. We have two central themes: first, that gender relations are central to the making of middle classes and modernity in the region and, second, that representations of gender occupy a central place in the contests about meanings and identities accompanying these processes.

Our main objective is to open up a series of questions about the links between gender, modernity and globalisation in the region. This is not meant to be a textbook on 'Asian women', but an intervention into debates within both mainstream social science about the region and feminist debates about women's place in 'development'. Indeed, one of our main aims is to break down the category 'Asian woman', most explicitly along class lines. This introduction is an attempt to clarify the analytical aims of the volume by placing its concerns within the academic debates to which it speaks. It is organised around feminist interactions with four areas of academic discourse: the 'new rich'/affluent Asia; modernity and globalisation; class and state; and, finally, 'positionalities', that is, the arguments about who has the right to make knowledges about whom/what.

GENDERING AFFLUENT ASIA

The booming economies of Asia have assumed a prominent place in global imaginings about the future of the world. Multiplying images of Asian modernities abound: of astonishing economic and urban growth; of remarkable change in social indicators like falling mortalities and rising income and levels of education; of massive consumption in huge postmodern shopping malls; of business hoping for instant riches; and of activists hoping for outbreaks of democracy among new middle classes. But such optimism is also tempered with stories about the costs of so-called 'development': the widening gaps between rich and poor; continuing human rights violations; scams and alleged corruption; the links between authoritarian, technocratic oligarchy and development; the costs of massive urbanisation with choking air pollution, traffic jams and continuous power brownouts and blackouts; the impact of globalising incorporation and new electronic technologies; and, of central interest here, a whole set of strongly voiced social anxieties across the region focussing on issues of 'family' and 'culture' – especially the 'Asian Family' and 'Asian values', women's place and women's sexuality.

In the flurry of writing about the new rich and the newly affluent of Asia, astonishingly little attention has been paid to gender relations in contemporary East and Southeast Asia. This exclusion is intriguing, given that anxieties about gender relations seem to be a central feature of many Asian leaders' pronouncements about the future and of some of the principal cultural contests in the region. There is much prophesying about globalisation, especially about the profound shifts in society and values that increasing affluence and indeed virtual realities will produce. The next century, we are told, will be the Asian century. It is striking how rapidly the leaders of the various countries have incorporated 'globalisation' into their core rhetoric about the Asian road to modernity, which is often implicitly or explicitly anti-Western. But this critique of the West is not aimed at the economic, the streams of globalised capital flowing through the region. Rather, 'culture' is the problem: the 'Asian Family' and 'Asian Values' will be the way for the region's states to negotiate the next century and millennium. Economy and culture are thus segmented from each other. In its most developed form an anti-Western discourse of '*westoxification*', which sees all things western as toxic, has become part of official state ideology. Thus, as our chapters on Malaysia, China and Singapore show, these countries are to avoid the 'excesses' of western culture as they steer a path through new prosperity. While the nature of work is transformed by industrial capitalist expansion orchestrated by the state, and by the large-scale entry of women into paid employment in the 'modern' sector, leaders extol the virtues of the Asian Family and Asian Values. The Asian path to modernity is to be made in the Asian Family and is implicitly women's work.

We are interested, therefore, in conceptualising the links between gender and modernity and globalisation. Does it matter if women and gender are marginalised in and excluded from academic accounts of regional developments? What happens if we bring women's (and children's) experiences of modernity into an account of these transformations? What kinds of theories of society and social change have writers operated with at all levels, from the academic to the common sense, that allowed them to exclude issues of gender? What happens if we leave men's experiences as gendered subjects out of the story as well? And how do we negotiate the pitfalls of 'positionalities', given the difficulties in reconstructing theory within a world dominated by Euro-American scholarship?

Our argument that politics in its widest sense is made in the kitchens, living rooms, bedrooms, workplaces and malls of Asia as well as in the stock exchanges and parliamentary chambers is scarcely a new one for feminists and other social theorists, even if it is still resisted by political scientists (cf. Pettman 1996). As John Gledhill, among others, has argued, political science places excessive emphasis on the state, formal political institutions of government and the centralisation of power. Quoting Abélès (1992: 17), he suggests that we need instead to appreciate the multilayered complexity of political reality: this includes political action in everyday life and the symbols and rituals associated with everyday political actions; the concretisation of 'political culture' occurs at the point where power is affirmed and contested in social practice (1994: 22).

Our main theme links gender and the making of affluent classes by focussing on the reworkings of so-called public and private spheres, especially the reworkings of ideologies of 'family' and 'domesticity' and their relationship to women's work outside the home. We need, however, to clarify our use of the 'private'. Feminist scholars in Euro-America have successfully dissected a whole body of western thinking about 'politics' and 'power', showing just how masculinist Western political discourse has been.[2] They have been especially critical of political thought's division of society into fixed domains of 'public' and 'private', treated as if they were universal, real social spaces (see Moore 1988). While the two spheres have been seen as varying historically within mainstream thought (Elshtain 1981), this conceptualisation has generally ideologically relegated women to a private, invisible domain outside politics, where their roles as biological reproducers and domestic labourers are assumed to keep them from any larger role in society.[3] The effect is to marginalise and trivialise what are seen as women's concerns, with little exploration of the circumstances under which both men and women may become gendered political subjects. The malestream public/private division is also highly ethnocentric, reflecting ideas about gender divisions formed and elaborated within the development of Western modernity.

Western feminists in the 1970s hoped that an understanding of the 'private' sphere, especially domesticity, would provide the key to understanding women's oppression. Rosaldo (1974), for example, saw women as universally located and subordinated in a private, domestic sphere, although she later questioned its universality (1980). Some Radical and Cultural feminists promoted the private not as the source of women's oppression but as the site of the good, nurturant essential, feminine outside of polluting male power. But other increasingly critical feminist responses have ranged from prescriptions for restructuring the two realms politically to a rejection of such a dichotomy.[4] Feminists have pointed to the multiple and shifting connections between the 'private' realm of the household and/or family and sexuality on the one hand and the market and state on the other. Thus, what has been defined as 'private', like sexualities, has in fact been increasingly politicised in the modern era.[5] Indeed, some suggest that in a post-modern world such dualities are collapsing completely. Private spheres throughout contemporary Asia, we contend, are constantly shifting, being reworked and redefined by economic, political and ideological forces, and the aim of the chapters here is to document and analyse some of these shifts. The construction of these supposedly private spheres has been a very public process in which state, economy and religion have all played extensive parts.

A main argument of the volume, then, is that domesticity and households in their varied forms are crucial sites for producing middle classness. We have found the work of the feminist historians Leonore Davidoff and Catherine Hall on the nineteenth-century English middle class very useful (1987). Their study shows how the processes creating a new middle class were thoroughly gendered, especially the construction of a domestic ideology and its constant reworkings. Their principal argument is that class and gender always operate together – consciousness of class always takes a gendered form. Seeking to dissolve the public/private divide, they argue that men who sought to be someone were in fact embedded in networks of familial and female support which underpinned their rise to public prominence (1987: 13). They conclude that the language of class formation was gendered and that manliness

and femininity were constantly being challenged, tested and reworked both in imagination and in the encounters of daily life (p.450).

In drawing on Davidoff and Hall's study we do not mean to evade the vast historical and social differences between nineteenth-century Europe and what we can call the neo-modernities of Asian consumer culture. Indeed, in some ways the issues surrounding domestic relations in affluent Asia could not be more different: the situation of women working outside the home is a key issue in the present-day reworkings of the domestic within the globalising new orders of the region. Professional women frequently have domestic helpers, either paid servants or dependent relatives; other 'working' women without servants have an exhausting double day; and only a section of the middle classes seems to espouse the housewife role, one often supported by servants. Nonetheless, Davidoff and Hall's central argument theorising the links between domestic relations and middle class formation is methodologically most instructive.

The contributors share an interest in the ways these reworkings of the 'private' link to wider changes. In particular, they explore the relationship the contests around the private have to the ever-growing consumption that is part and parcel of the new affluence. We see consumption as a pivotal concept to use in thinking about the place of gender in the new affluence. Jonathan Friedman notes the 'spectacular' aspects of capitalist consumption, based on the desire for new identities and accompanying strategies that render any particular set of consumer-based distinctions obsolete after relatively short periods of stability (1990: 313) (see also de Grazia 1996). In other words, consumption is central to the constant search for and the construction of the 'new', including new identities, that is the hallmark of modernity and postmodernity. While he does not look at gendered aspects of consumption, his argument about linking market and identity can be usefully appropriated by feminists trying to think about gender and globalisation in affluent Asia: household consumption patterns provide a way of tying gender directly into theorising the connections between macro-level global processes and local complexities and specificities. In particular, the development of elaborate new femininities based on the consumer/wife/mother and the consumer/beautiful young woman in the region can be seen as central to the very development of these burgeoning economies. For example, Stephanie Fahey in Chapter 8 quotes Pelzer's comment about beauty contests signalling to the world that Vietnam is open for business (1993), a theme that resonates through a number of the chapters. In questioning the nature of the 'identification of femininity, of the female sex, of womankind generally with sumptuary laws, shopping sprees and domestic display' de Grazia notes that acts of consumption and exchange in Western societies 'have long been obsessively gendered, usually as female' (1996: 1). In globalising Asia, this identification is no less gendered, and no less female.

Both state and other areas of national-level discourse in the Asian region explicitly deploy ideas of private and public which closely resemble the Western model, albeit with some local inflections. It would be easy to see this as a product of globalisation, given the long engagement with colonial and post-colonial ideologies within the world system. Nonetheless, the effects of the rapidly circulating images of private and public within the global media in the region cannot be underestimated. Some household forms in the booming urban areas of the region's cities have indeed come to resemble the monolithic private sphere of Western modernity. But as several chapters show, many images of the domestic circulate, and are best understood as products of highly specific local developments. Media attention to the problems of 'working' women and the juggling of everyday lives suggests some permeability of the public/private divide. Moreover, as we argue, the form of the so-called private sphere is very much the site of a series of contests throughout the region. What should family life be like in these brave new worlds? How much should it be like the West, and how much should it distance itself?

These contests around the 'private' are especially acute in the area of changing subjectivities. The contributors document some of the widespread cultivation of 'modern' ideas about intimacy, the individual and the interpersonal within the region. Books, magazines and newspapers (and to a much lesser extent the broadcast media) impart reams of advice about psychological well-being and interpersonal relations. These developments herald the growth of thoroughly modern subjectivities and a seemingly globalised elaboration of the domestic and the personal, which is welcomed by some, disparaged by others. Nirmala PuruShotam, for example, shows that in Singapore this is allied to a regime of bodily improvement and indulgence, with marketing outlets for cosmetics, clothes and gyms to match. It is no novelty to argue that the growing desire for and consumption of goods from the global marketplace can crudely structure corresponding subjectivities. The reception and processing of messages about family, love and sexuality from the same marketplace, however, point to a much more dialectical and contested process. The forms of emerging subjectivities within these complex scenarios is an issue for several of the chapters.

In Chapter 4 on Malaysia, based on anthropological research into the middle classes, I suggest that current reworkings of domestic ideology

and practice are key aspects of the cultural production of 'new' Malay middle classness economically, politically and culturally. They are also a key site for the expression of ambivalence around Malaysian modernity, especially the concern within the Islamic revivalism popular among the new Malay middle classes with the effects of modernity on women's behaviour. Contests around the remade 'private' spaces of Malaysian modernity are predominant issues for these middle classes in particular, with frequent debate in the media about the pressures and costs of juggling work and home, the nature of Muslim family life and law, proper and good Malay and Asian families and lifestyles. It is argued that an exploration of gender relations provides important ways to theorise the interplay between consumer capitalist culture, economy, polity and religious practice in the country.

Nirmala PuruShotam's chapter on doing middle class in Singapore (Chapter 5) also looks at the ways in which domesticity and consumption are crucial in constructing new middle classness. She emphasises the hard (and mostly invisible) work by women that goes into reproducing a middle-class way of life for themselves and their families. That way of life, she argues, is structured with reference to major texts/background knowledge which are common to most Singaporeans, a 'fear of falling'. This fear, which other writers on Singapore like Chua Beng Huat have noted (1995), places on women the burdens of reproducing a way of life that is at once about the better life and about their subordination. Even while it imprisons them, she suggests, this way of life gives women access to a body of knowledge that can bring about a questioning of their subordination. She traces the working of these 'texts' in consumption practices, in the ideology of the normal family, and within feminist alternatives.

Krishna Sen takes up similar themes in her chapter on middle-class women in New Order Indonesia (Chapter 2). She notes that most people working on issues of women and gender in Indonesia have pointed in one way or another to the construction of 'woman' primarily as reproductive mother rather than as productive worker. She shows, however, that through the last decade, both state policy and media texts have been redefining the 'Indonesian woman' as a working woman. But this 'new' woman, she argues, is constructed largely within a middle-class imaginary and implicitly excludes working class and rural women.

Kathryn Robinson's work on provincial Soroako on the island of Sulawesi (Chapter 3) suggests that women, even middle-class women, outside the Indonesian metropoles are largely constructed within a domestic/maternal frame. She argues that in Indonesia's emerging capitalist order, women's 'producer selves' are represented not only by their entry into paid work, but also by the reframing of their sexuality/fertility in terms of the rationalising doctrine of family planning. The ideal mother produces two well-spaced, healthy and well-educated children, who take their place as productive workers and loyal Indonesian citizens. In relation to their consumer selves, women's sexuality is subjected to the pressures of consumption, which take the form of exhortations to romantic love in a Western mode. This can be seen to incorporate discursive elements of the marketplace. The chapter looks at the tensions between these two tendencies and their implications for the reconstitution of femininity in contemporary Indonesia.

While both Sen and Robinson see the recomposition of femininity in Indonesia as drawing its force from the imperatives of globalisation, the difference in the descriptive content of their chapters is striking evidence of our fundamental assumption in this book: that the differential articulation of the region into global capitalist modernities prevents any generalisations about gender regimes even within the borders of a particular nation-state. Thus, while the middle-class professional woman of Sen's chapter sheds aspects of her domesticity, the wife of the mining worker in Robinson's chapter adopts an increasingly elaborate housewife form, modelled on the bosses' wives from the big city.

Beverley Hooper's chapter looking at the re-creation of femininity and its commercialisation in contemporary China provides yet another account of an Asian engagement in the global market (Chapter 6). She sees the new images of women as one of the most visible manifestations of the growth of consumerism. The move from austerity to consumer ethics has had a powerful impact on women in China. She considers the implications of these developments for women, examining the creation and manipulation of women's desires in their roles both as gendered subjects within consumer society and as sexualised objects of consumption. Charting the development of femininities from the revolution, she tracks the imposition of defeminised appearance and behaviour for women, the 1980s' 'pin-ups', beauty contests and the development of an elaborated housewife form. Exploring both these issues and the shifts in official ideology to a closer emphasis on 'family', she asks how far we can see some convergence between Chinese and Western patterns of consumer culture.

Stephanie Fahey's account of changes in the cultural images and social position of women in post-revolutionary Vietnam (Chapter 8) has, as we might expect, similarities with Hooper's account of China. In Vietnam, too, economic renovation and globalisation have produced a rampant growth in consumerism and an associated emphasis on household rather than communal, cooperative or state ownership. Women,

Fahey suggests, have been caught in a variety of ways in these changes. They have lost formal employment but have increased participation in petty commodity trade and commodity production. Renovation has also generated a complex of conflicting images, from the business woman who earns more than her husband to the demi-goddess who might bless one with profits and male children. Based mainly on observation of the emerging middle class in the north, the chapter suggests that Vietnamese women's response to economic renovation is mediated by the nation's history of revolutionary war and by older cultural practices that survived the war and communist legislation to be reconstituted in the present.

DIVERGENT MODERNITIES AND GLOBALISATION

To explore the links the links between gender, the public and private and the new affluence we need to look at the issues involved in theorising gender's relationships with modernity and globalisation in the region. We suggest that both an Asianist and a feminist reading of some of these debates can radically unsettle wider understandings of the modernisation process, an unsettling which is intensified when the readings are combined (see Stivens 1994b).

As Anthony King argues, any discussion of modernity until recently has necessarily been a Western discourse, with Western labels, concepts, periodisations and categories (King 1991: 154).[6] Central concepts such as westernisation, modernisation, development and tradition have been deployed in ways that frequently erase the history and the specificities of the non-Western world.[7] Moreover, models of development have often assumed that the rest of the world will follow a trajectory close to that of industrialisation in the West as part of a worldwide, global, universalised pattern of modernisation, or indeed Westernisation.[8] Even when such work acknowledges the specificities of the non-Western world, it often presumes an inevitable convergence between 'Western' and 'Eastern' patterns (cf. Robison and Goodman 1996). As Pieterse notes, the modernity/globalisation couple is frequently another term for 'westernisation', with an assumption that the process begins in and emanates from Europe and the West (1995: 46).[9]

Johann Arnason has pointed out in relation to Japan that a move to the more concrete in thinking about modernity can play a significant role in destabilising the category 'modern' (1987), allowing for the conceptualisation of divergent and multiple modernities within a globalising whole (Kahn 1993). Some recent critical theory has suggested we need to redefine the project of modernity in multidimensional rather than unidimensional terms to escape some of the preoccupation with economic features of modernity (see Robertson 1992; Turner 1990). Featherstone and Lash, for example, suggest that the range and pluralisation of responses to modernity mean that it may well be preferable to refer to 'global modernities' (1995: 3).[10] This links with an underlying theme of this volume, the nature of Asia's divergent modernities.[11] These modernities are probably best characterised as neo-modernities: that is, the current developments in the region qualify more as Asian versions of modernity, rather than as post-modern, globalisation notwithstanding (see Kahn 1993). The modernities of metropolitan China, Indonesia, Singapore, and of the peripheral Yangtze River basin or the mining town of Soroako, we argue, cannot be plotted across a single historical trajectory. There are many 'Asias' and as many modernities.[12]

As we noted, the current triumphalist rhetoric in the region about modernity as progress is tempered by critical and anxious voices worrying about the costs of being modern. But many Asian representations of current developments are a long way from the *fin de* (twentieth) *siècle* despondency of Euro-American intellectuals pondering the decline of the rust-belt city and unresolvable social divisions. While the middle classes of Euro-America contemplate their growing insecurity after a decade or two of restructuring and downsizing, the middle classes of Asia are represented by many scholars and activists as looking to a period of growing affluence and democratisation. Darker visions of modernity are suppressed in these discourses, left to activists and intellectuals decrying the authoritarianism and human rights violations of many regimes.[13] As Nirmala PuruShotam's chapter on Singapore suggests, however, the compliance of the middle classes is produced not just through repression but through other far more subtle means, including rising affluence itself and women's own policing of their ongoing construction of a middle-class way of life.

The Euro-American modernity debates, of course, have moved on to globalisation, debating its character and relation to modernity and postmodernity (Featherstone and Lash 1995: 1). In popular discourse, especially in the West, globalisation has taken on a reduced meaning, usually referring to the effects of current economic rationalist moves towards 'free' trade, restructuring and a rolling back of the state, combined with some reference to the information revolution. Robertson, the major sociological theorist of these processes, has suggested that globalisation is best defined as 'the crystallization of the entire world as a single place' (1987a: 38 quoted in Arnason, 1990). Globalisation clearly represents different processes from the earlier imperialist projects of nation–states (cf. Arnason 1987): the control of critical flows of information and capital[14] produces a single social and cultural space in which the nation–state is supposedly in decline. Western discussions of contemporary developments are preoccupied with a shift from 'industrial society' to 'informational world', seeing a circulation of seemingly empty and universalist signs in the world informational system and their recasting into different configurations of meaning (Featherstone and Lash 1995).[15] Featherstone and Lash, however, point out that globalisation as the stretching of social relations across time and space is proving difficult to theorise. With problems in speaking of a 'global society', 'a central implication of the concept of globalisation is that we must now embark on the project of understanding social life without the comforting term "society"' (ibid.: 2). It is clear, however, that we are not to forego the uncomforting and highly problematic term 'culture' (see Kahn 1996b).

Several of our contributors have found ideas about globalisation as multidimensional helpful (cf. Pieterse 1995), especially Friedman's and Appadurai's work. Friedman argues that the ethnic and cultural fragmentation that many see as part and parcel of postmodernity and the modernist homogenisation produced by globalising forces are not two arguments, two opposing views of what is happening in the world today; they are two constitutive trends of global reality (1990: 311).[16] Appadurai has posed an influential model of a number of 'scapes' within the global cultural economy (1990), including ethnoscapes, mediascapes, technoscapes, finanscapes, and ideoscapes. These 'are not objectively given relations but deeply perspectival constructs, inflected very much by the historical, linguistic and political situatedness of different sorts of actors: nation-states, multinationals, diasporic communities, as well as sub-national groupings and movements' and even intimate face-to-face groups (ibid.: 296). In his scheme these are the building blocks of 'imagined worlds', characterised by radical disjunctures among them.

GENDER, MODERNITY AND GLOBALISATION

If the making of current modernities in affluent Asia has been a gendered process, how do we think about this process, given that theories have often been both Eurocentric and male-centred? There are very few writings addressing the relationships between gender, modernity and globalisation, and except for Janet Wolff, they mostly ignore the world beyond Euro-America.[17] In an influential article Wolff has argued that women's experiences of modernity have been ignored because the primary object of discussion has been the (so-called) public sphere: women are positioned tacitly or explicitly outside its frame (Wolff

1985). Two recent books by Barbara Marshall (1994) and Rita Felski (1995) have attempted longer explorations of the many relationships between gender and the modern from somewhat contrasting viewpoints: Marshall's is more resolutely sociological, Felski investigates the cultural politics of modernity in nineteenth-century Europe, to 'unravel the complexities of modernity's relationship to femininity through an analysis of its varied and competing representations' (p.7).

There are more than women's experiences of modernity at stake here. A feminist reading can destabilise the very terms of the modernity debates in interesting ways (Stivens 1994b; cf. Felski, 1992, 1995). As Felski observes, 'the periodisation and the criteria used to define the concepts modern and post-modern appear profoundly altered when women become the focal point of inquiry instead of men' (1992:139). A feminist critique of the political thought underlying the modernity/postmodernity debates shows modernity to be a thoroughly masculinist construct, based on a whole series of concepts drawn from the European intellectual inheritance – like civil society, class and rationality: these systematically exclude women by taking the abstract male as an unacknowledged point of reference in their analysis of the supposed progress towards the rationality of modernity, of bureaucratisation, of capitalist development, of the growth towards the large-scale society as against the small-scale 'community' (Stivens 1994b, cf. Marshall, 1994).[18] The concept of rationality itself has been seen to be premised on a series of highly dubious, socially and historically specific and gendered binary oppositions that pose women, woman and the female as always negative, as lack. The modern, autonomous, individual subject of this new order is implicitly a man.

Second-wave Western feminist theories of social change, however, have also been problematic, inheriting ambiguous and contradictory narratives from classical social theory. These have seen modernity as endangering premodern 'tradition' and the feminine, but have also associated the feminine with the modern itself on occasion.[19] Liberal feminism, for example, has often represented modernity as an improvement on pre-capitalist 'traditional' forces, which are seen as regressive relics. In such cases, there is no analysis of 'tradition' as constantly reconstituted and reinvented. Recent post-modernist feminist theorisings have all but ignored the mostly materialist Women-in-Development literature, not only because they distrusted economistic grand narratives but also because of a Eurocentric disregard for the world beyond Euro-America. Women-in-Development perspectives in their turn have been especially vulnerable to the moves away from the *social* towards the *cultural* in the humanities and social sciences.

Globalisation, like modernity, turns out to be a problematic concept for feminist analysis. Wolff, critiquing the indifference of globalisation writings towards gender issues,[20] points out that we cannot discuss culture without discussing gender. Identity is always gendered identity, political and other ideologies operate through notions of gender difference, and discursive oppositions are also complexly interwoven with meanings and discourses of gender (1991: 169). Her argument parallels those here when she suggests that:

> contemporary relations of the world-system must be unavoidably implicated in the sexual division of labour and the practices and ideologies of the separation of ['public' and 'private'] spheres . . . [W]e must be prepared to investigate the interrelations of public and private, of the economy and the domestic, of male and female roles, and of ideologies of work and politics and ideologies of gender in our attempt to theorize the global dimensions of culture and society.
>
> (ibid.: 170)

Similarly, as a number of our contributors argue, globalising forces are critical for understanding the differential productions of 'woman' in our various case study countries, drawing as they do on rapidly circulating and continuously produced representations of gender and women.

GENDERING STATE AND CLASS

For students of modernity and democracy reared on the liberal democratic models of modernity, the current experience of capitalist growth fostered by authoritarian, often militarised, regimes in Asia must be profoundly unsettling. The region's states have been heavily involved as the 'midwives' of development (Robison and Goodman 1996: 4), with 'development' itself the central and guiding state discourse. The 'new' middle classes of the region are widely seen as the children of these hypertrophic (Kahn 1993) states, which, as in Indonesia and Malaysia, shelter a fragmented and state-dependent bourgeoisie or upper class and a complex set of entrepreneurial, bureaucratic and professional elements within the middle classes (there are many terms for these strata).

Feminists have argued robustly that the state is gendered, but the legacy of androcentric and ethnocentric political thought has again proved troublesome. Like political scientists, some feminists have tended to conflate the state with its administrative apparatus and to assume that the state is highly effective in securing the conditions of women's subordination (but see Yuval-Davis and Anthias 1989). As

Franzway *et al.*, Pateman and others have argued, the liberal theory of the state has tended to naturalise gender inequality by seeing such inequities as the products merely of social contracts between individuals.[21] Socialist feminism has often seen the relationship between the state and the private sphere as one of functional interdependence. Women's labours, especially domestic labour, are seen as contributing to the support of a capitalist/patriarchal state.[22] Claims by others that the state is 'patriarchal' have also proved controversial: they have been seen as obscuring variations in women's situation and male dominance historically. Even useful analyses like Franzway *et al.*'s (1989), which discuss how the state is gender-structured, tend to see it as a monolithic patriarchal entity, rather than as a site of conflicting sets of social relations. But Pringle and Watson (1992) go some way towards providing a more nuanced account, employing a version of feminist poststructuralism to argue for the state as a series of arenas, a plurality of discursive forums where women's (among other) interests are constructed in the process of interaction with specific institutions and sites (see also Butler and Scott 1992).

Discussion of these more theoretical issues about gender and the state has not been common in work on Asia, nor has Asia figured much in Euro-American theorising.[23] There is, of course, a growing body of work on female participation in party politics and government and policy implications for women in the region and on the effects of administrative apparatuses on women's lives, especially the misogyny of bureaucracy.[24] The role of state authoritarianism and associated militarisation has especially profound implications for women, as Cynthia Enloe has pointed out (Enloe 1989; see also Hilsdon 1995): the important question is how women's experiences of such militarised states differ from men's.[25]

Mina Roces' chapter adds to this literature in exploring the ways the dynamics of power and politics are gendered in the Philippines (see Chapter 10). She focusses on official/unofficial power in the practice of kinship politics (defined here as the use of political power to benefit the kinship group). She suggests that an understanding of kinship politics is vital to understanding the gendering of politics and the workings of the state and contestations within it. She explores the ways in which women exercise power behind the scenes as wives, daughters, sisters, mothers and sometimes mistresses of male politicians, even though men have the monopoly over the official symbols of power. She suggests that although men dominate Philippine politics, women are not denied access to significant sources of power and active political agency. She sees this kinship politics as both shaping women's access to power and its practice and providing a pre-eminent arena in which women can exercise power.

The nature of class in contemporary Asia has been an important issue for our project. There are considerable difficulties in conceptualising both the structure and the size of these classes. 'Class' of course has been one of the most contested terms in classical social theory, with endless disputation about the relationships between class, status and power. The middle class has been a highly ambiguous term within classical and modern social theory, with multiple meanings and predictions about its fate. A standard account would note the difficulties in identifying the middle strata and groups in classical class theory, especially within Marxist theory based on the notion of a capitalist exploiting the surplus value of (working-class) labour; it would also note the varying prognoses of the fate of the middle classes, especially the claims about the failure of the Marxist theses about the polarisation of classes into working and capitalist. The New Times postmodern arguments, however, have raised serious doubts about identifying classes as concrete entities in late modern/high modern/post-modern society (cf. Walby 1992; MacCannell and MacCannell 1993).

All these difficulties are compounded when the debates based on Euro-American experiences are transposed to contemporary Asia. There is a disparate set of groups within the affluent or 'new rich' categories, including an upper stratum of large capitalists, managers, and members of political elites, and a middle stratum of smaller business owners, managers of middle-range enterprises, professionals, middle level entrepreneurs, salaried men and women and clerical and administrative groupings. Some of these groupings are newly emerging, others are more long-standing. In all our case studies, the overall picture of the emerging class structure is far from clear. Scholars like Robison have warned against lumping the lower and upper levels of Asian middle strata together when all they share are some similarities in consumption (1990). While the lower middle classes of Euro-America are widely seen as becoming proletarianised, even the lower levels of these strata in contemporary Asia may well be counted and count themselves as affluent and as clearly middle class. The groupings within Asian middle strata are better seen as comprising a number of classes or class fractions, rather than as a unified, single class. Such fractions will differ according to context.[26] Whether we want to see them as consumption classes is a moot point. A number of levels of these middle strata appear to share significant parts of their lifestyle with the *nouveau riche*, for example. Moreover, in some circumstances, working-class members are also clearly part of the growing consumption marking the new orders.

The theorisation of the region's ruling and new middle classes has mostly proceeded with little reference to important feminist work like Carol Pateman's on rethinking citizenship and the highly gendered political thought underlying liberal democracy (1988).[27] We noted the recent optimisms about possible moves towards democratisation with the growth of new middle classes. Yet there has been little attention outside feminist circles to the issue of women as active members of classes and the place of men as well as women as gendered political subjects in the various social movements characteristic of the region.[28] As Gilmartin *et al.* argue for China (1994) the oppositional political subject has been constructed as male.[29] Moreover, the optimism about democratisation has mostly ignored the struggles of many women in the region for a democratisation of household and male–female relations more generally.

Attempts to include gender in conceptualisations of class have not been straightforward. Past feminist debates on this issue were driven by the arguments about whether class or gender/patriarchy came first. Some sociological attempts to expand stratification theories have been little improvement on the malestream accounts, merely adding women to elaborate occupational hierarchies.[30] But some recent work theorising class as always constituted in relation to ethnic or gender relations has been useful (e.g. Walby 1992). The implication is that class always has gender and ethnic dimensions (and gender is always constituted in relation to ethnic and class dimensions). Gender relations will thus be a crucial part of any study of class formation. These perspectives form a thread throughout the discussions in this collection, although our chapters mostly do not address the issues surrounding ethnicity directly (apart from Chapter 4). But the gendered dimensions of class are raised explicitly in the chapters by Krishna Sen on Indonesia, Maila Stivens on Malaysia, Nirmala PuruShotam on Singapore and Nerida Cook on Thailand. Cook, for example, is concerned to explore the nexus between the particularities of Thai women activists' class position and their positioning *vis-à-vis* prostitution. Sen looks at the ways in which the affluent professional women's redefinition of gender regimes is premised on and reproduces class privileges within Indonesian political and commercial discourses.

Also useful has been work exploring the links between domestic labour, paid labour and women's class situation. But much discussion has proceeded with a model of women as located within households formed through marriage. Our case studies also point to the vital part the work (both material and ideological) of women not living in marriage-based households plays in creating and reproducing class relations; as both consumers and as producers, as unmarried daughters of households, independent women, and, importantly, as maids, single or married but separated from their own household.

GENDER AND THE POLITICS OF MEANING

As the discussions of the representations of 'woman' in our case study countries show, current contests around the representation of this globalising order concentrate extensively on issues of national culture and women's place within them. Work on women in Asia in the last decade suggests that at the same time as more and more women are entering employment outside the household a nostalgic vision of femininity is being invoked in the widespread production of the modern Asian woman and the Asian Family across the region. Several national leaders have been prominent advocates of this family form, notably in Singapore, where it has been tied to an explicit reconstitution of Confucianism. Indeed, Asian leaders seem preoccupied with issues of national identity and women's and the family's role in producing that identity. Asian Family ideology both manufactures consent and contains dissent.

The Asian Family discourse is much wider than state propaganda machines, however, as the chapters on Singapore and Malaysia especially make clear. The public and the modern are gendered as male in much of this rhetoric. But this masculinity is to be tempered by a complementary idealised femininity located in modern family life 'eastern' style. This vision of complementarity draws on long-standing notions of relative male–female equality and complementarity within popular and scholarly ideologies in Southeast Asia (see for example Atkinson and Errington 1990); it is also present in some local feminist thinking (e.g. Maznah Mohamed and Wong Soak Koon 1994, for Malaysia). In the Asian Family discourse women are the bearers of this vision of family, its keepers, its producers; the family is the bulwark against the social costs of modernity (and of dissent) and the dangers of fragmenting national and personal identities produced in the current (post)modern order. The autonomous and sexualised modern woman threatens to break this complementary dualism of public and private, male and female, tradition and modernity.

Accounts of western modernity have pointed to the deeply nostalgic visions of femininity within modern sociological and critical thought (Stauth and Turner 1988; Felski 1995: 35).[31] Felski suggests that the yearning for the feminine as 'emblematic of a non-alienated, non-fragmented identity is a crucially important motif in the history of the cultural representations of the nature of modernity . . . an authentic point of origin . . . a recurring symbol of the atemporal and asocial at the heart of modernity' (1995: 37–8).[32] The workings of nostalgia, not simply for the non-modern, but as expressions of anti-Western modernity, like the reconstituted Asian family, are discussed by PuruShotam and McLaren in dealing with the reinvention of Confucianism and by Stivens in dealing with Islamic revivalism. It is hardly surprising, then, that the anxieties about the threats posed to the 'Asian Family' and to women's 'traditional' roles seem to have become a favoured site for expressing more general tensions and ambivalences about the costs of modernity and 'development' in both mainstream political and cultural forums and in some dissident circles.

The prevalence of nationalist ideology making and its reliance on images of Asian women and the Asian Family in a globalising age raises some questions. Social theory often asserts that the nation–state, a product of the age of imperialism, is in eclipse, yet nationalist image-making flourishes. This seeming paradox has been noted by Anthony King (1991: 153) and Parker *et al.* (1992) among others. King suggests that we can see a strengthening of the project of national identity on the periphery even as it erodes at the core (1991: 153), although his use of this dichotomy seems problematic. Simpler assumptions about national culture as a homogeneous entity that must necessarily break down with globalisation also do not allow for the multiple images of the nation now flowing forth into the media and indeed cyberspace in all the countries of the region (see Mee n.d.). Kahn has termed this a post-modernisation of national identity for the Malaysian case – there is no longer a single fixed idea of national identity but multiple and competing ones (personal communication). The frequency of anti-Western modernity messages within nation-building exercises may account for the prevalence of nostalgic, gendered images within these discourses. Our argument that the 'private' is a pivotal, contested nexus between the global and the local may also provide one explanation.

Perhaps one of the most powerful examples of this politicisation of gender has been the role Flor Contemplacion, a Philippine maid in Singapore, has assumed in the Philippine national imagination. She was hanged in Singapore in 1995 for the alleged murder of her charge and another maid. For some sections of the Philippine population Flor rapidly became a multilayered symbol of national martyrdom and the suffering that the economic forces of structural adjustment had unleashed on the country, with 'Chinese' (i.e. Singaporean) connivance.

The themes of reconstituted 'tradition' and nostalgia for the feminine within the modern are explicit in Anne McLaren's chapter on cultural revival and women's culture in China's Yangtze River Basin (see Chapter 7). Her piece illustrates through a detailed case study how the growth of affluence produces complex reworkings of gender images in regions some distance from national centres, reworkings which enter into national image-making about the nation. Looking at a state-sponsored revival of women's expressive culture – oral traditions – McLaren sees a merging of fractured aspects of China's folk inheritance with commercialised interests and mass communication in women's production of these cultural forms. Seeing considerable disadvantages for women in such neotraditionalism, she highlights the complex ways that the hybrid and reconstructed images of 'traditional' Chinese femininity are invoked to produce a national discourse about Chinese-style modernity. She sees the effects of globalisation and state cultural revival as by no means homogeneous or unidirectional: 'traditional' folk genres have absorbed elements of mass culture, and other invented traditions, offering an idealised depiction of 'nativised' Chinese women for the tourist industry. She suggests that future studies of the cultural construction of femininity in China will have to take into account not just the impact of the global economy and mass communications, but also the influence of state cultural policies and crucially, how these are manipulated locally by particular groups as women participate in the formation of a highly gendered and sharply contested notion of how to be female, Chinese and modern, but not Western.

POSITIONALITIES AND THE NEW AFFLUENCE

Our arguments about how we might begin to analyse the processes producing new affluence in Asia point to a number of issues surrounding positionality. Writing about women and gender from either inside or outside the region is an anxious and ambiguous process, as several of our contributors suggest: it involves us immediately in struggles about who has the right to make knowledges; and it raises questions about the central concepts in the debates both about gender and about development, modernisation and modernity in Asia.[33] A by now large body of feminist theory has mounted a devastating critique of the male-centred assumptions of much Western social and feminist theory (Barrett 1992: 202). But reconstructing theory has proved more problematic than feminists might have hoped, even as their efforts played an important if sometimes overlooked part in post-modern unsettlings of theories in the West.[34] These unsettlings, however, have brought their own problems for feminists everywhere (Nicholson 1990). Western feminists have expressed considerable anxiety about current theorisings. They see post-modernist critiques of grand unified theories as undermining the idea that all women as women share some common struggle; and some worry that the concepts of women and gender have become so fragmented by racial, class and historical particularity that they threaten to self-destruct as analytical categories (cf. Bordo 1990). If that is the case, then where will the supposedly unified feminist project be?

It also became difficult to sustain the idea of 'woman' as a single, undifferentiated category in the face of widespread challenges from women outside Euro-America. The latter argue that Western intellectual agendas have dominated scholarship globally; that Western feminist theories are part of this colonial hegemony; and that 'non-Western' women are posed as forever 'victims' of development or modernisation, seen as unable to act as social subjects in their own right (Mohanty *et al.* 1991; Lazreg 1988), and marginalised from 'Western' feminist politics, theory and practice.[35] Western feminists have responded to these counterchallenges somewhat equivocally, often only admitting 'different' women's voices into their debates as they become more and more insistent on being counted.

The critique of Western feminist ethnocentrism, however, poses problems for post-colonial feminisms in turn. Does the western hegemony of thought and representation 'permit' counter discourses (cf. Lazreg 1988)? That is, is it possible to escape these dominating frameworks in order to construct local, if not 'authentic', knowledges? This ties into a related concern about positionalities: who may claim the right to 'speak' about whom and for whom? It is especially relevant for this volume to note that it is the 'post-colonial' middle classes themselves, journalists, artists, academics, among them many women, who are simultaneously creating, living in and contesting their own middle-class cultural forms. The role of these intelligentsias can become extremely complex in such contexts. Some of them espouse the somewhat second-hand globalised, post-colonial (actually mostly US academy-based) agendas of speaking as and for the subaltern underdogs; their position is made even more complex when they sometimes embrace versions of anti-Western modernity. Thus some critics, characterising themselves as the 'authentic' interpreters of their own culture, or as the 'authentic' 'political' representatives of counter-hegemonic discourses, have expressed considerable resentment about First World women appropriating 'Third World' women's experiences for feminist scholarship. The elite situation of 'Third World' intellectuals, however, can undermine such claims to authenticity. They have to distance themselves from their own privileged practices, tied as these are into global scholarly enterprises, even on unequal terms. Moreover, such claims tend to pose opposition to the West in terms of essentialist ideas about authentic voices, often legitimised by the romanticism of Third-Worldism and neo-nationalism (cf. Chatterjee 1993; Harris 1986). The supposed authentic voice of the marginalised, the subaltern, including both 'high' and 'popular' cultural productions, is in fact often mediated and produced by elite or middle-class intellectuals and intelligentsia. As Edward Said among others has suggested, the very terms of the debates within which these issues have been explored, the essentialised 'West' counterposed to an equally essentialised 'Third World', are a central problem (1986).[36]

The anxieties about holding on to the idea of 'woman' as a unified political category resonate in interesting and challenging ways in the Asian region. It is not surprising that Western feminist theories have been received coolly in the region. Nor is it surprising that women's movements in Asia have been ambivalent about avowedly 'feminist' projects. Several of our chapters deal with aspects of these reactions. Although Asian feminists and 'womanist' (a term some women in Malaysia, for example, prefer) have sometimes been reticent about becoming involved in what are sometimes perceived as 'Western' women's movement issues like domestic violence, they have been active in a series of causes, as noted. It was mostly only in the 1980s, however, that the region saw the simultaneous emergence in a number of countries of organised overtly 'feminist' action against domestic and sexual violence, with many women's refuges being set up, mainly by women of the 'new' middle classes. The label 'Western' has often been used to describe – and discredit – feminist initiatives in the region. Recent years, however, have seen some shift away from the polarised positions within these debates, most notably at the 1995 Beijing Conference on women, where the idea of unity within a diversified global women's movement seems to have been a dominant theme. Affluent Asian women's ambivalences about both local and global feminist projects are very different from those besetting an inward-looking Euro-American academy preoccupied with post-postmodernism and refuting 'post-feminism': with the shift of the world economy to the Pacific Rim, Asian feminists may feel themselves located far from the anxieties besetting Western feminisms about how to sustain a feminist project within a fractured post-modern world. There is enormous energy in regional feminist projects, like the recent campaigns about domestic violence in Malaysia, on domestic servants throughout the region and on issues concerning prostitution in Thailand. As Nerida Cook's chapter on Thailand shows clearly, however, the part that middle-class women play in such controversies is exceedingly complex (see Chapter 9).

These issues pose some key questions about feminisms in the region. When does feminist practice become named as such? How far do the political actions of new rich and other affluent women base themselves on a modernist, politicised conception of gender? Is it possible to argue that current feminist agendas and practices in the region are direct products of the present neomodernities? While this runs the risk of appearing to construct yet another evolutionary sequence, this argument could be an attractive one for newly affluent Asia in the 1980s and 1990s: mass migration to the cities in the wake of state-led industrialisation, growing middle classes, and rising female education all produce a critical mass of educated women who begin to articulate their new discontents in modernist terms. But it ignores the long history of women's political actions on their sex's behalf in the region. Nonetheless, can we see the present rise of new middle classes as providing some degree of political empowerment for women, unlike the processes in European industrialisation when the rise of such classes has been seen by some to produce a widening gap between the public influence of men-as-men versus women-as-women?[37]

As suggested, it is precisely the women of the new middle classes of Asia who are simultaneously creating, living in and contesting their own (middle-class) cultural forms, speaking for and as the subaltern and as members of reforming groups. These themes recur in a number of the chapters, but are explicit in Chapters 5 and 9. Nirmala PuruShotam examines in some depth the ways that middle-class women in Singapore both produce and move beyond the 'normal family' and middle classness to versions of feminist action, including theatrical performance and overtly political action. Cook's chapter on the controversies about Thai prostitution is a detailed exploration of the complex parts that middle-class women play in the politicking around this issue. Tracking the history of prostitution, the involvement of middle-class women in campaigns, and perceptions of Thai women, she looks at the ways that prostitute women have been represented and the campaigns that have been set up to 'save' them. She argues that in spite of the disproportionate amount of attention Thai prostitution has received from both local and worldwide media, it cannot be ignored in any analysis of modern Thai women's experience. A focus on prostitution both from outside and, increasingly urgently, from within the country with panics about HIV/AIDS, has inevitably implicated Thai womanhood in general and thus significantly influenced the context within which the identities of educated women of the emerging middle class are discursively constructed. In turn, the meanings attached to prostitution in Thailand have been significantly reshaped by women activists' political and discursive practices.

Any discussion of the politics of knowledge production would be incomplete without some note of the contributors' own positionalities. As a project based at Murdoch University, this volume is of course mainly Australian-based, although the contributors are a relatively diverse group: two of us come from 'Asia' originally and another is based in Singapore; we all have long experience of researching in Asia. We come from a number of disciplines – anthropology, sociology, Asian studies, political science and communication studies – but all of us have been working in the basically transdisciplinary context of gender studies where formal disciplinary boundaries have become less important. The common concerns and methodologies of the different chapters of this volume illustrate this traversing of boundaries clearly. We also share aspects of the privileged globalised middle-class lifestyle which is a central issue for this book. Indeed, for some of us, the problem has sometimes been what some might see as an over-identification with our informants' everyday life dilemmas. These contexts need to be fully acknowledged. The location of Australian scholarship on Asia and academic production in general is an interesting one: it is of the West and yet on its margins, reading across varying positions from within an Asian-Pacific context, while being located within a national project that has until very recently at least identified itself as 'multicultural'. It is a truism that such marginality can recombine knowledges in novel ways.

CONCLUSION

This introduction has set out some of the issues involved in analysing gender relations in affluent Asia. It has been especially concerned to argue that we need to do far more than add women to the debates, suggesting that recent social change has been an inherently gendered process and that we need to concentrate on the reworkings of the 'public' and 'private' in order to understand the development of new affluence, middle classness and indeed modernity in the region. We saw the relations surrounding consumption as a key way to think about the nexus between the global and the local and argued for linking women's roles coordinating the rising consumption of the newly affluent to the creation of proliferating identities as 'modern' Indonesians, Malaysians, Singaporeans, Chinese, Thais, Vietnamese and Filipinos.

We are intrigued by the scale of the image-making tied to this burgeoning consumption, especially the sexualisation of women, which seems to be developing on an unparalleled scale with affluence and globalisation. In an age of the mass media, such representations can be both instantaneous and far-reaching. The development of these elaborate new femininities is a contested and indeed troubled process. Issues of family, gender, home, masculinity, femininity and sexuality are central sites for the cultural expression and reworking of ideas of the 'modern' and for the expression of worries about the costs of development and modernity. It appears to be no accident that the so-called 'private' sphere and gender relations have become a favoured site for the expression of these tensions, given the pivotal role that women as consumers occupy in mediating the global and the local, and production, consumption and identity through elaborated domesticities. The chapters look at the involvement of middle-class women in the struggles around these issues, as objects, producers and critics of these imaginings.

Some of our findings clearly qualify some of the more triumphalist rhetoric about the new Asian affluence. As a number of the contributors make clear, the experiences of women within these new orders cast a very different light on some of these processes. The chapters show women's agency in transforming economies and ideologies, the costs of development directly experienced by these women, some of women's experiences of authoritarian states, the juggling of everyday life, the contradictory searches for new forms of autonomy through intimacy, and the living of critical engagements with modernity through such movements as feminism and revivalist religion. Our case studies seriously challenge developmental models that do not take into account the divergent, even contradictory, engagements of Asia in globalisation processes.

As we argued at the beginning of this introduction, our main aim is to open up a series of questions about gender within the cultural economy of globalising Asia. We stressed that this is not meant to be a comprehensive textbook. If areas like ethnicity and the concerns of peasant and working-class women are somewhat marginal in this particular collection, this is not because we think them any less important fractures in the category called 'Asian woman'.

Feminist research is inseparable from feminist politics and feminist ethics. It is not our place to pronounce about the future for Asian feminisms, although our main objects, the 'new' middle-class women, will clearly be important players in those struggles. This book is a contribution to those struggles, part of an ongoing challenge to the mainstream androcentricism of Asian Studies and to the mainstream Eurocentricism of Women's Studies. We hope we have pushed the debate a little further, adding new doubts, fractures and questions to feminist research agendas.

NOTES

1 We prefer to term our object the 'newly affluent' rather than the new rich: our use of Affluent Asia in our title has an ironic edge to it, given the issues of inequality that the new affluence raises and the ways that affluence is produced and experienced by both the better-off and the more disadvantaged.

2 See Moller Okin (1979), Pateman and Gross (1986), Benhabib and Cornell (1987), MacKinnon (1987), Showstack Sassoon (1987), Jones and Jonasdottir (1988), Stivens (1991), Butler and Scott (1992).

3 As I argue elsewhere (1991), it can be difficult in any case to identify the so-called domestic domain where a clear division of 'public and 'private' has not (yet) been produced by local versions of modernity. I am thinking particularly of the case of rural sectors. Similarly, Women-in-Development writing has often itself been mired within some of the dualist western tradition. For example, it often tended to see an increasing relegation of women to subsistence sectors with capitalist development, while men work in the capitalist sector: this sector supposedly reproduces capitalist relations/the urban sector or some other object in what is sometimes a rather epistemologically confused account (cf. Moore 1988). This closely resembles the housewife/male breadwinner scheme, and is equally problematic.

4 See discussion in Pateman and Gross (1986), Benhabib and Cornell (1987), Showstack Sassoon (1987), Jones and Jonasdottir (1988), Pateman (1988), Stivens (1991).

5 As Foucault among others has argued. See Jones and Jonasdottir (1988) for discussion.

6 The recent interest in postmodernity and globalisation has been one of the main factors reviving interest in old debates about industrialisation, modernisation, the periodisations and logics within modernity. and its alleged social accompaniments such as a development of the individualised self and modern subjectivities, a breakdown of 'family' and of kinship ties, the separation of the household from the so-called productive economy and the rise of the citizen. In the face of this destabilising of the idea of modernity, the classic sociological formulations about its development gave way to new periodisations, including postindustrialism, late capitalism and the death of history.

Understandings of postmodernity in turn have been queried by critics such as Callinicos (1989), Lash (1990) and others who see the post-modern as merely a moment within the modern. An increasingly complex literature confronts a bewildering array of meanings of modernity and postmodernity (Boyne and Rattansi 1990) and a bewildering range of authors from Baudelaire to Baudrillard. (For some writers distressed by the current eclipse of large socialist metanarratives, 'modernity' has become a code for capitalist development, part of what some have seen as a widespread apologetic post-Marxist coding).

7 As Said notes, this erasure has been achieved through such concepts and the wholesale importation of Western epistemologies to the so-called periphery. Western intellectuals' concentration on the post-modern order, Said argues, excludes the very real concern of many people beyond Euro-America (he

cites the Arab and Islamic world) with modernity itself (1993: 399). The arguments that Paul Gilroy makes in exploring the relationship between the black Atlantic diaspora and modernity can help to dissolve some of the problems posed by the dualisms of the modernity debates. Suggesting that black individuals have drawn on the tradition of the modern through practice of affirmation and critique, he sees this diaspora as constituted as a 'non-traditional tradition, an irreducibly modern, excentric, unstable and asymmetrical cultural ensemble that cannot be apprehended through the Manichean logic of binary coding' (1993: 198). I make similar arguments in Stivens (1996).

8 See Hobart (1993) for discussion of ideas of development.

9 The historical amnesia about the history of ideas like imperialism, development and modernisation within some of this writing is striking. We share some of the concern of Pieterse and others that we are in fact seeing a resurrection of the tired sociological debates about modernisation under another name.

10 The status of the nation–state within these wider understandings of modernity, however, is highly confused and contradictory.

11 It is not being assumed here that current neomodernities in Asia are in any way the first manifestations of the modern. As I have argued elsewhere, the local societies have to be understood as arising within the modern order which we may well see as stretching back a number of centuries (Stivens 1996; cf. Reid 1993).

12 See Stivens (1994b). There has been a group working on issues associated with divergent modernities in Melbourne over the last few years, and several workshops, including two organised by Johann Arnason.

13 Felski suggests that modernity differs from other kinds of periodisation in having a normative dimension: 'one can be "for" or "against" modernity in a way that one cannot be for or against the Renaissance, for example' (1995: 13). This claim seems oddly neglectful of the rich normative and political meanings associated with such periodisations as 'feudal' or 'colonial', however. We might invoke here Bauman's famous argument that the highly rationalised technologies of the final solution in Germany were a logical development of modernity, not a retreat from progress and civilisation into barbarism and irrationality (1989).

14 See Castells and Hall (1994).

15 The widespread concern in the literature to periodise globalisation is relevant here. Writers like Pieterse (1995), Harvey (1989) and Lash and Urry (1994) see it as an epoch contemporaneous with postmodernity. Friedman, disputing this, sees globalisation as fundamentally civilisational in character, long pre-dating even Wallerstein's global system of modernity (1995).

16 Friedman tries to chart the logics of the apparent chaos of the modernity/postmodernity debates in the interplay between world market and cultural identity (1990: 312). As noted above, he sees this interplay occurring importantly through consumption. Featherstone and Lash, again, acknowledge the problems with applying the Western 'tradition-modernity-postmodernity' developmental sequence, but do not explore this in relation to the shifting centres of the contemporary world order (1995).

17 But see Marshall (1994), Felski (1992, 1995), Wolff (1985, 1991), Chow (1991).
18 Felski, however, notes Gail Finney's arguing for the imaginative centrality of female psychology and sexuality to representations of modernity in the European *fin de siècle* (1989), which Felski contrasts with Berman's exclusively masculine pantheon.
19 See Felski (1995: 3) for discussion of the latter.
20 There is for example no index entry for 'women' or 'gender' in Featherstone *et al.* (1995) although the volume does deal with 'family' in an abstract sense and social policy in a couple of chapters.
21 See Pettman (1996) for a discussion of the gendering of the state, especially conceptualisations of the state as a (male) person. See also Afshar (1996).
22 See discussion in Sassoon (1987). This functional dependence has been viewed in differing ways, however. In 1978, McIntosh noted that feminism had borrowed from the libertarian and radical left the idea of the state as a directly repressive mechanism. She preferred to see the state as intervening less conspicuously in the lives of women, often in fact denying them the protection given men. 'The state frequently defines a space, the family, in which its agents will not interfere but in which control is left to the man' (1978: 257). See also Stivens (n.d.c.).
23 But see Stivens (1990, n.d.c.), Pettman (1996), Afshar (1996), Paspart and Staudt (1990), Charlton *et al.* (1989), Kandiyoti (1991), Moghadam (1994a, 1994b), Rai (1996), Waylen (1996) on theorisation about the state in 'Third World' societies. For Southeast Asia, see Chua Beng Huat (1995), Stivens (1990) and for China, see Croll (1978), Gilmartin *et al.* (1994), Judd (1994).
24 See Stivens (1990) for a bibliography. See also Afshar (1987), Radcliffe and Westwood (1993), Silverblatt (1991), Mohanty, Russo and Torres (1991), Judd (1994), Moghadam (1994a, 1994b), West and Blumberg (1990).
25 See Pettman (1996), Rai (1996), Waylen (1996).
26 See Kahn (1996a). See also Tanter and Young (1990) and Robison and Goodman (1996) for discussion of the varying new classes of Asia.
27 For example, Tanter and Young (1990) contains no discussion of women apart from Susan Blackburn Abeyasekere's protest about the absence of women at the end of the conference, reported in the volume.
28 But see Rodan (1996).
29 See Blackburn (1991), Manderson (1991) and Stivens (1991) for Southeast Asian discussions. Some exceptions include Reynolds (1994), Young (1991).
30 Thus we have elaborate measures of women's social mobility in great detail, as in Crompton and Mann (1986).
31 See Felski (1995) for discussion.
32 Felski goes on to note the deeply ingrained assumptions about the necessary links between modernity, alienation and masculinity which underpin an influential intellectual tradition from Hegel to Jacques Lacan. 'Within this tradition, nostalgia and the feminine come together in the representation of a mythic plenitude, against which is etched an overarching narra-

tive of masculine development as self-division and existential loss' (1995: 37).

33 See Stivens (1994a, 1994b).

34 As one trained in anthropology, I am most familiar with that discipline although some of the epistemological issues relate to other disciplines as much as to anthropology. But I find myself in total sympathy with Henrietta Moore when she notes ruefully (1994: 2) that while she remains passionately committed, she finds her relations with the terms 'feminist' and 'anthropologist' 'strenuous, nuanced and unrelentingly complex'. See my discussion of these issues in Stivens (1994a).

35 The ethnocentrism of Western feminists is one measure of the ethnocentrism of the received social theory models within which they work. As a generation of post-colonial critics has alleged, such theorising has tended to write from a Euro-American standpoint, assuming that its issues and concerns generated in highly specific circumstances were easily transposable to other parts of the world. See discussion in Nencel and Pels (1991), Stivens (1994a, 1994b), Moore (1994).

36 In the present context, moreover, many see the idea of the Third World as an obsolete term referring to an earlier stage of the world order.

37 But see Enloe (1983, 1989), Yuval-Davis and Anthias (1989) and discussion in Stivens (1992, 1994b).

BIBLIOGRAPHY

Abélès, M. (1992) 'Anthropologie Politique de la Modernité', *L'Homme*, 121, Jan–March, XXXII, 1: 15–30.

Afshar, H. (ed.) (1987) *Women, State and Ideology*, London: Macmillan.

—— (ed.) (1996) *Women and Politics in the Third World*, London: Routledge.

Akbar Ahmed (1992) *Postmodernism and Islam*, London: Routledge.

Appadurai, A. (1990) 'Disjuncture and Difference in the Global Cultural Economy', in M. Featherstone (ed.) *Global Culture: Nationalism, Globalization and Modernity*, London: Sage.

Arnason, J. (1987) 'The Modern Constellation and the Japanese Enigma', *Thesis Eleven*, 17: 4–39.

—— (1990) 'Nationalism, Globalization and Modernity', in M. Featherstone (ed.) *Global Culture: Nationalism, Globalization and Modernity*, London: Sage.

Asad, T. (1992) 'Conscripts of Western Civilisation', in C.W. Gailey (ed.) *Dialectical Anthropology: Volume 1, Civilization in Crisis: Anthropological Perspectives*, Gainesville: University Press of Florida.

Atkinson, J. M. and Errington, S. (eds) (1990) *Power and Difference*, Stanford: Stanford University Press.

Barrett, M. (1992) 'Words and Things: Materialism and Method in Contemporary Feminist Analysis', in M. Barrett and A. Phillips (eds) *Destabilizing Theory*, Cambridge: Polity.

Barrett, M. and Phillips, A. (eds) (1992) *Destabilizing Theory*, Cambridge: Polity.

Basu, A. (ed.) (1995) *The Challenges of Local Feminisms: Women's Movements in Global Perspective*, Boulder: Westview.

Bauman, Z. (1989) *Modernity and the Holocaust*, Cambridge: Polity.

Benhabib, S. (1992) *Situating the Self: Gender, Community and Postmodernism in Contemporary Ethics*, New York: Routledge.

Benhabib, S. and Cornell, D. (eds) (1987) *Feminism as Critique: Essays on the Politics of Gender in Late Capitalist Societies*, Cambridge: Polity.

Blackburn, S. (1991) 'How Gender is Neglected in Southeast Asian Politics', in M. Stivens (ed.) *Why Gender Matters in Southeast Asian Politics*, Clayton: Monash Centre of Southeast Asian Studies.

Bordo, S. (1990) 'Feminism, Postmodernism and Gender-Scepticism', in L. Nicholson (ed.) *Feminism/Postmodernism*, New York: Routledge: 133–56.

Boyne, R. and Rattansi, A. (eds) (1990) *Postmodernism and Society*, New York: St Martin's Press.

Butler, J. and Scott, J. (eds) (1992) *Feminists Theorize the Political*, London: Routledge.

Callinicos, A. (1989) *Against Postmodernism*, Cambridge: Polity.

Castells, M. and Hall, P. (1994) *Technopoles of the World: The Making of Twenty-first Century Industrial Complexes*, NY, Oxford: Oxford University Press.

Charlton, S., Everett, J. and Staudt, K. (1989) *Women, the State and Development*, Albany: State University of New York Press.

Chatterjee, P. (1993) *The Nation and its Fragments: Colonial and Post-colonial Histories*, Princeton: Princeton University Press.

Chow, R. (1991) *Women and Chinese Modernity: The Politics of Reading Between East and West*, Minneapolis: University of Minnesota Press.

Chua Beng Huat (1995) *Communitarian Ideology and Democracy in Singapore*, London: Routledge.

Croll, E. (1978) *Feminism and Socialism in China*, London: Routledge and Kegan Paul.

Crompton, R. and Mann, M. (1986) *Gender and Stratification*, Cambridge: Polity.

Davidoff, L. and Hall, C. (1987) *Family Fortunes: Men and Women of the English Middle Class 1780-1850*, London: Hutchinson.

Ebert, T. L. (1996) *Ludic Feminism*, Michigan: Ann Arbor.

Elshtain, J. B. (1981) *Public Man, Private Woman: Women in Social and Political Thought*, Oxford: Martin Robinson.

Enloe, C. (1983) *Does Khaki Become You? The Militarization of Women's Lives*, London: Pluto.

—— (1989) *Bananas, Beaches and Bases: Making Feminist Sense of International Politics*, London: Pandora Press.

Featherstone, M. and S. Lash, (1995) 'Globalization, Modernity and the Spatialization of Social Theory: An Introduction', in M. Featherstone, S. Lash and R. Robertson (eds) *Global Modernities*, London: Sage.

Felski, R. (1989) 'Feminist Theory and Social Change', *Theory, Culture and Society*, 6: 219–40.

—— (1992) 'Whose Post-modernism?', *Thesis Eleven*, 32: 129–40.

—— (1995) *The Gender of Modernity*, Cambridge, Massachusetts: Harvard University Press.

Finney, G. (1989) *Women in Modern Drama: Freud, Feminism and European Theater at the Turn of the Century*, Ithaca: Cornell University Press.

Fox-Genovese, E. (1991) *Feminisms Without Illusions: A Critique of Individualism*, Chapel Hill: University of N. Carolina Press.

Franzway, F., Court, D. and Connell, R. W. (1989) *Staking a Claim: Feminism, Bureaucracy and the State*, Sydney: Allen and Unwin.

Friedman, J. (1990) 'Being in the World: Globalization and Localization', in M. Featherstone (ed.) *Global Culture: Nationalism, Globalization and Modernity*, London: Sage.

—— (1995) 'Global System, Globalization and the Parameters of Modernity', in M. Featherstone, S. Lash and R. Robertson (eds) *Global Modernities*, London: Sage.

Giddens, A. (1992) *The Transformation of Intimacy: Sexuality, Love and Eroticism in Modern Societies*, Oxford: Polity.

Gilmartin, C. K., Hershatter, G., Rofel, L. and White, T. (eds) (1994) *Engendering China: Women, Culture and the State*, Cambridge, Mass., London: Harvard University Press.

Gilroy, P. (1993) *The Black Atlantic: Modernity and Consciousness*, London and New York: Verso.

Gledhill, J. (1994) *Power and its Disguises: Anthropological Perspectives on Politics*, London: Pluto.

Grazia de, V. (ed.) (1996) *The Sex of Things: Gender and Consumption in Historical Perspective*, Berkeley: University of California Press.

Hall, C., Lewis, J., McClelland, K. and Rendell, J. (eds) (1993) *Gender and History, Special Issue on Gender, Nationalisms and National Identities*, Summer, 1993, Oxford, New York: Basil Blackwell.

Harding, S. (1986) 'The Instability of the Analytical Categories of Feminist Theory', *Signs* 11(4): 645–65.

Harris, N. (1986) *The End of the Third World: Newly Industrialising Countries and the Decline of an Ideology*, London: I.B. Tauris.

Harvey, D. (1989) *The Condition of Postmodernity*, Oxford: Basil Blackwell.

Hilsdon, A. (1995) *Madonnas and Martyrs*, Sydney: Allen and Unwin.

Hobart, M. (1993) *Critique of Development: The Growth of Ignorance*, London: Routledge.

Humphries, J. (1977) 'Class Struggle and the Persistence of the Working-class Family', *Cambridge Journal of Economics* 1: 3.

Jayarwardena, K. (1986) *Feminism and Nationalism*, London: Zed.

Jones, K. and Jonasdottir, A. G. (eds) (1988) *The Political Interests of Gender*, London: Sage.

Judd, E. R. (1994) *Gender and Power in Rural North China*, Stanford: Stanford University Press.

Kahn, J. S. (1993) *Constituting the Minangkabau: Peasants, Culture, and Modernity in Colonial Indonesia*, Providence and Oxford: Berg.

—— (1996a) 'Growth, Economic Transformation, Culture and the Middle Classes in Malaysia', in R. Robison and D.S.G. Goodman (eds), *The New Rich in Asia: Mobile Phones, McDonalds and Middle Class Revolution*, London and New York: Routledge.

—— (1996b) *Culture, Multiculture, Postculture*, London and New York: Sage.

Kandiyoti, D. (ed.) (1991) *Women, Islam and the State*, London: Macmillan.

King, A. (1991) 'The Global, the Urban and the World', in A. King (ed.) *Culture, Globalization and the World System: Contemporary Conditions for the Representation of Ideology*, 148–53.

Lash, S. (1990) *Sociology of Postmodernism*, London: Routledge.

Lash, S. and Urry, J. (1994) *Economies of Signs and Space*, London: Sage.

Lazreg, M. (1988) 'Feminism and Difference: The Perils of Writing as a Woman on Algeria,' *Feminist Studies* 14(1): 81–107.

MacCannell, D. and MacCannell, J. Flower (1993) 'Social Class in Postmodernity: Simulacram or Return of the Real?', in C. Rojek and B. Turner (eds) *Forget Baudrillard*, London and New York: Routledge.

McIntosh, M. (1978) 'The State and the Oppression of Women', in A. Kuhn and A. M. Wolpe (eds) *Feminism and Materialism*, London: Routledge and Kegan Paul.

MacKinnon, C. (1987) *Feminism Unmodified: Discourses on Life and Law*, Cambridge, Mass.: Harvard: Cambridge University Press.

Manderson, L. (1991) 'Gender and Politics in Malaysia', in M. Stivens (ed.) *Why Gender Matters in Southeast Asian Politics*, Clayton.: Monash Centre for Southeast Asian Studies.

Mani, L. (1990a) 'Contentious Traditions: The Debate on Sati in Colonial India', in Kumkum Sangari and Sudesh Vaid (eds) (1990) *Recasting Women: Essays in Indian Colonial History*, New Brunswick: Rutgers University Press.

—— (1990b) 'Multiple Mediations: Feminist Scholarship in the Age of Multinational Reception', *Feminist Review* 35 Summer: 24–41.

Marshall, B. L. (1994) *Engendering Modernity: Feminism, Social Theory and Social Change*, Cambridge and Oxford: Polity.

Maznah Mohamed and Wong Soak Koon (eds) (1994) 'Feminism: Malaysian Critique and Experience', *Kajian Malaysia*, Special Issue, Vol XII, Nos 1 & 2, December.

Mee, W. (n.d.) 'National Difference and Global Citizenship on the Internet', in J. Kahn (ed.) *Culture and Identity in Southeast Asia*, Singapore: Institute of Southeast Asian Studies.

Moghadam,V. A. (1994a) *Gender and National Identity, Women and Politics in Muslim Society*, London: Zed Books.

—— (ed.) (1994b) *Identity Politics and Women: Cultural Representations and Feminisms in International Perspective*, Boulder: Westview.

Mohanty, C., Russo, A. and Torres, L. (eds) (1991) *Third World Women and the Politics of Feminism*, Bloomington: Indiana University Press.

Moller Okin, S. (1979) *Women in Western Political Thought*, Princeton: Princeton University Press.

Moore, H. (1988) *Feminism and Anthropology*, Oxford: Basil Blackwell.

—— (1994) *A Passion for Difference*, Bloomington: Indiana University Press.

Nencel, L. and Pels, P. (eds) (1991) *Constructing Knowledge*, London: Sage.

Newland, K. (1991) 'From Transnational Relationships to International Relations: Women in Development and the International Decade for Women', in R. Grant and K. Newland (eds) *Gender and International Relations*, Bloomington: Indiana University Press.

Nicholson, L. (1990) *Feminism/Postmodernism*, New York: Routledge.

Parker, A. Russo, M., Sommer, D., and Yaeger, P. (eds) (1992) *Nationalisms and Sexualities*, London and New York: Routledge.

Paspart, J. and Staudt, K. (eds) (1990) *Women and the State in Africa*, Boulder, Co.: Lynne Riemer.

Pateman, C. (1988) *The Sexual Contract*, London: Polity.
Pateman, C. and Gross, E. (eds) (1986) *Feminist Challenges*, Sydney: Allen and Unwin.
Pelzer, C. 'Social-cultural Dimensions of Renovation in Vietnam: Doi Moi as Dialogue and Transformation in Gender Relations', in W. S. Turley and M. Seldon (eds) *Reinventing Vietnamese Socialism: Doi Moi in Comparative Perspective*, Boulder, Co.: Westview Press.
Pettman, J. J. (1996) *Worlding Women: A Feminist International Politics*, Sydney: Allen and Unwin.
Pieterse, J. N. (1995) 'Globalization as Hybridization', in M. Featherstone, S. Lash and R. Robertson (eds) *Global Modernities*, London: Sage.
Pringle, R. and Watson, S. (1992) 'Women's Interests and the Post-Structuralist State', in M. Barrett and A. Phillips (eds) *Destabilizing Theory: Contemporary Feminist Debates*, Cambridge: Polity.
Radcliffe S. A. and Westwood, S. (eds) (1993) *Viva: Women and Popular Protest in Latin America*, London: Routledge.
Rai, S. (1996) 'Women and the State in the Third World', in H. Afshar (ed.) *Women and Politics in the Third World*, London: Routledge.
Ramazanoglu, C. (1988) *Feminism and the Contradictions of Oppression*, London and New York: Routledge.
Reid, A. (ed.) (1993) *Southeast Asia in the Early Modern Era: Trade, Power and Belief*, Ithaca, NY: Cornell University Press.
Reynolds, C. (1994) 'Predicaments of Modern Thai History', *Southeast Asia Research* 2(1): 64–90.
Robertson, R. (1992) *Globalization*, London: Sage.
Robison, R. (1990) 'Problems of Analysing the Middle Class as a Political Force in Indonesia', in R. Tanter and K. Young (eds) *The Politics of Middle-class Indonesia*, Monash Papers on Southeast Asia No. 19, Clayton: Centre of Southeast Asian Studies.
Robison, R. and Goodman, D. (1996) *The New Rich in Asia: Mobile Phones, McDonalds and Middle-Class Revolution*, London and New York: Routledge.
Rodan, G. (1996) *Political Oppositions in Industrialising Asia,* London: Routledge.
Rosaldo, M. (1974) 'Woman, Culture and Society: A Theoretical Overview', in M. Rosaldo and L. Lamphere (eds) *Woman, Culture and Society*, Stanford: Stanford University Press.
—— (1980) 'The Use and Abuse of Anthropology: Reflections on Feminism and Cross-cultural Understanding', *Signs* 5(3): 389–419.
Said, E. (1986) 'Intellectuals in the Post-colonial World', *Salmagundi*, 70–71, Summer, pp. 44–64.
—— (1993) *Culture and Imperialism*, London: Chatto and Windus.
Showstack Sassoon, A. (ed.) (1988) *Women and the State*, London: Hutchinson.
Silverblatt, I. (1991) 'Interpreting Women in States: New Feminist Ethnohistories', in M. di Leonardo, *Gender at the Crossroads of Knowledge*, Berkeley: University of California Press.
Stauth, G. and Turner, B. S. (eds) (1988) *Nietzsche's Dance: Resentment, Reciprocity and Resistance in Social Life*, Oxford: Blackwell.

Stivens, M. (n.d.a) 'Modernising the Malay Mother', in M. Jolly and K. Ram (eds) *Modernities and Maternities in the Asia Pacific region*, Cambridge: Cambridge University Press (in press).

—— (n.d.b.) 'The Hope of the Nation: Moral Panics and the Construction of Teenagerhood in Contemporary Malaysia', in L. Manderson and P. Liamputtong Rice (eds) *The Emerging Adult: Young People, Sexuality and Courtship in South and Southeast Asia*, London: Harwood Press (in press).

—— (n.d.c.) 'Thinking Again about Gender and the State in Indonesia', in A. Budiman (ed.) *The State and Civil Society in Indonesia*, 2nd edn., Clayton: Centre of Southeast Asian Studies. Monash University.

—— (1990) 'Thinking about Gender and the State in Indonesia', in A. Budiman (ed.) *The State and Civil Society in Indonesia,* Clayton: Centre of Southeast Asian Studies, Monash University.

—— (1991) (ed.) *Why Gender Matters in Southeast Asian Politics*, Clayton: Monash Centre of Southeast Asian Studies.

—— (1992) 'Perspectives on Gender: Problems in Writing about Women in Malaysia', in J. Kahn and F. Loh (eds) *Fragmented Vision: Culture and Politics in Malaysia*, Sydney: Allen and Unwin, Honolulu: Hawaii University Press.

—— (1994a) 'The Gendering of Knowledge: The Case of Anthropology and Feminism', in N. Grieve and A. Burns (eds) *Australian Women: Feminist Perspectives*. Sydney: Oxford University Press.

—— (1994b) 'Gender and Modernity in Malaysia', in A. Gomes, (ed.) *Modernity and Identity: Illustrations from Asia*, Bundoora, Melbourne: La Trobe Asian Studies, La Trobe University Press: 66–95.

—— (1996) *Matriliny and Modernity: Sexual Politics and Social Change in Rural Malaysia*, Asian Studies Association of Australia, Women in Asia Series, Sydney: Allen and Unwin.

Suryakusuma, J. (1996) 'The State and Sexuality in New Order Indonesia', in L.J. Spears (ed.) *Fantasizing the Feminine in Indonesia*, Durham, NC and London: Duke University Press.

Sylvester, C. (1993) *Feminist Theory in International Relations*, Cambridge: Cambridge University Press.

Tanter, R. and Young, K. (eds) (1990) *The Politics of Middle Class Indonesia*, Monash Papers on Southeast Asia, No. 19, Clayton: Centre of Southeast Asian Studies, Monash University.

Turner, B. S. (ed.) (1990) *Theories of Modernity and Postmodernity*, London: Sage.

Walby, S. (1992) 'Post-Post-Modernism', in M. Barrett and A. Phillips (eds), *Destabilizing Theory*, Cambridge: Polity Press.

Waylen, G. (1996) 'Analysing Women in the Politics of the Third World', in H. Afshar (ed.) *Women and Politics in the Third World*, London: Routledge.

West, G. and Blumberg, R. L. (eds) (1990) *Women and Social Protest*, New York: Oxford University Press.

Wolff, J. (1985) 'The Invisible Flâneuse: Women and the Literature of Modernity', *Theory, Culture and Society* 2 (3): 37–46.

—— (1991) 'The Global and the Specific: Reconciling Conflicting Theories of Culture', in A. King (ed.) *Culture, Globalization and the World System: Contemporary Conditions for the Representation of Ideology*, London:

Macmillan, in association with the Department of Art and Art History, University of New York at Binghampton, NY.

Young, K. (1991) 'Political Science and the Neglect of Gender', in M. Stivens, (ed.) *Why Gender Matters in Southeast Asian Politics*, Clayton: Monash Centre of Southeast Asian Studies.

Yuval-Davis, N. and Anthias, F. (eds) (1989) *Woman/Nation/State*, Basingstoke: Macmillan.

2 Indonesian women at work

Reframing the subject

Krishna Sen

This chapter looks at shifts in the discourses about Indonesian women in the current phase of their enmeshment into global exchanges. It tries to understand the interplay of class and gender in the changing constructions of women in Indonesia. Through a reading of key state policy documents and advertising images in the 1990s, I argue that the 'working woman' operates as an increasingly central, though highly contested, signifier in contemporary Indonesian politics and popular culture.

From the point of view of this chapter, the precise numbers of women in paid work is less important than the recognition that in the 1990s, in sharp contrast to the 1970s, the working woman is replacing the 'housewife' as the paradigmatic female subject in political, cultural and economic discourses in Indonesia. The working woman is everywhere, from the major policy statements of the government such as the GBHN[1] to radical political posters, to advertisements. She is even in Garuda Indonesia's inflight magazine![2] In accounting for the rise of the 'working woman' as a central figure in many Indonesian institutional discourses, this chapter makes two key arguments: first, that the working woman is one of the icons around which Indonesia's position as a modern nation in a global economy and culture is legitimised; second, that this iconic figure is premised (explicitly and implicitly) on the professional rather than the proletarian woman.

This does not mean that the mother and wife are set to disappear from all Indonesian texts. Kathryn Robinson in Chapter 3 shows clearly that the domestic sphere continues to frame many constructions of femininity in Indonesia. This chapter, however, deals with official and commercial texts emanating from metropolitan Jakarta, which are addressed principally to an urban middle-class audience in Indonesia and the world outside. The importance of these texts lies not in their universal appeal to all Indonesians or even to the majority of Indonesians, but rather in the large section of the citizenry they exclude: the proletarian, the rural, the provincial. This chapter is in part about reading some of these silences.

FRAMING THE SUBJECT

Academic research on women in Asia overwhelmingly characterises the working woman as a labourer in the multinational factory floor. Spivak, perhaps the most famous Asian feminist academic, has suggested for instance that 'collusions between local forms of "patriarchy" and transnational capital have made the subproletarian woman "the paradigmatic subject" of the international division of labour' (Spivak 1988, cited in Ong 1991: 281). Within this feminist–Asianist discourse, the title 'Indonesian women at work' raises expectations that the subject of the chapter is the poor and exploited woman living in dirty slums and working long shifts on assembly lines (see, for example, Grossman 1979).

Similarly, feminist academic and activist accounts of Indonesia focus on women as victims of the nation's modernisation and its rapid incorporation into global capitalism since 1965. For those familiar with this literature, the title of this chapter might evoke the image of Javanese women out of work through farm mechanisation (e.g. Ann Stoler 1975), or the elderly street seller transformed into an icon of Indonesian womanhood by Lea Jellinek's evocative ethnography (1978). In the 1990s those images have been supplemented by Jakarta's younger kampung women of Alison Murray's (1991) *No Money No Honey* and the *Factory Daughters* of Diane Wolf (1992). The archetypal target of feminist critique in contemporary Indonesia is, however, the institutionally 'housewifed' woman of New Order government policy.[3] The single most cited passage on Indonesian women is probably Hull's (1976) account of the 'five duties' of women promoted by the PKK (Organisation for Family Welfare) within the New Order government. These ideals, widely publicised in the early 1970s (Sullivan 1991: 64), were:

1 Producer of nation's future generations.
2 Wife and faithful companion to her husband.
3 Mother and educator of her children.
4 Manager of household.
5 Citizen (Hull 1976: 21–2).

On the other hand, the critical accounts of wealth and power in New Order Indonesia, whether from a liberal position (e.g. Crouch 1978) or from a Marxist one (e.g. Robison 1986), implicitly assume the citizen/

subject to be male (cf. Chapter 1). Agency, whether in reproducing or challenging the political and economic structures of Indonesia, is thus ascribed almost exclusively to men. In all of these scenarios women play the roles of victims or, at best, survivors against great odds.

Against this malestream and feminist mainstream, this chapter focusses on a growing minority of women who belong to the middle classes in their own right as participants in the economy in the public sphere of society, and not only as daughters, wives and mothers of male members of those classes. Indeed, the chapter aims to rethink the category of 'middle-class woman' – she is neither left out of production and politics (as in malestream writing), nor merely victimised by those processes (as in the feminist–Asianist mainstream). She is not domesticated (as middle-class women appear to have been in the early Anglo-European transition to capitalism), nor does she share the working conditions of working-class women. The ambiguous location of Indonesia's 'new middle-class working woman' thus provides a useful heuristic category around which to rethink the politics of class and gender. I suggest that women's ideas and practices, their work and play, are increasingly significant in the operation of government and market. Without taking into consideration the images, actions and policies that these women are generating, it will be impossible to understand the continuities as well as the transformations in the particular conjunction of capitalism and patriarchy that is involved in the current phase of Indonesia's 'modernisation'.

In the framework of contemporary feminist research, the right to write about a society to which one does not 'belong', of which one is not a 'native', is under challenge. The 1995 women's conference in Beijing made it clear yet again that we continue to conceptualise our identities and speaking positions largely on the basis of national boundaries. I need then to take account of my position as an Indian woman speaking about (though by no means on behalf of) women in Indonesia to an imagined global feminist and academic readership. Of course, I could don a pan-Asian identity and argue that speaking about an 'other' becomes a sensitive issue mainly in relation to a 'West–Rest' contradiction that is bound up in the history of colonialism. Here I want to flag a response more pertinent to this chapter to that persistent feminist question: 'who can speak about what/whom?'

Jonathan Friedman in his book *Cultural Identity and Global Process* (1994) suggested a useful way of thinking about identities in the global capitalist framework. He argues that the 'practice of identity encompasses a practice of consumption and even production' (p.115, see also Chapter 1 in this book). Identity, then, depends not on colours of skins and accidents of place of birth but rather on what we eat and wear, the movies we watch and the computers and dishwashers we use to do our work. In that sense, my 'practice of identity' is very similar to the Indonesian 'middle-class working women' who are my main 'informants' for this chapter, and who are its subject matter. At any rate, my 'practices of consumption and production' are closer to theirs than their practices are to those of, say, the Javanese peasant woman, the tribal woman in Irian Jaya or the Achenese female domestic servant in Medan.[4] Indeed, it is my similarity to the metropolitan middle-class professional Indonesian woman – our shared world of gendered images and ideas, and our class-based (consumption and production) differences from the sub-proletarian woman in Indonesia and elsewhere in Asia – that forms a central feminist problematic of this chapter.

AFFLUENT WORKING WOMEN

Reviewing the research on gender in the context of the rise of the Anglo-European middle class in the nineteenth century Anne Phillips writes: 'Class began and continued as a muddle, but as "middle" and "working" came into sharper focus in the course of the century, they did so partly through the roles they allotted to their women' (Phillips 1992: 95). She goes on to argue that 'middle-class' status became increasingly dependent on the exclusion of women from productive work while at the same time 'women from the working class were being called out of their homes into fields, mines, factories, and . . . into domestic service for the rich' (ibid.: 96).

Such a clear division between the culturally distinguishable 'housewife' and 'working woman' is impossible to sustain in the context of advanced capitalism. In the late twentieth century, in the West as well as in most of Asia, there are growing numbers of women in a highly diversified range of white-collar jobs (albeit, not the same or even the same range of jobs as men's – see Adkins 1995). I have tried, therefore, in this chapter to distinguish 'working women' from 'working-class women' – to emphasise that today's affluent women are not by definition women of leisure.

Dick Robison has commented that 'studies of the Indonesian middle class are in their infancy both in terms of theorising this social category in its Indonesian context and assembling a systematic and comprehensive set of data to support any wide ranging quantitative conclusion' (1996: 84). Such lacunae in the current research on Indonesia are all the more obvious when one tries to focus on women. Furthermore, as feminists have consistently argued, class analyses of most societies have been overwhelmingly 'gender blind'. The question of women's class identity is further complicated by the contradictions of their location in productive and reproductive economies.[5] In the current state of research, it is impossible to identify precisely which Indonesian women and how many can be placed in the category of 'working middle-class women' or even a more descriptive category such as affluent working women (that is, which professions, what income segments, in what geographical locations). It is possible, however, to document the emergence of the figure of the 'working woman' in Indonesian discourses – from policy papers to national statistics to various forms of popular culture and the media.

The ideology of early New Order refused to recognise women as workers. Ali Murtopo, one of the most powerful military figures in the 1970s, reportedly claimed, 'in Indonesia . . . generally it is only men who work . . .' (*Angkatan Bersenjata* 2 July 1973). Somewhat ironically, feminist critiques of that period confirmed that ideological position by documenting the ways in which New Order 'modernisation' programmes were pushing women out of paid work. For instance, Morgan, summarising the data from the 1970s writes: 'Rice-hulling has cut women's income by $55 million and reduced half-time employment by more than 8.3 months for 1 million women; yet income for the men who work in the new mills has increased by $5 million . . . Imports and mechanisation have forced 90 per cent of women weavers (over 1 million women) out of work . . .' (1984: 315) and so on.

By the mid-1980s, research on women's employment in the Third World had started to call into question the assumption that there was a single irreversible systemic tendency within dependent capitalist development marginalising women from production (see Scott 1986). The Indonesian figures clearly show significant rises in female employment throughout the 1980s and 1990s. Even when economic growth slowed down in the mid-1980s (to 2.5 per cent in 1985) female labour participation continued to rise – from 32.6 per cent in 1980 to 39.21 per cent in 1990. During the period 1989–1994 'the female labour force grew at an average annual rate of 5.5 per cent compared with only 3.6 per cent for the male labour force' (Indonesian Country Report 1994). By 1994, out of a total labour force of 86.3 million, 36.1 million were women (Richard and Jenny Mann, 1994: 14).

Although women's earnings continue to be about two-thirds that of men's,[6] in an increasingly diversified work context there is a small but growing number of women whose earning capacity is not only greater than that of the vast majority of working women, but also the vast majority of working men. In 1992 just over 11 per cent of women earned wages of more than Rp.150,000 per month, whereas some 75 per cent of male workers earned less than that figure (BPS and UNICEF 1993: 61–2). In a nation of stark inequities in wealth and power,[7] however, these sorts of statistics on wages do not provide us with a picture of the dramatic contrasts in the earnings and consumption practices of its citizens. In Jakarta, and to a lesser extent in other major cities, there is a very visible minority of wealthy women (and men) whose purchasing power is many times the Rp.150,000 which marks the national statistical institute's highest wage bracket.

Patterns of women's employment provide some indication of the numbers of working middle-class women. In the public service, for instance, women's participation has grown rapidly, doubling in the decade to 1984 (Logsdon 1985: 79–87) and most rapidly in the middle management levels. Latest figures from the Bureau of Statistics show that women hold almost 40 per cent of *Golongan* (level) 2 and 32 per cent of *Golongan* 3 positions, although only about 13 per cent each of the top and bottom levels of the bureaucracy (BPS and UNICEF 1993: 50). The proportion of employed women in professional jobs has risen consistently since the early 1980s (Office of Minister of State for the Role of Women 1989: 23). In 1993 4.88 per cent of all working women were categorised as professional, administrative and managerial, as against 4.07 per cent of the working male population. There is an increasing proportion of women in the legal and medical professions (BPS and UNICEF 1993: 52). According to a study of women managers in Southeast Asia about 6.6 of all 'administrative and managerial workers in Indonesia' are women (Hoffarth 1990:17).[8] While the proportion of women 'managers' in Indonesia is among the lowest in Southeast Asia, the study concludes that the management sector is growing rapidly throughout the region, 'with marked improvement in women's participation in it' (ibid.). Of course, such figures are by no means adequate for a comprehensive empirical account of the affluent middle class, nor, indeed, can we mount any argument on the basis of such data without knowing how categories (such as managerial) were defined. Whatever the real numbers, however, there appears to be a growing awareness of women in high offices in the private sector. For instance, the 'Who's Who' of Indonesian executives (*Top Eksekutif Indonesia*) included 3 women in its list of 89 in its first issue published in 1992, while in its second issue published in 1994 nine out of 79 were women. There is also plenty of anecdotal evidence that suggests that some of the business empires built up in the last 25 years may come to be inherited by daughters rather than sons.

POLICIES

The rise of the New Order in Indonesia has frequently been associated with the consolidation of capitalist modernisation in Indonesia (see Robison 1986). Feminist critics both within and outside Indonesia have also seen the New Order as the consolidation of a patriarchal state (see Suryakusuma 1991; Kacasungkana 1992). In that sense, the Indonesian instance fits all too neatly into a standard feminist critique of capitalist modernisation, which argues that modernisation has led to '[t]he differentiation of spheres, the increasing division of labour, [and] the "functional" specialization of women into "reproductive" work' (Marshall 1994: 28). But, as Marshall points out, such generalisations are often 'at the expense of a more adequate consideration of the potential of modernity to imagine new possibilities for women which would entail working through the double-edged character of differentiation of spheres, seeing openings for new means and contexts of identity formation' (ibid.).

In a speech to a Catholic Women's Organisation in 1967, President Suharto said that the disappearance of the difference between men and women under the 'Old Order' [sic] was one of the main features of its political and social instability (cited in Douglas 1980). In its first decade the New Order government proceeded to institutionalise an ideal of gender difference through two key institutions – PKK and Dharmawanita. Until the establishment of the Ministry for the Role of Women in 1983, the government's policies regarding women most frequently involved some participation of these two institutions. PKK was initiated in 1974, and through it 'women's participation in national development became law' (Sullivan 1991: 62). Although its members are not paid as government servants, Sullivan has described the PKK as 'functional units of local government, whose main task is to implement the Applied Family Welfare Programme and its many projects at the neighbourhood and village levels' (ibid.: 62–3). Dharmawanita is an older organisation that pre-dates the establishment of the New Order government. But in 1974 membership of this organisation became compulsory for all women civil servants and civil servants' wives. According to PKK's ideals listed above (see page 35), a woman is first a reproductive agent, then a faithful wife and mother, and an unpaid domestic worker and consumer. She is a citizen last and paid productive worker not at all.

The constitution of Dharmawanita states as its objective: 'the guidance and development of civil-service wives' organisations with the aim of increasing their participation in National Development *in accordance with the nature/duty (kodrat) and position of women as wife and housewife.*'[9] The structure of the organisation reproduces precisely this identity of woman as wife. Nationally the wife of a senior Minister heads Dharmawanita. In each government department, wives in the Dharmawanita hierarchy are placed in accordance with their husband's position in that department. Similarly, in the PKK the office bearer's position depends on her husband's position within the hierarchy of the government bureaucracy.

Unlike many other states in Southeast Asia, the New Order's commitment to capitalist development did not lead to the construction of women as cheap fodder for large-scale capital. In Malaysia and the Philippines, for instance, governments in the early 1970s introduced legal changes to make women's labour more readily available to manufacturers (Grossman 1979). In New Order Indonesia, however, protective legislation for women workers initiated in the late 1940s, such as restrictions on women's night work and working in mines, lifting weights over 25 kg, 3 months paid maternity leave and 2 days a month 'menstrual leave', remained largely intact. On the other hand, through most of the New Order period women have been targets of governmental policy and expenditure mainly in relation to 'family planning'. We could argue, then, that discourses and practices of New Order policy constructed women as biologically specified reproductive workers. Given the structures of Dharmawanita and PKK, women's only legitimate access to state power was as wives of powerful male functionaries of the state.

By the early 1980s, however, cracks were starting to appear within the state-sponsored woman-as-wife-and-womb paradigm. In 1978, 'women' became a separate category in the GBHN. This was explicitly part of Indonesia's response to the United Nation's International Women's year. The previous year a 'Junior' Minister for Women's Affairs (Menteri Muda Urusan Wanita) had been appointed. This became a cabinet position in 1983, with the formal title 'Office of the Minister of State for the Role of Women' (henceforth Women's Affairs), again as part of Indonesia's participation in a global event, the International Women's Decade. Even the most cursory look at the statements and publications coming out of this ministerial office since the mid-1980s shows a growing emphasis on women's paid and productive role in the economy.

By the late 1980s a similar emphasis comes into play in the government's overall policy position. In 1978 and 1983 the GBHN emphasised that a 'woman's role in national development' must be 'in harmony with the development of her responsibility and role in the family's health and welfare'. The 1983 GBHN added that the 'role and responsibility of women in development had to mature through education and training in various sectors *suitable to their needs and abilities*' (my emphasis). In the 1988 formulation that clause was reworded to remove any assumption of women's particular 'needs and abilities'. It now said 'women's skills and education had to be upgraded especially to enable women to take advantage of work opportunities in various sectors'. The 1993 GBHN removed the reference to women's gender-specific role in child-rearing, which had appeared in every previous edition of the document.

Ever since the 1978 GBHN declared that women had a role to play both in national economic development and in the family, one of the buzzwords in the women's policy area had been *peran ganda* or the dual role of women. This suggests that the early New Order ideal of the woman-as-primarily-mother-and-wife had begun to change. While popular media in Indonesia, and indeed in much of Southeast Asia, enthusiastically embraced the career woman as attractive wife and super-mum, Indonesian feminists increasingly came to see women's dual role as a double-burden, putting them at a disadvantage *vis-à-vis* men. In the preparation of the draft for the 1993 GBHN, key officials in Women's Affairs tried to introduce the idea that *peran ganda* or dual role should refer not just to working women, but to working men as well. That terminology did not receive formal official sanction, but the 1993 GBHN affirms that 'the promotion of women's role in the welfare of the family is to be implemented alongside the promotion of awareness of [the] parent's (male and female) role and responsibility in the education of children . . .' (GBHN 1993, cited in Sjamsiah Ahmad 1993: 18).

How did a liberal feminist agenda find its way into government policy and shift its focus away from the domestic role of women? Gossip is often the best way to understand political processes in Indonesia. According to Jakarta gossip, ever since the establishment of the cabinet position in Women's Affairs there had been differences between the successive female ministers holding that portfolio and Dharmawanita heads (who, as mentioned earlier, are always the wife of a senior minister). There were some personality and funding issues involved – a tussle to control the dispersal of development funds for women. But the rivalry between 'women's minister' and 'minister's wife' can also be seen as symptomatic of a wider strain between female civil servants and wives of civil servants.[10] It seems to be common for women civil servants to resent their obligations to Dharmawanita and their bosses' wives who put additional demands on these working women in the name of that institution. Some have never participated in any Dharmawanita activity. At least one senior female bureaucrat told me that she had written formally to her male boss pointing out that she was not the subordinate of his wife. In general, female civil servants do not seem to take their obligations to Dharmawanita seriously.

Interestingly, there are several common grounds occupied by the Ministry of Women's Affairs and the women's organisations which have developed outside the New Order state apparatus. Both the Ministry and the new Indonesian women's organisations came into existence in the early 1980s, in the aftermath of the United Nation's declaration of the 'International Decade for Women', and in the context of an increasingly global definition of women's issues. Furthermore, the implicit rejection of Dharmawanita by the women civil servants is matched by the explicit critique of Dharmawanita, particularly its basis in the woman-as-wife paradigm, by the non-government women's organisations.[11]

In the early New Order period, women's only access to state funding and legitimate political agency was as wives in the Dharmawanita and PKK. After the late 1970s, however, with women's rising employment in the civil service, a small but growing number of women had access to the power of the state in their own right, as functionaries. With the establishment of the Ministry of Women's Affairs, there was a further legitimate institution (in addition to and very different from Dharmawanita and the PKK) within the New Order state to articulate policies and ideologies about women. The 'femocrats'[12] and women academics who have been involved in government planning processes clearly see themselves as liberating Indonesian women from the domesticity which is the ideological justification of Dharmawanita. Thus, the shifting paradigm in 'women's policy' in Indonesia in the 1990s comes, at least in part, out of a contradiction between two sources of power that women in affluent classes in Indonesia acquired in the New Order – as wives of bureaucrats in the early years of the New Order and later as femocrats. The new emphasis on the working woman in government policy reflects the growing influence of the nascent democracy, but does not necessarily imply a recognition of the growing female labour force or the needs of working-class women.

Although official discourse on gender proceeds largely on the assumption that women are a single unified category, the class position implicit in the recasting of the government's policy on women becomes clear when we look closely at the wording of the current GBHN. As noted earlier, the 1993 GBHN not only continues the shift of policy focus to women in the work place, but also attempts to place some of the domestic responsibility onto men. Of the five paragraphs devoted to 'women's role', two talk about the joint roles and responsibilities of men and women. Paragraph I insists on the equality of men and women in all public roles 'as citizens and as human resources for development'.

This role includes men's and women's responsibility to 'build a healthy, prosperous and happy family along with the nurturing of children, adolescents and youth in the effort to fully develop the Indonesian character (*manusia Indonesia*)'. Paragraph III deals with the family, household (part of which I have quoted earlier) and 'Methods for creating family welfare'. It calls for the 'promotion of awareness of the parents' (male and female) roles and responsibilities in the education of children and adolescents based on religious values (*nilai-nilai agama*) and national cultural values (*nilai-nilai budaya bangsa*)'.

It is significant that government policy is beginning to define gender equality not only as women's access to jobs but also in terms of men's shared responsibility for looking after children. Both popular culture and official discourse of family health and welfare had tended to assign all blame for failures of children to mothers. (See for example my discussion of genres of films that depict the working woman as an unfit mother, Sen 1994: 131–56.) But what is left unsaid in the GBHN's shifting definition of women's and men's work is equally significant. The section from GBHN quoted above refers to parents' joint responsibility in the education of children, and in the overall cultural or philosophical guidance of children. But it refers to no other aspect of domestic work or indeed the physical labour of raising children.

This very selective inclusion of domestic responsibility into the gender equity agenda is understandable when we take into account the Indonesian professional women's (including the femocrats) domestic arrangements. In middle- and upper-class households, the physical work is performed largely by domestic servants. The female (and male) civil servants who draft government policies do not themselves have to undertake domestic chores. Indeed, the professional woman's ability to establish herself in a career depends on the continuation of inequalities of wealth and power, which make it possible for her to be released from domestic work. The professional woman's claims to equality with men of her class do not require the man to share domestic work, since the burden of domestic labour can be passed on to the displaced rural poor and to female members of the urban working classes. In contemporary Indonesia (unlike many Western contexts), housework cannot be described as unpaid appropriation of *women's* labour. Rather, it represents one of the least regulated and lowest-paid sectors for the *appropriation of working-class women's labour.*[13]

The feminist lawyer Nursjahbani Kacasungkana has pointed to the contradictions in the interests of professional and proletarian women in relation to recent criticisms of aspects of labour laws by some women's groups. As noted, Indonesian women workers have the right to 2 days a month menstrual leave under the Labour Act of 1948 (Article 13, UU Kerja No.12 1948). In the early 1990s IWAPI, the Association of Indonesian Business Women, led the criticism against this provision on the grounds that it was 'contradictory to the aims of women's emancipation . . . [because] the large numbers of women who make use of this right only serve to lower the productivity of the companies for which they work and, as a result, many companies are reluctant to employ women'. Kacasungkana argues that IWAPI's attempt to repeal the law (the motion was moved but defeated in parliament in 1992), had general support from 'middle-class women who work as white-collar employees' and no longer make use of menstrual leave provisions. To them the biologism of this leave provision appears 'discriminatory' and 'old-fashioned'. The large majority of women in blue-collar work, however, continue to make use of the provision which remains important, particularly due to the high level of malnutrition and ill-health amongst these women (Kacasungkana 1992: 17–18).

The redefinition of the reproductive mother-woman as the productive worker-woman in recent government policy and political discourse more generally has the potential, then, to remove special protective regulations for women labourers, which depend on foregrounding women's biological specificity as reproducers. The case of menstrual leave provisions underline the enormous socio-economic differences among Indonesia's 'working women' and the contradictions between their aspirations. The same ideological move that cracks the glass ceiling for professional working women may further deepen the exploitation for the vast majority of proletarian women. Thus, the politics of sex in contemporary Indonesia cannot be separated from the politics of class.

PICTURES

I have argued so far that in the 1990s we can observe major reorientations in the conceptualisation of women in governmental policy frameworks in Indonesia. I have argued further that the new paradigmatic female figure, the 'working woman', is being cast by and principally in the interest of middle-class professional women. I will argue here that we find the same class-specific resistance to the woman-as-housewife ideal if we look at advertising. This is not to suggest that the housewife image has disappeared, but rather that it is steadfastly occupying only the lower end of the advertising market.

I could have chosen any cultural practice to demonstrate the confluence of policy and popular imagery, but advertising is an obvious choice

– partly because it sits quite unequivocally in that cusp between economics and culture where consumption practices and cultural identities come together, and also because anecdotal evidence suggests that there has been a phenomenal expansion of women in creative positions in the advertising industry in the late 1980s. Images of women in domestic and maternal roles continue to be the mainstay of advertisements of everyday consumer items like food, beverages, toiletries and household cleaning products. These account for a good third of the total advertising expenditure in print and television (Indonesian Association of Advertising Agents 1993–94: 54). A few women in the industry told me about their attempts to change their clients' assumptions that only women should appear in domestic roles in detergent or food advertisements. One Melbourne-trained creative director[14] claimed that in her 7 years in the industry, she had steadfastly avoided the 'mum in the kitchen' image, even though the majority of her clients were from the food industry. On the other hand, she has used 'dads' in two successful food advertisements – although both were somewhat ironic representations of men's domestic skills!

While men only rarely appear in food, detergent or baby product advertisements, except in a few humorous episodes, images of professional women are increasingly common in advertisements for banks, real estate, cars and computers. This advertising is not, as one might expect, addressed exclusively to the male, who works in the office and makes the big financial decisions. Some are addressed to the professional female. Even skincare products have started to target specifically this professional woman, her 'working woman' image defined by the tall office blocks around her, the diary and the laptop computer. The written text of the Ponds 'advertorial'[15] (Figure 2.1) in *Femina*, (4 October 1995) (the oldest and one of the most successful women's magazines in Indonesia), starts thus: 'Women of today are increasingly participating in a variety of professions which demands activity outside of the office. [They work as] journalists, television reporters, architects, sales officer [sic], account executive [sic] (the last two terms in English in the original) and in a variety of other jobs that involve frequent travel.' Of course, advertisements which are arguably addressed primarily to men also use images of women. And in these too the woman is marked clearly as a working woman (see the advertisement for 'Alctel Communication System', *Tempo* 28 May 1994, Figure 2.2).

As indicated earlier, the ways in which the female subject is interpellated into Indonesian advertisement texts is changing. In the 1970s, and even in the first half of the 1980s, advertisements were not on the whole addressed to a consumer, specifically defined as a 'professional

Figure 2.1 The ‘professional woman’ in Ponds advertorial, *Femina*, 4 October 1995

Untuk pemecahan soal-soal sistim komunikasi, bicaralah dengan mitra setempat anda.

Di seluruh Indonesia kami sedang membantu memecahkan soal-soal komunikasi dengan membangun pelbagai macam sistim komunikasi yang maju. Sebagai bagian dari Alcatel Alsthom, kami percaya bahwa pemecahan yang paling efektif adalah yang didapatkan dari pekerjaan yang dilakukan dalam kerja sama yang erat dengan para pelanggan kami.

Misalnya, kami telah memasang lebih dari 10.000 km sambungan digital mikrogelombang dengan kapasitas tinggi yang merupakan tulang punggung dari sistim transmisi jarak jauh Indonesia. Di bidang komunikasi mobil, bersama dengan Satelindo, kami akan memasang jenis jaringan GSM yang paling mutakhir yang meliputi 18 kota dengan kapasitas yang bisa menerima 350.000 langganan.

Alcatel. Mitra anda yang dapat diandalkan tentang sistim-sistim komunikasi.

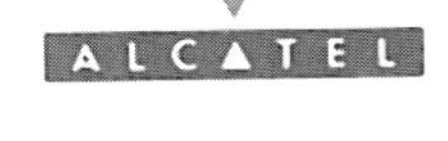

Figure 2.2 The ‘professional woman’ in advertisement for Alctel Communication System, *Tempo*, 28 May 1994

woman'. As a case in point, we might look at advertisements carried in *Tempo*, the most successful Indonesian weekly after 1965, virtually a flagship for the entire middle-class readership. To compare advertising in it over the years, I picked at random an issue each from 1971, the first year of the magazine's publication, 1986 and 1994. In the April 1971 issue there were two advertisements with female images, one clearly domestic (advertising a stove), the other simply a woman in appealing posture, with no specific social identity attached. In the 16 August 1986 issue, when advertisements were now in colour, there was not one female image that could be identified as a working woman. By contrast, in the May 1994 issue (just weeks before the magazine was banned by the government), almost every female image in advertisements was that of a professional woman. Even the vitamin advertisement, where one might expect a domestic scene, is addressed to the working couple, 'facing a busy Monday schedule' (see Figure 2.3).

Such an apparent transformation in the image of women in advertisements, however, is by no means unique to Indonesia. Studies of advertising in American women's magazines from the 1950s to the 1980s show a similarly increasing presence of the 'working woman' (Busby and Leichty 1993: 247–64). Nor does the increasing presence of the professional woman indicate that the domestic-maternal female is losing her appeal to *all* Indonesian readers/consumers. In 1994, for instance, the readers of the very popular women's magazine *Kartini* voted a Nestlé's milk product advertisement (see Figure 2.4) as their favourite. It was the highly conventional image of a young mother with pre-school-age child. The advertisement works by addressing the woman as a mother responsible for the health and growth of the child, responsible for determining choices in household consumption. All of these aspects of a woman's domestic work are referred to in the written text of the advertisement. We need to ask, then, what considerations determine the choice of the 'working woman' image in any particular advertisement.

The advertisements I refer to above are for a diverse range of goods and services and appear in magazines like *Tempo*, *Femina* and *Kartini*. These magazines differ in a variety of ways, but from the advertisers' point of view one difference is crucial – the so-called 'socio-economic status' (SES) of the consumer to whom the advertised goods are to be sold. Related to that is the readership/audience of the medium in which the advertisement is placed. The advertising industry divides the audience/consumer into four categories, from A at the top to D at the bottom, according to personal disposable income. Some advertising professionals I interviewed identified a 'super A' category, which has

Figure 2.3 The 'working couple' in advertisement for Vitness vitamins, *Tempo*, 28 May 1994

only recently come to be recognised by the industry. This group is a very small minority with an exceptionally high level of disposable income of perhaps over Rp.1 million (approximately US$4,000) a month. Most of my informants in the advertising agencies, however, seemed unwilling to attach precise income or expenditure figures to the SES categories.[16]

"Aku dan Kau suka Dancow"

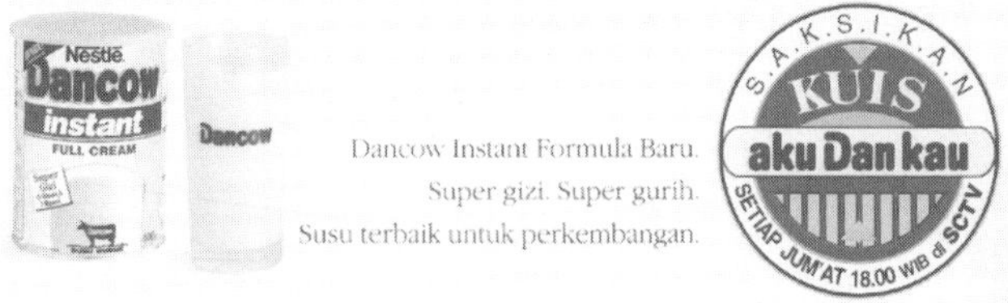

Figure 2.4 Targeting the 'domestic-maternal female': advertisement for Dancow range, *Kartini,* 1994
Source: reproduced with permission of Pt. Nestlé Indonesia

Matra, a leading men's magazine analysing its own readership provides the following monthly Rupiah expenditure figure for each category:

A1 over 700,000 (roughly US$3,000)
A2 500,000–700,000
B 300,000–500,000

C 150,000–300,000
D 100,000–200,000

Like the advertising executives I interviewed, *Matra* appears to have no interest in those who fall below category D (*Matra* April 1995:136). A comparison of the advertisers' categories with the categories of wages used by the Statistical Institute suggests that a large majority of Indonesians in fact remain outside the advertisers' concerns altogether. As noted earlier, according to 1993 BPS figures only 11 per cent of females and 25 per cent of males earned more than Rp. 150,000 a month. In looking at advertisements, then, we are looking at differences among a high- to middle-income minority within the total population. However, even within this minority the differences are clear. The higher we go up the advertisers' SES categories, the more certain the displacement of the figure of the 'domestic woman'.

The *Kartini* readership, predominantly in the advertisers' B–C 'socio-economic status' category, indicated in late 1994 a continuing attachment to the woman in a domestic setting. By contrast in *Femina* and *Tempo*, with readerships in A–B categories, advertisements in the 1990s are dominated by images of the professional woman. However, the gender revolution in advertising images comes most fully into play when we look at those directed to the women in the 'Super A' SES category.

The advertisement for Thalia Le Spa (see Figure 2.5), a highly exclusive health club was created by a thirty-something, successful woman creative director. According to her, this advertisement for an expensive luxury item was addressed primarily to the 'Super A' consumer and first appeared early in 1994 in *Dewi*, the most exclusive Indonesian language women's magazine on the market. Later in the year, with its original English caption translated into Indonesian, the advertisement reappeared in *Femina*. The two-page advertisement centres on a naked, white, male torso with a caption in large print: 'True beauty for you and your man.'

The male body in this advertisement came out of an international image bank to which most advertisers around the world subscribe. The identifiably white male was not only beheaded, but all his body hair was removed by computer imaging technology to make it conform to what the creator of the advertisement thought would appeal to the tastes of her female audience. This image, highly unusual both in Indonesian advertising and in the country's media more generally, was made possible by the circulation of images internationally and the technology that allows these images to be manipulated. More importantly, it was made possible by the advertisers' hypostatised female readers/consumers who

Figure 2.5 Addressing the 'Super-A' customer: advertisement for Thalia Le Spa

were not 'faithful companions to husbands' nor the ideal 'reproducers of the next generation' of Indonesian citizens! The woman addressed by this advertisement is a far cry from the wife-reproducer of early New Order policy, who is replicated in the image of the young mother in the Nestlé's advertisement popular with *Kartini* readers.

The 'Thalia Le Spa' advertisement heralds a new breed of woman, both as producer and consumer, who works hard, pays her own bills and whose fantasies might include a white man. Her hard work is evoked in the written text of the advertisement: 'natural beauty can only be achieved with your own great effort.' The collective desires and fantasies which this advertisement evokes cannot be fully elaborated within the domestic sphere – whether we understand that 'domestic' in the sense of the household or the nation. In other words, this text invokes the subject as a woman who is not just sophisticated, wealthy and professional, but also as one whose experiences and aspirations include a world beyond the limits of the nation.

A sense of enmeshment in the world is also one of the driving forces in the shift to the working woman in the policy discourse discussed earlier in this chapter. In documents, speeches and policies coming out of the Ministry of Women's Affairs the plea to recognise the importance and needs of the working woman is inevitably justified by explicitly referring to 'globalisation'. Examples of this abound. The preface to the first 'Gender and Development Training Material' published by Women's Affairs in 1993 starts thus: 'The promotion in women's role is not only a matter of national concern, but a global concern, the concern of all nations in the world' (Office of the Minister of State for the Role of Women 1993: iii). Sjamsiah Ahmad, one of the four Ministerial Assistants in Women's Affairs closed her analysis of the 'equal partnership of men and women' in the current GBHN with the following: 'The foregoing provides some information and opinion on the promotion of women's role in Indonesia and as a world movement in the era of globalisation . . .' (1993: 23). In the 1990s it is difficult to find a single speech by Ministers of Women's Affairs (two in succession in the last 5 years) which does not refer to globalisation. But apart from acknowledging that the UN International Women's Year led to the insertion of women's special interests into the GBHN (Moerpratomo 1990: 1), there seems to be little discussion of why globalisation should require Indonesian women to become men's equals in the public arena of work. More often than not globalisation is seen as an inexorable force transforming gender relations: 'The challenges of progress and globalisation oblige us, whether we wish to or not, to see the role of men and women within a regime of equal partnership . . .' (Moerpratomo, Minister of Women's Affairs, 1992: 3).

As indicated earlier, the femocrats have, in a sense, been bred by globalisation, which pushed the Indonesian government into particular policy initiatives and institutional arrangements with regard to women.[17] Many of them also had long experience as students and scholars abroad and some as functionaries of the United Nations. Their advocacy on behalf of Indonesian women at the national and international level depends on a global discourse of gender equity.

SEX, CLASS AND KITCHENS

Globalised language and images of gender equity are clearly being adopted and adapted to challenge patriarchal policies and practices in Indonesia. But global patterns intrude on the construction of the affluent working woman in Indonesia in contradictory ways. As noted earlier, the central figure in contemporary Indonesia's gender equality agenda – the working woman who does no housework – does not appear in the history of Anglo-American capitalism.[18] In the West, increasingly, most women work at home and outside it – although they are stratified due to their highly differentiated work and income. How that housework is done also marks differences in lifestyles and consumption patterns which, on a day-to-day basis, women recognise as their location in different social classes. The hi-tech designer kitchen is one of the signifiers of this difference in lifestyle. And even though the central figure in my narrative about Indonesia does not perform domestic chores, the fashion kitchen sets in concrete, so to speak, her differences not only from less affluent women of her own society but also, ironically, from her Western counterparts.

Since at least the early 1980s, wealthy households have tended to have two kitchens: one commonly called the 'dirty kitchen' (*dapur kotor*) at the back of the house, close to the servants' quarters, and a 'clean kitchen' (*dapur bersih*) attached to the living area of the family. It is hard to establish what proportion of houses have two kitchens, but architects with whom I spoke seemed to suggest that a second kitchen would be included in the overwhelming majority of renovations in Kemang, the old wealthy suburb of Jakarta, and in almost all new architect-designed houses in exclusive Pondok Indah, the archetypal 'new rich' suburb of Jakarta. Typically the Pondok Indah houses are two or three storey, and cost anywhere between Rp. 0.5 and 1 billion (roughly US$400,000) to build at early 1990s prices. But two kitchens are also showing up in the smaller houses of single professional women. At the other end of the housing market, the construction cost for government housing is between Rp. 7 million for the 'very simple' category (RSS, Rumah Sangat Sederhana) and Rp. 9 million for the 'simple' category (RS, Rumah Sederhana), that is, roughly US$3,000–4,000 (Gatra 22 April 1995: 85). In other words, a simple house can be built for as little as 1 per cent of the cost of some of the Pondok Indah houses.

The microwave oven, an essential item in the designer kitchen, does not affect in any way the pattern of domestic food preparation, which continues to be done in the 'dirty kitchen' by maids. The fridge in the clean kitchen contains soft drinks and wines and packaged foods to which the family can help themselves. It is where, one woman architect told me, her 'husband enjoys cooking omelettes at weekends'. The hi-tech kitchen represents entertainment, relaxation, weekend family time together and, of course, social status, but not the real and indeed messy work of preparing food, which is done in the 'dirty kitchen'.

'[A]rchitecture and urban form not only result from social change but also help bring it about' (King 1984: 9). In that sense the two-kitchen house further reinforces the affluent woman's freedom from domestic labour, making her simultaneously more equal to men and more unequal to women who do the domestic work. The dirty kitchen, out of sight at the back of the house, or more commonly in the basement, is perhaps the most potent symbol of 'a society increasingly divided, both socially and spatially, according to class' (ibid.).

There probably is something to celebrate in the challenges to gender hierarchy that come into play in new policies and popular imagery directed by and at the New Order's new wealthy working women. As advertisers, architects, femocrats and high-income consumers of goods and services, these women use and help transform the languages and images of gender classification. Ambiguously located in the particular conjunction of local militarist patriarchy and global capitalism, their ability to challenge some existing hierarchies depends on the advantages they derive from their location in other socio-economic hierarchies. Consequently, in New Order Indonesia, the erosion of functional (work-related) and social (status-related) divisions between the sexes is necessarily premised on inventing new divisions between the classes.

NOTES

1 The GBHN, *Garis Besar Haluan Negara*, that is, the Broad Outlines of State Policy is restated every 5 years. It is a statement of the major policy principles that underlie the government's economic planning, the *Repelita* or Five-Year Plan.

2 The Garuda inflight magazine carries a regular column 'The State of the Economy' written by Dorodjatun Kuntjoro-Jakti, one of the leading economists of the country. Returning from a field-trip mainly spent collecting data for this paper, I was struck by Professor Dorodjatun's December 1994 column titled 'Women Make their Presence Felt in the Workforce'. What was particularly interesting to me was the way in which the article presented the rising number of women in the labour force as one of the symptoms of Indonesia's industrial modernisation.

3 'New Order' refers to the current Indonesian state and government headed by President Suharto. 'New Order' was established after a violent military coup in October 1965, which brought General Suharto to power. What is crucial for this chapter is the association of the New Order with (in Robison's terms) 'the rise of capital'. Most critics and supporters of the New

Order would agree that the single most important difference between the New Order and the leftist nationalist Sukarno government it replaced was the enthusiastic (if at times a little ambivalent) embrace of capitalist development, including global capitalism, in post-1965 Indonesia. This chapter thinks about gender within this broad understanding of the New Order in Indonesia.

4 This point about my similarity with the informants and subjects of this paper comes through in a remarkable way in one of the taped interviews with two successful women in the advertising industry (December 1994). (Incidentally, like myself, one of them had gone to university in Melbourne.) As we talked about their least successful work, one of them recalled a shampoo advertisement she had been assigned to do for Unilever, which was to be directed mainly to a rural low income audience. She found it very difficult to prepare the visuals for this advertisement since she had no confidence in her ability to imagine what appeals to a rural woman. In the end she opted for a black and white shot, drawing on images of simplicity that the mention of village evoked for her. Apparently, market research discovered that the audience in the rural periphery of Jakarta did not like the advertisement. She was not surprised: 'Kita kan tidak tahu selera mereka' (We don't know their tastes!). Interestingly too, in sharing this story of her difference with women living within a 100-km radius of her, she used 'kita', the Indonesian language 'we' which includes the addressee, thus including me on her side. National differences in this instance were evidently, for both myself and my informants, less important than other markers of identity.

5 In other words, answers to questions such as 'whose wife are you?' and 'what job do you do?' could produce contradictory class identities for women. And how, for instance, do we attribute class status to the widow of a successful village businessman who after the death of her husband is forced to work as a domestic help? During field work in April 1995 I heard a number of accounts of such dramatic changes in women's social position particularly through widowhood or divorce. Whereas the growth of the Indonesian economy in the last two decades has expanded the middle class, without the rule of law that in the West secures that class status to a large extent, the hold of the new members on their middle-class status remains fragile and not grounded in the network of wealthy relatives which supports older middle-class groups.

6 According to 1992 figures (BPS and UNICEF 1993) women's average wage was Rp. 78,723 and men's Rp. 133,748 per month.

7 In a recent interview, Ginanjar Kartasasmita, the Minister for National Development Planning, commented that, by World Bank criteria, Indonesia's income distribution is in the 'low inequality' category. However, the Minister also acknowledges that the most recent figures from the national Statistical Institute shows that inequality is rising (*Republika* 13 October 1995).

8 The figures are sourced to ILO *Year Book of Labour Statistics*, cited by Annette Prissey in 'Trends in Female Employment', unpublished report, 1990.

9 My emphasis. Anggaran Dasar Dharmawanita, (5 August 1974, Chapter II, Clause 8b). *Ibu rumah tangga*, literally translates as 'household mother'.

10 Of course in many instances women civil servants are also wives of male civil servants. This appears only to heighten the contradiction in the roles of woman-civil-servant and wife-of-civil-servant. In some instances the woman is senior to her husband, or her boss's wife, with a lower rank in the civil service, is her superior in the Dharmawanita structure by virtue of her husband's position.

11 I have explained in some detail elsewhere that Indonesian women's organisations were destroyed or coopted into the state in the aftermath of the civil war of 1965–66. From the mid-1980s onwards a new breed of women's organisations began to re-emerge in Indonesia as part of the NGO movement. Most of these women's organisations were led by urban middle-class women and started with funding from international donor agencies concerned with women and development issues (see Sen in Blackburn, n.d.). By the late 1980s women's NGOs had mushroomed and diversified from a fairly uniform liberal feminist agenda to almost the entire political spectrum, with Islamic women's groups at the one end to forms of socialist feminism at the other. Nonetheless, the majority of the women's NGOs remain tied to some form of global liberal feminist agenda.

12 The term 'femocrat' was coined to describe women with feminist agenda who entered the Australian bureaucracy in the Whitlam era, particularly via the Office of Women's Interest established by the Whitlam government. It seems to me that there are enough parallels between that Australian situation and the Indonesian one. In both cases the state created new institutions which in turn opened up spaces within the bureaucracy for women in general, but more particularly for women administrators as 'advocates of the interest of women as a gender class' (Yeatman 1990: 61). Indeed, as in Australia, so in Indonesia, the location of female bureaucrats in certain state institutions (e.g. in the Ministry for the Role of Women in Indonesia) requires these women to identify with women as a gender class. In this chapter, I use the term femocrat in order to evoke this conjunction of state interest (in the Indonesian instance the desire of the government to appear as a good international citizen by taking part in safe international events such as the Women's Year) and liberal feminism, which produced the Indonesian woman bureaucrat with womanist agenda.

13 There have been a few attempts to regulate the pay and working conditions of domestic workers, but these have not received much support from mainstream women's organisations. Kacasungkana describes a seminar on that topic organised by the government's National Legal Planning Agency (BPHN) and the Indonesian Women's Congress (KOWANI, which is the federation of all major women's organisations) in 1992. 'Many women present at the seminar (most of whom were members of KOWANI) raised objections', on the ground that any government regulation would damage 'familial feelings' (*rasa kekeluargaan*).

14 Creative Director is the highest position in the creative department of an agency. There are still only a handful of women in these positions.

15 'Advertorial' is a commonly used term in media analysis. It refers to advertisements which appear as articles or editorial pieces. These generally have quite a large amount of written text and a typeface that matches the magazine's articles. Often these are only identifiable as advertisements because the word 'advertisement' appears somewhere in the margin.

16 Much of the information on the advertising industry is drawn from my interviews with people working in middle to upper level positions in advertising agencies. I spoke to several women working in small locally owned agencies and to men and women in one large multinational advertising agency. Most of these interviews were conducted in November–December 1994.

17 See note 12

18 The working-class woman who relies on the domestic labour of other members of the household like daughters does, however, appear.

BIBLIOGRAPHY

Adkins, L. (1995) *Gendered Work: Sexuality, Family and the Labour Market*, Philadelphia: Open University Press.

BPS (Baden Pusat Satistik, Indonesian Statistical Bureau) and UNICEF (1993) *Indikator Sosial Wanita Indonesia,* Jakarta: BPS.

Busby, L. and Eighty, G. (1993) 'Feminism and Advertising in Traditional and Nontraditional Women's Magazines 1950s-1980s', *Journalism Quarterly* 70: 2.

Cooley, L. (1992) 'Maintaining Rukun for the Javanese Household and the State', in van Bemmelen, S., Djajadiningrat-Nieuwenhuis, M., Locher-Stolen, E. and Touwen-Bouwsma, E. (eds), *Women and Mediation in Indonesia*, Leiden: KILTV Press.

Crouch, H. (1978) *The Army and Politics in Indonesia*, Ithaca and London: Cornell University Press.

Douglas, S. (1980) 'Women in Indonesian Politics: The Myth of Functional Interest', in S. Chipp and J. Green (eds) *Asian Women in Transition*, London: Pennsylvania University Press.

Friedman, J. (1994) *Cultural Identity and Global Process*, London: Sage.

Grossman, R. (1979) 'Women's Place in the Integrated Circuit', *Southeast Asian Chronicle*, 66.

Hoffarth, V. (1990) *Women Managers in Southeast Asia* (Vol 1, Corporate Managers), Manila: Women for Women Foundation (Asia) Inc.

Hull, V. J. (1976) *Women in Java's Rural Middle Class: Progress or Regress?,* Jogjakarta: Gajah Mada University Working Paper Series No.3.

Indonesian Association of Advertising Agents (1993–94) *Media Scene 1993–1994: The Official Guide to Advertising in Indonesia*, Jakarta.

Jellinek, L. (1974) *The Life of a Jakarta Street Trader*, Working Paper series, Melbourne: Centre of Southeast Asian Studies, Monash University.

—— (1978) *The Life of a Jakarta Street Trader: Two Years Later*, Working Paper series, Melbourne: Centre of Southeast Asian Studies, Monash University.

Kacasungkana, Nursjahbani (1992) 'Engendering a New Order, Engendering Democracy: A Reflection on the Use of Women in the New Order', unpublished paper presented at the conference on 'Democracy in Indonesia', Monash University, December 1992.

King, A. D. (1984) *The Bungalow: The Production of a Global Culture*, London: Routledge and Kegan Paul.

Logsdon, M. (1985) 'Women Civil Servants in Indonesia: Some Preliminary Observations', *Prisma* 37: 77–87.

MacEwen Scott, A. (1986) 'Women and Industrialisation: Examining the "Female Marginalisation" Thesis', *The Journal of Development Studies* 22(4): 649–80.

Mann, R. and Mann, J. (1994) *Women's Role in Development*, Toronto: Gateway Books.

Marshall, B. L. (1994) *Engendering Modernity: Feminism, Social Theory and Social Change*, Oxford: Polity.

Moerpratomo (1990) Minister for the Role of Women, 'Enhancing the Role of Women in Development', presented at the Meeting with Delegation from Nigeria, Jakarta, 14 September 1990.

—— (1992) 'Sambutan Menteri Negara Urusan Peranan Wanita Pada Pembukaan Latihan Pelatih Kepemimpinan Wanita Angkatan Ke VIII', Jakarta, 20-29 February 1992.

Morgan, R. (ed.) (1984) *Sisterhood is Global: The International Women's Movement Anthology*, New York: Anchor Press.

Murray, A. (1991) *No Money No Honey: A Study of Street Traders and Prostitutes in Jakarta*, Singapore: Oxford University Press.

Office of the Minister of State for the Role of Women (1989) *The Changing Role of Women With Special Emphasis on Their Economic Role: Country Report of Indonesia*, Jakarta.

—— (1993) *Bahan Pelatihan Gender dan Pembangunan*, Jakarta.

Ong, A. (1991) 'The Gender and Labor Politics of Postmodernity', *Annual Review of Anthropology* 20.

Philips, A. (1987) *Divided Loyalties: Dilemmas of Sex and Class*, London: Virago.

Phillips, A. (1992) 'Classing the Women and Gendering the Class', in L. McDowell and R. Pringle (eds) *Defining Women: Social Institutions and Gender Division*, Cambridge: Polity Press.

Robison, R. (1986) *Indonesia: The Rise of Capital*, Sydney: Allen & Unwin.

—— (1996) 'The Middle Class and the Bourgeoisie in Indonesia', in Robison and Goodman (eds) *The New Rich in Asia: Mobile Phones, McDonalds and Middle-class Revolution*, London, Routledge.

Sen, K. (1994) *Indonesian Cinema: Framing the New Order*, London: Zed.

—— (n.d.) 'A Feminist Review of the New Order in Indonesia', in S. Blackburn (ed.) *Gender in Asian Politics*, Sydney: Allen & Unwin.

Sjamsiah Ahmad (1993) 'Mewujudkan Kemitraan Pria-Wanita Dalam Mensukseskan PJPT II', unpublished paper, presented at the National Workshop on Equal Partnership between Men and Women, University of Brawijaya, Malang, Indonesia, 5–7 July.

Spivak, G. (1988) 'Subaltern Studies: Deconstructing Historiography' in Guha and G. Spivak (eds.) *Selected Subaltern Studies*, New York: Oxford University Press.

Stoler, A. (1975) 'Some Socio-Economic Aspects of Rice Harvesting in a Javanese Village', *Masyarakat Indonesia* 2(1): 51–87.

Sullivan, N. (1991) 'Gender and Politics in Indonesia', in M. Stivens (ed.) *Why Gender Matters in Southeast Asian Politics*, Clayton: Monash Centre of Southeast Asian Studies.

Suryakusuma, J. (1991) 'Seksualitas Dalam Pengaturan Negara', *Prisma* 7, July.

Wieringa, S. (1992) 'Ibu or the Beast: Gender Interests in Two Indonesian Women's organisations', *Feminist Review*, 41.

Wiryani, U. (1986) 'The Second Sex in Indonesia', *Inside Indonesia* 7.
Wolf, D. (1992) *Factory Daughters: Gender, Household Dynamics and Rural Industrialisation in Java*, Berkeley: University of California Press.
Yeatman, A. (1990) *Bureaucrats, Technocrats, Femocrats: Essays on the Contemporary Australian State*, Sydney: Allen & Unwin.

3 Love and sex in an Indonesian mining town

Kathryn Robinson

> Politics, broadly understood as the competition for power, generates new ways of constituting the subject and the social order within which humans dwell. Serious talk about sexuality is thus inevitably about the social order that it both reproduces and legitimates.
>
> (Laqueur 1990: 11)

INTRODUCTION

This chapter attends to new ways of constituting the subject and the social order in an Indonesian community caught up in the transformations wrought by the modernising development programme of Indonesia's New Order. The community, Soroako in South Sulawesi province, has since the early 1970s been the centre of a foreign-owned nickel mining and processing plant, one of the the first of such large projects initiated by the New Order.[1] Changes in economic, social and personal life are all elements of this emerging social order which manifests both the homogenising imperatives and the incoherence and contradictions arising from 'global cultural flows' (Appadurai 1990). In particular, the chapter focusses on changes in 'the social patterning of desire' (Connell 1987) in adult sexual relations which relate to discursive forms of the global order and of the Indonesian New Order state.

The economic forces which have produced the new 'middle classes' of affluent Asia have had transformative effects for people not directly benefiting from being members of an urban rich or self-consciously modern stratum. The social and cultural effects of the processes variously described as 'modernisation' or 'globalisation' operate irrespective of affluence. One does not have to have a high disposable income to desire consumption of new commodities, or to aspire to associated lifestyles. This chapter looks at a community, only some of whose members qualify as the newly affluent, but all of whose lives are affected by these processes.

The processes of change associated with transformations of the contemporary world have been variously labelled as 'development' or 'modernisation', terms which imply progress and evolutionary inexorability. In these models, cultural and social transformations are treated as epiphenomena of (presumed fundamental) economic transformations. More recent theorising of change in Third World societies has relied on notions of 'globalisation', with a focus on changes in lifestyle, consumption, and culture. Much of the globalisation literature strives, in the manner of the earlier theorists, to identify grand schema, universal historical trajectories and predictive models. In contrast, Arjun Appadurai characterises the 'new global cultural economy . . . as a complex, overlapping disjunctive order, which cannot any longer be understood in terms of existing centre–periphery models' (1990: 296). Appadurai argues against attempts to conceptualise contemporary 'global interactions' as cultural homogenisation or the closely associated process of commoditisation. 'At least as rapidly as forces from various metropoles are brought in to new societies they tend to become indigenised in one or other way' (ibid.: 295). Models emphasising the inexorability of the forces of homogenisation simplify the actual processes which can 'be exploited by nation states' in relation to their own citizens, 'by posing global commoditisation (or capitalism or some other such external enemy) as more 'real' than the threat of its own hegemonic strategies' (ibid.: 296). That is, the homogenising discourse is available to national elites who can represent Westernisation or foreign domination as a more powerful threat than local forms of domination.[2]

Appadurai directs our attention towards local responses and the constitution of local, national and ethnic identities in the context provided by the global economy. His notion of 'global cultural flows' addresses the multiple and contradictory character of change in the modern world, the combination of homogenising and particularising forces. It encompasses both the particularity of local manifestations and the unity of the transformative impulses. That is, it allows a more decentred notion of power than implied in analyses which give a pivotal role to a single generative principle (such as economic growth, class relations, or historical narratives).

Appadurai provides us with a view of a world in which cultural flows move in often incoherent and contradictory fashions, in which they are refashioned by local elites in the service of their own power and in which individuals rework the impetus to consumer agency so that it is felt as individual agency. Notions of individual agency are especially powerful in the arena of gender identities and sexual relations. One of modernity's most powerful discourses is that of the autonomous individual seeking personal fulfilment in their sexual relations (see Giddens 1994). This chapter seeks to identify changing gender relations as a core component of the changes associated with the global order.

The 'women and development' literature lurches between two extreme models: one arguing that development has led to a worsening position for women, and one arguing that it is capitalist development which offers women liberation from the constraints of traditional forms of patriarchal power (cf. Chapter 1). Connell's (1987) analysis of gender and power rests on the notion of the gender order which he sees as a 'historical composition' rather than a system (or something arising from a generative nucleus, 1987: 116–17. This historical composition arises on the basis of inequalities of power, the sexual division of labour and the social patterning of desire, or 'cathexis', 'the construction of emotionally charged relations with 'objects' (i.e. other people) in the real world' (1987: 112). The gender order operates through institutions like the state, the family and the workplace. Connell's mode of explanation is not dissimilar to Appadurai's approach to the global order in its retreat from the quest for a single generative principle, and its emphasis on the intersecting flows of power. Gender identities can be added to the local, national and ethnic identities which Appadurai sees as caught up in the dynamic interaction of the local and the global.

THE LOCAL IN THE GLOBAL: THE SOROAKO NICKEL PROJECT

The village of Soroako is an Indonesian community located in the sparsely populated interior of the island of Sulawesi. In the 1970s it became the centre of a nickel mine and processing plant owned by a multinational company. After Suharto's New Order was ushered in by the 1965 coup the regime sought out foreign investment; the contract with International Nickel of Canada to exploit the nickel deposits in the vicinity of Soroako was one of the first foreign-funded projects. It led to an infusion of personnel and massive capital investment in infrastructure in the region of Soroako village, beginning in the late 1960s (Robinson 1986). The transformation of social relations in what had previously been a subsistence-based village economy was sudden and cataclysmic, as people lost their land and independent livelihood to the project.

The immediate and transparent new form of power in Soroako was class-based: the domination of physical and social space by the company and its installations. The community found itself with an 'elite' of expatriate and Javanese and Sundanese mine managers, immigrant mine personnel of varying occupational categories, both middle- and working-class, while the local Soroakans were transformed into a proletariat, with the only agricultural land available now some distance from the village. Accompanying these processes was the transformation of the gender order, in particular the imposition of a sexual division of labour, 'domesticating' women as they became housewives dependent on their labourer husbands. Previously, they had been equal participants in production in the agricultural economy, but this almost disappeared with the project's monopolisation of land (see Robinson 1986; 1983).[3]

At the same time forms of personal relationship were in flux, in particular those relating to issues of cathexis in adult sexual relations – young people were questioning the arranged marriage as the basis for family formation and as a cornerstone of personal life. There was a growing demand by young people to choose marriage partners on the basis of romantic love, with sexual attraction as the spark.

CHANGES IN PERSONAL LIFE

In his analysis of intimacy Giddens suggested that romantic love is historically related to the realisation of the self as a quintessential fact of modernity. So, rather than the 'political economy' of the personal, his analysis focusses our attention on important questions about the ability to realise one's 'self' in personal relationships, like marriage and sexual relationships. For Giddens, the appearance of romantic love in history is a step in the movement towards the 'pure relationship' which heralds a new form of potentially revolutionary social transformation. The 'pure relationship' is one entered into 'for its own sake', for what can be derived by each person from a sustained association with another (1994: 58). This is not necessarily tied to marriage. He sees it as part of a 'generic restructuring of intimacy' related to the development of a 'plastic sexuality' (ibid.).[4]

Giddens' argument has an apocalyptic quality. Romantic love is a step on the road to the perfectibility of human society, achieved through fundamental change in the character of intimate relations. The ideas of romantic love and associated ideas about the fulfilment of sexual desire have proven to be extremely motile in the global economy, he suggests. Their manifestation in particular settings, however, cannot be assumed to be the working out of a unilinear progress towards a better world. As Appadurai comments, cultural flows in general have a necessarily 'perspectival' quality, as each 'scape' intersects with other kinds of global flows (such as money, people, media images). Giddens' argument does lead us to attend to the heightened significance of particular culturally mandated forms of cathexis as part of the 'assemblage' of modern gender orders, but we cannot lose sight of its relation to other forms of power and domination. The historical moment is not a cross-section in a linear path forward, but rather a particular assemblage which exhibits historicity.

Indeed, if we look at these changes in the context of Soroako, we can see global cultural flows operating through a number of intersecting mechanisms. The forces which are delivering the (apparently) emancipatory movements towards personal autonomy are simultaneously emmeshing the people in a global economic order which incorporates new forms of domination. The gender order is an important aspect of a broader transformation in the structures of domination, for example transformations in sexuality with the state-sponsored adoption of modern contraception. What can appear as a gain in personal autonomy can also be seen as a shift from a social world in which personal life is enmeshed in local forms of domination based on kin relations (especially sex and generation) to one in which global economic and cultural flows provide new forms of subjection.

THE GENDER ORDER OF THE NEW ORDER

The development project of the New Order displays particular presuppositions about the nature of the transformation to a modern society: the emphasis on capital investment, big projects and a rationally ordered citizenry is part of its vision of modernity (see van Langenberg 1986).[5] The project of the New Order has also rested on a refashioning of the gender order. In this an 'emphasised' femininity (see Connell 1987) has been promoted as part of a social order in which the domination of a hegemonic masculinity is fundamental to its authoritarian character, manifested in militarism, and the elevation of the power of the patriarch as an aspect of state power (*bapakism*, see Suryakusuma 1996). Women are offered citizenship on the basis of their difference from men (Robinson 1994). Although women are increasingly to be found as workers in the modern capitalist sector in Indonesia, and, as Krishna Sen argues in Chapter 2, the working woman is becoming an icon of modernity in some quarters: women's role in reproduction has been emphasised by the state at the expense of their 'producer selves', at least until very recently. This has been most obvious in the reframing of women's sexuality in terms of the rationalising doctrine of family planning. The ideal woman is the mother who produces her two well-spaced, healthy and well-educated children, who take their place as productive workers and loyal Indonesian citizens (Robinson 1994). New Order ideology has strongly valorised the wife as the '*pendamping suami*' – the companion at the side of the husband. For elite women, this role must be maintained even at the expense of their role as mothers. Their first duty is to be at their husband's side on official occasions, even if this means 'abandoning' their children to another carer. The ideal of the New Order mother has been disseminated through the communication media, especially radio and television. Thus family planning advertisements on television present the harassed mother of many small children contrasted with the calm, well-groomed mother of two well-spaced children.

Dominant official models of femininity enshrine an image of fragility and helplessness. The national dress is a modified version of peasant costume – the wrapped batik cloth and the blouse (by way of the costume of the elite women of Javanese courts).[6] In the modern form, however, the cloth is wrapped tight, accentuating the bottom, which is further accentuated by the posture arising from standing in high-heeled slippers. The wrapped cloth is held in place with a corselet accentuating a tiny waist. The blouse strains against pointed breasts, achieved through extraordinary bras not unlike those for which Madonna is famous, and the transparent blouse reveals the contours of the underwear. The face is heavily made up, and the hair fixed with the addition of a hairpiece in the form of a large flattened bun, all held together with a hairnet. The overall effect is to confer immobility. It is said that women never stay long at Jakarta cocktail parties and do not eat or drink because of the impossibility of going to the toilet. This is a highly stylised feminine body, not like the working body of peasant women with strong shoulders and arms, skirt wrapped loosely to allow free movement in walking and working.[7] In spite of the circulation of highly desirable images of the modern woman (such as cosmetics billboards with Princess Diana look-alikes), images of women in traditional costume are frequently used to sell modern products, like the innocent-looking young women with robust bodies and round faces wearing regional costumes on calendars promoting *kretek* (clove cigarettes).

This model of femininity has not prevented women from participating in even the highest levels of public life (see Lev 1996). There is tension between the objective conditions of life of women who work, for example, as high-level civil servants, and the official promotion of women's relation to the state being through their bureaucrat husbands. Some of these elite women have resisted this dominant model, even to the extent of having more gender-equal formulations of government policy, for example in the GBHN (see Chapter 2). However, for the bulk of Indonesian women, and particularly those living outside the major urban centres, state policy is experienced through mass campaigns, like the Family Welfare movement (PKK) and the Family Planning campaign. The 'Five Responsibilities of Woman' (*Panca Dharma Wanita*), which have been endorsed by the government and adopted by the major women's organisation, are: appendages and companions to their husbands; procreators of the nation; mothers and educators of children; housekeepers; and members of Indonesian society (Suryakusuma 1996: 101; see also Hull 1976, Sullivan 1994, Robinson 1994 and Chapter 2).

But the effects of state policy are not modulated only through resistance by women in particular sectors of Indonesian society. There are also the effects of the exposure of the economy to global cultural flows as a result of New Order economic policies like opening up the economy to foreign investment and international labour migration to and from the country. In this context, Indonesian women are interpellated as 'modern' subjects by a sexualised femininity. The modern idiom of romantic love is engaged with through commodified modes of communication (pop music cassettes, television soap operas) and is related to the consumption of commodities associated with the manufacture of sexual desirability. The 'mediascapes' (Appadurai 1990) of pop music, television soap operas and movies are important vectors of these ideas. Indeed, one of the aspects of the mining company's presence in Soroako in the 1970s which people appreciated was the ability to embrace modern consumer items. One of the most popular consumer items in the 1970s was the cassette player, on which were played Dang Dut songs (rhythmic, Indian influenced tunes). These seemed to represent a particular construction of romantic love, one based on models of modern forms of emotional slavery, in which the slave is under the master's arbitrary control. The lyrics represent the power of feeling (an abject form of love); 'Love at first sight', and 'I hate you but I miss you' were the refrains of the songs most popular at the time of my initial fieldwork.

The government's programmes can also lead to unexpected consequences. Contraception has, until recently, been available mainly through the government-sponsored Family Planning programme with the aim of limiting the fertility of married women. However, there is evidence from other parts of Indonesia that after several decades of continuous exposure to modern contraception, women are beginning to think about it in terms of liberating their own sexuality.

These forces redefining women's subjectivities have been experienced most forcefully in Soroako through the activities of the mining company. The company has instituted its own versions of government policies such as a wives' organisation and a family planning programme. In these programmes, the elite wives have become the bearers of contemporary middle-class Indonesian culture to the local people. These elite women are models of the Panca Dharma Wanita, not working but helping their husbands in their careers, and supporting the organisations for which the men work.

THE MORAL ORDER AND MASCULINE POWER

Cultural practice and the feminine ideal

Soroako in the 1970s was caught in a moment between the enforced puritanism of the Darul Islam rebels and the effects of new cultural flows as diverse people and ideas moved into their changing world. Darul Islam, which had been fighting for the constitution of an independent Indonesia as an Islamic state, controlled much of rural South Sulawesi in the years 1950–65. They enforced a puritanical repression of sexuality and banned free mixing between men and women, proclaiming compliance with this repression as a badge of Islamic identity. They had also dismantled old practices such as the circle dances associated with flirtation and courtship. As a consequence of their campaigns, Soroako had been 'made over' in the image of the Bugis and Makassarese cultures of South Sulawesi. The women of Soroako, like Muslim women all over South Sulawesi, carried the burden of their family's honour. Restrictions on movement and behaviour for young women had moral authority. Modest dress required that the head and shoulders be covered, and the blouse and sarong be worn loose. Young women had to avoid any contact with men who were not close family.

While honour implied an obligation on men as well, for them it was more reactive than pro-active. So, for example any man who was a classificatory 'uncle' would take it upon himself to chastise a young girl if her public demeanour was felt to be transgressive. The reactive obligations of honour, which obliged a man to retaliate with physical violence against another man who had 'violated' a kinswoman, could be avoided by making sure they were never seen to meet publicly (for example by disappearing into a house if such a man were spotted in the distance). No such avoidance was possible for women, who found all aspects of their everyday lives affected by moral codes.[8]

Changes in definitions of femininity, however, were afoot. The defeat of the rebellion by the central government in 1965 was followed swiftly by the 1965 coup ushering in Suharto's New Order and the arrival of the mine. The spatial organisation of the mining town which engulfed the village incorporated divisions of space along class, race and gender lines. A public domain of markets, shops, schools and hospitals was incorporated. Unskilled workers lived in makeshift slums in contrast to the comfortably appointed houses provided for skilled and professional company employees. Because of the segmentation of the workforce on racial and ethnic lines, Indonesian and expatriate company employees tended to inhabit different 'suburbs'. The residential areas of the mining town, including the village, were a world of women in the daytime; there were specific male spaces in the bars and restaurants. The mining town, therefore, represented a complex 'ethnoscape'. Migrants from all over Indonesia and the world were incorporated in terms of the structures of the mining company and the global ecnomy. The Soroakans found themselves no longer in a world where everyone understood their social networks in idioms of kinship, but rather the more complex 'networks of networks' which Hannerz (1991) has called the 'global ecumene'.[9]

While young women have since 1981 travelled to a nearby town to attend high school, women are allowed less physical mobility than men. The customary forms of marriage and the moral norms of surrounding sexual behaviour were predicated on a social universe in which people were mobile over a very limited territory, which could be mapped in terms of real (known) social relations. The villagers' own self identity saw them as linked by common kinship (see Robinson 1986). Appadurai's term 'ethnoscape' refers to that aspect of the global economy in which people are constantly on the move (workers, tourists, immigrants). In the case of Soroako, men are more mobile than women, most immigrants and all but a handful of indigenous Soroakan emigrants being male. Their movement has been in response to fluctuating national and international demands for labour – some have even gone as far as the Middle East. While only a minority of Soroakan men responded to the changing circumstances of the winding down of the company workforce in the late 1970s by migrating elsewhere, there were large numbers of men who migrated into the project. These men often had wives elsewhere and established temporary liaisons in Soroako. For women this represented considerable problems. They often did not know if the liaison was temporary or not. If the suitor was an immigrant, parents felt they lacked adequate control over the process of arranging an appropriate marriage for their daughters, because they did not know the suitor's past history, or his family.

The complex 'ethnoscape' of the mining town meant that the women needed to negotiate new forms of social spaces in their everyday housekeeping activities, such as shopping, washing and collecting water from public standpipes. It also meant that new forms of activity were available to them. Both the expatriate women and Indonesian immigrant women, in particular other non-elite groups like the Torajan women, observed standards of dress and demeanour within public spaces like the markets which distinguished them from the locals. The Torajans, who had come in some numbers from the nearby Christian region of Tana Toraja, were less concerned than the Muslim Soroakans about the connection between modesty and dress, and felt more able to move about freely wearing such clothing as sleeveless dresses. Many had come on their own in quest of work as household servants (see Robinson 1991). The elite Indonesian women, many of them from Java, behaved in terms of an urban middle-class sense of propriety, driving little cars, and wearing Western-style clothes.

By the late 1970s, many of the Soroakan women were experimenting with wearing a modifed form of Western dress, usually (long-sleeved) blouses and (below-the-knee) skirts. Many also were cutting their long hair. This was considered particularly appropriate dress for activities within the 'modern' sector, like shopping at the company town site, or meetings of the women's association established by company managers' wives.

The 'new rich' women, wives of the highly paid managerial level employees of the MNC mining company, have brought new moral sensibilities to the definition of women's roles in their promotion of 'the national feminine' which they regard as a normative standard (see Robinson 1983; 1994). Through the company-sponsored women's association they endeavoured to inculcate their standards of feminine behaviour in the village women, manifested in dress and demeanour and practices such as cooking and childcare. The power of ridicule and shame was used to reinforce the moral authority of their message. For example, village women who participated in a cooking competition were publicly chastised for their 'wrong' use of spices. I attended a demonstration of how to behave in a hotel restaurant and on an aeroplane (how to eat bread and butter, how to use salt and pepper shakers) intended for wives of men recruited off-island who would travel home by air. For the managers' wives, their membership of the national elite gave them moral authority, based on their economic power, their social position and greater experience of the 'new' Indonesia.

The elite women, however, did not see themselves as promoting a set of cultural ideals and practice which were global in their orientation. Rather, they were to be bearers of a modern Indonesian constellation of beliefs and practices. The expatriate community was not regarded as a model for their behaviour, although they did see themselves as a model for the 'backward' people of inland Sulawesi. They saw villagers as too bound up with kinship and obligation, while 'expats' were too individualistic. ('We go to visit them and they're eating and they ask us to wait outside,' one woman complained to me.) Their own balance of self-interest and sociality was just right, and assumed to be enduring; they rejected my suggestion that they themselves might be caught up in a transition to more individualist ways of ordering their social relations.

The elite definitions of femininity were reinforced by economic changes in the sexual division of labour. These changes eroded the importance and possibility of agricultural production, where women had previously been equal participants. Women increasingly were dependent housewives, responsible for a domestic sphere in which forms of commodified consumption were dominant. Women had been equal participants with husbands and brothers in the pre-project agricultural economy (Robinson, 1986). By 1981, however, only 5.7 per cent of married women saw themselves as farmers, while 85.7 per cent reported their occupation as 'housewife'.[10] Definitions of femininity and new ideas about interpersonal relations were part of an assemblage of personal relations, economic relations (the division of labour) and the exercise of state power by an elite who had benefited from the transformation of the economic and gender orders.

Marriage, sexuality and romantic love

For older village residents, the association of family honour with female modesty was strong. Sexual behaviour was tightly regulated. Young women were not to be alone in the company of any man who was not a forbidden marriage partner. When I first arrived in the village in the 1970s, for example, the indigenous headman told me proudly that he had forced several (immigrant) couples to marry after the man had been seen too often calling at the young woman's house.

The moral order of restrictions and prohibitions on women's (especially young women's) behaviour was enforced by men and women, including old women who enjoyed more personal freedom. In this society where bilateral kinship and inheritance had not been strongly challenged by patriarchal tendencies within Islam, older women enjoyed authority within the family. Widows controlled family estates which were not distributed among the children until after the woman's death. Older women also had an important voice in family decisions about arranged marriages. Their authority was being eroded, however, by modern notions: these include state-driven presumptions about male 'household heads' and the emergence of challenges to customary inheritance patterns by views about the pre-eminence of male rights in Islam.

Marriages following 'traditional custom' were arranged by the bride and groom's parents, with an eye to the successful establishment of a new household. But this did not mean that passion and sexuality were considered unimportant in marriage. During my fieldwork, the wedding night was always accompanied by ribald joking and teasing about the future pleasures of marriage. Sex was regarded as a pleasurable aspect of marriage. Some healers (*dukun*) did a steady trade in aphrodisiac potions and amulets with which women sought to rouse a husband's sagging interest. Interestingly, it was women from elsewhere who were regarded as most skilled in this matter. It was, however, assumed such pleasures would follow marriage, not that they were a sufficient basis for marriage. There is evidence that young people had been more free to express mutual interest in the context of the circle dances before these were banned by Darul Islam as contrary to the behavioural norms of Islam. In these dances, young men and women joined hands to dance in a circle to the beat of drums, while singing flirtatious songs.

Although Islam sanctions polygyny in certain contexts, women saw it as a threat. The only outbursts of unruly public behaviour by women which I witnessed or heard about were between co-wives. One called out to her adversary after a particularly bitter dispute about household property, 'I'll cut his penis in half. You can have half and I'll have half.' Her contemptuous evocation of her husband's sexuality pointed to the issue not being sexual jealousy as such but men's economic power and control. Women feared for their own and their children's economic security should he take a second wife. The economic basis of marriage is indicated by women's responses to polygyny, which do not valorise cathexis (through protestation of sexual jealousy) but rather economic dependence, as a consequence of the sexual division of labour.

In developing his analysis of the significance of romantic love in the historical development of the 'pure relationship', Giddens makes use of Sharon Thompson's study of romantic love among American teenagers. For them, she discovers, '(s)ex, as it were is a sparking device, with romance as the quest for destiny' (cited Giddens 1994). This is the precise inverse of the relation between romance and sex as expressed by Soroakan people, whose sensibilities had been formed prior to the changes associated with the project. Finding a mate was understood in terms of meeting up with one's *jodoh*, or predestined marriage partner. Destiny, or rather a kind of predestination, decided one's path to romantic experience. Sex was a delight which was available to those so blessed. Unmarried older women would joke that their *jodoh* had been lost, echoing these assumptions of predestination. In contrast, the notions of romantic love being promoted in popular songs rested on this model of sex as a sparking device, exemplified in the Dang Dut song *Pertemuan Pertama* (First Meeting), in which the first glimpse of the beloved 'sparks' the passionate attachment.

There was no pressure for a marriage to be consummated immediately, although excessive resistance on the part of a young woman occasioned the intervention of a *dukun*, to ensure desire for her husband developed. Also, the sexual pleasures marriage afforded were all of a piece with the importance of having children. People spoke of the good fortune of those young women who did not have a menstrual period after their wedding. This meant that the marriage had been consummated and pregnancy had rapidly followed. For both men and women, personal satisfaction in marriage was in becoming a parent. As one man commented, 'Why do we men marry except in quest of children?'

On the night before the wedding, his female kin would escort the groom into the sitting room of the bride's house. He would be subjected to merciless teasing by her female relatives and guests, the male kin and guests sitting elsewhere. At the time of weddings in particular, but also at other times, one would hear what Abu-Lughod (writing about Egyptian Dedouin) calls 'sexually irreverent discourse' in which women 'make fun of men and manhood' (1990: 45). She reads such discourse 'as a form of women's resistance to dominant definitions of sexuality and sexual difference which are forms of male power'. As a form of resistance, it is symptomatic of where power lies and how it is exercised (ibid.).

On the whole, women, especially women already married, supported the feminine behaviour which propped up customary kinship-based power and a moral order which supported male authority. But in a shocking deviation from what had been their taken-for-granted world, a woman in 1984 murdered her husband, stabbing him while he was asleep. It transpired that he had been drinking and sexually abusing his daughter. She had gone to the village officials, who were also her kin (uncle and cousin), and was told to return home, to maintain the sanctity of her marriage; that is, they stressed the importance of maintaining the institution of marriage and woman's responsibility in this. When the husband once again abused the daughter, the wife waited until he fell asleep, stabbed him, and then went to fetch the village officials. One of them told me, 'when we went to the house, there wasn't a single grain of rice' (i.e. he had spent all the household income on drink). They were shocked and saddened, but there was no groundswell of opinion that she had done the right thing, nor any sense of regret by the officials that they might have handled it differently, even though all were alarmed and saddened by the sordid events.

This tragic tale reflects the changes in cultural flows bringing newly imagined sexual possibilities into the multi-ethnic community. Prostitution flourished in the otherwise male spaces – the bars and restaurants. This set new terms for sexual encounters. Some of the young men described to me how they would go to a bar, order a bottle of beer between a group of them and have a hostess come to sit with them so that they could flirt with and grope her (*meraba-raba*). Once video recorders became available in the village, men also had access to pornography. One man described how he sat around with other men masturbating as they watched pornographic videos – a new kind of sexual imagining indeed!

Although there was a presumption of male authority, older women in this bilateral society had a strong voice in matters relating to disposition of land and arrangement of marriages. Married women generally supported the idea of arranged marriage: 'If you marry whom your parents want and he turns out to be no good, they have to take you back. Anyway, our parents love us and would not do what they thought was not best for us.' Some married women claimed that they had resisted marriage, or rather resisted the consummation of a marriage, because they resolutely opposed their parents' choice. Resistance to arranged marriages, however, has become more common since the 1980s. Marriage was once the quintessential expression of kinship-based power, manifesting the moral authority of older relatives to determine the fate of the young. Resistance to arranged marriage points to the emerging gender order and forms of domination within which personal relations are constituted. An old man whose son had left his wife for an immigrant woman felt so shamed that he retreated to his garden on the far shore of the lake and refused to arrange a marriage for his younger son, for fear he would be shamed again by behaviour which was morally incomprehensible to him. (He had arranged the marriage between his first son and a classificatory niece.)

In 1974–75, the Indonesian government passed a marriage law which claimed the right of the state to authorise the conditions under which a marriage can occur: this included setting a minimum age at marriage, and legislating for free consent by both parties to a marriage. Another objective of the legislation demonstrated the instrumentalist rationality of the New Order: to support the initiatives of the Family Planning programme through delayed age at marriage. Thus elements of the emancipatory rhetoric of the Indonesian women's movement were harnessed in the service of forms of state power. The marriage law also prohibits a man from marrying a second wife without the first wife's consent. State regulation of marriage, of course, does not automatically change behaviour, but it does provide a discourse about individual will and men's and women's rights in marriage, which operates against the norms of arranged marriages. That is, once people are aware of the provisions of the law, these are available to be used as a basis to challenge kinship-based forms of power. Indeed, young people in Soroako were citing the new marriage law in claiming their rights to free choice marriage, and government officials were at least verbally supporting their legal rights.

CHANGING SEXUAL RELATIONS

The opening of a high school in a nearby town had given young women as well as young men the chance to further their education, and a few even aspired to attending university in the provincial capital. Whereas in the past few girls had been encouraged to pursue education beyond grade three, interestingly, parents were now showing no particular preference for educating sons. 'How do you know which of them has brains?' one man replied when I asked about sex preference in schooling. Another example of young women's breaking away from the moral imperatives of femininity which had dominated their mothers' lives was the teenage girls' participation in the local volleyball competition. They won this against the more middle-class inhabitants of the town site. Participation in the competition necessitated their wearing short skirts in public, running and jumping on the court, showing physical prowess and fighting to win – a very different kind of demeanour from that hitherto the norm for young women in the public gaze. They were trained by a middle-aged village woman, who carried out her duties in a tracksuit and had only begun 'experimenting' with Western-style dress less than 10 years previously.

Most surprising to me were two hastily arranged weddings that occurred during my short stay in the village in 1985. In both cases the bride was already pregnant, including one daughter of a village official who had been instrumental in forcing marriages for far lesser breaches of propriety in the mid-1970s. The wedding ceremonies were modest celebrations, in itself something of note, as weddings are the major occasions for public affirmation of a family's status according to the size of the party and the prestige of the guests (see Robinson 1986: Chapter 10). Six years earlier the older sister of one of the young women had proudly told me that the helpers at her wedding were so numerous that they were 'like ants'.

A further incident suggested a major shift in moral sensibilities. I sat with two women I knew well while they were discussing an allegation by a female student that the son of one of them had 'gotten her pregnant'. In the 1970s, such an allegation, regardless of whether or not it was true, would be shaming. (For example, I had one old friend who, on the first night his son did not sleep at home, sought him out at his girlfriend's house and forced them to marry. This was in spite of the fact that the father thought they were too young to marry.) The women were quite savage in their condemnation of the girl, one of them stating with a rhetorical flourish, 'I'll take her up to the hospital and we'll see who's pregnant.' Their strong response was no doubt fired by a desperate wish for the sacrifices made for the son to pursue his education to come to fruition. His graduation from high school would be in jeopardy if he had to marry and assume the responsibilities of fatherhood. The changes in teenage behaviour, but also in adult attitudes to teenage sexuality, were dramatic.

If pre-marital sex was a phenomenon in the 1970s it was well hidden. In contrast, in 1985, I had ample evidence that it was becoming more common, not the least from hastily arranged marriages. A young friend told me how she took advantage of her widowed mother's absence from the house working in the gardens to allow friends to meet there for illicit encounters. She obviously found pleasure in her subversive activity. The new conditions of life in the larger and more socially and economically complex mining town led to more opportunities for activities not governed by customary norms. People had to juggle the new desire to educate their children with the need to support their families in the changed economic circumstances; these included the loss of agricultural land to the mining concession, the dependence on wage labour and then the loss of waged work as the company retrenched its workforce after the initial development stage of the project. Young women would be left in charge of the village house to oversee the education of younger siblings while the parents stayed away on the farm, often some distance away, as noted. Cathexis in interpersonal relations between young adults no longer developed in the context of the arranged marriage, but rather in an environment where the young people acted out their own felt desires.

Young women's rejection of the marriage partners chosen by their parents was evidence of their resistance to the control of their sexuality and person. There were several instances of young women threatening to run away with their boyfriends if the parents did not agree. In terms of customary norms even such a threat would be shameful. A number of women were successful in getting their way. While I saw several brides who tearfully endured a marriage ceremony to men of their parents' choice, I saw other weddings in which the young women put up significant resistance. One ran away several times, until the ceremony was finally held. For several weeks after the ceremony, I would see her at the mosque with the single girls, attending the evening prayers during Ramadan. She and her friends made it clear that she was resisting the husband's efforts to consummate the marriage, although he was living in her parents' house. In a curious engagement with a modern icon (associated in advertisements with women's 'freedom'), one of her friends pointed out she was wearing jeans as part of her strategy to foil his attempts; compared to a sarong the jeans functioned as a kind of a chastity belt. There was an interesting postscript: when I visited them several years later, in their own house with two children, they presented as a 'modern' couple with a companionate style marriage. They sat side by side and both joined in a free-flowing discussion about family planning, with a degree of equality and openness which struck me as unusual.

In the transformed world of the company town young women in Soroako resisted their parents' choice because of romantic visions – they either had a preferred partner, or felt no romantic desire for their parents' choice. In one particular case, a woman rejected an arranged marriage in spite of the fact that by local standards the man was spectacularly wealthy.[11] In another case it was explained to me that the young woman was resisting 'because he's [the young woman's] *saudara'* (sibling, in fact her first cousin)', and that he was already 'old' (probably about 30); the romantic ideal was someone youthful and perhaps an outsider.

What do these changes mean for men in terms of marriage? Both men and women have customarily been subjected to the power of older kin in arranging marriages. In the company town it was young men who earned wages and the highest wages. This gave them the ability to act on their own desires in terms of marriage and many did. The basis of this change, however, was not just the import of new 'ideoscapes' which included individual desire/will and romantic love. The incorporation of this ideoscape into Soroako is itself intimately related to the shift from a 'peasant' economy, where wealth was in the form of land controlled by elders, to a more fully capitalist economy where households were dependent on wages, earned (mainly) by younger men.

Many young men were able to build a house, the most significant form of savings in this community, before marriage, or soon after, allowing the couple to establish their own domestic space much more quickly. This establishment of neolocal residence was a significant transformation in the gender order, breaking the pattern of uxorilocal residence, another significant component of control of the young by the old. In the growing urban space of the mining town, the village was squeezed on all sides by company-controlled land. Housing land was at a premium, as immigrants flowed into the region, while local government officials (from outside the village) were corruptly involved in regulating access to land. They would refuse to recognise claims of customary rights by indigenous people and give permission to immigrants to build (in what was euphemistically described as a *sistem amplop* (envelope system, that is bribery, Robinson 1986: 197). The most certain way to secure a customary claim, to protect the village estate against squatters and interlopers, was to build a dwelling, as unoccupied land was the most likely to be sold corruptly. The new houses were mostly built in the new section of the village, scattered among the houses built by the immigrants flooding in to work for the company. Neolocal residence, however, went unchallenged by the elders because of the paramount need to protect their remaining rights to residential land after the mining company had been allowed to appropriate their agricultural land (Robinson 1986).

The growing incidence of neolocal residence allowed young couples in the most erotically active phase of their relationship to inhabit a private space in more intimate circumstances than had hitherto been the case, underscoring the significance of forms of cathexis grounded in sexual attraction as the 'spark' for romantic love. During my 1985 trip, I would occasionally stumble across scenes of easy intimacy between newly-weds in their privatised homes. Customarily, newly-wed couples were offered the limited privacy of a bedstead in the sitting room of the house (rather than in the communal sleeping room) where they were under the scrutiny of the bride's family, but in their own homes couples appear to have developed new kinds of intimacy, with the marital relationship acquiring greater significance in their personal life than it had in the past. That this was in part a consequence of the economically and politically driven trend to neolocal residence was indicated by the fact that this kind of intimacy was also observable in neolocally dwelling young couples in which the young women had (unsuccessfully) resisted arranged marriages. On the other hand, residence in the new areas of the village left women more isolated from their kin, which presumably was also a factor in the changing character of their relationship with their husbands.

The separate household also had consequences for another aspect of the gender order, the sexual division of labour. The man's wage labour paid for the new fashions in house forms, with concrete floors and internal bathrooms. These, however, created more housework for the woman and exaggerated her identification with domesticity.

WOMEN AS REPRODUCERS

The Indonesian state-sponsored family planning programme presents a particular image of embodied femininity. Here the emphasis is not so much on the disciplining of feminine sexuality as on the taming of its product. The fecundity of women's bodies is presented as a threat to the economic well-being which the development doctrine (*pembangunan*) of the New Order promises: not so much a threat to the nation as a whole (although this is the thinking behind the national programme) as a threat to the well-being of the nuclear family. The family planning literature stresses the rational control of bodily functions and feelings. Later age at marriage is part of the agenda, along with the use of modern contraceptives. The notion of 'control of fertility' promoted by the programme is not one based on ideas of the connections between women's autonomous control of their fertility and personal autonomy, as in Western feminist discourses.[12] Rather it is about the rational control of women's bodies and the harnessing of the energy of mothers to produce model Indonesian citizens and workers. Through the mass programme for family planning and the related Family Welfare Movement (PKK), campaigns reach out into the villages of Indonesia to incorporate women into the Indonesian nation, defining their citizenship in terms of their roles as wives and mothers.

Modern forms of contraception are replacing 'traditional' sexual customs and practices through which Indonesians have, directly and indirectly, regulated their fertility. The methods being promoted are all female methods and create an image of female sexuality as always ready, the complement of a hydraulic male sexuality which needs immediate gratification. The programme does not endorse the customary notions of fertility regulation which placed an onus on men as well as women. For example, a man whose wife had too many children too quickly was regarded with scorn, as someone who did not shoulder his responsibilities for his wife's fertility and well-being. The sanitised propaganda of the programme ignores issues of sexuality, although users are acutely concerned about issues of sexuality and their gendered bodies. For example, I frequently encountered a belief that male sterilisation would result in the wife's becoming adulterous.

Women's concerns about the negative effects of contraception were not taken seriously by the health services. Their worries often related to the disruption of the ordinary functions of women's bodies, such as menstrual irregularities. Women complaining of pain or irregular bleeding with IUDs or injectables, for example, were urged to put up with it. Couples who chose the non-invasive method of condoms were listed as problems to be chased up, to 'upgrade' their methods, by family planning workers.

In Soroako, as noted, the mining company had its own family planning programme, established in the early 1980s, based on the model of the official government programme (see Robinson 1989). Like the national programme, it was promoted by fieldworkers who visited people in their homes. They encouraged women to use the methods which ensured the most control for the programme, but were most invasive of women's bodies (IUDs and injectables). In line with their status as examplars of modern Indonesian womanhood, the elite women in the company town had very high levels of contraceptive use, and in particular very high rates of sterilisation compared to the national average. Thus in two of the areas of the townsite inhabited by managers and their families, about one third of the women had been sterilised. Around 75 per cent of wives of skilled workers and junior managers used modern contraceptives in 1985, compared with about 50 per cent in the country as a whole. Male sterilisation was also common, especially among senior managers, where it was the choice of 28 per cent of couples using modern contraception.

The flow of ideas ('ideoscape') of romantic love and its valorising of sexual desire (especially the sexual desire of young women) cuts across the alternative 'ideoscape' of the rationalising family planning programme. Both of these models of femininity can be seen as a consequence of the intersecting processes of globalisation, through technological change (technoscapes/finanscapes) and the circulation of new images and ideas (mediascapes/ideoscapes). The images of femininity in the Family Planning programme are direct products of state policy and serve the interests of the powerful architects of the New Order. The linking of fertility regulation and a particular mode of economic development also reflects the interests of the Big Players in the global economy (see Robinson 1996). New Order ideology operationalises the ideoscape of modernity, incorporating notions of the individual citizen and his/her rights and responsibilities, and ideas of the rational control of (out of control) natural bodies. The government uses the family planning programme as a way of integrating the diverse peoples of the archipelago, as a cornerstone of the project of constituting the sentiment of citzenship through incorporation in a state programme. It effectively uses modern media to spread this message, but there are also competing images of sexualised femininity resulting from the engagement with 'global cultural flows' (Appadurai 1990). The new constructions of sexualised romantic love draw their power from the circulation of images made possible by new technologies (cassettes, videos, films and television), the circulation of which it is increasingly difficult for governments to control, even when there is a will to do so.

CONCLUSION

The development strategy of the New Order has led to profound changes in Indonesian society, not least in the gender order. Some of these changes are a direct consequence of the exercise of state power, through government programmes designed to remake the people of the archipelago into a unified citizenry. Other changes have resulted from the strategy for the New Order economic transformation of the country along capitalist lines. This has extensively affected the division of labour, including the sexual division of labour. The refashioning of Soroakan women's sexuality by the forces emanating from these New Order strategies, mediated by the nickel project, operates in ways that are by no means predetermined, fixed, or certain. People's lives become increasingly more complex due to the flux and intersection of cultural flows which the government cannot contain and control. The modernising capitalist forces, which they hope will bring wealth, also involve the constitution of consumers, and a resulting valorising of autonomy for the individuated self.

Women might be experiencing themselves increasingly as subjects of romance and their choice of partner as an act of pure will. But women's engagement with these new forms of femininity signifies their insertion into relations of power and domination which derive from the dynamics of a global order. Their act of free will can be seen as a form of self-subjection in the context of new forms of power, both state and non-state. The education system, and programmes like family planning, depend on the separation of kin groups and the regulation of the individual. They are thus closely linked with the new gender order in which women's economic independence has been eroded by the imposition of a sexual division of labour involving the 'domestication of women'. Romantic love, although apparently arising not from the external force of state power, but from the individual's own desire, would seem to be securely located in the economic and cultural imperatives of the global order.

NOTES

1 I have studied the effects of the project for the local people in several periods of fieldwork: July 1977–March 1979; December 1980–January 1981 and throughout 1984–85 when I was teaching in the university of the provin-

cial capital, and had several opportunities to visit Soroako and to have a number of Soroakan people visit me in the city.

2 This is similar to what Laura Nader (1989) has called Occidentalism.

3 This seems to be particularly intensified in mining communities: see Robinson (1996).

4 In an appraisal of these historical changes in Europe, Luhmann comments that romance could not sustain the marriage relationship in a long-term fashion, hence the invocation of the old puritan notion of companionship (1986: 51).

5 Democracy is identified by Appadurai as part of the 'master narrative' – in Indonesia the brief experiment with parliamentary democracy having given way to notions of 'Panca Sila democracy' as the autochthonous political system of the Indonesian people.

6 See L. Sears who reports Jean Gelman Taylor's suggestion that Indonesian women's national dress was invented in the 1950s and 1960s (Sears 1996: 38).

7 There are alternative models of femininity, for example that reinforced by the popularity of child performers on television. There is a kind of precocity in their jaunty confidence in front of the cameras, but a desexualised femininity/asexual flirtatiousness in the cute stylised movements and the direct gaze to the camera. Is this a model for adult femininity?

8 In 1977, some houses in Soroako had small circular windows, which you could peep out of, but which were impenetrable to the gaze of a passer-by. They represented a less strenuous screening of a hidden female world than elite houses in other parts of South Sulawesi, where young women peeped through ornate ventilators to observe guests in the sitting room, in order to prepare snacks and drinks appropriate to their status. This was seen as having utility in protecting female demeanour, the house as the haven within which young unmarried women were safe.

9 Hitherto, divisions of space were focussed on the dwelling house, with exclusion of some men from the kitchen, the realm of women. There were also sex-segregated areas of the mosque. This gender separation relates to moral sensibilities rather than the division of labour and male sexuality, which are significantly demarcated by spatial separation in the mining town (see Robinson 1996).

10 A further 6.6 per cent said they were 'self-employed', mostly running small shops. Source: census of Soroako village conducted by P.T. Inco Medical Services (1981).

11 In contrast, Abu-Lughod (1990) argues that young Bedouin women resist the partner chosen by parents if the man cannot generate the cash they see as necessary to support a modern lifestyle.

12 Rather, images of women's autonomy from the strictures of motherhood are used to sell the goals of the programme, in a similar manner to the way in which organisations like the Rockefeller Foundation promote equity for women as a way of achieving reduced fertility (Robinson forthcoming).

BIBLIOGRAPHY

Abu-Lughod, L. (1990) 'The Romance of Resistance: Tracing Transformations of Power through Bedouin Women', *American Ethnologist* 17(1): 41–55.

Appadurai, A. (1990) 'Disjuncture and Difference in the Global Cultural Economy' in M. Featherstone (ed.) *Global Culture: Nationalism, Globalization and Modernity*, London: Sage.

Connell, R. W. (1987) *Gender and Power*, Sydney: Allen and Unwin.

Friedman, J. (1994) *Cultural Identity and Global Process*, London: Sage.

Giddens, A. (1992) *The Transformation of Intimacy: Sexuality, Love and Eroticism in Modern Societies*, Cambridge: Polity.

—— (1994) 'Men, Women and Romantic Love', in *The Polity Reader in Gender Studies*, London: Polity.

Hannerz, U. (1992) 'The Global Ecumene as a Network of Networks', in A. Kuper (ed.) *Conceptualizing Society*, London and New York: Routledge.

Hull, V. (1982) 'Women in Java's Middle Class: Progress or Regress?', in P. van Esterik (ed.) *Women of Southeast Asia*, Northern Illinois University Centre for Southeast Asian Studies.

Langenberg van, M. (1986) 'Analysing Indonesia's New Order: A Key Words Approach', *RIMA* 20(2).

Laqueur, T. (1990) *Making Sex*, Cambridge Massachussets: Harvard University Press.

Lev, D. (1996) 'On the Other Hand?', in L.J. Sears (ed.) *Fantasising the Feminine in Indonesia,* Durham, N.C. and London: Duke University Press.

Luhmann, N. (1986) *Love as Passion: the Codification of Intimacy*, Cambridge, Mass.: Harvard University Press.

Nader, L. (1989) 'Orientalism, Occidentalism and the Control of Women', *Cultural Dynamics* 2(3): 265–76.

Robinson, K. M. (1983) 'Women's Work in an Indonesian Mining Town', in L. Manderson (ed) *Women's Work and Women's Roles in Southeast Asia*, Canberra: A.N.U. Development Studies Centre.

—— (1986) *Stepchildren of Progress: The Political Economy of Development in an Indonesian Mining Town*, Albany, NY: SUNY Press.

—— (1989) 'Choosing Contraception: Cultural Change and the Indonesian Family Planning Program', in P. Alexander (ed.) *Creating Indonesian Cultures*, Sydney: Oceania Monographs.

—— (1991) 'Housemaids: The Effects of Gender and Culture on the Internal and International Migration of Indonesian Women', in G. Bottomley *et al.* (eds) *Intersexions: Gender/Class/Ethnicity*, Sydney: Allen and Unwin.

—— (1994) 'Indonesian National Identity and the Citizen Mother', *Communal/Plural* 3.

—— (1996) 'Women, Mining and Development', in R. Howitt, J. Connell and P. Hirsch (eds) *Resources, Nations and Indigenous Peoples*, Melbourne: Oxford University Press.

—— (n.d.) 'Government Agency, Women's Agency: Feminism, Fertility and Population Control', in M. Jolly and K. Ram (eds) *Borders of Being*, Cambridge: Cambridge University Press, forthcoming.

Sears, L. (1996) 'Introduction: Fragile Identities', in L. Sears, *Fantasizing the Feminine in Indonesia*, Durham, NC and London: Duke University Press.

Sullivan, N. (1994) *Masters and Managers*, St Leonards: Allen and Unwin.
Suryakusuma, J. (1996) 'The State and Sexuality in New Order Indonesia', in L.J. Spears (ed.) *Fantasizing the Feminine in Indonesia*, Durham, NC and London: Duke University Press.

4 Sex, gender and the making of the new Malay middle classes

Maila Stivens

In 1994 the Malaysian Prime Minister Datuk Seri Dr Mahathir Mohamad was widely quoted making a series of blistering attacks on the Islamist group *Al Arqam*, likening the group's women (sic) to 'sex slaves' trapped in a form of 'prostitution'.

> 'The movement is more inclined to the satisfaction of their (leaders') desires, especially in women and sex,' the Prime Minister reportedly said.
>
> 'Islam is only used as a mask. They marry and divorce at will and some of their [polygamous] marriages are very temporary . . . When they get bored they divorce.'
>
> '[The group's leader] Ashaari himself has at least four wives.'
>
> (Tan Kim Bock 1994: 1)

Dr Mahathir was also quoted as saying 'that in every religion there were groups like the *Al Arqam* whose preoccupation was women and sex and how to make polygamy acceptable' (*Bernama* 1994).

The Deputy Prime Minister and other ministers took up the refrain, suggesting that the group's ideas of marriage had deviated from true Islamic teaching (*Star* 26 August 1994: 2) and that the government would help 'Arqam's women' (*Star* 24 August 1994).

These statements dwelling on the allegedly feudal sexualities of this Islamist group might seem surprising. *Al Arqam* had been a successful *dakwah* (missionary)[1] group, with an estimated 10,000 members. The group had set itself up in an Islamic 'commune', where the members wore Arab robes and allegedly used horses. But then in 1994 they were banned by the government, producing an outcry from a somewhat unlikely source of support, human rights activists. The Prime Minister's grounds for the banning were that *Al Arqam* represented a threat to national security. To the obvious surprise of many local journalists,

Al Arqam turned out to be a thoroughly middle-class group with a substantial following among the affluent Malay middle classes and included computer programmers, engineers, accountants and other highly late modern, perhaps hyper-modern, occupational groups (Wan Suhaimi Saidi and Hanim Adnan 1994). The group was revealed to have extensive economic interests in 'modern' economic enterprises, including supermarkets and computer services. Some of the Prime Minister's rhetoric, however, highlighted its sexual and family practices, which were depicted as feudal, backward and as being against Islam.

How might we explain the Prime Minister's highly sexualised characterisation of *Al Arqam* and the politicisation of gender it implies? One argument might see the sexualising of the group as merely a rhetorical device, deploying gendered themes to demonise the group in a society where overt public discussion of sexuality is most unusual. But a more convincing argument might be that Mahathir was having some difficulty in differentiating *Al Arqam's* version of an Islamic future for Malaysia from his own in a context marked by great ambivalences about modernity. His recourse to a sexualised polemic dwelling on particular aspects of morality neatly positioned *Al Arqam* outside the corporate (civilised) Islamic modernity seen as the way forward for new Malays and a new Malaysia by the government. Mahathir might also be viewed as trying to appeal to the modernist liberal feminism of some elements in the women's arm of his party, UMNO (United Malays' National Organisation).

I shall argue that this episode exemplifies the ways that gendered images have become central to cultural contests about being 'modern', Malay and Muslim in late modern Malaysia. Some saw the outbursts about *Al Arqam* as merely part of a tendency for a populist and recently hugely popular prime minister to let his 'big mouth' run away with itself. The pronouncements, however, can be seen as the markers of an extremely interesting intersection of modernity, religion, nation and gender at a crucial point in Malaysia's development. I am especially interested in the terms under which 'women' as a category enter into public discourse and rhetoric about national and ethnic identity within present-day reworkings of Malay imaginaries.

This chapter explores the issues involved in talking about the relationships between gender, power and Malaysian modernities against a background of findings from my recent research.[2] Over the last few years I have been engaged in a research project looking at gender and public and private spheres in middle-class Malaysia. This has involved extensive historical and sociological research into the growth of the

Malay middle classes and long interviews with 100 households (60 in Seremban, 14 in Kuala Lumpur and 26 in Penang).[3] I suggest that contests around femininities are crucial both to the production of new Malay middle classness and (neo- and post-) modern consumption, and to the critiques of current versions of modernity in the country. Drawing on John Gledhill's ideas about power being affirmed and contested in social practice noted in Chapter 1 (1994: 22), I hypothesise that the recent politicisations of gender are intimately tied to ideological unsettlings and remakings of the private/public divide within the modernising project in Malaysia. I see this remaking of public and private as having a number of dimensions: first, large numbers of women have entered middle-class and working-class employment in urban areas with the recent spectacular state-led industrial growth in the country. This has profoundly affected labour patterns. Second, there appear to be extensive changes in subjectivities. There is also growing Islamicisation as Malaysia partakes of recent Islamic globalisations. This Islamicisation has multiple links to the reworking of public and private, as I shall show. In addition, there are moves for women's rights, especially among women of the middle-class intelligentsia as they explore their relationships with global feminisms.

Contests around the remade 'private' spaces of Malaysian modernity are predominant issues for the middle classes in particular. There is frequent debate in the print media about the pressures and costs of juggling work and home. The nature of Muslim family life and law is similarly a pervasive concern within cultural productions about Malays. This has been embedded within the larger discourse about the 'Asian Family' discussed in Chapter 1. The Malaysian Deputy Prime Minister, for example, speaking on Wanita (Women's) Day in 1994 of the *Arqam* banning, said that:

> 'Islam stresses on (sic) fairness and justice for everybody but these values have been misinterpreted by the group for their own personal interests . . .
>
> 'To me, not only the National *Fatwa* (Religious Ruling) council, government agencies and departments, but women themselves should take a firm stance in rejecting this deviant group,' he added.
>
> . . . 'We have to protect and defend our definition of family values and institutions and not be influenced by the definition promoted by the West . . . The east (sic) has its own values and culture which strongly depended on the strength of the family institution.'
>
> (*Star*, 26 August 1994)

As in this quote, the model of a 'toxic' West and its social ills operates as a constant point of reference in contests about family, creating meanings about proper and good Malay and Asian families and lifestyles.

PARADIGMS AND POSITIONALITIES

The late modern anxieties about positionalities and problematic intellectual inheritances, which I discussed in Chapter 1, have rightly made some scholars cautious about importing authoritative Western feminist frameworks into such locales as Malaysia. I have argued elsewhere that there are many reasons to be uneasy about writing about Malaysian women (1992): any attempt to explore the relationships between gender and power in the country will be at best an ambiguous affair. I noted some of the political and epistemological problems to be faced, including loss of scholarly authority, furious and sometimes obsessive debates about positionalities in general and subaltern status in particular, and the distortions of hegemonic Western epistemologies. A particular question concerns the extent to which scholarly and media agendas are produced within locally specific contexts, and how far they represent an imposition of a globalising culture's agendas. Some (female) Malaysian scholars have reacted to various feminist pronouncements about Malaysian women with ambivalence. They have felt justifiable resentment, irritation and sometimes hostility about 'expatriate' scholars making off with materials for their own ends. But as argued in Chapter 1, the claims of some Malaysian intellectuals to be providing (more) authentic knowledge of their own conditions (e.g. Maznah Mohamad and Wong Soak Koon 1994) run the risk of overlooking their own location within dominant Western ways of knowing and their own elite position. As Leila Ahmed argues in her book on gender and Islam, discourses of resistance (outside the so-called) West can be seen as inextricably informed by those of the West (1992: 2; Spivak 1987. See also Stivens 1992). This context can undermine claims for authentic, pure, indigenous knowledges.

GENDER, MODERNITIES AND GLOBALISATION

In Malaysia, as elsewhere in the region, the concepts embedded in Western epistemologies have clearly colonised debates about modernity, Westernisation and globalisation, and gender's relationships to these processes. As I argued in Chapter 1, feminist and Asianist readings can both usefully destabilise the idea of modernity.[4] In the Malaysian context, where revivalist Islam has considerable support among the middle classes, the idea of modernity has become further destabilised: it is located within a cluster of tensions surrounding the role of religion in the modern Malay world and its relationship to capitalist 'progress', development and 'tradition'. Ayatollah Khomeini's idea of 'westoxification', in which a toxic Western way of life poisons the rest of the world, has real currency among a substantial portion of Malays, who look to a future Islamic state as an alternative path to modernity.

These oppositional posings of 'East' and 'West' might suggest that the divergent globalisations of 'Westernisation' and 'Islamicisation' are not part of a larger global whole. In Chapter 1, however, I suggested that Jonathan Friedman's arguments about the ethnic and cultural fragmentation and the modernist cultural globalisation and homogenisation of the world as two constitutive trends of global reality can be useful in rethinking some of the connections between the 'global' and the 'local' in such contests as Malaysia.

NEW MALAYS, NEW MIDDLE CLASSES

The juncture of gender, class and nation expressed in the *Al Arqam* depictions has found one focus in the somewhat shadowy figure of the coming Malaysian neomodern order, the *Melayu Baru* or new Malay. The new Malay became prominent in 1993, featuring regularly in media cultural productions about a new, confident group of Malays 'less misty-eyed about the traditional nationalist values espoused by UMNO [the United Malays National Organisation, the Malay party within the ruling coalition], and more inclined to an aggressive, business oriented approach to politics' (*Far Eastern Economic Review*, 15 July 1993: 15).[5] In turn, the figure of the new Malay striding forward into the fully developed Malaysia envisaged in Prime Minister Mahathir's Vision 2020 has been a site of extensive contests about the future of Malay culture within modernity. These contests are direct heirs of earlier debates about the place of Malays in colonial Malaya and post-colonial Malaysia (see Roff 1967; Mahathir Mohamad 1970). The main dilemma today, however, is posed squarely in terms of the old tradition/modernity couple: some local scholars and commentators have called for the emergence of a new Malay equipped with the 'necessary skills and fighting spirit to tackle the future' (Wan Hashim quoted in *Asiaweek*, 12 January 1994: 3). They have been very exercised about how Malays might take their new place in society without losing their heritage and culture: 'How is the *Melayu baru* to be a global and local *Melayu*?' asks Asma Abdullah (*New Straits Times*, 23

December 1993: 30). 'Modernity, many may argue, does not sit easy (sic) on the Malay psyche', notes Askiah Adam (1994: 12). She concludes that, 'for the new Malays, defined by (industry board director) Nik Mahmood as possessing all the dynamic qualities of modernity while retaining those positive essential values of traditional Malay culture, it could possibly be a simple matter of reconstructing the good past in the hopeful present and then sculpting it according to the dictates of an optimistic future' (ibid.).

In some ways the current tensions about new Malayness (both within the Malay 'community' and with other ethnic groups) are not particularly new: they have surfaced at different points in local history, particularly in the nationalist period, when anxieties about the dislocations of colonial identity featured.[6] In 1978, 20 years after independence, the Malaysian social scientist Nordin Selat described the confused middle classes 'made in London' and riven by ethnic non-accommodation (1978). But what really stands out in all the present commentary about the future of Malay society is the way that the development of these new classes is seen as a *cultural* phenomenon, a cultural project (cf. Kahn 1996a). The overt concerns are not with the massive economic growth and rising affluence and consumerism. These are positively gloried in by some political and media rhetoric, although there is some Islamic dissent about the materialism of 'Westernisation'. However, there is direct concern with ways in which modernity and corporateness are seen to pose a threat to Malay 'culture'. It is not, however, the culture located in the rural idyll of colonially reconstituted communitarian peasant villages (*kampung*). Instead, ideas of being Malay have clearly cut loose from the core, expressivist, modern Malay identity associated with the imagined villager living in the imagined *kampung*. The *kampung* itself has become many things, including a background prop for advertising and fashion shots. My co-researcher Joel Kahn has recently interpreted this surface play of signs and images of old and new Malayness as evidence of a post-modernisation of Malay identity.

While there are a number of versions of the newly imagined Malay, one feature seems certain, his gender: he is implicitly understood to be a man.[7] The national, indeed neonationalist, emphasis on corporate Islam in some of the discourse about *Melayu baru* seems similarly to exclude women. We could well, adapting European historians' terminology, label it a version of muscular Islam. At the same time, new Malayness locates itself discursively in a field where women are specifically posed as bearers of families' moral and religious worth and of 'tradition' – indeed, of the nation. In much commentary, then, the new middle-class Malay is undeniably a male citizen subject, whose wife and children are addenda, inhabiting a private space outside of politics. The assumption that the public sphere is coded as masculine is all too clear. A dominant sub-text is that only men are seen to make political culture: women and gender are excluded from political subjecthood in much popular discourse and local Malaysian scholarly discussions (as in Pathamanathan and Haas 1994). There is, however, considerable rhetoric about women's place in nation-building in official documents (like those prepared for the Beijing Conference, see Jamilah Ariffin, 1994, and '*Malaysian Women Today*', prepared by the Ministry of National Unity and Social Development, Women's Affairs Division, Nagaraj 1995) and there are some prominent women politicians.

The absence of women from specific depictions of the new Malay – the new man – is interesting, given that representations of women feature strongly in many of the cultural productions of affluent middle classness and achievement, especially those surrounding consumption.[8] But these are not uniform: there are many and diverse, if not fragmented, images of 'modern' and 'middle-class' women depicted widely in the media, especially in the proliferating women's magazines aimed at the middle-class market and in advertisements. Women, moreover, are deployed as metaphors for often conflicting aspects of modernity in popular, religious and official discourse. For example, there is often an implicit modernist identification of 'new' women with the newly arrived affluent order in the celebrations of middle-class female achievement. Thus *Nona* magazine profiled a group of successful women in its centenary issue. But the dangerously sexual(ised) woman of modernity noted for nineteenth-century Euro-American discourse by a number of feminist writers (cf. Felski, 1995) also makes an appearance. The elision between modernity and unacceptable sexuality has been overt in representations of young factory workers, dubbed *Minah Karan* (Electric Minah, Fatimah Daud 1985; Ong 1987). A rash of articles appearing in 1994–95 about the teenage girl indulging in 'promiscuity' (*boh-sia*)[9] is just the latest example of the use of sexualisations in moral panics about the dangers of modernity, especially Western-style modernity.

What versions of new Malayness are open to women when the 'modern' itself is sometimes elided with the dangerously sexual? For women to claim the identity of a new Malay so overtly could well bring them a series of problems *as women*, especially the compromises involved in embracing particular versions of 'modern' identity. These dangers are less clear in the case of another modern woman, the manager, who has become a somewhat more prominent figure in the last decade. (From 1970 to 1990, however, women administrators and managers only rose from 0.1 per cent to 0.6 per cent of all female employment while the percentage of all employers who were women rose from 7 per cent [of 121,200] in 1980 to 8.5 per cent [of 169,400] in 1990, Siti Rohana Yahya 1993, quoted in Jamilah Ariffin 1994: 16–18.) Some of the elision of the modern and sexual is also evident in representations of middle-class women in glossy upmarket magazines. *Jelita*, for example, explicitly aimed at a Malay readership, features young Malay women in short-skirted power suits in advertisements, posed in the internationalised demi-erotic style of global advertising. Such images, which form an analogue to the male version of the mobile phone-toting yuppy version of the *Melayu baru*, nonetheless suggest the dangers in such self-presentation, glamorous as it might appear. Magazines and newspapers regularly picture patrons in the international hotels and their restaurants which are a central playground and site of display for the new middle classes; (their special menus run to $120 RM or more, about US$52 per head). The masculinity of the new (middle-class) Muslim Malay represented as inhabiting such global spaces is not directly problematic for his moral and business identity: he is even pictured holding an orange juice, not alcohol. But the femininity of a new woman slides more easily into moral ambiguity. It is clouded with the eroticisation of the commodity inherent in neomodern/post-modern consumption in contemporary Malaysia.

Of course, magazine features about real life Malay female managers treat them quite differently. Respectful of their achievements, the stories discuss their problems and achievements soberly. The women, usually in their thirties or older,[10] are pictured in extremely modest dress and often veiled, mostly wearing a *moden* (modern) *baju kurong* (long tunic and sarong underneath), or, less often, a *kebaya* (a more fitted tunic and considered somewhat more 'sexy', recently more popular). Managers and professional women within such stories can escape some of the sexualisation of the modern/post-modern woman: they are located discursively firmly within concerns with 'juggling' the demands of home and work, public and private and with the negotiation of power with male employers and employees.

Defining middle classes

Who are these new Malays? The outward signs of the rise of the middle classes in Malaysia and their accoutrements of housing and cars have been dramatic. Large areas of the cities have been turned over to new middle-class housing areas, the condominium phenomenon has been attracting much attention within popular culture and academia, and traffic jams choke all points of entry to the city. For many of the young, especially, the large post-modern shopping centres with their globalised patterns of entertainment have become the social centres of their lives, where they hang out ('loaf', *lepak*), speak English to each other and incur the wrath of their elders for their inactivity.[11]

There is little work on the new middle classes as yet, especially the non-Malay sectors (but see Saravanamattu 1989; Crouch 1996). In general commentary these classes are seen as the children of the New Economic Policy (NEP), implemented in 1970 after ethnic tensions between Malays and Chinese erupted in 1969.[12] This policy has been central to subsequent restructuring of the economy. The NEP aimed to progressively redistribute wealth to the poorest sections of Malaysian society, the Malays, through affirmative action, including a large-scale campaign to improve Malay education and pressure on employers to take on Malay employees. Khoo Kay Jin sees this as a response to Malay business and intelligentsia demands for a more interventionist state protecting 'Malay' interests, a shift of power to technocrats and bureaucrats (1992: 50).[13]

Nonetheless, state intervention in industrialisation produced spectacular economic growth (Jomo 1993; Kahn 1996a), with an average growth rate 1970–90 of 6.5 per cent (in spite of a recession in the mid-1980s) and over 8 per cent 1990–95 (*Mid-Term Review of the Sixth Malaysia Plan 1991-1995*: 28). The distribution of benefits from these changes is more debatable. Certainly, unemployment has been low, although fluctuating: the official figures for 1994 and 1995 were 2.8 and 2.9 per cent (*Economic Report, Ministry of Finance* 1994/5).[14] The extreme labour shortages of recent years have encouraged large-scale illegal immigration, especially from Indonesia. Other measures such as life expectancy, infant mortality and literacy all showed extensive improvements over the same period. Inequalities in income distribution seem to have been greater than in the east Asian NICs, rather less than in the rapidly growing Latin American economies, and roughly the same as the USA and Australia (Kahn 1996a).[15] From the early 1980s, there appears to have been some growth of small entrepreneurship among rural Malays benefiting from preferential government contracts in areas such as construction, agricultural marketing and processing (Shamsul 1986). At the same time, the mass of property development has produced a large sector of professionals and entrepreneurs serving the construction and financial sectors in the major cities. A number of critics of the NEP argue that a main outcome of the NEP has been the fostering of these new middle classes rather than the planned rural poverty alleviation.

The two features most-commented-on of the contemporary role of the Malaysian state in managing modern capitalism are the hypertrophic public sector and the global factory regime (Kahn 1996a). Government expenditure formed 39 per cent of GDP in 1987, one of the highest rates in the world, with large growth in public enterprises concentrated in the financial and industrial sectors (Kahn 1996a). The recent policy of Malaysia Incorporated, however, has moved the emphasis to a partnership between state and the private economic sector, with economic liberalisation and structural adjustments since the late 1980s undermining state investment (Jomo 1993). UMNO's own financial interests add a further, critical complexity (Gomez 1990).[16] Malaysia today appears to be planning for a Singapore-style Second Industrial Revolution, shifting away from the model of the low-wage factory to the high tech, highly skilled economy. The aim is to avert the problems posed by loss of investment to lower wage areas and Malaysia's own labour shortages (Kamal Salih and Young 1989; Kahn 1996a).

The other area attracting comment has been the global factory regime. The figure of the 'unskilled' (but often over-educated for the tasks expected of her) female factory worker in the labour-intensive, Free Trade Zone factory has been an object of great interest to feminists worldwide. Indeed, she has often come to signify Asian modernity for many a documentary maker and other commentator: she appears as both the sexualised figure of the new working-class Malaysian woman, the subject of local demonisation as Electric Minah; and as the workerist, victim figure in some First World feminist rhetoric about a conspiracy between capitalism and patriarchy. The concentration on these world market factories, however, misrepresents the structure of the contemporary Malaysian industrial economy, ignoring the relative isolation of FTZs from the rest of the economy, other important areas of employment and the role of the state in the economy.

I pointed out in Chapter 1 that we have considerable difficulties in conceptualising both the nature and the size of these allegedly new classes throughout the region and their impact on the economy and polity. The problems with the Eurocentric debates are compounded when we transpose the debates about the 'middle class' to contexts like Malaysia. I would argue that we need to query the identification of the many disparate groups forming these middle strata as a class at all (see Kahn 1996a). At the least, we need to see these strata in contemporary Malaysia as comprising a number of classes. Such schemes also exclude issues of gender, as I noted.[17] Given the all-important specificities of Malaysian developments, we cannot assume a homogeneous, collective class identity or homogeneous class practices among the various fractions that are identified as middle class. Yet what struck my co-researcher Joel Kahn and myself immediately and forcefully was that large numbers of our informants had little difficulty in identifying themselves as 'middle class'. Many volunteered such a self-description, and had a clear idea about what being middle class involved in terms of income and everyday practices.[18]

The standard ways of identifying 'class' in Malaysia have followed occupational categories. If we use these problematic classifications from the censuses to give a pragmatic overall picture of recent changes,[19] it appears that 'middle-class' (professional, administrative and technical, clerical and related) *male* occupations among Malays comprised 3 per cent of all occupations in 1931, 3.4 per cent in 1947, 5.1 per cent in 1957, and 9.3 per cent in 1967. Although these are crude occupational categorisations, they suggest that there was a small, slowly growing, mainly urban middle class until the post-colonial period. By 1980, however, these figures appear to have risen to as high as 24 per cent of the work force (Crouch 1985: 31–2). Using the same measures, Saravanamuttu estimates that by the late 1980s 37.2 per cent of workers were in middle-class occupations (1989), while Crouch gives a figure of 32.6 per cent (see Table 4.1). The 'bourgeoisie', 'upper' or 'ruling' class disappear from many such schemes.[20]

Crouch suggests that by 1990 Malay and other *bumiputera* (literally 'sons of the soil', i.e. Malay and other indigenous group) employees made up almost half of both the white-collar and working-class employment categories, compared to about a third in 1970, although Malays were still underrepresented in the administrative/managerial and sales categories (1996: 238). There was also a doubling of public sector employment[21] and, with ongoing privatisation, growing numbers of new middle-class occupations within private economic sectors. From the early 1980s, small entrepreneurship among rural Malays appears to have benefited from preferential government contracts in areas such as construction, agricultural marketing and processing (Shamsul 1986). Crouch, however, casts doubt on the size of the larger Malay entrepreneurial class produced by the NEP.[22]

Table 4.1 Malay occupational structure 1957, 1979 and 1990

	1957	*1979*	*1990*
Middle class	15.5	20.0	32.6
	(4.0)	(5.9)	(11.3)
	(11.5)	(14.1)	(21.3)
Working class	18.9	27.3	27.6
Agriculture	56.4	44.9	28.3

Source: Crouch (1996: 183).[23]

It is extremely difficult to extract figures for women from the available data. It appears that few women are entrepreneurs, although women's workforce participation has risen steadily, reported at 44 per cent in 1992 (Jamilah Ariffin 1992:33) and 47 per cent in 1993 (*Mid-term Review of the Sixth Malaysia Plan 1991–1995*: 239). Education has expanded greatly, with large numbers now attending tertiary institutions and increased opportunities for girls and women.[24] Jamilah Ariffin estimates that in 1986 10.1 per cent of employed women were professional and technical workers, the proportions having risen from 5.3 per cent in 1970 and 5.6 per cent in 1975 (1992: 40; 1994: 16). Siti Rohani Yahya gives a figure of 9.4 per cent for 1990 (cited in Jamilah Ariffin 1994: 16). Only 0.1 per cent of women employed were in the administrative and managerial category in 1970, rising to 0.6 per cent in 1990. If one includes clerical workers, in fact a slightly greater proportion of women than men were in white-collar work in the early 1980s (19.9 per cent as compared to 14.6 per cent, Siti Rohani Yahya quoted in Jamilah Ariffin 1994: 16).[25] By 1990, these figures had risen to 24.1 per cent and 16.2 per cent respectively (ibid.). A different set of figures about employment status shows 9 per cent of employers being women in 1985, rising to 11 per cent in 1987, 1988 and 1989, but falling back to 9 per cent in 1990; the figure of 27 per cent of women being own account workers remained constant over the same period, however (Ariffin 1994: 29). But most of the latter are in fact in agriculture and forestry and so outside the present purview.

An account of the processes of Malaysian middle-class formation needs to look at the 'old' middle class. I have argued elsewhere that this 'class' arose within the structures set in place by the colonial order in managing the colonial economy and polity (Stivens 1996). The significant social inequalities in Malayan society in the colonial and early independent years, I suggest, should not be seen as a class division between large rural capitalists (large landowners) and peasants/rural proletariat, following many of the models of rural differentiation. Rather, the significant relations were between a rural 'middle-class' fraction heavily involved in mediating between the state, a peasantry differentiated to varying degrees and the reconstituted 'aristocracy' of the sultans and rulers. This rurally based middle class included local officials, school-teachers, the police and small entrepreneurs (Stivens 1996). Many of my urban informants had their origins in this rural middle class and I would argue that it has had important links to the present generation of new middle-class urban dwellers.[26] The role of rural school-teachers in the nationalist movement, particularly in UMNO until the New Economic Policy (NEP) took hold, has been legendary.

(Women formed a sizeable portion of school-teachers, so the decline of this pressure group within UMNO in recent years has a gendered dimension (see Manderson 1980).)

DOMESTICITY, FAMILY AND CLASS

My informants are living their everyday lives in a context where 'family' is highly politicised, especially within the Asian family discourse. Ideas of family, home and work are being profoundly reorganised and continuously contested within middle-class daily life. As suggested, I see this contestation about 'family' as closely implicated in the production of middle classness and of masculinity and femininity.

Middle-class women's class situation in contemporary Malaysian discourse is generally subsumed in that of the household/husband. Analytically, however, this subsumption is embedded in the problematic division between public and private: this assumes that men and (occasionally) women in their 'public' work practices are members of 'classes' but domestic work is somehow outside the economy and polity. Yet the domestic work within the supposed private sphere that women (and some men) do can be seen as integral to the everyday cultural production and re-production of middle classness. This echoes the arguments of Davidoff and Hall (1987) discussed in Chapters 1 and 5. Davidoff and Hall's study showed the links between the domestic and the processes forming the middle classes in Britain in the nineteenth century. They argue that these processes were thoroughly gendered, focussed on the construction of a domestic ideology and its constant reworkings. Although the Malaysian specificities are critical, especially women's 'double role' in both production and consumption, there are significant structural parallels, not least the expression of ambivalences about modernity in so-called fundamentalist religion discussed below. The situation of women working outside the home in a globalising neomodern/post-modern order is a key issue in present-day reworkings of the domestic in Malaysia.

A first obvious and critical point about my informants' lifestyles is that the levels of prosperity of the families were often dependent on women's extensive involvement in work outside the home, although the women interviewed mostly earned considerably less than their husbands. Of the sixty Seremban households interviewed (a section of a housing estate) 65 per cent had two sources of income. Almost all the women in the other samples in Penang and Kuala Lumpur were working, but this was in part an effect of the sample selection. The majority said they enjoyed their work, although a sizeable proportion were interested in promotion. I am not detailing their work and household management experiences here, although these are being fully explored in some detail in the writing up of this project.

The juggling act my informants' lives involved dominated the interviews. Child care problems, the demands of the school co-curricular (extra) activities, parental transporting of children and timetabling were primary concerns. The commodification of time is an abiding and deeply gendered issue for Malaysian modernity. As one woman informant put it, 'Rush, rush, rush!'. This 'juggling' discourse, with which my interviewees totally identified, will be instantly recognisable to contemporary middle classes globally.

Woman at Work is an English language magazine published in Kuala Lumpur, which mainly features European and Chinese-looking models in its advertisements for imported watches, clothes and beauty aids but appears to have a multi-ethnic readership. (Speaking English, especially as a form of display in public spaces, has become very prevalent among middle-class Malays, precipitating something of a crisis within national/nationalist language policy.) In June 1995 the magazine carried an advertisement for a forum on 'How to Balance A Career and a Family':

> A Career or a Family? Women are often in quandary (sic) when it comes to this dilemma. Does (sic) the two go hand in hand? Our society places pressure on women to stay at home for the children but more and more women have careers that they are quite reluctant to give up. So they have to juggle both and juggling career and family can bring a great toil (sic) not just on working mothers but on their families and their careers too.
>
> If you find yourself in this predicament and you are about to pull your hair, please don't! Come join our forum and share juggling strategies with other like-minded women.
>
> This month's forum will be facilitated by Ezuria Mohd Hashim, a management development trainer and marketing consultant with Colybrand Sdn Bhd – a business unit of Coopers and Lybrand. Ezuria holds an MBA in International Business from the University of New Haven USA. She is married with three children.
>
> (*WAW* June 1995: 135)

To be held 2–4.30 pm at a local hotel, it charged a very modest 20 ringgit for non-members of Women N-atwork.[27]

Male inputs into domestic work among my informants were variable, but generally not great. The pressures of household juggling with increasing female workforce participation arguably have led to some restructuring of male–female relations in Euro-America. But the availability of servants for the more affluent in Malaysia generally may well be one of the most important factors deflecting or at least deferring a renegotiation of male–female relations within households. Male domestic inertia is left relatively untouched, at least among the better off. The new conjunctures may be producing greater change in other less well-off groups, however, with juggling forcing greater male participation. In the interview groups and on the housing estate in Seremban where I stayed for 2 months, men were active in one part of the juggling exercise, the transporting by car of children to school and to after-school lessons. The after-school activities included music and dance tuition and extra tutoring to improve school performance. These activities are clearly a vital component of the new middle classes' educational and class re-production projects.

This underlines the importance of working-class servants in the lives of many middle-class Malaysians. Many people would find the achievement of the requisite upper middle-class lifestyle and standards of domestic management difficult to achieve without the services of maids. Nurseries and creches are rare and apparently of questionable quality. There is kin help with childcare for some. The labour market for various kinds of maids/babysitters, however, is unregulated: quite a number are illegal migrant workers. A recent registration of illegal immigrants, for example, netted 100,000 workers, including 19,912 domestic workers (Heyzer and Wee 1994). It is estimated that there may be between 500,000 and 800,000 illegal workers in the country (ibid.). Moreover, as in Singapore, there is an ethnically segmented labour market for maids, with Filipino maids earning the highest rates.[28]

In fact, I was surprised to find that only a minority overall of the study households employed a servant: a quarter of the Seremban study households had paid domestic help, about a half of the Penang sample, but over 80 per cent of the KL households. People said that they could not afford even the cheaper and often illegal migrant servants, because they had mortgages and other debts on consumer items. In any case, valuing their privacy, a number did not like the idea of having someone in their often quite small houses. Stories about the 'problems' with these maids feature regularly in the Malaysian press, mostly telling us how unreliable these women are and what trouble they cause their employers. This discourse was also common among academics who might be expected to view the situation somewhat more critically. Even though those attending a seminar I gave on some of this material in 1995 at the University of Malaya were all social scientists, they echoed the media's concern with the faults of maids rather than sympathising with the maids' difficulties.[29] Stories about the maids' problems and the trade in maids, an issue for feminists in the region (see for example Heyzer and Wee 1994), appear much less frequently. This is a site of particular tension for those professing such oppositional politics, because quite a few of them also employ servants.[30] Like other members of the middle classes, their social position is supported by these arrangements.

The academics at the 1995 seminar suggested another reason why women are unable to get men to 'help' much in the house. They stressed the power they saw the threat of polygamy giving men over women. A husband displeased with a wife's attempts to negotiate household responsibilities might simply take another more pliable wife, they said. Even though the polygamy rate is low (1–3 per cent plus of Muslim marriages, Jones, 1994), this insecurity points to the power of polygamy in the female imagination – there is a long history of reformist female concern about marriage laws. A few cases among the very men who might be seen as particularly 'modern' – entertainers, academics and other members of the intelligentsia – have achieved wide publicity, leading perhaps to some exaggeration of its frequency. They have also been the object of feminist ire. The anxiety about husbands also finds expression among the middle classes and others in the alleged widespread use of magic to keep a husband's affection. This reconstituted modern magic involves such rites as burning a used sanitary pad and crumbling the residue into the husband's food to keep him faithful.

The continuing power of these anxieties is nonetheless interesting, given the relative financial independence of many middle-class women, an independence and even 'autonomy' which some of my interviewees explicitly recognised and valued.[31] This power has to be seen in the context of changing marriage patterns and subjectivities. The last decades have seen a decline in arranged marriage and a rise in 'free-choice' marriage among Malays, with an associated modernist ideology of companionate marriage and a search for intimacy. This search for versions of intimacy can be documented throughout the 'women's' magazines. Malay marriages in the colonial period were represented in the anthropological literature in a highly authoritative tone as governed by 'pragmatism', and with little attention to subjectivities.[32] But as I argue elsewhere (1996), the role of earlier historical constructions of love and passion in relationships between men and women may have been underestimated. I am not sure that the alleged new emphasis on romance is as much of a departure from previous patterns as might be thought,[33] nor that it is to be seen as an effect of globalising subjectivities and sexualities. It might be better understood as refigured within the present conjunctures. But there is an explicit discourse among Malay women that modernity has offered 'freedom' from the constraints of 'arranged' marriage.[34] In the present context, polygamy may well transgress both these changing subjectivities and versions of family life espoused by different agents like the reformist Muslims (such as the Sisters in Islam group) and modernist state ideology (as in Mahathir's comments at the beginning of this chapter).

The stress on companionate marriage does not seem to have undermined the pressures felt by women in allegedly non-standard marital careers. Pressures against divorced (and widowed) women (*janda*) have long been reported in the anthropological literature (see for example, Djamour 1965) and my female informants provided much direct evidence of this. Some of them told me how difficult their situation was if they were living as a single (divorced) parent; hence the widespread fear of infidelity, polygamy and divorce, perhaps. One professional woman had even received poison-pen letters from colleagues for having been divorced from her husband and for trying to bring up her child on her own while holding down a responsible position. (Such letters were a common method of 'social control'.) She and a number of others found their Islamic belief a great source of comfort and solace when faced with such difficulties, of which more will be said below.

THE 'ASIAN FAMILY'

As I noted in Chapter 1, there has been a massive cultural production of ideas about the Asian family throughout the region in the last few years. The dominant state-level ideology of family in Malaysia is complex, involving an implicit assumption that the desirable 'Asian family' is an extended one with an entrenched ideology of familism. It looks to a golden and, in some ways, feminised past. At the same time, somewhat contradictorily, the Malaysian state in some of its official pronouncements suggests that the nuclear (sic) household is becoming the dominant 'family' form (Stivens 1987) and that modern Malaysian society must accommodate these changes without going down the Western path. A number of panics are imported, like those relating to the divorce rate in much of Euro-America. Journalists talk about rising divorce in Malaysia and dangers to (elementary) family life without noting that Malay divorce rates have in fact fallen spectacularly in the last 50 years, from yearly rates of over 90 divorces per 100 marriages a year in some places to rates of about eight or nine divorces per 100 marriages per year. Jones, however, reports that in Kuala Lumpur and Penang divorce rates are on the rise again.[35] In the 1970s and early 1980s, familism was linked to various campaigns about population control, mostly imposed by outside agencies. But the last decade has seen a shift from family limitation to the cooption of a long-standing pronatalism within Malay society to encourage women to marry young and have lots of children in order to fulfil the 1984 '70 million [population] policy' (Stivens 1987, n.d.a).

In Malaysia, these campaigns have restated an often crudely patriarchal version of family life, with the father as the clear head and protector of the family and the mother as a warm and supportive helpmate. Women are enjoined to look to their role as mothers (although there is much rhetoric aimed at *parents* and families): their job is producing the producers of newness, the children who are the hope of the nation. These messages have been prominent within a series of developed government campaigns in the last few years, especially the campaigns around the 'happy family' and its location in the wider discourse about the Asian family. A back cover of *Ibu* (Mother) magazine in 1991 (see Figure 4.1) illustrates some of this discourse. It shows a boy (probably Indian, but his ethnicity appears to be deliberately unclear), astride the picture, neatly dressed in grey school pants, with blocks of flats in the middle distance. The caption celebrates the Selangor Development Corporation, and reads 'We are building housing, you are building happy families'. The rest of the advertisement (which appeared in a number of other magazines as well) outlined the hopes and efforts of parents (mainly mothers?) in raising their children.[36] Figure 4.2 shows the front cover of the same issue of *Ibu*.

The happy family campaign and the Asian family discourse have an uneasy relationship with different versions of a Muslim future. Some of the *Dakwah* groups argue that motherhood and child care are women's true vocation. Islam, they say, unlike the West, upholds and values women's full participation in society, but sees women and men as having essentially complementary roles. Given the robust involvement of *Darul Arqam* for one in a range of highly modern capitalist enterprises (see Wan Suhaimi Saidi and Hanim Adnan 1994), these pronouncements about a woman's place being in the home may be somewhat rhetorical. Both government and many branches of religion, however, are united in a view of the need to 'strengthen' the family by promoting the idea of the Asian family. There have been large numbers of newspaper and magazine articles over the last few years exhorting the populace to observe family values. These ideas of the Asian family gain their meaning almost entirely in relation to the purported post-modern anarchy and chaos of the 'Western family' (as in the remarks by the deputy Prime Minister quoted above) and the toxic effects of Western-style modernity.

How did my informants see Malay and Malaysian family life? A sizeable proportion produced statements that closely resembled the public

Figure 4.1 Targeting the 'Asian Family': advertisement for Selangor Development Corporation, *Ibu*, 1991

discourses about the Asian family. Their own practices did in fact support wider kin relations, although the reasons for this lie more in the continuing discursive power and practical uses of kinship and the absence of social security (see Stivens 1987). As I had foreseen, my interview households were mostly very involved in helping kin, both rural and urban. This provides further evidence for my suggestion elsewhere that the rise of the so-called 'nuclear' family (as against

Figure 4.2 Visions of a Muslim future: cover of *Ibu* magazine, November 1991

elementary family household) in Malaysia was in some ways mythical (ibid.). I suggested there that the pressures of industrialisation reshaped kinship relations, producing a modified and often female-centred extended family form to support the work and family trajectories of urban life. My informants might be living in smaller, mostly elementary family households, but the elementary family has been a feature of pre-industrial Malay kinship patterns (ibid.). It is also possible that the continuing importance of kin ties in their own lives has been read as legitimating Asian family discourses. These describe a version of a lived reality which reassures them that they were not becoming modern in an undesirable way.

MASCULINITIES, FEMININITIES AND MIDDLE-CLASS IMAGINARIES

The models of the patriarchal father and the new Malay might suggest that the Malaysian state has been concerned to promote particular versions of masculinity, the thrusting economic rationalist of corporate Malaysia or the firm and upright father at home. Yet in spite of this there seems to me to be no clear state project of masculinity comparable to the developed exhortations about femininity.

The image of the hypermasculine, new corporate Malay can be seen to be constructed wholly as the antithesis of the emasculated, fatalistic and negligent Malay of the colonial 'lazy native' discourse (see Syed Hussein Alatas 1977). Prime Minister Mahathir spelled this out in his tract *The Malay Dilemma* (1970, banned 1970–1981). Arguing for the need for the Malays to be elevated to the level of the other races in the country, he pictures them as a debilitated race affected by inbreeding, a too easy life and habits of excessive courtesy, politeness and indulgence of children. This is a clear internalisation of the colonial discourse, a version of the familiar depiction of the (male) colonial subject as lacking masculinity (cf. Hall 1992). (I think, nonetheless, that some of the post-colonial literature on the feminised and Orientalised colonial subject tends to homogenise vast historical and geographical differences and make unwarranted generalisations.)[37] The rejection of the emasculated past that is explicit in many of the ideas about the new Malay, however, has an uneasy relationship with the nostalgia of the present imaginings about the Asian family.[38]

There are a number of versions of new masculinity apparent in popular culture, including the new Malay, preferably allied to the local versions of the 'family man' of the reinvented Asian Family. But as we saw, some of my female informants had a further version that loomed large in their anxieties about husbands, the feckless and duplicitous Lothario. The latter is enshrined in a number of cartoon book guides for men about how to be a *buaya* (literally, a crocodile, which translates as 'wolf' in Anglo-American imagery). This ties in to a widespread representation by Malay women of Malay men as unreliable and 'irresponsible'.[39] Arguments about the industrial revolution in nineteenth-century Euro-America have stressed the ways that versions of masculinity were constructed around the breadwinner role. Active trade union participation to obtain and protect the family wage embedded ideas of manliness in the breadwinner role for the working class (Humphries 1977). Davidoff and Hall note for the middle classes a similar link between the worlds of public and private in forming masculinity, in which masculinity becomes closely tied to thrift, a work ethos and domestic responsibility. Mahathir's Vision 2020 produces a parallel version of masculinity in its embrace of a 'dry' economic rationalist blueprint for a corporate Islamic future of thrift and hard work.

It is significant that, in spite of the masculine character of the New Malay in 'public' political discourse, much of the massive volume of cultural productions about Malay modernity in present-day Malaysia is decidedly feminine and is overwhelmingly feminine in the act of consumption. I am thinking of magazine advertisements in particular. These acts of consumption are highly socially stratified and deeply gendered.

The all-important role of the members of these classes as consumers is critical here in producing meanings about modern womanhood and its relation to Malay identities. I am not talking about the haute-bourgeois consumption of the elite and the upper middle classes but the ordinary everyday consumption by the affluent and less affluent middle classes. This has had untold effects in shaping modern Malaysia and the emerging middle-class project, often quite literally. For example, the demand for middle-class housing and cars has altered the environs of the major cities beyond all recognition, as noted. The desires for shopping centres, for restaurants, for the accoutrements of modern life are areas where issues of gender and women may be ignored by the male intelligentsia and commentators, but they are not ignored by advertisers. They spend fortunes on consumer profile studies, providing us with a series of cultural depictions of the consumer: such schemes include categories like 'the yuppies', 'the not-quite-theres', 'the conservatives' and 'the traditionalists' (Adnan Hashim 1994). Here women come into their own, with explicit recognition of their role as consumers.

My informants mostly read two or more of the many middle-class women's magazines. The majority of these emphasise glamour, domesticity and motherhood, apart from magazines like *Woman at Work*. But each of the magazines appears to have perfected the art of niche marketing, producing multiple images of modern Malay and Malaysian femininities. While images of chaste, modern Muslim wives, keepers of the family and indeed Malay modernity proliferate in the magazines and in other parts of the media, these are far from monolithically uniform: some of the 'modern' glossies aiming more upmarket, like *Jelita*, downplay this, picturing women, as does *Woman at Work*, in the globalised zones of corporate Malaysia, whereas *Ibu* (Mother) is full of stories about how to conduct Islamic family life at a much less exalted level. Thus we can see a close identification of Islam and Malayness in *Ibu* which is skirted in *Seri* if not ignored, and accommodated but not embraced in *Jelita. Ibu* tries to reconcile domestic ideology with the idea of the new modern 'working' supermum.[40] It might be tempting to see the messages in *Ibu* magazine as part of a globalising production of domesticity inflected with local specificities, in this case of an Islamic modernity, or a simple reflection of government fiat. There are substantial parallels, for example between the views about family life, the need for thrift and hard work in *Ibu*'s texts and the ethics of Vision 2020 as propounded in official publications.[41] Parents/mothers are constantly being exhorted to encourage the values in their children that will help produce a disciplined and developed future. But even *Ibu*'s text is fragmented by advertisements deriving from the latest in globalising semiotics, with images playing on the erotics of consumer desire.

If there is a dominant sub-text in such magazines, it is that Malaysian women are being centrally placed as producers of contemporary urban culture and middle classness. The images of urban middle-class women, especially of mothers, in these cultural productions provide a mass of advice: how to create a home in these new and sometimes modest, sometimes not so modest dwellings, with detailed instructions for women readers on modern household consumption and decor; how to avail themselves of reinvented cuisines; how to conduct interpersonal relationships, especially those between men and women; how to juggle busy work and home lives; and how to produce happy, clever, industrious and indeed nation-building children. The labour of the maids who play such an important part in producing upper middle-class lifestyles is more or less totally suppressed from this imagery.

Women's focal role as coordinators of consumption and the producers of elaborated domesticities parallels that reported for consumer capitalist culture worldwide. There is obviously much pleasure and much work in this process of consuming images and commodities and producing domestic comfort. But while some of my informants were presenting houses and selves that were closely modelled on the blueprints circulating, many did not succeed or wish to succeed in producing the utopian domestic retreats pictured in the magazines. Their houses did not contain the elaborate interiors pictured in some of the upmarket publications, but were mostly very 'ordinary' comfortable middle-class houses, the ubiquitous developer's model of terrace or semi-detached single- or two-storey concrete houses of the middle-class estates and condominiums. They were mostly furnished with comfortable, far from opulent furniture, a selection of modern electrical and electronic devices like one TV, a video player, a rice cooker, and some books in some cases, especially in academic households. This reflected their levels of income: the Kuala Lumpur (KL) and Penang informants' monthly incomes clustered in the $M3,000–$M5,000, for example, with a substantial minority earning more. The Seremban informants were a bit lower on the income scale. The magazines' version of Malaysian domesticity is an explicitly urban phenomenon. The pictures of modern decor all feature 'townhouses' or condominiums. The rural house belongs to another cultural set altogether, deployed only in relation to the 'traditional', the site of either 'heritage' or 'traditional' village (*kampung*) values. But even those are post-modernised, no longer internal to new Malay identities, but an accessory for feminine fashion consumption.

Images of mothers are, of course, central to much of this cultural production. Long-suffering, self-denying Malay mothers and their sentimentalised relationships with their children will be familiar to those acquainted with Malay literature and other cultural productions and this picture is replicated in some of the present-day media. Contemporary images of mothers build on the models of family and mothering constructed in local and colonial discourses of Malay parenting. The latter depicted mothers as indulgent, loving and nurturant, but also in the end as too indulgent, indeed fatalistic and ultimately positioned within the dominant colonial discourse about the 'lazy native' (see Stivens n.d.b). But contemporary middle-class projects, while developing these themes, see present-day parenting as an altogether more purposeful activity, often pictured as occurring within a revived spirituality. Thus we get a growing amount of advice in newspapers, magazines and books as well as through government speeches to parents (mothers) about how to bring up children properly. My informants in Penang, however, told me that they rarely read such advice books, relying on newspapers and magazines instead.

The fashion pages of these magazines would make a study in themselves. Detailing reworked, modern (*moden*) versions of 'traditional' Malay women's dress, these advertise the outfits available at special boutiques in glitzy shopping centres, with marked hierarchies of elaborateness and price. We can note immediately the contemporary reconstitution of the colonial pattern of males adopting Western dress (except when they go to the mosque or get married) whereas women are constructed as bearers of a recreated nationality/nationalism and or Islamic piety in their everyday dress (cf. Taussig 1993). Many of my women academic informants, like many other middle-class women, feel constrained to wear 'Malay' dress to work. While some magazines like *Jelita* and *Woman at Work* show women in international 'power suits', these are not widely worn by Malays. On the other hand, the infrastructure of airconditioning in buildings and cars has allowed the adoption of what is now no longer 'colonial' but global dress to go to what seem absurd lengths in a humid, tropical climate. 'Western' suits, even with waistcoats, are standard for men. (I note that Singapore *Vogue* for May 1995 – also sold in Malaysia – had a cover story about how the trenchcoat is fashion's *greatest* cover up.) It is noteworthy that it is only when women get married that there is an increasingly approved wearing of Western dress, the ubiquitous white wedding dress, while men wear 'traditional' Malay dress. The white dress is usually worn at one point during the ceremonies; currently, it appears at the 'dinner' that is now held on the evening of the wedding day, in middle-class circles at least. This dress has also been subject to various 'Malayanising' and 'Arabising' reworkings. Recent editions of middle-class magazines have carried stories with enormously elaborate instructions about how to have the latest, most fashionable, reconstituted 'traditional' Malay wedding; in these the decorations, presents and so on surrounding the wedding clearly have an iconic status as Malay 'culture' even as the ceremonies partake of thoroughly global practices. It is no accident that a number of hotels in Singapore and KL have for at least 25 years carried 'cultural' shows which feature re-enacted weddings.[42]

The question as to how these images are received, interpreted and acted upon is another whole issue. In spite of the dominant 'domestic' subtext, my sense of these cultural productions is that they provide many and fragmented images of masculinities and femininities. There has been no simple convergence of state, religious and popular cultural views about a woman's place in the home, for example. These fragmentations might be interpreted as active cultural contests about how to live Malay middle classness in neomodern/post-modern times or perhaps as evidence of the thoroughly post-modern fragmenting of Malay identity argued for earlier.

MODERNITY, COMPLIANCE AND ANXIETY

In general, a majority of my interviewees said that they were happy with their work, homes, suburbs and possessions, and they were overall hopeful about their own and their children's future. This might be read as a somewhat remarkable level of contentment with the new order. A particular issue for debates about the new middle classes of the region, as I noted in Chapter 1, is the supposed developing taste of these classes for liberal versions of freedom and democracy.[43] This has been more muted in Malaysia than in some of the other countries in the region like the Philippines and Indonesia. In the Malaysian case it is commonly asserted that the delivery of stunning economic growth through the New Economic Policy has proved self-legitimating for the ruling national front. Such arguments have gained extra currency from the large gains by the government in the 1995 election.

Yet my informants, especially women, also expressed a clear set of more existential anxieties about their entry to modernity and its costs. Women's troubles with 'juggling' and their insecurity about their husband's affections were part of a set of wider concerns. Far from being full of the optimism and remade nationalist spirit alleged by the New Malay discourses, a substantial minority spoke of a range of feelings: considerable ambivalence about how far they wanted to embrace the 'new' and, for some, considerable personal stress and even misery. A few informants were enormously dissatisfied with the lives they were living, especially, as noted, the difficulties in being a divorced middle-class mother. One woman even disowned her own ethnicity, finding Malay friendship groups oppressive, with gossip and observation meaning little privacy and much pressure. For some an embrace of re-emergent Islam was a solution: about a quarter of my informants explicitly supported revivalist Islam, with a number privileging their Muslim identity over being a Malay. This placed them outside both the traditionalist Malay identity and secular versions of the new Malay. The tensions around modernity/post-modernity obviously qualify the highly optimistic national-level rhetoric about the booming Malaysian economy and the Vision 2020 Utopianism.

It is worth stressing here that it is middle-class Malaysians, journalists, artists and academics, among them many women, who are simultaneously creating, living in and contesting their own middle-class cultural forms. The role of intellectuals becomes extremely complex in this late modern context. Many have espoused the somewhat second-hand global post-colonial (actually mostly US academy-based) agendas of speaking (for) the subaltern. Such positioning is made more complex by a partial embrace of an anti-Western Islamic modernity. The relationship of that most middle class of movements, the women's movement of the 1970s on, to Malay dissidences about modernity is particularly ambiguous. I have suggested elsewhere that Western feminisms, products of the specificities of North Atlantic modernity, have clearly not always chimed with the particularities of Malaysian post-coloniality (1992, 1994a, 1994b): the definitions of women's concerns have inevitably been localised and contextual. Women's organisations have been extremely active in critiques of the conditions of women workers like operatives in multinational factories and maids. They were more reticent, however, about becoming involved in what have sometimes been perceived as 'Western' women's movement issues like domestic violence, although a long campaign against domestic violence recently resulted in legislation aimed at dealing with this issue.[44] Many women's refuges were only set up in the mid to late 1980s in several countries in Southeast and East Asia.[45] But while adherence to formal feminisms might be ambivalent, versions of local and imported feminist agendas feature in many of the women's magazine discussions at both implicit and more overt levels. Such interventions have been one of the major players surrounding the reworking of the 'private'.

MIDDLE-CLASS WOMEN AND THE POLITICS OF RELIGIOUS PRACTICE

The support for revivalist Islam among sections of the new middle classes, especially university students (Nilufer Narli 1986), casts a further critical light on understandings of modernity in Malaysia and its relationship to gender. The contests around the Islamicisation of Malaysia in recent years have become critically centred on the nature and costs of 'development', with revivalist groups mounting rigorous critiques of the perceived costs of 'Western-style' modernisation. Indeed, one might argue that religion and modernity are mutually self-defining in contemporary Malaysia. Although such critiques have involved some attempts to set up alternate Islamic financial institutions, they do not direct their attention to the economic and political costs of modernity so much as to the perceived cultural/moral costs (see for example Ustaz Ashaari Muhammad 1993). And, as indicated, this critique has become crucially centred on issues of women's modesty, chastity and sexuality. Contests about women's place have been a continuing and critical feature of the core tensions within Malay politics between modernist and traditionalist Islam over the last century, with particular emphasis on issues of polygamy and covering the body.[46] The subtext to these contests is that women have been deployed as bearers of correct religious dress and behaviour and as keepers of a hopefully revivified private sphere, the 'family'.

The rising tide of veiling in the country has assumed a central symbolic place in everyday protestations of faith, and, I would argue, of ethnicity. The decision to veil or not to veil, and the meanings attached to the proliferating versions of the veil were dominant issues for the informants I interviewed in Penang, for example. However, the interpretation of the meanings of this renewed veiling is somewhat fraught. It has been argued that working-class women have found in Islamic practice a sense of social worth denied by the social order, whereas middle-class women are essentially victims of a governance by Islam (Ong 1987; 1990). Some of my informants claim that the veil is often merely a fashion accessory, and point to the multiple styles in circulation, some with elaborate and highly decorative beading and fringing! I would argue that for urban middle-class Malay women, the veiling and covering of their bodies appear to have taken on a number of meanings, a neonationalist symbol of a specifically Malay modernity that has deep ethnic and class repercussions (cf. Ong 1990), a powerful symbol of what we might see as an Islamic modernity, and an (ultimately unsuccessful) means to escape some of the pervasive sexualisations of modernity by constructing an alternative 'private' sphere. The meanings deployed around the figure of a Malay woman have become inseparable from a critique of the ills of Western modernity. The class dimension is particularly developed through the sexualisation of working-class women, especially women working in factories owned by international corporations. These images of available women gain much of their meaning from an implicit comparison with the supposed chastity and respectability of middle-class women. (As a footnote, I could report the frequency with which I have heard claims that carefully veiled middle-class employees were in fact involved in extra-marital affairs.).

The tensions between so-called First World and Third World feminisms are central to conceptualising the relationships of women and gender to Islam. Some local scholars – members of oppositional middle-class factions – have argued that Western feminism is inappropriate in the Malaysian context, and that the veil and Islamic practices confer equal but separate power. In this account, then, a somewhat different 'public' and 'private' is created from that argued for by modernist feminists and by the state. This argument links up to an international movement by some Islamic feminists working for a reinterpretation of Islam (e.g. Mernissi 1991, writing from a Middle Eastern context; Amina Wadud-Muhsin 1992, writing from Malaysia). The central tenet here is that the Koran can be reread as a text setting out a social justice agenda whose gender egalitarianism has been suppressed historically in many Muslim states.

My informants have been clearly articulating aspects of these renewed contests in their conversations during the interviews. A significant proportion are living the revived spiritualism of the Islamic resurgence at a very intense level, with many stressing the absolute centrality of Islam in their lives. They were very anxious to discuss their decisions to wear the veil or not, and to disabuse me of any orientalist notions they thought I might entertain about this practice. Putting on the veil was often a long, deeply considered and sometimes anguished move, involving much consultation with friends and relatives. It was also a highly political gesture, a means for them to engage with neo-modernity/postmodernity on terms that seemed to be more of their own making. A number of my informants, however, shared none of these views: they voiced secular modernist critiques of the Islamic 'atmosphere' at various places of work, of the thwarted potential for Islam as a force for reform and were peeved at receiving anonymous letters and flyers pressuring them to conform in dress and behaviour to 'more Muslim' ways.

Leila Ahmed, in her book on women and gender in Islam takes up many of the arguments from the post-colonial debates about the power of Western discourses in constructing images of women in Arab societies. She returns to the obsessive interest of the West in the veil and the meanings those wearing the veil attach to it, especially its prominent meaning in many nationalist and liberation movements as a rejection of the West. I noted her argument that discourses of resistance (outside the so-called) West can be seen as inextricably informed by those of the West (1992: 2; cf. Spivak 1987). 'Ironically', she points out, 'it was the discourses of the West, and specifically the discourse of colonial domination, that in the first place determined the meaning of the veil in geopolitical discourses and thereby set the terms for its emergence as a symbol of resistance' (1992: 235). She argues that the re-emergent veil 'attests, by virtue of its very power as a symbol of resistance to the uncontested hegemonic diffusion of the discourses of the West in our age. And it attests to the fact that, at least as regards the Islamic world, the discourses of resistance and rejection are inextricably informed by the languages and ideas developed and disseminated by the West to no less a degree than are the languages of those openly advocating emulation of the West' or those who are 'critical of the West but nonetheless ground themselves in intellectual assumptions and political ideas, including a belief in the rights of the individual', which arose with Western modernity and spread over the world as a result of Western hegemony (1992: 235).

In Malaya/Malaysia the veil *per se* has not been the site of more general political contest in the way in which it was during the colonial period in some other Muslim countries like Egypt or Algeria (see Ibrahim bin Abu Bakar 1994). That in itself is interesting. Its adoption by the members of the new middle classes at the present juncture provides ready support for Leila Ahmed's arguments about the relationship of this protest against the West being simultaneously of the West. It is easy to see it as clear assertion of difference from Western versions of being modern. But we also, I would suggest, need to locate veiling beyond such an occidentalist framework. Is it a coincidence that this powerful, compressed female symbol of being Muslim/Malay/middle class appeared in the late 1970s and early 1980s with the internationalisation of Islamic revivalism and the intensifying drive for industrialisation by the Malaysian state? That is, is the Malay Muslim embrace of re-emergent Islamic practices to be seen solely as a resistance to Western hegemony within terms set by the West, an expression of a number of ambivalences about Western-style modernity? Or should we also explore its place within the globalisation of Islam and the complex relationship of this globalisation to the Malaysian development of an alternative modernity?

CONCLUSIONS

This chapter has argued that the current reworkings of domestic ideology are key aspects of the cultural production of the 'new' Malay middle classes, providing important ways to theorise the interplay between consumer capitalist culture, economy, polity and religious practice. I suggested that the shifting relations and representations of the so-called private sphere are central to the construction of Malay middle classness economically, politically and culturally. It is at the point of consumption that we can most clearly demonstrate the thoroughly gendered processes involved in this construction. The development of elaborate new femininities in the region based on the consumer/wife/mother can be seen as critical to these connections. I also concentrated on how the 'private' has become a favoured site for the expression of tensions and ambivalences about the costs of modernity: issues of family, gender, home and sexuality are central sites for the cultural expression and reworking of ideas of the 'modern', Malay and Muslim. The constitutive ideologies of masculinity and femininity central to these processes are not simply translated into practice but only realised through long and often conflict-laden processes in which the defining ideologies and practices of being modern and middle class are reworked. The anxieties about the threats posed to the Asian family and about women's 'traditional' roles are both clear examples of the ambivalences about modernity. Islamic revivalism's discourse about 'Westoxification' in some Muslim circles has focussed very deliberately on the dangers for family life produced by modernity and, specifically, 'modern' sexualities. It is no accident, I would suggest, that *Al Arqam*'s rhetoric about the decadence of the West has focussed on sexual themes, nor that when Mahathir came to ban the organisation, he produced his own line of rhetoric about *Al Arqam*'s 'women' being 'sex slaves'.

The cultural constructions of Malay neomodernity verging on post-modernity are making some extremely interesting plays on the story lines of old and new and are thoroughly entangled with colonial inheritances and globalising cultural intrusions. State rhetoric has a problem with the constantly shifting 'tradition' modernity couple, tying one or other or both terms to various other areas of discourse, as in the widespread linkage of modernity with Westernisation or Westoxification. It could be seen as trying to steer a path between the internationalisation of Malaysian society and the construction of highly particular Malay identities which do not rend apart the ethnic accommodations of the last 25 years. A central challenge in looking at this material is a familiar tension: on the one hand we have the clearly globalised patterns emerging of a state-driven production of a consumer capitalist culture and the similarly globalised patterns of Islamic re-emergence; on the other we have the highly particular and often self-consciously constructed specificities of Malaysian developments, especially forces critiquing different versions of modernity.

Yet there are considerable difficulties in analysing these patterns overall. While I have argued for a post-modern fragmenting of images of women overall, the figures of both the Muslim middle-class woman and the sexualised working-class woman have become highly politicised, compressed and powerful symbols of versions of modernity within contemporary reworkings of the Malay imaginary. The veiled middle-class woman in particular is a symbol of a specifically Malay modernity that has deep ethnic and class repercussions. Both figures in many ways represent a rejection of the 'traditional' woman associated with the nationalist Malay rural idyll. But they might also seem to betoken a neomodernist reassertion of an essentialist figure of the 'modern Malay woman' in the face of the simultaneously multiplying and fragmenting images of modern womanhood. We can also speculate about why national-level imaginings and their ambivalences about modernity have been so fixated with gendered themes in the last two decades. As I asked in Chapter 1, is this an artefact merely of increased feminist scholarly observation, or is it a sign of something else within a globalising late modern New World Order, a global unsettling of 'public' and 'private'? Such symbolisation is hardly a phenomenon limited to Malaysia, although it has its own specificities: the challenge again is to explore the relationship between the global and the particular in this as part of a larger unitary whole.

NOTES

1 *Dakwah* groups are missionary Islamist, revivalist groups. The main ones have been *Pertubuhan Kebajikan Islam Malaysia* (Malaysian Muslim Welfare Organisation), the *Jamaat Tabligh* (Tabligh) and *Darul Arqam*, a more anti-establishment group (see Khoo Boo Teik 1994).

2 I am currently engaged in writing up two related projects on *Work and Family in the New Malay Middle Classes* (1990–93) and *Public and Private: Gender and Southeast Asian Modernities* (1995–96) funded by the Australian Research Council. This research has involved a 2-month period of residence on a Seremban middle-class housing estate in 1987–88, and a number of trips gathering materials in Malaysia, Singapore and the UK since. I am extremely grateful to Lucy Healey, Goh Beng Lan, Hah Foong Lian, Zainab Wahidin, Linda Pang, Norani Othman, Clive Kessler, Azizah Kassim, Jomo Sundaram, Ikmal Muhd Said and Joel Kahn for their help during the current project. Earlier versions of this chapter were delivered to: the Asian Studies Association of Australia, Women in Asia Conference, Melbourne, 1994; The Anthropology Association of Australia Annual Conference, 1994; the Workshop on Sex and Power in Affluent Asia, Murdoch University, February 1995; and the European Association for Southeast Asian Studies, Leiden, 1995.

3 The men had a variety of 'middle-class' occupations, including positions in school teaching, the civil service, technical services, army, police, and a range of professional occupations in both the civil service and private sectors. Private sector jobs included positions in management, personnel, banking, fashion, architectural practice, as well as self-employed business. The women had a range of jobs including company management, medical staff, clerks, teachers, lecturers, and analysts.

4 See Stivens (1994b) for further discussion of these issues in the Malaysian context.

5 See Muhammad Haji Taib (1993), Rustam Sani (1993a; 1993b).

6 I have a number of texts from magazines and books from the 1920s on addressing the problems with the new and the dislocations of colonial identity. See also Syed Hussein Alatas (1977), Lockhart (1936).

7 I am maintaining that he is male, even though the term *Melayu baru* is gender free and Malay lacks a gendered third person singular pronoun.

8 Thus an official publication about a seminar organised to discuss Vision 2020 made a valiant effort to show four women participants in one picture but another 18 pictures feature men only and a further one shows 32 members (12 women) of the Seminar Secretariat (who presumably did all the work organising the Seminar) with the Coordinator of the Seminar. Women participants got a list of their own at the back (seven out of 117), but apparently none gave a paper (Malaysia, 1991).

9 See Stivens (n.d.b).

10 A study of women managers found that 84 per cent of them were above the age of 30, that only 21 per cent were single, and 76 per cent of those

with children had three or fewer children (Sieh Lee Mei Ling *et al.* 1991).

11 There was a sizeable moral panic in 1994–95 about the dangers to the moral fabric of society of youth *lepak* (hanging out, loafing) and, as noted, of *boh-sia* (girls engaging in 'free sex/promiscuity').

12 The target of the New Economic Policy was a 30 per cent *bumiputera* (Malay or indigenous) ownership of the economy by 1990 (cf. 2.4 per cent in 1970), and 10.3 per cent in 1978. Other Malaysians were to own a 40 per cent share and foreign interests 30 per cent (cf. 63.3 per cent in 1970, Majid and Majid 1983: 69). While the NEP target of 30 per cent ownership of shares in the corporate sector was not met, holdings did rise to 20.3 per cent in 1990 (Crouch 1996). The restructuring continues with the new Development Policy (Askiah Adam 1994: 12). Latterly, Prime Minister Dato' Seri Mahathir Mohamad has promoted his Vision 2020, according to which Malaysia is to become a fully developed industrialised country by the year 2020. The development of a vigorous, entrepreneurial middle class is seen as integral to development (Mahathir 1991). See Kassim (1992), Khoo Kay Jin (1992).

13 Khoo Kay Jin sees the NEP as overturning the relationship between state and economy, spelling the end of an alliance between the state and private capital in which the state was content to support the efforts of private accumulation and to ameliorate the discontents of the rural poor and the Malay intelligentsia (1992). Development expenditure doubled its proportion of GDP over the 1970s, with public enterprise expenditure rising from 37 per cent of the total annual federal budget in 1970 to 56 per cent in 1974 (Khoo 1992). Kahn, drawing on Khoo Kay Jin's analysis of the cleavages within UMNO in the late 1980s, suggests that Mahathir and Anwar, with the support of big players in the corporate sphere, were pushing an authoritarian economic rationalist modernism as against the Semangat '46 , who with the support of middle-level Malay business people were loath to see the 'traditionalist' policies of UMNO replaced by pure economic rationalism (1996a).

14 The figures were 5 per cent in 1982, 6.9 per cent in 1985, 8.6 per cent in 1987, 4 per cent in 1991 (Jomo 1993: 336), 3 per cent in 1993 and one of the lowest rates in the world, 2.3 per cent in February, 1994 (*New Straits Times*, 20 September 1994, quoted in Kahn 1996a). The youth figure is believed to be three times higher than the national average (Khoo Kay Jin 1992: 54).

15 Elsewhere, I am working on the relationship between the processes of class formation and the macro-level economic changes in the country, including the development of export-led industrialisation, a rapidly growing state sector and the growth of party capitalism (Gomez 1990, cf. Kahn 1996a).

16 UMNO played a critical role in dispensing political patronage, producing significant electoral support. Malay business people with close links to UMNO were given preference in obtaining licences, credit and government contracts (Crouch 1996: 37).

17 See Crouch's account for greater detail of the workings of this patronage, including share deals and company board seats (ibid.).

18 See PuruShotam, Chapter 5, for an extended analysis of the ways in which Singaporeans identify as and construct being middle class.

19 The 1990 census only came out in 1995–6, so most analyses have not had the benefit of its statistics.

20 There are of course multiple problems in using these classifications, including assumptions about the nature of the static classifications staying uniform over the decades, a privileging of occupation as the main indicator of 'class' and an absence of the proprietorial and aristocratic fractions from the classifications. They have also of course often omitted women entirely.

21 H. Osman Rani and Ismail Muhd Salleh suggest that there has been enormous growth in public sector employment, from 398,000 in 1970 to an estimated 859,000 in 1992. But it could be noted that the population also doubled during this period to about 17 million. The overall percentage of the work force in public sector work also only rose from 11.9 per cent in 1970 to a peak of 15 per cent in 1981 before declining to 12.2 in 1992 (1994: 208–9).

22 Crouch argues that this does not imply the growth of a strong Malay entrepreneurial class, because large numbers of shares were in fact held by government agencies ostensibly on behalf of Malays and by the giant trust fund, PNB (1996).

23 See Crouch (1996) for discussion.

24 See *Economic Report*, Ministry of Finance, Social Trends section (Malaysia, 1995), for figures on enrolments, women's wage force participation, variously reported at 46 and 47 per cent for 1993, and measures of infant morality and life expectancy. The special efforts made to advance the Malays under the New Economic Policy did, however, expand girls' and women's educational achievements. Thus the proportion of Malay girls and young women aged 10–19 attending school rose from 32 per cent in 1957 to 47 per cent in 1970 and 67 per cent in 1980. This contrasts with the absence of education for most Malay women over the age of 50 in the 1980 census. Those completing the Lower Certificate of Education or its equivalent rose from 2.2 per cent in 1957 to 10.4 per cent in 1970 and 37.9 per cent in 1980 (Jones 1994: 30).

25 The percentage of women working in the service sector rose from 10.7 per cent in 1975 to 15.1 per cent in 1986 (Jamilah Ariffin 1992: 40).

26 I argue elsewhere (Stivens 1996) that the rural 'rich' of the peasant class differentiation debates, land holders with 10 or more acres often bought with the proceeds of school teaching or bureaucratic salaries, are better thought of as a rural middle class with strong links to the colonial and post-colonial state. I suggest that the 'peasantry'/state relation was a more significant site of structural relations of inequality than putative class differences within the rural economy throughout the colonial and post-colonial periods and that the state in its many and shifting manifestations was clearly central to the generation of inequality within rural society. I suggest that modern state formation rather than capitalist development *per se* provided the main impetus for social differentiation within villages (cf. Kahn 1993: 276): village elites, officials, schoolteachers, and the 'rich' had strong economic, political and cultural links to the state.

27 This network was set up through the magazine.

28 As PuruShotam notes (quoted in Heyzer and Wee 1994: 65), Thai maids in Singapore are paid S$200–250, Indonesians, S$160–300, Sri Lankans $160–280 and Filipinos $300, due to checks imposed by their government). Many of these maids are illegal immigrants (the majority Indonesians, ibid.: 44) with zero legal rights in their employment. Those legally imported

into Malaysia by agents are subject to a 2-year contract with a $RM2000 agent's fee levied (ibid.: 56). Cynthia Enloe and others have noted the international, political aspects of this trade and the ways that this demand from the more affluent in the region (and of course way beyond, even as far as the UK and the USA) has profound political and economic implications for the global economy: remittances from such workers are seen as propping up the Philippines economy for example (Enloe 1989). The absence of properly regulated child care in the employing countries is a key aspect of these processes.

29 Another academic informed me that her parents could not be told that their granddaughter had a Filipino maid, because they would disapprove of their grandchildren being cared for by a Christian. In this case a Philippine woman was preferred by the child's parents because she was highly educated and spoke good English.

30 This was the cause of some considerable tension in an international conference at the University of Melbourne which I was involved in organising (*Linking our Histories*, on international migration, 1994). The rhetoric of the (mostly) servantless Australian attenders evoked obvious embarrassment from many of the professional women from the Asia-Pacific region.

31 See Stivens (1996) for a discussion of difficulties with the concept of 'autonomy' as applied to Malay and other Southeast Asian women.

32 See for example Swift (1958).

33 Virginia Matheson Hooker is working on romance in Malay popular culture in the first decades of the twentieth century.

34 See Stivens (1996) for a discussion of these views among informants in my earlier study. About half of all marriages were 'free-choice' in the Negeri Sembilan villages I first researched in the mid-1970s. I suggest that the urban context, where women may lack the kin support previously available in rural areas may well offer women increased dependence on men and new oppressive versions of femininity.

35 See figures in Djamour (1965), Jones (1994). The arguments put forward to explain this fall by writers include growing urbanisation, female education, rising age of marriage and the growth of companionate marriage. See also Stivens (1996).

36 See Stivens (n.d.a, n.d.b) for further discussion of child rearing and child bearing.

37 Interestingly, women in my previous study area of Negeri Sembilan were exempted from this depiction, as strong 'matriarchal' women (Taylor 1929: 13). See Stivens (1996).

38 Feminist discourse about the relative equality of the sexes in Southeast Asia oddly echoes the colonial perceptions of a lack of machismo among Southeast Asian men (e.g. Atkinson and Errington 1990).

39 I saw a central contradiction in my earlier research on the 'matrilineal' social system of Negeri Sembilan between some men's considerable work and concern for their wives', sisters' and children's property and a group who were regarded as highly unreliable *husbands*, who could only be brought to task even imperfectly through recourse to the Islamic legal system and often were not. I asked: were the latter group somehow peculiarly a product of *adat perpatih* ('matrilineal customary law'), driven by their lack of authority to run out on their responsibilities towards children and

others, or at least to seek their fortune alone in migrant work? Or was their perceived irresponsibility simply part of a more general male irresponsibility (Stivens 1996, cf. Hart 1991)?

40 In relation to globalisation and global cities, it is interesting to note that supermum is 'Mum' in Malaysian English, whereas 'Mom' seems to have taken over in Singapore, a truly global city.

41 See the Vision 2020 Seminar proceedings, Malaysia, 1991.

42 Again, this is clearly not confined to Malaysia, but is a more international phenomenon, the history of which is unclear. The meaning of these images of women as bearers of these ethnic and/or nationalist imaginaries must, however, have shifted considerably over this time.

43 The Malaysian experience suggests that the scenarios of middle classes pushing modernist democratic reform which are favoured in some Southeast Asian Studies circles need to be treated with caution. Kahn suggests that in fact the legitimacy of modern forms of political domination has been seen by a number of writers like Wallerstein to rest more on legitimation in the eyes of the middle strata than on the legitimised domination of 'working classes' and other 'subaltern' groups (1996a).

44 I am grateful for information from one of the anonymous readers that the Women's Aid Organisation in 1990 commissioned Survey Research Malaysia (the longest established and largest market research agency in Malaysia) to integrate questions related to domestic violence into its monthly *Flexibus* (a survey on consumer preferences). There is also a series of vigorous newsletters produced by women's organisations like the Women's Crisis Centre (in Penang).

45 I am not implying that there has not been a long history of action on women's issues, only that expressions of considerable ambivalence about the current women's movement in the West have formed part of an occidentalist post-colonial rejection of things Western within some discursive forms (see Stivens 1992). See the discussion in Chapter 1.

46 See Ibrahim bin Abu Bakar's recent account of modernist Islam in Malaysia (1994).

BIBLIOGRAPHY

Abu Bakar I. bin (1994) *Islamic Modernism in Malaysia: The Life and Thought of Sayid Syekh Al-hadi 1867-1934*, Kuala Lumpur: University of Malaya Press.

Adnan, H. (1994) *Advertising in Malaysia*, Kuala Lumpur: Pelanduk Publications.

Ahmed, L. (1992) *Women and Gender in Islam: Historical Roots of a Modern Debate*, New Haven: Yale University Press.

Akbar, A. (1992) *Postmodernism and Islam*, London: Routledge.

Amina Wadud, M. (1992) *Quran and Woman*, Kuala Lumpur: Penerbit Fajar Bakti.

Arnason, J. (1990) 'Nationalism, Globalization and Modernity', in M. Featherstone (ed.) *Global Culture*, London: Sage.

Askiah, A. (1994) 'A Corporate Culture with Local Values', *New Straits Times*, 5 October 1994: 12.

Asma, A. (1993) 'Oh to be a Global and a Local Melayu', *New Straits Times*, 23 December 1993: 30.

Atkinson, J. M. and Errington, S. (eds) (1990) *Power and Difference*, Stanford: Stanford University Press.

Crouch, H. (1985) *Economic Change, Social Structure and the Political System in Southeast Asia*, Singapore: Institute of Southeast Asian Studies.

—— (1996) *Government and Society in Malaysia*, Sydney: Allen and Unwin.

Davidoff, L. and Hall, C. (1987) *Family Fortunes: Men and Women of the English Middle Class 1780-1850*, London: Hutchinson.

Djamour, J. (1965) *Malay Kinship and Marriage in Singapore*, London: Athlone Press.

Enloe, C. (1989) *Bananas, Beaches and Bases: Making Feminist Sense of International Politics*, London: Pandora.

Fatimah Daud (1985) *Minah Karan*, Kuala Lumpur: Berita.

Felski, R. (1992) 'Whose Post-modernism?', *Thesis Eleven* 32: 129–40.

—— (1995) *The Gender of Modernity*, Cambridge, Massachusetts: Harvard University Press.

Friedman, J. (1990) 'Being in the World: Globalization and Localization', in M. Featherstone (ed.) *Global Culture: Nationalism, Globalization and Modernity*, London: Sage.

Gledhill, J. (1994) *Power and its Disguises: Anthropological Perspectives on Politics*, London: Pluto Press.

Gomez, E.T. (1990) *Politics in Business: Umno's Corporate Investments*, Kuala Lumpur: Forum.

Hall, C. (1992) *White, Male and Middle Class: Explorations in Feminism and History*, London: Polity.

Hart, G. (1991) 'Engendering Everyday Resistance: Gender, Patronage and Production Politics in Rural Malaysia', *Journal of Peasant Studies* 19, 1: 93–121.

Heyzer, N. and Wee, V. (1994) 'Domestic Workers in Transient Overseas Employment: Who Benefits, Who Profits?', in N. Heyzer, G. Lycklama à Nijeholt and N. Weeraloon (eds) *The Trade in Domestic Workers: Causes, Mechanisms and Consequences of International Migration*, Kuala Lumpur: Asia Pacific Development Centre; London and New Jersey: Zed Books.

Humphries, J. (1977) 'Class Struggle and the Persistence of the Working Class Family', *Cambridge Journal of Economics* 1: 3.

Kassim, I. (1992) 'KL Intellectuals to Submit Suggestions on Vision 2020', *The Straits Times*, 9 December 1992: 13.

Jamilah Ariffin (1992) *Women and Development in Malaysia*, Kuala Lumpur: Pelanduk Publications.

—— (1994) *Reviewing Malaysian Women's Status: Country Report in Preparation for the Fourth UN World Conference on Women*, Kuala Lumpur: Population Studies Unit, University of Malaya.

Jomo K.S. (ed.) (1993) *Industrialising Malaysia: Policy, Performance, Prospects*, London and New York: Routledge.

Jones, G. (1994) *Marriage and Divorce in Southeast Asia*, Kuala Lumpur and Melbourne: Oxford University Press.

Kahn, J.S. (1993) *Constituting the Minangakabau*, London: Berg.

—— (1996a) 'Growth, Economic Transformation, Culture and the Middle Classes in Malaysia', in R. Robison and D. S. G. Goodman (eds), *The New*

Rich in Asia: Mobile Phones, McDonalds and Middle-class Revolution, London and New York: Routledge.

—— (1996b) *Culture, Multiculture, Postculture*, London and New York: Sage.

—— (1996c) 'The Middle Class as an Object of Ethnological Study', in Muhammad Ikmal Said and Zahid Emby (eds) *Malaysian Critical Perspectives: Essays in Honour of Syed Husin Ali*, Kuala Lumpur: Persatuan Sains Sosial Malaysia.

Kamal Salih and Young, M.L. (1989) 'Changing Conditions of Labour in the Semiconductor Industry in Malaysia', *Labour and Society* 14: 59–80.

Khoo Boo Teik (1994) *Paradoxes of Mahathirism: An Intellectual Biography of Mahathir Mohamad*, Kuala Lumpur: Oxford University Press.

Khoo Kay Jin (1992) 'The Grand Vision: Mahathir and Modernisation', in J.S. Kahn and F. Loh Kok Wah (eds), *Fragmented Vision: Culture and Politics in Contemporary Malaysia*, Sydney: Allen and Unwin and Honolulu: Hawaii University Press.

Lockhart, R.H.B. (1936) *Return to Malaya*, London: Putnam.

MacCannell, D. and Flower MacCannell, J. (1993) 'Social Class in Postmodernity: Simulacrum or Return of the Real?', in C. Rojek and B. Turner (eds) *Forget Baudrillard*, London and New York: Routledge.

Mahathir, Mohamad (1970) *The Malay Dilemma*, Singapore: Donald Moore for Asia Pacific Press.

—— (1981) *Malaysia: The Way Forward*, Working paper presented by Y.A.B. Dato' Seri Dr Mahathir Mohamad, Prime Minister of Malaysia, at the Inaugural Meeting of the Malaysian Business Council, 28 February, Kuala Lumpur.

Majid, S. and Majid, A. (1983) 'Public Sector Land Settlement in West malaysia', in D.A.M. Lee and D.P. Chaudhri (eds) *Rural Development and the State*, London: Methuen.

Malaysia (1991) *National Seminar, 'Towards a Developed and Industrialized Society: Understanding the Concept, Implications and Challenges of Vision 2020'*, Proceedings, Kuala Lumpur: Socio-Economic Research Unit, Prime Minister's Dept.

Malaysia (1993) *Mid-Term Review of the Sixth Malaysia Plan 1991-1995*, Kuala Lumpur: Economic Planning Unit, Prime Minister's Department.

Malaysia (1995) *Economic Report*, Kuala Lumpur: Ministry of Finance.

Manderson, L. (1980) *Women, Politics and Change: The Kaum Ibu UMNO Malaysia, 1945-1972*, Kuala Lumpur: Oxford University Press.

Maznah Mohamed and Wong Soak Koon (eds) (1994) *Feminism: Malaysian Critique and Experience*, *Kajian Malaysia* Special Issue, XII (1 and 2), December.

Mernissi, F. (1991) *Women and Islam: An Historical Enquiry*, Oxford: Blackwell.

Muhammad Haji Muhd Taib (1993) *Melayu Baru*, Kuala Lumpur: ITC Book Publisher.

Murugesu Pathamanathan and Haas, R. (eds) (1994) *Political Culture: The Challenge of Modernisation*, Kuala Lumpur: Friedrich Naumann Foundation.

Nagaraj, S. (1995) Malaysian Women Today, Kuala Lumpur: Ministry of National Unity and Development, Women's Affairs Division.

Narli, A.N. (1986) *Malay Women in Tertiary Education: Trends of Change in Female Role Ideology*, unpublished PhD thesis, University Sains, Penang.

Nordin Selat (1978) *Renungan*, Kuala Lumpur: Utusan.

Ong, A. (1987) *Spirits of Resistance and Capitalist Discipline: Factory Women in Malaysia*, Albany: Suny University Press.

—— (1990) 'Malay Families, Women's Bodies and the Body Politic', *American Ethnologist* 17(2), May.

Osman Rani, H. and Salleh, I. (1994) 'The Public Sector' in K.S. Jomo (ed.) *Malaysia's Economy in the Nineties*, Kuala Lumpur: Pelanduk Publications.

Roff, W.R. (1967) *The Origins of Malay Nationalism*, New Haven: Yale University Press.

Rustam Sani (1993a) *Melayu Baru dan Bangsa Malaysia: Tradisi Cendekia dan Krisis Budaya*, Kuala Lumpur: Utusan.

—— (1993b) 'Phoenix-like, a new kind of Malay arises', *BT* 27–28 March 1993.

Said, E. (1993) *Culture and Imperialism*, London: Chatto and Windus.

Saravanamattu, J. (1989) 'Kelas Menengah dalam Politik Malaysia: Tonjolan Perkauman atau Kepentingingan Kelas', *Kajian Malaysia*, 7(1 and 2): 106–26.

Shamsul A.B. (1986) *From British to Bumiputera Rule: Local Politics and Rural Development in Peninsular Malaysia*, Singapore: Institute of Southeast Asian Studies.

Shyamala N. (1995) *Malaysian Women Today*, Kuala Lumpur: Ministry of National Unity and Social Development, Women's Affairs Division.

Sieh Lee Mei Ling, Phang Siew Nooi, Lang Chin Ying and Mansor, N. (1991) *Women Managers of Malaysia*, Kuala Lumpur: Faculty of Economic and Administration, University of Malaya.

Spivak, G.C. (1987) *In Other Worlds*, New York: Methuen.

Stivens, M. (1987) 'Family and State in Malaysian Industrialisation', in H. Afshar (ed.) *Women, State and Ideology*, London: Macmillan.

—— (ed.) (1991) *Why Gender Matters in Southeast Asian Politics*, Monash Papers on Southeast Asia No. 23, Clayton: Monash Centre of Southeast Asian Studies.

—— (1992) 'Perspectives on Gender: Problems in Writing about Women in Malaysia', in J. Kahn and F. Loh (eds) *Fragmented Vision: Culture and Politics in Contemporary Malaysia*, Sydney: Allen and Unwin, Honolulu: University of Hawaii Press.

—— (1994a) 'The Gendering of Knowledge: The Case of Anthropology and Feminism', in N. Grieve and A. Burns (eds) *Australian Women: Feminist Perspectives*, Sydney: Oxford University Press.

—— (1994b) 'Gender and Modernity in Malaysia', in A. Gomes (ed.) *Modernity and Identity: Illustrations From Asia*, Bundoora, Melbourne: La Trobe University Press.

—— (1996) *Matriliny and Modernity: Sexual Politics and Social Change in Rural Malaysia*, Sydney: Allen and Unwin.

—— (n.d.a) 'Modernising the Malay Mother', in M. Jolly and K. Ram (eds) *Modernities and Maternities in the Asia Pacific Region*, Cambridge: Cambridge University Press.

—— (n.d.b) 'The Hope of the Nation: Moral Panics and the Construction of Teenagerhood in Contemporary Malaysia', in L. Manderson and P. Liamputtong Rice (eds) *The Emerging Adult: Young People, Sexuality and Courtship in South and Southeast Asia*, London: Harwood Press (in press).

Stivens, M., Ng, C. and Jomo K.S. (with Jahara Bee) (1994) *Malay Peasant Women and the Land*, London and New Jersey: Zed.

Swift, M. (1958) 'A Note on the Durability of Malay Marriages', *Man* 58: 155–9.

Syed, H.A. (1977) *The Myth of the Lazy Native: A Study of the Image of the Malays, Filipinos and Javanese from the 16th to the 20th Centuries and its Function in the Ideology of Colonial Capitalism*, London: Cass.

Tan Kim Bock (1994) 'Sex Slaves', *Star*, 23 August 1994.

Taussig, M. (1993) *Mimesis and Alterity: A Particular History of the Senses*, London and New York: Routledge.

Taylor, E.N. (1929) 'The Customary law of Rembau', *JMBRAS* 7(1): 1–55.

Ustaz Ashaari Muhammad (1993) *The West on the Brink of Death*, London: ASOIB Books.

Walby, S. (1992) 'Post-Post-Modernism', in M. Barrett and A. Phillips (eds) *Destabilizing Theory*, Cambridge: Polity.

Wan Suhaimi Saidi and Hanim Adnan (1994) 'Into the Arqanomics Maze: The Al-Arqam Business Empire', *The Star*, 1 August 1994.

5 Between compliance and resistance

Women and the middle-class way of life in Singapore[1]

Nirmala PuruShotam

> How, then, does one register one's many disagreements from within this solidarity? For some years I have thought that one simply could not do so, that dissenting speech would probably be a betrayal of that solidarity. More recently, though, I have come to believe that such a position of willed neutrality is politically wrong, morally indefensible . . . . Suppression of criticism, I have come to believe, is not the best way of expressing solidarity.
>
> (Aijaz Ahmad 1992: 160)[2]

INTRODUCTION

In Singapore, a majority of women appropriate the label 'middle class' and work hard to reproduce an associated way of life for themselves and their families. This way of life embodies 'liberation' in local parlance for women: they are engaged in a middle-class life world with its attendant benefits, benefits denied to their mothers and grandmothers. I begin this chapter with a brief discussion of the Singapore middle class, arguing that to be middle class is to engage in the continuous reproduction of a middle-class way of life. That way of life is structured with reference to major texts/background knowledge that are common to most Singaporeans – living with a fear of falling (I am drawing on Ehrenreich's 1989 use of this term) and living within the normal family. This fear of falling places on women the burdens of reproducing a way of life that is at once about the 'better' life and about their subordination. Even while it imprisons them, this way of life gives women access to a body of knowledge that can bring about a questioning of their subordination. This raises a crucial question: are the meanings and experiences of being middle class creating, in any way, a new set of social interests that pressure the state to give women a new place in an established order?[3]

I address this issue as a feminist middle-class woman in Singapore. These categories are placed upon me both by others, as well as myself. While some writers use the word 'feminist' notionally, my use of the term is very specifically oriented to a conscious platform. Feminism, then, importantly involves a political position that is anti-patriarchal and, moreover, very sensitive to the inequities of the patriarchal system even at its more kindly. Indeed, I am clearly aware that women in a patriarchal system can and do enjoy the 'goodwill' of men as breadwinners and protectors: it is this that enables the re-production of patriarchy by women, without whose cooperation patriarchy would not be so easily assured of its continued social existence. For this reason, my work as a feminist activist, especially in the period in which this chapter was written, was inspired by a deep and abiding concern with consciousness-raising, especially pertinent to women who do not suffer the overt abuses of patriarchy. Those women, perhaps needless to say, include myself – married, middle class, professional and a mother. I do not write on behalf of all middle-class women in Singapore, but I do write as an 'insider', implicated in the conditions and contradictions that I try to analyse and transform.

THE MIDDLE CLASS IN SINGAPORE

The experience of 'social reality' in Singapore is tied to a socio-historical context, and perceptions of that context. The history of the island and its people is commonsensically understood as tracing its roots to a British colony, beginning with the arrival of mostly extremely poor immigrants. Singaporeans share a view that this began to be fundamentally changed in the early 1960s: economic policies and concomitant urbanisation processes have effected profound changes for the majority of the population,[4] with shifts from labour-intensive light manufacturing to high technology industries more recently. These transformations have included changes in housing type, job and career choices, higher wages, expanded educational achievements, ownership of household technologies, televisions, video cassette recorders, etc., ownership of stocks, real estate and an expanded access to leisure activities.[5] There are clear differences in terms of the distribution of the benefits that economic and social policies have produced. But there is also a common recognition of 'betterment': both the actual experience of it and, via social mobility, the continued expectation of its continuation in the future for almost every Singaporean. This generalised sense of progress is condensed in the everyday life use of the label 'middle class', a social category used by a majority of Singaporeans about themselves, both individually and with reference to their families. The term also has been used, particularly by the ruling elite, to characterise Singaporean society as a whole.

My central preoccupation in this piece is this intersubjective use of the term 'middle class'. My basic assumption is that the appropriation of this label involves everyday life work, to ensure the continued production of upward mobility. Further, the production of upward mobility is understood and judged in terms of the consumption of 'better' goods, services and ideas than 'before'. This involves the expectation that children will do better than their parents. Thus Singaporeans who live in three-room public housing flats, five-room public housing flats, and private apartments in middle-class condominiums would all refer to themselves as middle class, although 'objectively' and subjectively there would be an instant recognition of the differences between these three sets of living arrangements. But these people also share experiences of mobility through the housing progression. The work of constantly upgrading one's home is tied to a complex of other work, including the expectation of better employment opportunities, wage increments and the like. Betterment is not just about expanding material goods. It can and has become a demand also for expanded political and general social rights.

Texts for the way of life of the middle classes are as diverse as their sources, their authors and their users. This accounts for both the high level of divergence within the parameters of the term 'middle class' and the possibility and plausibility of the choice of 'middle class' as a term of self-reference by a widely divergent group of people, often not even connected – and in oppositional tension to each other in terms of experience and politics. But these people are also similar in important respects. First, to be middle class is to have a vast arena of choices within which to continually attain/experience betterment. Second, to be middle class is to do the work of making the relevant choices from within this vast arena. It is not just a matter of making choices *per se*; the choices must add up to a complex whole. This is because, third, choices must be balanced by a realistic appraisal of what is possible, given the Singapore context. This is underscored by the notion that the wrong choices can cause the loss of upward momentum, the stuff of middle classness.

The everyday life problematic of being middle class is at the same time a political problematic. On the one hand, if the sense of being middle class is provided for and sustained, then the promise of modernity, the blueprint of governing parties worldwide, is achievable/achieved. On the other hand, if the sense of being middle class is thwarted, the legitimacy of governing party rule riding on the modernisation covenant could begin to crumble. The problem from the perspective of the ruling elite is to ensure that the measurement and experience of mobility are in accordance with the kind and degree of mobility which the government constructs in response to its own political interests, and limited by what it can deliver to the people.

EXPANDING GOODS, EXPANDING IDEAS

At one level, the ever-increasing range and variety of goods available via global capitalist production processes allow a continuous sense of change for the better. In important ways, capitalist production, with its built-in obsolescence, produces a sense of progress to be accomplished more easily than otherwise. But who is to decide what goods must be attainable or attained to support a sense of being middle class? In Singapore, the expanded range of material goods is perceived as related to the political climate, even as gifts of the state to the people. Indeed, the state overtly prides itself on its provision of goods and services. The amorphous mass that identifies itself as middle class may well use indicators of mobility by referring to goods that the state may not be able to provide.

For example, two important elements of upward mobility in Singapore are the car and the 'better' residence, but both are becoming increasingly difficult to afford. The government nonetheless struggles to ensure a continuing sense of improvement for the populace. In the realm of housing, the sense of mobility until recently came about through the availability of better flats. In the present heated/over-heated property market, however, this has become difficult for some sections of Singapore's middle class. Thus, the government has undertaken to improve existing housing estates in an upgrading exercise by which one gains extra space, additional features, and even additional value on public housing apartments. Without having to find new accommodation, many Singaporeans can express betterment in living conditions in this way.

Pursuit of betterment also involves ideational choices, the potent idea of mobility as an increasing sense of control over one's life. In other words, choice could involve the claim to be able to provide and produce ideas about new ways of being middle class. The government must, therefore, deliver the promise of the texts by which ideational choice is defined or indeed delegitimise some of those discourses. Thus, if the middle class aspires to alternative voices in parliament, those alternative voices are created by the presence of non-partisan nominated members of parliament. Opposition politicians are shown to be mostly irrelevant if not downright unnecessary nuisances who obstruct proper governing/government in Singapore. Further, 'progress' must be read into some situations, while it is erased from other situations. Thus the debate about the relevance of 'Western' democracy for 'Asian' societies attempts to cast aspersions on certain kinds of democratic institutions, practices and ideas. In this way, what could be seen as taken-for-granted aspects of betterment can now be reread with greater suspicion: is this really what we want? Is this really betterment?

I have been arguing that the material and ideational choices that underpin the discourses of being middle class both legitimise and challenge the Singapore regime. It therefore has to curb the extent, pace and content of the expansion of alternatives. This is merely the battle – and one that involves possibly the most overt negotiations. The real war engages the form of dominant texts, in which the work of the middle class translates into the reproduction of a particular complex of middle-class life. As I shall show, the middle-class way of life is negotiated and reproduced with reference to shared notions about the limits of the possible. That is, even while modern technology and communications make the range, form and content of choices appear limitless, the limits of possibility are brought to bear upon the range of choices. Paradoxically, the limits of the possible – defined importantly in relation to the normal, the moral and the contextually relevant – enable/coerce the middle class to *choose* to limit those expanding ideational and material choices that come with being and doing this class.

FEAR OF FALLING

In contemporary Singapore, there are at least two potent sources of legitimate limits to 'choices'. First, there are shared notions of Singapore society *per se*, which frame the way choices must be made. I refer to these shared knowledges as the 'fear of falling'. Such fear is general, that is, not gender specific. Choices are framed with reference to certain limits, summarised as responsible familial and national participation – demands are framed by what is *morally* possible. This moral legitimation is crucial in framing social, economic and political demands. The limits of the possible act as a brake on claims by both individuals and groups, and include perceptions of state authoritarianism and forces larger than the state such as God/religion and 'tradition'/racial heritage. Second, there are two basic 'biological givens' that are assumed to define persons, 'race' and 'sex'. In this chapter, I am concentrating on sex-based limits and their relevance for women's lives in Singapore. These limits are given meaningful legitimations in what I shall refer to as the 'normal family' ideology dominant in Singapore today.

The demand for more variety is not simply tied to the consumption of an increasing range of items. Choices are part of a complex whole, reflecting a fear of losing what has been gained and should continue to be gained. This fear of falling makes for a particularly interesting combination of alliance and tension, in which middle-class aspirations and the regime's frames for those aspirations are worked out. One of the most powerful aspects of the fear of falling refers to the official version of Singapore's international standing. Within this discourse Singapore is commonly and commonsensically represented as a small island highly vulnerable to the exigencies of the outside world. Underscoring this is a siege mentality, a continuing fear that something might happen outside of Singapore's control which would destroy all that has been gained thus far. A second, related, issue is the received economic history of Singapore, which sees the secret of Singapore's success as due to the achievements and continuing expertise of the ruling People's Action Party (PAP). This is closely tied to an acceptance of the PAP's free rein with one-party rule since Independence. Based on this reading of history, the government and the ruling party claim the authority to define the directions for the future as well. There are at least three sets of specific concerns about which the country must be continuously vigilant:

1 '*Westernisation*' The Singaporean/government notion of 'Western' choices refers to 'wrong' or 'bad' choices, which reflect what is wrong with developed countries today. These include values, attitudes and ideas, which summarily pit the individual and his/her concerns over and above societal concerns. Linked at once to particular material choices, certain ideas if left unchecked can and will bring with them problems of an undisciplined society with concomitant social problems, like illegitimate [sic] children, AIDs, increasing uses of illicit drugs and so forth. All these threaten the gains made thus far.
2 '*Welfarism*' What we can have today must be weighed against how much we must squirrel away for the future. The government sees itself as the strict head of the 'family of Singapore'. If it spares the rod, the children will ransack the candy store for more than they can afford, or more than is good for them. Thus the constant admonition that we cannot afford 'welfare'. This word, I would argue, is a catch-all term for increasing costs of living in Singapore, especially those tied to the recent privatisation of select public schools and all major hospitals and the increasing jumps in the costs of owning a home in contemporary Singapore. Fear of costs, which inhibits forward

momentum, must be weighed against the fear of falling in the future. One must guard against such problems by saving.

3 *Political liberalism* One of the most potent fears of falling concerns itself with the need for the 'correct' kind of political party and government to lead the country forward. As well, the government must have a free rein to ensure that its expert planning and programmes are not hindered by a strong oppositional voice, which will oppose merely for the sake of opposition. That will produce political instability which will scare investors away. If the populace wants different/non-People's Action Party (PAP) voices, these are possible without opposition party membership in parliament through such schemes as nominated members of parliament.

'Westernisation', 'welfarism' and 'political liberalism' are discourses authorised by the ruling elite as checks on what could be a wider range of material and ideational choices. They are top-down impositions, not consensual 'ordinary' middle-class concerns shared with the government. But all three discourses have also been challenged in varying degrees, generating yet another, fourth, fear – that of the middle-class squeeze. Thus, the concerns with rising costs of living, a heated property market, the high costs of owning a car, let alone its maintenance, and education issues are closely tied to a growing sense that the government is restricting the forward momentum in some of these areas, and thus making the climb upwards more difficult.

Alongside the squeeze there is a sense of powerlessness about changing the situation, which relates to the fifth fear, the fear of government reprisals. There has been a growing sense that the government is responsible for unnecessary curbs on acceptable alternative views and emasculating the political potential of the middle class. This understanding acts to put a brake on ideational changes, giving the middle-class push a certain preoccupation with material gains.[6] Yet, despite the tensions that these fears create between the middle class and the regime, it is important to recognise that they share a siege mentality which forges an alliance between them. As I shall argue, the ideology of the 'normal' family, and the brakes it puts on aspirations, are powerful factors in embedding this siege mentality.

THE NORMAL FAMILY IDEOLOGY

The idea of the 'normal' family rests, first and foremost, on a dual sex, dual gender category, dominant in contemporary Singapore. This is widespread in political discourse and a taken-for-granted orientation among large sections of the population. There is the shared notion that gender resides in the body, summarised in genitalia. 'Boy' or 'girl' invokes a range of 'normal', 'moral' measures by which the body so named is regulated. This regulation involves a contract, embodied in the discipline we engage in to accomplish being boy/man or girl/woman with respect to social notions and specificities. At the same time, tutelage over the body – overt policing – is legitimated. Through discipline, the ongoing body achieves its socially recognisable male and female genders. This general stance takes on a more specific form and content via the location of social bodies in corresponding socially recognisable spaces. Of prime concern here is the space and time which are recognisably 'middle class'. They give to the actors embedded in such space the self-awareness of their 'middle-class' position. The construction of this space and time involves reflexive and deliberate reference to a vast and notional complex of ideas, which – as mentioned – I refer to as the normal family ideology.

The normal patriarchal family ideology in Singapore arose, perhaps paradoxically, when women in the then incipient 'middle class' of the politically active 1950s clamoured for equal rights.[7] In doing so, they joined forces with a section of their middle-cum-upper class British rulers. Select aspects of the family were treated as especially problematic in terms of a largely colonial exposure to and reading of family lives. The custom of primary and secondary wives, named and understood as Chinese 'polygamy', disconcerted British legal administrators. In addition, the newly established voluntary Singapore Family Planning Association, run by English and English-educated welfare workers and medical personnel, noted the disturbing practice of women being married from as early as 10 years of age, continual pregnancies and the consequent overcrowding of homes and difficulties with housework. Women and therefore the family were read as being in danger.[8]

These readings fuelled the struggle for women's betterment by the middle class. Equal rights for women became a rallying call even for the PAP. One of their most important political documents of that time, *The Tasks Ahead. PAP's Five Year Plan 1959–1964*, included a section on 'Women in the New Singapore'.[9] Increasingly, mobility into the 'middle class' became identified with the production and consumption of a particular construct of the family, modelled as a social group comprising husband, wife and, preferably, two children. Prior to the late 1960s, such a unit was not the only norm for Singaporeans. Sections of the population were involved in secondary marriages, concubinage and larger household groupings of kin. As I have argued elsewhere (PuruShotam 1993: 3–4), families then and now are constructed, lived in and experienced in a multiplicity of ways. Indeed, some of the pre-1960s 'families' contradicted the norms of heterosexuality and patriarchy, viz., the Fukien-derived practice of male homosexuality and male-male marriages, and the Canton-derived associations of women entering into lesbian marriages. Today, in the place of such myriad norms there exists a single dominant ideology of the normal family, which derives its legitimacy from the following claims:

1 The Singaporean (Chinese) family is rooted in Asia (China) – a claim to antiquity that is at once moral and moral also because 'racial'.[10]
2 This family is arranged with reference to an age- and gender-based authority and power structure.
3 While the family's assumed antiquity gives its ageism and sexism a certain powerful morality, the same ageism and sexism are accepted as having been excessive in some ways. Accordingly, there is the claim/assertion that modernity has tempered the original version of the family, particularly with regard to excesses that related to the subordinate position of women in the family. In this respect, while essentially Chinese in form, the texture of the family here is importantly Singaporean. Women are subordinate but liberated; their bound feet have been freed for a wider range of spaces that they can enter into both literally and figuratively; but they must also be cognisant of their status as women in a patriarchy.
4 Westernisation threatens the family, particularly with respect to the authority of elders as parents, and elders as males. Specific aspects of this threat include women's rights, particularly in the form of feminist extremism. This is often presented as a singular phenomenon, best captured in the oft-repeated media-imagined story of bra-burning women in the West.
5 The meaning of an individual's life relates to its embeddedness in the family. Accordingly, all lives unfold along a normal continuum. Girls will become young women who will marry, produce children and raise them. These are their central tasks. Boys will grow up and marry too, but their familial responsibility is as breadwinners. Therefore their major concern is to engage in the public world. They are also the natural heads of their families.

In sum, the 'normal family' is a contemporary invention whose dominance hides the fact of its social creation. Women's significant role in the reproduction of this ideology means that they must reproduce their own subordination. Indeed, the hegemonic position of the 'normal family' lies in its reification – that which women themselves construct is understood as existing prior to the constructors themselves.

The normal family ideology enables the continuing existence and reconstruction of the assumption of the natural rightness of a dual sex, dual gender relationship. In this one sex, the male, is 'naturally', 'normally' and 'morally' superior to the other. Also, as noted, the ideology almost ensures the protection of the family from the dangers of Westernisation/Western decadence. This notion prepares the way for everyday life work in which deliberations concentrate less on the sins of patriarchy than on its fragility (!) Thus, while modernity provides a means to betterment, that betterment is always subject to a need to safeguard the family both from the dangers of Westernisation and to uphold patriarchy. Limits are thereby placed, not least by women themselves, on what women can expect to ask, and be given, as citizens of their country. More importantly, the normal family ideology allows women to imagine themselves to be on a normal life trajectory, in which they must work to acquire membership as 'girl', 'young woman', 'married woman' and 'mother'. In doing this work a woman becomes of her own accord a key producer of middle-class life generally and of her husband's and children's middle-class life in particular. This moral binding between their everyday work and the better life means that women of the middle class are engaged daily both in the reconstruction of a middle-class way of life, by definition a better life, and their own subordination in it.

WOMEN'S REPRODUCTION OF THE MIDDLE-CLASS WAY OF LIFE

It is a taken-for-granted assumption both among the general population and the political elite that Singaporean women have come a long way. Celebrating this, the PAP's Women's Wing published two books on Singapore women in 1993.[11] The authors generally maintain that the position of Singapore women has been favourable, especially 'when we remember what it used to be in the 1960s' (Wong 1993: 11). Many women would agree. Indeed, in conversation 'middle-class' women here openly suggest that they are better off – they are the 'modern', liberated women. Revealingly, the 'liberation' refers not so much to an ideological stance, as to a recognition that the contemporary Singaporean woman now has access to an expanded range of choices. This specifically refers to a social and economic context, seeing this as fashioned for them by the Singapore government. As Aline Wong (1993: 11), chair of the Women's Wing and now Minister of State for Education and Senior Minister of State for Health notes: '[t]hat we [women] have arrived so far is due, in no small measure, to the economic and social policies of the government under the People's Action Party which has been the ruling party since Singapore's independence.'

At one level, it is difficult to gather together and name such a wide and varied range of expanding ideational and material choices for women. Thus, among the many and varied changes for the better are a host of seemingly unrelated phenomena: monogamous marriage involving romance and courtship and not arrangement by parents; educational and career opportunities; private homes with a kitchen and two or more bathrooms; access to interior design experts and beautiful homes; disciplined bodies sheathed in the latest imported designer wear with cosmetics, costume jewellery and hair styles to match; magazines and books written specifically for women – the almost endless list is evidence of how far Singapore women have come.

At another level, there is something importantly singular about these diverse phenomena. They comprise choices that spell first, 'woman' as a general social construct and, second, 'woman' as a specifically middle-class construct. In both instances, further, the experience of middle class and middle-class betterment is linked to a woman's entry into and situation within the family of marriage and procreation. To enter into marriage is to make oneself eligible: expanded material and ideational choices are, along these lines, most bountiful. To take just one example, a large range of locally published and eagerly read magazines for women sell a middle-class way of life via the products they advertise in their glossy pages and the ideas they present in their articles. These products and ideas involve men-as-experts pronouncing about female bodies and female minds. After all it is heterosexual eligibility that one must strive for, given the normal family. My favourite love-to-hate 'advice' article of this kind was published in *Go* (November 1990: 78). In that issue's cover story, titled *'Our Bodies. The Bits the Singapore Man Likes Best'*, two men reveal:

> What are the parts of the female body that makes [sic] their hearts beat faster? Not surprisingly, a clear eighty per cent expressed a fondness for breasts. But unlike their Western counterpart, prone to drool over the Dolly Partons of this world, the Singapore man prefers proportions to size [sic].

This article is presented as an example not so much of social control as of a version of liberation. Such commentaries are taken as signs of 'frank' and honest discussion, with open references to women's 'sexuality'. Such openness would not have been possible in the 'old-fashioned' past. Women are free to hear men talk of them and thus learn from that talk about what men want, so they can therefore perform better as 'woman'.

The material and ideational are not only available but are consumed in large measure, figuratively and literally. The range of means by which women can 'modernise' their bodies has grown astoundingly. Being middle class has meant seeing the proliferation of experts that one can avail of to redo the body; including beauticians, dietitians and cosmetic surgeons. A *Sunday Times* news report (13 June 1993) proudly announced that Singapore women today 'are bigger, going by their bras':

> This indicates that Singapore women are not only getting bigger built but better developed too' said Mr Lam (spokesperson for Japanese bra manufacturer, Wacoal Singapore) . . . . (T)wo Minister of Health nutritionists said the findings could be attributed to better nutritional intake in recent years.

Not surprisingly, as one Singaporean fashion designer commented, 'over the last decade customers (have become) more confident of their fashion sense and their bodies' (as quoted in the *Straits Times* 24 November 1993). She also noted that bodies had become thinner. This thinner but bigger-busted and constantly modernising body of the single woman in particular is also placed in a space that she can colour with the romance which is the 'modern' way to find a husband. A woman's sexuality is expressed primarily in her appearance and seen as legitimate because it brings with it the potential to enter into a heterosexual marriage and to produce children. Indeed, much of the means to a middle-class way of life involves being wife and husband.

Take for instance ownership of an apartment, one of the most sought after embellishments of 'class' mobility in Singapore. An estimated 86 per cent of the resident population live in public housing, Housing and Development Board (HDB) flats (Housing and Development Board 1993/4: 70). One of the criteria for eligibility to own such flats is the 'family formation rule': this states that unless a woman is 40 years old or more, or a man is 50 years old or more, s/he will not be 'eligible to rent or purchase a HDB flat without having to form [sic] a family nucleus' (Wong and Yeh 1985: 246). This is because:

> [t]he HDB operates on the general principle that a family unit is in more need of housing than an unmarried individual. At the same time, for many social and practical reasons, it would wish to discourage individuals, whether young or old, to [sic] live on their own . . . . [T]he HDB also actively promotes the extended family as an institution through several specially formulated housing schemes . . . introduced in the seventies and eighties . . . (such as)

> . . . Reside Near Parents/Married Children Scheme . . . and the Multi-Tier Family Housing Scheme.
>
> (ibid.: 252)

The need for a family nucleus comprising a man and his wife was explicitly spelled out in a 1994 National Day Rally Speech by the Prime Minister. He lamented the fact that unmarried mothers by virtue of being mothers were eligible for public housing: 'This rule implicitly accepts unmarried motherhood as a respectable part of our society. This is wrong. By removing the stigma, we may encourage more women to have children without getting married,' (as quoted in the *Straits Times* 22 August 1994). From then on such women would be denied the right to buy public flats directly from the HDB, but could only obtain them from the resale market at a substantially inflated price.

Owning an apartment is the entry point for yet another crucial aspect of middle-class everyday life. Doing up a home provides one of the most important ways of doing middle-class culture. The furnishing market in Singapore is estimated to be worth US$1.4 billion a year (*Asia Magazine* 1995: 12). Translate this into a timetable involving window shopping, gazing at books on interior decoration, actual buying, actual decorating involving hours with a decorator, and maintenance of a set middle-class standard of cleanliness and presentability. There is a pleasurably endless variety of work involved in dressing up the home in which a woman will reign, subordinate only to her husband. It is also a means to present a social self and a family that has a recognisably middle-class way of life.

In these homes too, women become mothers of two to three well-spaced out children. As mothers they take on added responsibilities. They must ensure that their children are properly socialised. Upward social mobility for the family will be continued through them. Women's choices have greatly expanded here too. There is, for example, a vast array of paraphernalia and a proliferation of relevant expertise by which they can ensure that their babies will have a head start in life. They work hard to find and consume material like *How to teach your baby to think*, or read, or do maths, or have encyclopedic knowledge. Such books are often shelved with other child care books in the section entitled 'of interest to women' or 'for women'. If they are sorted under the shelf titled 'child care', then these shelves are located next to 'women' shelves, such as 'health and women', 'cookery', or just 'women'. Women also arrange their child's enrolment in the growing numbers of speech and drama school courses which promise access to English, the language of mobility, as spoken by the presumably more inherently qualified teachers from the UK, USA, Canada, Australia and New Zealand. Drama and other schools that 'improve' the minds and bodies of children are filled with women bringing children in for their classes and waiting until the hour is up to ferry them home or to another class.

Much of the work that women do, then, creates a complex way of life that can be and is loosely recognised as middle class. This work not only creates middle-class life for themselves, but also ensures its accomplishment for men and children, in important ways. The work is clearly burdensome, given that middle classness for women also involves their being 'working mothers'. The multiple careers imposed on women obviously disturb illusions about middle-class life as a wholly attractive option. The related burdens have led women to question the way of life that they have undertaken. Yet there is a powerful Singaporean aspect of this that mitigates the onerousness of the middle-class family way of life. Upward social mobility still holds out real promise for the transfer of the tedious, mundane and boring tasks that are part of the less rewarding aspects of doing the middle-class family to first, labour- and time-saving household technologies and, second, to other women.[12] These other women include full-time foreign domestic maids, brought in from the Philippines, Malaysia, Indonesia, Sri Lanka, India, Thailand and Burma.[13] One may not have such a maid, but to be of the middle class means that one can aspire to have such help in the future. The problem with the middle-class way of life, then, is not so much that it is a problem in and of itself; rather, it is a reflection of one's lower place in that same class: future mobility will iron out the wrinkles.

SOCIALLY RELEVANT FEMINIST ALTERNATIVES

I have already mentioned that the middle-class way of life that women reproduce with reference to the normal family ideology is both their betterment and their imprisonment. The experience and recognition of imprisonment, however, involve interpretive work and therefore a body of social knowledge which can give social meaning to it. Are the frustrations and difficulties of being 'woman' merely the fate of woman, or are they a consequence of actions that can be challenged and changed? Middle-class education and other resources have allowed Singapore women access to texts that can provide another way of understanding the middle-class family way of life, and choices about how to modify that way of life. The most politically powerful body of such texts can be loosely grouped together as 'feminist alternatives'. As with all social knowledges, available texts are dormant until called up and used to interpret and construct social realities. Feminist alternatives are no different. Given the normal family ideology in particular, feminist alternatives can be treated as interesting but not very relevant aspects of middle-class perspectives. They are not very real or accomplishable, however, especially in unquestionably patriarchal contexts. Further, 'everyday life' involves the doing of the mundanely normal. The unquestioned normal needs to be breached.

At this point I should like to explore these complexities by outlining three characteristic orientations that middle-class women can and do take in negotiating life constructs for themselves and others: the 'modern not feminist' perspective (often summarised in statements like, 'I am liberated/modern but not feminist'); the moderate feminist perspective (which is clarified by the statement that, 'We are *Asian feminists*'), and the radical feminist perspective (a designation that some Asian feminists give to certain views that they are nervous about). The terms 'modern/liberated', 'moderate' and 'radical' are derived really from their occurrence in everyday life discourse and are being used here strictly with reference to their more local meanings.[14] I shall look at these three orientations more closely below, but it is important to stress that they are not meant to be treated as exclusive categories of women within the middle class. Any one person can hold one, two or all of these sets of views. Thus, one can be 'modern' about some things, but not 'feminist'; moderately 'feminist' in relation to some others; and radically feminist about others. For example, a woman may not question her own hiring of a foreign domestic maid using strictly contractual terms of employment. Yet in another situation she may bemoan the difference between women's and men's pay.

Generally, the combination of these attitudes, contradictory or otherwise, varies in relation to the person's location in a trajectory of social time, marked by location within or outside of a marriage, and the experiences within it. Thus women who have had a marked feminist-based repugnance against the foreign domestic maid scheme have shelved this and gone on to use the scheme after they themselves become mothers. Feminist texts then become relevant and useful, even if notionally and in an unquestioning manner, when they correspond in some important ways to the normal family-embedded trajectory that a woman occupies at different points in her life. These personal life experiences shape the way the different texts are interwoven into a perspective which can change from moment to moment. Such personal life experiences are at once social too, for, as I have argued, the paradigm of the normal family and the life trajectory of a woman embedded within it ensure a certain shared knowledge by which life is reconstructed. The majority of women in Singapore, sooner or later, will make their way out from their family of origin into a family of procreation of their own by a heterosexual marriage. This process itself embeds them in a materially and ideationally expressed ideological meaningfulness.

'Modern' orientation draws unquestioningly from the dominant family ideology. Such an orientation arises from a context in which the experience of the middle-class way of life is perceived as unproblematic for the most part. There is little sense of gender-based discontent within the dominant texts of middle-class modernity. The perception is that women have advanced and will continue to do so. Equality has happened and will continue to happen. Further, equality is understood in given gender terms – it is an equality based on the principle of complementarity, which gives women a secondary place next to men.

Such an orientation appears to have been the socially dominant one among Singaporean women till as late as the early 1980s. Through the 1960s up to this time middle classness was achieved fairly easily, and came to be seen as a gift of the government, making the work of women in this respect invisible. A rude social awakening came in early 1983. On 14 August 1983 the then Prime Minister of Singapore, Lee Kuan Yew, gave a National Day Rally speech which has resonated down to the present. Lee began this speech by recounting the success story of Singapore since 1959. On the one hand, the story was a celebration of Singapore's economic achievements: since 1959, against great odds, Lee and his government had wrested immense progress for Singapore society economically and (thereby) socially; on the other hand, the story was given a new twist. The very crucial changes that this progress brought about, which underscored the economic and social mobility of women in Singapore, was, according to him, regrettable in some important respects:

> Our most valuable asset is in the ability of our people. Yet we are frittering away this asset through unintended consequences of changes in our education policy and equal career opportunities for women. This has affected their traditional role as mothers. It is too late for us to reverse our policies and have our women go back to their primary role as mothers, the creators and protectors of the next generation. Our women will not stand for it. And anyway they have already become too important a factor in the economy. Therefore we must amend our policies, and try to reshape our demographic configuration so that our better-educated women will have more children to be adequately represented in the next generation . . . . They need incentives not disincentives.[15]

Lee was here regretting changes in education and work opportunities for women – two of the most significant of the expanding choices that marked being and doing middle class. Not surprisingly, it shook women up – and continues to do so, for time proved that Lee's speech heralded a long new moment for Singaporean women: new only because the patriarchal bases of Singaporean society were made clear, and that somewhat ironically set women thinking about them more critically. Thus Lee set in motion a train of speeches and policies pertinent to women in Singapore society which continues today. Lee is now senior minister in Goh Chok Tong's cabinet. But the present Prime Minister has made it clear that his position on women and the family largely perpetuates the concerns expressed by his predecessor:

> Singaporeans living in HDB flats have seen big improvements in their standard of living. Aside from owning more luxury consumer items like hi-fi sets, 37,000 HDB homes have (full-time foreign) domestic maids, with 4,000 of the maids in three-room HDB flats. And each year, almost one in two HDB families have some members who go abroad for holidays . . . Our institutions and basic policies are in place to sustain high economic growth. But if we lose our traditional values, our family strength and cohesion, we will lose our vibrancy and decline.
>
> (Quoted in *Business Times* 22 August 1994)

Like Lee, Goh sees the threat to traditional values contained within the normal family as deriving from the changes in women's position and the demands they can now make. The fundamental problem – the one that allows women to live alone, to treat divorce as acceptable and to not bear (enough) children, is seen to be due to the challenges to patriarchy that changes in women's status have unwittingly brought about. Goh noted that women must accept that they live in a patriarchal society and should realise that it is 'not possible nor is it wise to have total sex equality in all areas' (Goh 1993: 29). To augment this, the government will introduce legal and administrative rules that will block women from certain kinds of gains, such that they will have access to certain 'rights, benefits and privileges' only through 'the head of the family, so that *he* can enforce the obligations and responsibilities of family members' (Goh Chok Tong, as quoted in the *Straits Times* August 22 1994, emphasis mine).

From the very start, women recognised the threat in all these statements, a threat that drew them towards feminist knowledges and made feminisms potentially more relevant in their lives. Suddenly middle-class women in Singapore awoke to a sense of fear that continuing middle-class betterment could be thwarted by the very source bringing them what they saw as the good and modern life. The modern viewpoint was not as easy to hold on to as before. Thus, the shock, dismay and anger that followed Lee's first speech came especially strongly from the ranks of professional middle-class women, who decided to found the Association of Women for Action and Research (AWARE). Registered in 1985, this was the first feminist organisation to arise since the virtual disappearance of women activists from the political scene in the early 1960s. Today AWARE boasts close to 700 members, who are middle class both 'objectively' and subjectively. Individuals and other middle-class women's professional and social organisations, particularly under the auspices of their umbrella body, the Singapore Council of Women's Organisations (ORGANISATIONS), also began to engage in debates about the question of women's place in Singapore. In all these deliberations women entered into a conscious relationship with the examination, selection, re-production or rejection of notional and specific knowledges, which they referred to as 'feminist'.

Yet there was something enigmatic in this turn of events. First, feminist debates obviously did not take place in a vacuum. Given the powerful position of the normal family ideology, deliberations on feminisms became occasions to wed feminist alternatives with ideas and elements from the ideology of family. In their search for texts to counter the ruling elite's position about women's place, middle-class women were struggling to retain a middle-class way of life resting on this family ideology. Feminist questioning did not come from a questioning of the middle class itself. Instead it came in response to the stated regrets of a respected leader considered to be one of those directly responsible for the betterment of middle-class Singapore women. Feminism was being used, in an important way, to support a way of life that was at once in contradiction with some of its tenets.

Second, this rather strange marriage between feminist knowledge and a patriarchal family orientation did give women a political voice in a society in which political voices were restrained, to say the least, by the fear of reprisals against anything resembling oppositional politics. As I shall show below, the negotiations between the ruling elite and women centred around a shared language, in which both appeal to the texts pertinent to fears of falling and the normal family ideology. Women's use of these texts is of strategic importance, although it is not used as mere strategy. Herein lies the crux of the problem. Texts can be used to reread women's position. Claims made about women within them are seemingly accepted but also used to pressure creatively for change.

A further, third, complication is that the newly created space for negotiations between middle-class women and the ruling elite was in itself a middle-class desideratum. These were heady times in Singapore:

women and their organisations were heralded as the newly emerging civic society. Women's organisations and their leaders became symbols of yet another aspect of middle classness. This symbolism was underscored by the attention the government paid to AWARE in particular. But the negotiations demanded the use of a language that the ruling elite would be willing to negotiate in, a language that called for both sides to attend to the powerful limits that the normal family imposed, supposedly, for the good of the nation and hence women too. Additionally, women's new-found organisational vigour was to be protected for fear that the organisations might be deregistered if women in these organisations breached the unspoken terms by which negotiations with the ruling elite are possible.

As a corollary, a body of knowledges that was, and is, labelled moderate feminism was constructed and used in the language of women who could legitimate its rightful place in contemporary Singapore. 'Moderate feminist' views acknowledge their reliance on feminist texts to critique various instances of inequality within the structures of patriarchal family ideologies and patriarchal families, but they are also highly mindful of 'Asian' concerns, which moderate legitimate limits on what is normally and morally possible for women in Singapore. Clearly there is a central tension here. Asian-ness is importantly located in the normal family, the core of which is patriarchal. Patriarchal families, in which men are heads of household, refer, implicitly at least, to a patriarchal society in which the members of the male ruling elite are heads of state in like manner. Moderate feminism then is selective feminism in which certain ideas and ideologies cannot be publicly admitted. In this way middle-class women's politics arises and takes shape within a constantly shifting continuum of compliance with and resistance to patriarchal ideologies and practices. To illustrate some of the implications of this I shall look at the example of the unequal medical benefits for women in the civil service, not least because this issue was one of the few issues that has provoked strong reactions from middle-class women and women's organisations in recent times.

THE MODERATE FEMINIST ORIENTATION: BETWEEN COMPLIANCE AND RESISTANCE

In spite of the principle of equal pay for equal work adopted in 1966, female civil servants are not entitled to the same medical benefits as their male counterparts unless they are widowed, divorced or separated. In the main, medical benefits for male civil servants extend to a male employee's wife and children, while only the individual female worker is covered. Although this situation had existed for a long time it only surfaced for the first time as a public issue when a former male member of parliament, Ong Leong Boon, raised it in 1976. It surfaced again in 1986 when another, female, member of parliament, Yu-Foo Yee Shoon, appealed for a change to this ruling. Finance Minister Hu, however, claimed that the economy was not performing satisfactorily enough for an extension to be possible at this time (*Straits Times* 13 February 1994).

When Yu-Foo asked for reconsideration of the issue in early 1993, Hu said that the scheme 'may see a change' in the latter part of the year (*Straits Times* 12 March 1993). Hopes were so high that at least one large statutory employer proceeded to prepare the grounds for extending similar medical coverage for spouses and children of its female employees in time for the next Budget announcements. Instead, to the shocked dismay of many, Hu announced in November 1993 that women would not be give similar coverage, although cost was not an issue at all. The increase in medical subsidy would amount to $8.1 million, just 0.4 per cent of the payroll, if the coverage was extended. The rationale was loudly and clearly about framing women's rights *vis-à-vis* the patriarchal family, as Hu made clear:

> It is the husband's responsibility to look after the family's needs, including their medical needs. This is how our society is structured. It would be unwise to tamper with this structure.
>
> (*Strait Times* 12 November 1993)

Clearly there were two issues here: the issue of medical benefits *per se* and the issue of women's place in the family and society. Reactions from the women's organisations and women activists in these organisations appear to have understood this.

In these debates there is a tendency to stay close to concrete concerns rather than the larger issues within which they are embedded. A statement and/or an announcement of incentives and, more so, disincentives, made by the ruling elite, *may* provoke a reaction. The issue of limited medical coverage for female civil servants saw one of the most acrimonious reactions in recent decades. But when Dr Richard Hu, the Finance Minister, introduced tax rebates in the 1987 and 1989 National Budgets to encourage women to have children earlier and to have more children, they were barely noticed. He had announced that $20,000 rebates would be offered to encourage parents to have a third and fourth child (*Straits Times* 3 August 1990). Another set of rebates were given in 1990, when Hu announced that 'rebates of $20,000, $15,000, $10,000 and $5 000 were to be given to mothers who deliver a second baby before they turn

28, 29, 30 and 31 years of age respectively' (*Business Times* 7 March 1990). Thus, 10,500 women were expected to benefit (sic) from these rebates in the 1991 Year of Assessment alone. Significantly, tax rebates did not bring forth much public protest, despite the apparent patriarchal objectification of women.

The protests that may follow particular concerns involve the use of one or more of the following approaches:

1 Letters are written by individual women and men, and/or representatives of women's organisations, to the local newspapers.
2 Questions and criticism are raised in parliament in the main by nominated member of parliament (NMP) Khanwaljit Soin, to whom I shall refer later. Soin arrived on the scene in 1992, when she was president of AWARE. She began her term with the firm public declaration that she was here to represent women; they were her constituency.
3 Less frequently, public forums are organised by AWARE, ORGANISATIONS (Singapore Council of Women's Organisations) and the National University of Singapore Society.
4 Sometimes, representations are made to the relevant Ministries behind closed doors. These may take the form of arguing against the policy *per se*, or arguing for relaxation of the ruling in relation to a special case.
5 Private conversations provide another means of airing frustration at the government's latest salvo against women.
6 I should also note a suggestion that appears to have first come up in a forum on 'Towards Equal Benefits', organised by ORGANISATIONS in December 1994, which encouraged women to 'speak up more. Talk to our MPs. We shouldn't be silenced' (*Straits Times* 13 December 1994). It does not seem to have been taken up in any prominent way, however. All six ways of protest importantly focus attention on the ruling elite, confirming that social change is the prerogative of the male elite and not the direct and powerful work that women can and could do on and for themselves. Consequently, energies are directed at berating the authorities, perhaps mocking them and ultimately appealing to them. The powerful programme of consciousness-raising which would empower women, both numerically and ideologically, is almost completely ignored.

The strength of the medical benefits protests is revealed by the variety of interests united by the issue. These included PAP party stalwart and MP Yu-Foo, columnists of the *Straits Times*, who normally take pains to explain the government's position on many other issues, voices of husbands and fathers protesting that their wives and daughters should not be discriminated against as they were part of the general workforce, and AWARE and ORGANISATIONS. Private debates were complemented by Soin's statements in Parliament, while more than the usual number of letters were published in the press. ORGANISATIONS organised a well-attended forum, 'Towards Equal Benefits', at which many took to the floor to voice their discontent. This was a splendid but, alas, brief time. The diversity of women and women's orientations that it brought together did not last. Further, the moment that enabled patriarchy itself to be seriously questioned very quickly narrowed back to concern with winning the State's patronage. This is best summarised in the words of one of the most active women of the time of the medical benefits clamour, Anamah Tan, President of ORGANISATIONS:

> Enough of confronting the policy-makers in public. We also know that if you go around beating your breast, you are not going to get anywhere. It's better to *present your facts in a reasoned and mature way* and doing this behind closed doors might *give politicians a chance to make a U-turn, if they want to.*
>
> (Quoted in *Straits Times* 13 February 1994: my italics)

The powerful moderate feminist orientation to the issue was legitimated by the ruling elite's apparently conciliatory tone, even if that tone was glazed with paternal sternness. Goh Chok Tong has made it very clear that he and his government are more than prepared to help women get ahead, even enjoy 'equal' status at home and in the country at large. He himself has duly noted, time and again, that the government's stance towards women has little to do with its attitude to women *per se*. Its real concern is with 'big national problems' that inevitably involve women (Goh Chok Tong 1993: 32). The message is simply that women's demands are acceptable and to be expected – and should be catered to. If and when they are not, it is *not* a matter of a stance against women, but a stance in aid of the family, given the modern forces that work against this almost sacred institution. The example of the 'Western family' as the typically 'broken family' is warning enough, according to the mostly male polity. As Prime Minister Goh put it, after a National Day Rally speech,

> It is only a small group of women in Singapore who thought that the [National Day Rally] speech [which reiterated the government's position on women's subordinate status to men] was anti-woman. They are wrong. It is not anti-woman. I mean, how can we be anti-woman in our values? We are pro-family.
>
> (Goh Chok Tong, quoted in *Straits Times* August 22 1994)

A host of supportive policies and statements suggest that it is not the government's intention to block women's advancement in spite of its fundamental beliefs about gender. Chief among these policy areas are the job opportunities they are seen to be providing for women. Here the reader should recall Prime Minister Lee's regret in 1983 that it is too late for the government to expect women to leave the workforce and return home full-time, a regret which acknowledges capitalist demands in the labour force. Middle-class women are both confident and secure that this cannot ever change. Indeed, their gainful employment is justified by the family's 'middle-class' lifestyle, which they help achieve. This includes the highly important contribution to the mortgage of the very house/apartment, whether HDB or private, in which their families live. The perceived need for women in the workforce has also meant that, from time to time, the patriarchal polity makes statements which admonish men to be more equal partners in the home, especially when a call for more women to enter the labour force is made. In the main, this means that they are to help women out in housework, child care and cooking. This appeal to men has come from as high up as the Prime Minister and has been taken up by a number of other male ministers as well.

The most important proof of willingness to expand avenues for women is possibly the incorporation of women into Parliament and even in the Cabinet. Since the late 1950s, women had more or less disappeared from the political scene. This absence was not socially recognised till as late as 1984, when three women from the professional 'middle class' were 'hand-picked by the PAP to stand for election to Parliament' (Wang Look Fung and Nancy Teo 1993: 291). Today, slightly more than a decade later, there are two elected and two nominated female members of parliament. As well, for the first time a woman Aline Wong, who was mentioned above, has been appointed to the cabinet, although not as a fully-fledged minister, but as Senior Minister of State for Education and Health. Further proof of dispensation is to be found in the presence in parliament of NMP Khanwaljit Soin. Despite her strong pro-women stand both inside and outside Parliament, Soin was renominated by the cabinet for her second, current, term in parliament. Moreover, Goh has supported Soin's requests for parliament to include more women amongst its members. Graciously and generously, considering both the long absence of women in parliament as well as the publicised reluctance of women to enter politics, Goh promised to see to it that there would be six women in Parliament, double the number at the time he made this promise, by 1996 (*Straits Times* 14 June 1993). He did, however, note that:

> It's a very demanding job. *Even for a man* . . . it's difficult. For the woman there is the home to look after too. Like it or not, in Singapore, we expect the women to play a bigger role in the home.
>
> (Prime Minister Goh quoted in *Business Times* 14 June 1993)

The position of many prominent women activists again demonstrated that the ruling elite and many middle-class women shared the language of the normal family ideology and its inherent texts about the real character of women being distinctive. For instance, amid the furore over the Government's announcement regarding the continuation of unequal medical benefits for women civil servants, Claire Chiang, then president of AWARE, is reported to have said, with reference to the need for women to represent themselves politically, 'I just don't feel that fire in the belly' (quoted in the *Straits Times*, 11 December 1993). At this same time, the president of ORGANISATIONS, Anamah Tan explained:

> Politics is not foremost in the woman's mind. Foremost is which tutor to get for her daughter, what class to send her to, ballet or piano, or both? You ask them if they want to go into politics, they'll ask you, 'Where got time'?'
>
> (*Straits Times*, 11 December 1993)

In the same vein, almost no one argued with Yu-Foo when, speaking at the first ASEAN Women Leaders Forum in 1994, she claimed that Singapore women stay out of politics by choice, because they care more about the family than their own advancement. Such commentaries on the question of women in politics are occurring in a context in which men too are reluctant to enter politics. Thus in recent years the government has continuously referred to the problem of getting 'talented' 'persons' (read mainly men) into politics and the cabinet. The lack of interested males, in contrast, has been explained as arising from the financial sacrifices men must make in the transition from life as chief executive officers to that of civil servants. Consequently, ministerial salaries have been raised substantially – in an effort to get the good *men* into politics.

This brings us to the perhaps the most crucial point about gender and the 'middle class' in Singapore. The limits that the government insists on work not only because it wields the stick with the carrot, but because they make sense to women in contemporary Singapore. The enduring subtexts about women's subordination are read tantalisingly as if the government is actually ambiguous about women. There is a sense of negotiability. Women can and do question inequalities – with specific reference to specific statements. The focus of their attention is the male polity, which sometimes appears very reasonable – especially when they give in to women's demands, as with the demand for political representation in parliament. Each win is a powerful example that you can, and must, negotiate. It also shows how to negotiate with the ruling elite. This puts a certain onus on women's negotiations among themselves: much time is spent on reforming their own strategies, reformulating their feminist knowledges and related language. Their efforts at moderating alternative knowledges with reference to the normal family and fears of falling are made all the more powerful by the ambivalent stance of the ruling elite on women. This has given to the moderate feminist orientation a certain smugness, making it the most overt and dominant one in Singaporean women's politics today.

But there is still the real presence of that feminist orientation that is described even by women who hold it as radical feminism. This is supposedly non-Asian, and by that definition, pro-Western. Where does this fit in the context of contemporary Singapore? Is this where the pressures for real changes for women could come from?

RADICAL INTERPRETATIONS OF THE FAMILY

As mentioned earlier, the term 'radical feminist' is being used here in its specifically Singaporean meaning, which is attached to and comes from the notion of Asian feminism. This sees the world as divided into two spheres of influence in which Western ideas compete with, challenge and could even destroy Asian ideas. This is not unlike the ruling elite's conceptualisation of 'Westernisation' as one of the processes that Singaporeans must guard against if all that we have won for ourselves is not to be lost. It is noteworthy that the notion 'Asian' derives its meaning not so much from the idea of what is Asian but from what is not-Asian (cf. Chapter 4). Thus Asianness becomes the stick to knock down certain ideas which are perceived to question dominant taken-for-granted ideas. Asianness is obvious, commonsensically understood – it needs no explanation.

One of the most powerful condensations of this body of Asianness refers, as I have shown, to the normal family ideology. In this way, radical perspectives themselves are almost doomed from the start, because they admit to being radical in the sense that they are not Asian. The language then borrows from the dominant text. It persists in reifying the normal family, failing to question the contemporary and constructed character of the normal family. Instead, the normal family as a modern invention providing a powerful means of disciplining women is reified as if it were the 'real' cultural heritage. The radical critique assumes that the ideology of the normal family is that of a truly Asian family: to reject the family is then to reject Asian culture. The more potent critique, the deconstruction of the family, is not available. This limits the radical position in the Singapore context, for both the family and Asianness are put on the stand. The argument is then couched in terms of what is wrong with us as Asians. It highlights the male chauvinism of Asian men in general, Asian husbands and Asian family practices. Their difference from those in the West becomes the basis of discourse. This division, moreover, gives strength to the notion that the Western family is different from the Asian family, undergirding the commonly held notion that Western family life is breaking down precisely because of its failure to be like the Asian patriarchal family. This removes the possibility of thinking about universal features of patriarchal families. In addition, by accepting the normal family ideology as the only Asian way of doing the family, the radical position fails to discover and/magnify the many choices about family which Asian cultures and Asian histories offer women that might run counter to dominant ideology. These include such examples as the institutionalised Cantonese practice of sisterhoods: these developed into a tradition amongst some women as an alternative way of doing the family, with or without marriage as an adjacent institution (PuruShotam 1993: 3–4).

Bearing this in mind, I would like to turn now to what I would argue are the most public radical statements about gender and the middle-class way of life, the works of Singaporean women playwrights, particularly Eleanor Wong and Ovidia Yu. Both Wong and Yu have struggled admirably to place the voices of the less visible views of women's plight on stage. Both, though, are also not yet 'mad' (i.e. 'lunatic') enough: their women, even at their most critical, cannot and do not manage to free themselves from the reins of the normal family. I have discussed this theme of gender in Singapore theatre elsewhere (PuruShotam 1995: 9–10), from which the following descriptions and arguments are derived.

Wong's *Mergers and Accusations* traces the relationship between Ellen Toh, a young, successful lesbian lawyer and a man, Jonathan Chin, also young, successful and a lawyer. The two end up marrying, have a child, and reverse gender roles: Jonathan stays at home as full-time 'mother' and 'housewife'. In a very crucial sense, Ellen and Jonathan play it strictly by the rules of gendered life trajectories. We are almost warned of this by Jonathan's careless response to Ellen's confession as a closet lesbian. Jonathan hears, but clearly does not listen. And he is not the only one who does not seem to reflect on crucial aspects of gender and gender relations that lesbianism – as an affront to 'normality', marked by Ellen's insistence on remaining in the closet, throughout the play – could have offered. The marriage and life after it become very close to the normal gendered way of doing family. First, the sequences that are expected to occur in a certain order are adhered to: marriage before children; postponement of career because of mothering; returning to work after the child's babyhood. Second, the trajectory is put into play without much thought to it, with the same unquestioning stance that makes it a seen-but-unnoticed backdrop in most everyday lives. This is especially marked because of Ellen's willingness to marry and then provide Jonathan with a baby. Yet she never expresses a wish to have a child. So what was in it for her? Indeed, at the beginning of the play she dismisses Jonathan's interest in children with a distinctly unmaternal: 'They all remind me of fish at that age.' Third, the sequences leave the related membership categories associated with them intact in the most meaningful way. This is why we have referred earlier to Jonathan as 'mother' and 'housewife'. Because Jonathan is precisely like a mother and housewife, his gender as male recedes and the gender behind mothering and housework takes over. Ellen is the financial provider, living like a man in the world that Jonathan makes for her at home. She even uses the home like men would: in and out as she pleases, spending hardly any time with her child Sam or Jonathan. And Jonathan complains as the stereotypical neglected wife might be expected to complain.

> *Jon*: So why didn't you call earlier? Weren't we supposed to have dinner together tonight? Sam wanted to show you her latest masterpiece.
> *Ellen*: I said we would – if I could get away.
> *Jon*: And you couldn't. Why am I surprised?
> *Ellen*: I'm really sorry. Maybe tomorrow night. . . . You and Sam come first.
> *Jon*: After work.
> *Ellen*: If you're in one of your moods, I'd rather not discuss this.
> *Jon*: Sorry. It's just been a bitch of a day. Sam's stomach started acting up again and the clinic was a madhouse. Took us two hours to see the doctor. Which made me miss the plumber so the bathroom's still flooded.

To compound matters, the treatment of mothering and housework is clearly patriarchal in orientation. On the one hand, Wong's Jonathan slips in where Ellen would otherwise have been. She refuses a job that is quickly and easily filled: Jonathan just does what other women *struggle* to do. The fact that housework and mothering is work, and like work in a legal firm, requires skills and training that women are put through throughout their lives is dismissed. This is reflective of Western feminism in the 1960s. The world of women is not examined in terms of the meanings and experiences within it. Moreover, this world is to be judged by the standards of the real world, in this case the law firm and the legal world that Jonathan used to share with Ellen. Indeed, both Ellen and Jonathan strongly support the necessity for the world to be peopled by patriarchal constructions of 'wife' and 'mother'. Ellen refuses marriage, at the beginning, not only because she is a lesbian, but even more so because marriage would mean demands on her as a wife and mother. Jonathan accepts this position, and so agrees to be that wife and mother in their marriage.

Jon: I'll quit to look after the baby.
Ellen: You'll wash and clean?
Jon: Like a demon.
Ellen: Change nappies?
Jon: Every hour on the hour.
Ellen: Buy the groceries.
Jon: With Sam strapped to my chest.

The social fact of the normal family and family work is unabashedly undisguised. We sympathise with Jonathan because he is such a good wife and mother to a philanderer, in the way we would sympathise with any good wife and mother.

> *Jon*: You still don't understand do you ? You're right. I *am* giving up. I *can't* handle this. Don't you see? I'm jealous . . . I'm jealous of the fact that you say you love me, but I can't seem to give you what you need, that you'd destroy your self-respect by fucking anything in a skirt that will have you rather than be content with me.

Yet it is Jonathan's gender that gives him the exit permit out of the female trajectory that he lives in for the first three years of Sam's life. Thus, while his complaints may well mirror myriad women's lives in the normal world, he can just decide to pack it in in a moment. There is no guilt, no angst, no tears here. Indeed, it is Ellen who does the crying. And the resolution is so simple: Sam is put under Jonathan's parents' care; and Jonathan, after an absence of three years from law, finds a job pretty quickly. He exits as only a man who is experimenting with a woman's trajectory can.

As I have also argued elsewhere (PuruShotam 1993: 3–4), the most astute evaluation of the normal life trajectory for women in a patriarchally gendered world comes from the mouths of Yu's three fat virgins in her play *Three Fat Virgins Unassaulted* (1991). Their words are laced with bitter, perhaps even bitter-sweet experiences. They tell it like it is not only because, like many of the women out in the real world, they have lived the trajectory, but also because they are not fooled by the small print in the gender contract that they have been living by. Yu's play is about three women conversationally examining their lives as women and the lives of women generally. The play goes right to the heart of the meaning of 'woman' as a gendered category, including the trajectory of being 'woman'. Marriage is recognised as the pivotal point within this trajectory. There is a clear signal that the social self of a woman is not possible until it is conjoined to a husband and to children. Indeed, the more children one has, the larger, even if more fragmented, her names and so her self will be. Women can and do have the alternative of not getting married, by becoming nuns, or earning lots of money. Still, an unmarried status is marked by the male world one lives in. Thus, women can mostly work in female jobs, epitomised by the profession of a secondary school-teacher. That is, female qualities and skills are defined in terms of a male ideological and consumer market. The body of a woman then, a real woman, cannot be sold for itself, to make money for the woman who owns it, but the body, its virginity, can be sold for a husband. Nuns, at the same time, are only hiding their fatness behind their habit – fatness being a symbol of unattractiveness to males and so the male world. Marriage therefore is practically unavoidable. The gender trajectory is shown to be nothing more than a poor choice in lieu of even poorer choices, in so far as its meanings derive from a male polity and society. If woman is to be located in a man's world, then the reality of a trajectory pivoted upon marriage, the gender meanings associated with it, must always be marked by three qualities: sadness, virginity, and fatness.

Sadness arises from the fact that a woman can never own her body. If it is not marked by possession by a man, then it lacks meaning. Yet after the fact of possession can come the fact of being discarded. Virginity that attracts is spent and so is the attraction. Sadness is also unavoidable when one becomes a woman. For, 'one is not born a woman but becomes one'; and one becomes one from choosing from a limited range of options – nun-virgin, unmarried virgin, educated virgin-with-a-profession, wise virgin for having married a rich man, and foolish virgin, for having married a poor man. It is a 'sadness that is harder for thin men with balding heads and paunches to understand. This has nothing to do with penis envy.' Virginity is a permanent disability. It marks the inexperience of women as an enduring reality in a man's world. Women will always be unsure how to react, what to be, when to do, for the rules of the games being played are not made by them nor for them. You can't even tell' where the dividing line between a joke and sexual harassment is, exactly'. Virginity is a mark of unattractiveness, that you have not (hopefully, just not yet) been desired, consumed by a man. So virginity is a waiting by 'the pure young virgin of 17'. But the waiting can never end. For consummation does not end it. Unlike food, the woman is still there to be desired, to be consumed again. Thus, after marriage particularly, there is always the return to virginity, 'the unwanted fat virgin of 27'. The trajectory is not developmental, evolutionary, progressive. 'Woman' as a meaningful gendered construct is condemned to a cycle of apprehensive pauses. Whether young or old, 'it's the same condition. Why do we see it differently?'.

Fatness is about the body of women and its preparedness for men. Sexuality, sexual attraction and so the desired loss of virginity involve having a desirable body; a thin one.

> *Virgin A*: I simply have to lose ten kilos before the annual dinner and dance.
> *Virgin B*: I signed up for a slimming course you know. Carrot juice and watermelon juice. That's all they allow you to take.
> *Virgin C*: It cost me five hundred dollars! Of course it works! . . .
> *Virgin B*: I hate to diet . . .
> *Virgin A*: But then why do you diet?
> *Virgin B*: My husband makes jokes about me in front of our friends.
> *Woman* (as B's husband): My wife is on a seafood diet. When she sees food she eats it.

At the same time, in trading virginity for marriage, a married woman, especially a wise one, gains a provider: he provides car, house, food, a social life; she consumes in accordance with what he provides, not what she wants or needs; she gains fat – a certain stolidity, a weightiness that makes it difficult to run away; and so she regains her virginity.

> *Virgin B*: Darling, I've decided that I'm going to pull my life together!
> *Woman (playing man)*: That's wonderful, Darling. How much money do you need this time?
> *Virgin B*: I don't – I didn't . . .
> *Woman*: Here, take this. Buy yourself something nice. No one can say that I am not a generous husband where you are concerned. I am always more than generous. I am more generous than any other husband I know who has a wife as fat as you are.
> *Virgin B*: Thank you, Darling. You are always so good to me.

> *Woman*: Darling, now let's go out to dinner to celebrate! What do you feel like eating?
> *Virgin B*: Oh Darling, the thing is, you see, my diet . . .
> *Woman*: You can start tomorrow!
> *Virgin B*: Oh . . . tomorrow we're supposed to be going to have dinner with your golfing friends . . .
> *Woman*: Darling . . . I don't like this. Are you saying appearance is more important to you than our relationship? . . . than spending time with my friends? Have you forgotten how lucky you are that I married you in spite of your fatness?
> *Virgin B*: No, no, no, Darling . . . Of course our relationship is important and I want to spend time with your friends. And I will never forget how lucky I am to have married you.

In sum, the meaningfulness of 'woman', the experience she is thus allowed to have, condemn her always to the sadness of being a fat virgin:

> *Woman*: For a woman to be a fat virgin, it is not necessary for her to be fat. Neither is it necessary for her to be a virgin. It is only necessary for her to be a woman.

Strangely, shockingly too, the words of this virgin actually mirror the argument in Prime Minister Lee's statements about women. 'Women', said Lee, 'need incentives not disincentives' to conform to what is required of them. To be woman in a middle-class society is, at once, to have a disadvantaged life, with built-in advantages for everyone including (therefore) women themselves. Fatness is disadvantageous, but not to be fat is not to have the choices and the means to consume the choices by which one gets fat. Virginness is restrictive, but conforming to restrictions brings rewards, with time. The underlying proviso is that women must do the work necessary to bring about those rewards, encapsulated in the middle-class way of life that they, their husbands and their children can enjoy. The middle-class way of life as a way of normal family life becomes a fundamental given.

In this way Wong's and Yu's radicalism is powerful but restricted. It is imagined not for the real world, but for the theatre. Woman and her sympathisers can laugh, even when the message is inherently sad. The laughter helps the tension of the real world that women continue to reproduce, that middle-class way of life which paradoxically cannot be reproduced if she chooses not to reproduce it. But middle classness offers a powerful constraint on women's politics: the family as it is, 'normal', reified, is the centre of middle-class reality, and the family is reified because it is 'normal', 'moral' and therefore without any acceptable alternative.

UNVEILING THE MIDDLE CLASS: WOMAN POWER IN CONTEMPORARY SINGAPORE

> [I]f domestic *ta'a* (obedience) is challenged by weak women, how can men be expected to lower their eyes in defence to the leader? The modesty of the Arab women is the linchpin of the whole political system. Entire chapters in the collections of *Hadith* . . . dictate to us how to braid our hair, how to lower our eyes, and how to slip on modesty like a camisole. . . . The civil codes reproduce in every article the picture of the family in the image of the caliphal palace, where *ta'a* is required and the will of the leader overrides that of all others. The battle of the 1990s will be a battle over the civil codes, which women challenge. . . . [T]hrough education and paid work, modernity has . . . [allowed women to] speak an unknown language. The equality they demand . . . is [condemned as] a foreign imported idea. [So women become] targets of intimidation and violence . . . that hark back to the past. Tomorrow the same thing can happen elsewhere. The reason is simple: women . . . [t]oday constitute one of the most dynamic components of the developing civil society . . . The relentless battle doesn't target just any woman. One precise category is aimed at: middle-class women who have had access to education and valorising salaried jobs. . . . Their obsession is with the woman who enjoys all the visible privileges of her modernity.
>
> (Mernissi 1993: 153, 157)

I selected this quotation with the intent to disturb, if not shock, those feminist friends and acquaintances who have argued that the Singapore woman today is not that badly off, is differently – better – positioned than her contemporaries elsewhere in the world; and, in any case, is in an enviable enough political position, because the ruling elite will negotiate with her and grant her requests if she can craft her language to suit the modern times. In this we have forgotten that, if the texts by which we do the world are better texts, it is in part because at the dawn of the birth of Singapore, women made their presence felt, their voices heard; they also took to the streets. They spent time deliberating upon how the world was constructed, and argued about how this must be done differently. A central principle of such deliberations and demands referred to a better life for all based on a concern with equal rights. This term encapsulated the desire for a world in which power would be better distributed. The perspectives of women, and by that token, children, would have an equal place with those of men in reconstructing life. That is, women struggled to deliberate upon given texts by which everyday life was reproduced, and, more significantly, they struggled to *author* the texts by which life would be reproduced in the future.

Sadly, by the time Singapore was expelled from the Federation of Malaysia, and came into its own, Singapore women were busily involved in doing their middle-class life largely according to texts constructed for them by a male polity. The eventual awareness of this in the 1980s, however, came not from the ground up, but from top-down statements about women, followed by policies affecting their lives. In the main, the concern has arisen from the fear of falling I have discussed above. At the same time, there has been a growing recognition that the dissenting female voices need to be aired in the corridors of male power. It is argued by some of the most powerful and prominent female activists that this male power both holds the means to grant the change and is open to persuasion.

This reading is tempting, given the fear of falling. Indeed, the Singaporean woman, it appears, can do anything she wants. She can be granted spaces in such relatively exalted niches as parliament and the cabinet. In any case, she will be reasonable about these possibilities, policing herself in terms of the demands that the family 'normally' makes on her. The middle-class woman, then, is in the enviable position of having access to all the 'visible privileges of her modernity'. Monogamy and romantic marriage have replaced polygamy. Schools, colleges and the university opened their doors to females. With that came employment opportunities and the 'supplementary' wage. Homes in which husbands rather than mothers-in-law presided could be jointly owned. Even the marketplace expanded, making and selling the woman material and ideational goods often catering to her body's needs, her mind, her lifestyle and the lifestyles which she desired for her husband and children. As I have shown, through these material and ideational choices, women continuously reproduce a middle-class way of life and society, mirroring the ruling elite's images of that class.

Yet something went wrong, or almost wrong, viewed from the perspective of the male political elite – something that should alert us women to the power that we possess and do not have to be granted from some external source. In reproducing their lives *vis-à-vis* the dominant ideology of the normal family, women are one of the key players in the ongoing construction of a particularly middle-class way of life that marks Singapore society as a whole. This means that if women choose to do everyday life differently, then the form and substance of this way of life itself, including the accomplishment of her current largely subordinate position, will undergo changes. The ruling elite is clearly very aware of the formidable place that the contemporary middle-class women of Signapore occupy. It is no coincidence that the elite's concern about the continuation of the middle-class way of life, as it has been reproduced thus far, takes women as its main subjects and objects of social control. Neither is it, to stress the point, a reflection of women's powerlessness and therefore a case of the elite's picking on a group which can be intimidated. Instead, the middle-class woman is the one who is intimidating.

First, despite the lack of a conscious or concerted plan, women began to actually realise and so prove their capacity to change the fabric of Singaporean society. They began making independent judgments, rereading their position in the normal family in liberating terms. They sought more and more education; they treated careers seriously and therefore postponed and sometimes refused marriage and children; or they limited the number of children they would bear and raise; they preferred to make time for themselves as persons, rather than as a social category tied to husband and child, family and state; and they exercised their right to divorce themselves from bad, and unequal marriages. If these new ways of reproducing personal lives take root, the middle-class way of life thus reproduced will surely be vastly different. Second, these acts were political acts, even if women were innocent of this aspect of their content. They bring with them the spectre of individual choice, individual rights, individualism *per se*, in a political context that not only openly dismisses the individualist conceptualisation of people as irrelevant, even dangerous, but which also embraces a highly particularised notion of communitarian democracy. This notion of democracy sees the state/ruling elite as the only component of society that has the expertise and the legitimacy, the right if you will, to decide what the community's interests are to be, and how these are to be implemented.[16]

That is why, like the 'Arab women' whom Mernissi discusses, Singaporean women must be constrained by civil codes. These may not be as specific, as neatly packaged and so clearly identifiable as those collected in the *Hadith*, but they are there nevertheless. Women can roam as far as is allowed by the normal family ideology, which encapsulates community interests defined by the male polity. The boundaries she must not cross are underscored by the context of myriad fears of losing her present privileges. In other words, the middle-class Singaporean woman is as much veiled as her Arab counterpart, albeit in her case she is veiled by 'the family'. This veil, this boundary, is an insidious one, because it is less visible in the separate, enclosed enclaves it constructs for women. Yet it does impose a powerful and limited boundary upon women. First, it imposes a calendar of life, a normal unfolding that flows from childhood, courtship, marriage, wifehood and motherhood.

Second, underlying this calendar is an omnipresent timetable of daily demands. Third, and as a corollary to both calendar and timetable, it creates and perpetuates experience and social reality in which the world is dichotomised into the realm of the private/female sphere, and public/male sphere. In such a dichotomous world, underscored by this timetable, women feel the pressures, including the emotional and psychic pressures, to do the family first – and only to enter public life if that timetable allows them some time to do so. Usually this requires the women to wait until their children, if not their husbands, are independent of them. Often by that time the contribution she feels she can make is by way of voluntary work in charitable organisations, or voluntary work in civic organisations, rather than contributing a powerful perspective for change arising from her experiences as mother, wife and so forth. Indeed, given the private–public conceptualisation of the world, these perspectives often tend to get dismissed as personal and irrelevant. Yet, as this chapter has argued, (and as is argued elsewhere in this volume) the private and the public are 'so deeply involved with each other that the impoverishment of one entails the impoverishment of the other' (Bellah *et al.* 1986: 163).

Unlike the *hijab*, the Singaporean family does not come with an actually available text, authored by the powerful figure of Allah, but is enshrined in nebulous texts, from nebulous sources. The 'Arab woman' learns the text of the Koran from the time that she is a child (Mernissi 1993: 77–80). She can use it to quote chapter and verse, and so, (as studies on the Arab women's movements show) can contest the polity's interpretations of gender (ibid.: 160–1). When texts are as nebulous as their sources, the oppressiveness of the normal family is disempowering, not energising. This is what makes Wong's and Yu's plays, in the end, so sad: women cannot see and so reread the frames by which they do their lives. Indeed, the normal family is perceived to be a reified institution, that just is: not a text from which women themselves create the social reality.

The sadness need not lock us out, however, for it provides a key. If a chord is struck, then there is space for women to come together and explore this sadness. That space must be used with greater creativity, more potent imaginings, to raise questions and heighten consciousness. We have the power already. It is locked up within us, and left locked because we fail to see that the key to our liberation must start with ourselves. We must recognise that this normal family is a modern-day construct that we have participated in creating and maintaining. It is a veil which hides us from the more pertinent and powerful perspective that a questioning attitude might bring us. We need to recognise that we do have the choice to drape the veil over ourselves, that we can choose to see and so craft questions and answers that can empower us. Are these texts mostly readings of a heavily male-dominant commentary on what 'woman' is? Or are these texts the work of our own constructions, committed to the perspectives and concerns that arise from our confidence in our own varied social realities? Thus, what kinds of texts do we want to use to reconstruct our world? What kinds of texts should be given political legitimacy?

This should involve a serious re-evaluation of women's place in the constitution of Singapore, as well as especial reference to the invisible or silenced promises in the Women's Charter. This Charter arose from the demands of women and men in Singapore in the late 1950s that the unequal position of women in Singapore should be rectified, with proper legislative backing. By the time the Charter was actually passed, in 1961, it had become yet another male document, with little in it of the original intention to ensure women's equal rights in Singapore. We need to revamp history, or at least add to it, with herstory. If Asian traditions must form the base of legitimate argumentations, then we need to realise the inhumane consequences of these traditions. We also need to be aware that the body of Asian traditions clearly includes those institutions and ideologies arguing for women's rights.

Singaporean women require a blueprint that will involve working with and forging bonds with ourselves: we need to recognise the gossamer threads we may desire are only a web of someone else's construction, a trap. We must start with the basics: ourselves, and an understanding of our real power as fully equal citizens of the nation we belong to and care about. Equality does not come from a top-down granting of concessions. Equality is a text built into our constitution. If this is given primacy, what sort of voice will we speak with, and what sort of world will we reproduce? It is not a question for one individual to answer, certainly; but it is a necessary question, a crucial beginning by which the potential power of the resource rich middle-class woman can be used to allow her class to come into its own. The reasons for this are simple: the contemporary Singapore woman has the potential to ensure the growth and development of the truly civil society to which both middle-class men and women in Singapore aspire.

NOTES

1 For four very special, insuppressible women: Chung Yuen Kay, Joan Bungar, Falaq Kagda and Stephanie Sim.

2 This paper has been particularly difficult. Apart from drawing my data from my field experience in Singapore and primary documentary sources, the

insights that I bring to bear upon the data cannot be pried from my experiences as a woman living in Singapore today. This includes my work as a feminist here. It is the presence of the insights from the latter that cause me particular anxiety. I grappled long and hard with what I have had to say. Indeed, in the first drafts of this paper, I decided to barely make reference to some of the most important points – in my opinion – that are now a part of this paper.

3 This reflects the question that Robison and Goodman (1996: 9) posed.

4 For greater details on the economic history of Singapore see Chia (1989).

5 In an examination of statistical data available for the middle class of two public housing estates in Singapore, Leong (1995) lists these factors as comprising the fields of life experiences that those Singaporeans who labelled themselves as 'middle class' were referring to. Leong also noted that in this respect no one factor dominated. Thus, for example, the identification with middle class was certain if a person lived in a particular type of apartment. But those who do not live in such apartments would use other means by which their sense of being of the middle class could be achieved.

6 This was given clear voice in a forum on the role of intellectuals in contemporary Singapore, that was organised by the editors of *Commentary*, the National University of Singapore Society's Journal. As one of the participants of the forum, Daren Tang, stated: '. . . for us, material pursuits take up most energy. This is tied to the fact that the fear people feel has been subsumed into the urge for material pursuits. All political and intellectual energies are directed towards that end. I don't know how entrenched these fears are, but if this is removed, in some ways people might be more willing to channel their energy towards other materialistic activities' (*Commentary* 1993: 59–60).

7 A fuller treatment of the historical development of this ideology is in PuruShotam (1993).

8 PuruShotam (1993: 17–20).

9 People's Action Party 1959 (Part 2), 17–19.

10 One of the central tenets of PAP rule in Singapore rests on the paradigm that Singapore is a multiracial society, constituted by four main races. These are defined as the 'Chinese', the 'Malay', the 'Indian' and the 'Other'. These biological differentiations between these groups, it is further assumed, are at the root of their sociocultural differences. Accordingly, to be 'Chinese' for instance is to acknowledge the biologically given social and cultural specificities that makes one properly 'Chinese'. Thus all real Chinese should learn to speak their officially defined mother tongue, Mandarin. An elaborated discussion of this is found in PuruShotam, forthcoming.

11 See Wong and Leong (1993) and Eng Wee Ling (1993).

12 I have delineated the various choices women have in this respect in PuruShotam (1992).

13 A detailed explication of this in terms of the politics of gender that this engenders is found in PuruShotam (1995b).

14 However, it seems clear to me that a complex of orientations, largely the feminist with the anti-feminist even, can and does exist outside of Singapore society too.

15 There are two other aspects in this speech that must be noted. First, Lee referred to his fundamental belief in research that ascertained that people are constituted of 80 per cent nature and 20 per cent nurture (Lee Kuan Yew

1983). He did not spell out the sex/gender connection in this. But it is imperative that we bear in mind the idea of genetic differences between males and females that is embedded in this kind of sociobiological argumentation. Second, the tactic of the government approach to the problem of women, as identified by them, is revealed here. Women need 'incentives' – the soft approach – to rectify the social problem that they are and could continue to be. Incentives to become 'good' women, I would argue, appeal to women to deliberate upon the normal and so moral thing women should be doing. This is compounded by the appeal that if women do not do the right thing as women, then 'our economy will falter, the administration will suffer, and the society will decline' (Lee Kuan Yew 1983). The limits of what is possible for women are to be placed on them only because the stakes are so high. Needless to say these very same stakes are what has enabled the continuation of upward social and economic mobility. The limits of what is possible for women are normal and moral; and are about the possibility, otherwise, of all of us together falling from the level we have been brought to.

16 See Chua Beng Hunt (1995: 184–202).

BIBLIOGRAPHY

Aijaz Ahmad (1992) 'Orientalism and After: Ambivalence and Metropolitan Location in the Work of Edward Said', in *Theory: Classes, Nations, Literature*, London and New York: Verso.

Asia Magazine (1995) 'Asia Blues', 2–4 June, 33 (K-17): 9–12.

Bellah, R. N., Madsen, R., Sullivan, W. M., Swidler, A. and Tipton, S. M. (1986) *Habits of the Heart: Individualism and Commitment in American Life*, New York: Perennial Library.

Business Times (1990a) '10,500 Women May Gain From Rebates', 3 March.

—— (1990b) 'Latest Tax Incentives a Boon to Young Mothers', 6 March.

—— (1990c) '10,500 Women May Gain From Rebates', 7 March.

—— (1990d) 'Call to Extend Procreation Incentives', 13 March.

—— (1993a) 'PM Goh Plans To Double Number of Women MPs by 1996', 14 June.

—— (1993b) 'PM Upbeat about Economy Over the Next Five to Ten Years', 14 June.

—— (1994) 'Strong Family Values Needed to Ensure Success: PM. Economic Policies Alone Not Enough to See Singapore Through', 22 August.

Chua, Beng Huat (1995) *Communitarian Ideology and Democracy in Singapore*, London: Routledge.

Chia, Siow Yue (1989) 'The PAP and the Structuring of the Political System', in K. Singh Sandhu and P. Wheatley (eds) *Management of Success: Moulding of Modern Singapore*, Singapore: ISEAS.

Donzelot, J. (1979) *The Policing of Families*. New York: Pantheon Books.

Ehrenreich, B. (1989) *Fear of Falling: The Inner Life of the Middle Class*, New York: Pantheon Books.

Eng Wee Ling (1993) *A Woman's Place: The Story of Singapore*, Singapore: Times Editions.

Foucault, M. (1972) *The Archaeology of Knowledge and the Discourse on Language*, New York: Pantheon Books.

—— (1977) *Discipline and Punish: The Birth of the Prison*, New York: Vintage Books.

Garfinkel, H. (1967) *Studies In Ethnomethodology*, Cambridge: Polity Press.

Goh Chok Tong (1993) 'Guarding the Sacred Institutions of Marriage and Family', in *Speeches: A Bi-Monthly Selection of Ministerial Speeches*, May–June: 28–33.

Housing and Development Board (1993/4) *Housing and Development Board Annual Report*, Singapore: HDB.

Jones, D. M. and Brown, D. (1994) 'Singapore and the Myth of the Liberalizing Middle Class', *The Pacific Review* 7(1): 80–7.

Lee Kuan Yew (1983) 'Talent for the Future', *Strait Times*, 15 August.

Leong Choon Heng (1995) *The Construction of a Contented and Cautious Middle Class*, paper presented at the International Conference on East Asian Middle Classes and National Development in Comparative Perspective, Institute of Ethnology, Academia Sinica, Taipei, Taiwan.

Mernissi, F. (1993) *Islam and Democracy: Fear of the Modern World*, London: Virago.

Mohanty, C. T. (1991a) 'Introduction: Cartographies of Struggle: Third World Women and the Politics of Feminism', in C. T. Mohanty, A. Russo and L. Torres (eds) *Third World Women and The Politics of Feminism*, Bloomington and Indianapolis: Indiana University Press.

—— (1991b) 'Under Western Eyes: Feminist Scholarship and Colonial Discourses', in C. T. Mohanty, A. Russo and L. Torres (eds) *Third World Women and the Politics of Feminism*, Bloomington and Indianapolis: Indiana University Press.

PuruShotam, N. (1992) 'Woman and Knowledge/Power: Notes on the Singaporean Dilemma', in Ban Kah Choon, A. Pakir and Tong Chee Kiong (eds) *Imagining Singapore*, Singapore: Times Academic Press.

—— (1993) 'The Normal Family: A Study of Ideological Reformulations Concerning the Family in Singapore', draft paper, presented at the Third Malaysia-Singapore Forum, National University of Singapore, Singapore.

—— (1995a) 'What is "The Asian Family"? Glimpses of the Past, Concerns for the Present, Relevance for the Future', *Awareness* 2, May.

—— (1995b) 'Not Mad Enough. Gender in Singapore Theatre', (unpublished working draft).

Robison, R. and Goodman, D. S. G. (1996) *The New Rich in Asia: Mobile Phones, McDonalds and Middle-class Revolution*, London: Routledge.

Singam, C. (1993) 'The Many Faces of AWARE', *Awareness: A Journal of the Association of Women for Action and Research*, 1(1): 31–7.

Straits Times (1983) 'Talent For the Future. Prepared Text of the PM, Mr. Lee Kuan Yew's Speech at the National Day Rally Last Night', 15 August.

—— (1990a) 'New Tax Incentives to Encourage Procreation. Latest Move Aims to Sustain Earlier Growth. Population Planning Unit's Director Explains Rationale Behind It', 8 March.

—— (1990b) 'Individual Tax Incentives. Why Only Younger Mums Qualify for Second-Child Rebate', 14 March.

—— (1993a) 'Medical benefits May Cover Civil Servants' Families', 12 March.

—— (1993b) 'PM's target: 6 Women in Parliament by 1996', 14 June.

—— (1993c) 'Benefits For Female Civil Servants Unchanged', 12 November.

—— (1993d) 'Profile of the Singapore Woman', 24 November.

—— (1993e) 'Woman's Place in the House', 11 December.

—— (1994a) 'First ASEAN Women Leaders' Forum. Singapore Women Stay Out of Politics by Choice: Yuhua MP. They Value Family and Child Care More Than Their Own Advancement', 26 January.

—— (1994b) 'PM's National Day Rally Speech. Three Lessons for Singapore', 22 August.

—— (1994c) 'Concern Over 'Anti-Women' Policies in PM Goh's Speech', 28 August 1994.

—— (1994d) 'See PM's N-Day Speech in 'Wider Context'. Be Less Emotional, Aline Tells Women', 3 September.

—— (1994e) 'Fewer Kids of Graduate Mums Could Lower Society's IQ Levels', 3 September.

—— (1994f) 'N-Day Rally Speech Was Pro-family, says PM', 8 September.

—— (1994g) 'Gender Roles: Debate Hotting Up', 10 September.

—— (1994h) 'Women and Public Policy', 24 December.

Sunday Times (1993) 'Women Are Bigger Going By Their Bras', 13 June.

—— (1994) 'Women's Groups to Discuss Medical Benefits with Government: Talks Will Take Place Behind Closed Doors', 13 February.

Wang Look Fung and Teo, N. (1993) 'Public Life and Leadership', in A.K. Wong and Leong Wai Kum (eds) *Singapore Women: Three Decades of Change*, Singapore: Times Academic Press: 284–317.

Wong, A. K. and Yeh, S. H. K. (1985) *Housing a Nation: 25 Years of Public Housing in Singapore*, Singapore: Maruzen Asia for HDB.

Wong, A. K., (1993) 'Singapore Women: An Overview', in A. K. Wong and Leong Wai Kum (eds) *Singapore Women: Three Decades of Change*, Singapore: Times Academic Press: 1–19.

6 'Flower vase and housewife'

Women and consumerism in post-Mao China[1]

Beverley Hooper

In March 1992, China's national women's newspaper complained that the country's burgeoning advertising industry was casting women in two contrasting roles, both of which had adverse implications for women's lives in modernising China:

> [There is] the open 'modern flower vase' type, luxuriously adorned and bejewelled, proponent of advanced consumerism' . . . [and] there is the traditional virtuous wife and good mother who is generally associated with kitchen utensils, washing machines, refrigerators, and other consumer goods related to housework.
>
> (*Zhongguo funü bao*, 20 March 1992: 3)[2]

Starting from a situation of imposed austerity and asexual representations at the end of the Mao era in 1976, post-Mao China presents a striking case study of the creation of a gendered consumer culture. This culture is only beginning to emerge, but women are already being utilised to create and manipulate personal desires, both as consumers and as sexualised objects of consumption.[3] This chapter examines the 'flower vase and housewife' roles currently ascribed to women in the context of China's modernisation, particularly the growth of a consumer society and culture set against reduced state control over people's everyday lives.[4]

The creation of a consumer society has been central to China's recent economic development. Per capita material consumption has risen at an average annual rate of 7 per cent since the inauguration of the post-Mao economic reforms in 1978, taking China from a state-controlled economy towards a market economy, somewhat euphemistically labelled the 'socialist market economy'. For most of the post-Mao era, China has had the highest growth rate in Asia, with GDP annual growth averaging 9 per cent. Annual per capita income has more than doubled. While it still stands officially at only $US655, one of the lowest figures in Asia, a more indicative income figure is the Purchasing Power Parity amount of $US3,945 (*Asiaweek* 24 October 1996: 67).[5]

Per capita statistics, however, give little indication of the increasing affluence and spending power of some sectors of the Chinese population, especially those living in urban areas, as income disparities increase. In addition to over one million households in the *yuan* millionaire bracket (approximately $US125,000), China has an expanding middle class like other industrialising Asian countries. By 1994 an estimated 4.3 million Chinese, admittedly still a tiny proportion of the population, were estimated to earn over 30,000 *yuan* ($US3,750) per annum, enough to allow people to enjoy many of the benefits offered by China's modernising society. Aspiring to the new middle classes were something over 100 million people with an annual income of more than $US1,000, a figure estimated to reach 270 million by the year 2000 (*South China Morning Post* 11 October 1994).

The government itself largely equates the achievement of a 'well off society' with what it terms a 'relatively comfortable life' (*xiaokang*). This includes 'raising the level of personal consumption' as well as improving people's working environment and housing (Zhu Qingfang 1993). In the mid-1970s, at the end of the Mao era, the 'three consumer desirables' were a transistor radio, a bicycle and a sewing machine. During the subsequent two decades, China followed a changing consumer goods 'wish list' pattern common to most developing Asian societies (Freedman 1972; Fukutake 1982). A range of goods – particularly television sets, refrigerators and washing machines – moved through the 'status symbol' category to become everyday household possessions, at least in urban areas.[6] By the 1990s, the 'three general desirables' were a video, CD player and air conditioner, while the 'three-super-products' – establishing a new level of consumer aspirations – had become a telephone, privately owned apartment and car (*Zhongguo qingnian* March 1993: 8–9; also Chan and Lin, 1992). Whereas the 'three desirables' of the mid-1970s were virtually the only consumer goods available, by the 1990s they represented merely the tip of a consumer goods iceberg.

According to a late 1994 report from DRI/McGraw-Hill, China's consumer market, already the second largest in Asia after Japan, will be the fastest growing in the world during the decade 1993–2003, expanding at an average annual rate of 7.5 per cent. Total expenditure on consumption is expected to treble from $US261 billion to $US743 billion. Almost completely isolated from the international market 20 years ago, China is now proving irresistible to foreign investors and producers. The level of foreign investment in China increased more than tenfold in the decade 1983–93. The market for imported luxury products might be small in population percentage terms, but 'it translates into millions of affluent customers' (*South China Morning Post* 11 October 1994).

While China's pattern of burgeoning consumerism and increasing integration into the global economy is a familiar one, what distinguishes China from many countries, though not from those undergoing a similar transition from socialism, is the dramatic change in the country's ideological environment. During the decade immediately preceding the economic reforms of the late 1970s, China had not only a low level of consumption but a virtual cult of austerity in an officially sponsored atmosphere of extreme self-denial (Hooper 1979). Since the 1980s this cult of austerity has given way to one of consumption, encouraged not just by Chinese and foreign producers but also by the Chinese government. As an early examination of Chinese advertising expressed it: '[l]uxury' goods have changed from being hated symbols of decadent capitalism to being touted as consumption incentives for those who work hard and show initiative' (Tse *et al.* 1989: 457).

Although most Chinese people probably paid little more than lip service to the austerity cult, manufacturers and trading companies have undoubtedly seen a need to educate the public to become 'modern consumers' rather than pursuing the more traditional behaviour of saving or having more leisure (ibid.; Campbell 1987). Advertising in China grew from zero at the end of the Mao era to over 30,000 companies and an annual turnover of more than $US1.2 billion in 1994 (*Shenzhou xueren* 23 June 1995). It has created a highly visible culture of consumption, introducing Chinese people to the world of personal desires through its images of the good life, beauty and fulfilment. While both sexes have been caught up in these developments, they have had distinctive implications for Chinese women.

RECREATING FEMININITY: THE CHINESE 'FLOWER VASE'

> '[Beauty contests] look upon women as nothing more than flower vases.
>
> (Chinese Women's Federation, reported in *Zhongguo funü bao*, 5 July 1993: 1)

One of the most visible manifestations of the growth of consumerism in China, set against the decline of state control, has been the recreation and commercialisation of 'femininity'. The minimal emphasis on gender distinctiveness ever since the 1949 communist revolution, a feature characteristic of most post-revolutionary socialist societies, reached its peak during the Cultural Revolution decade 1966–76. While to the keen observer the occasional 'clinched-in waist' and 'open gaze' continued to mark the woman's image as feminine, China probably came closer than virtually any other society in history to removing previous constructions of femininity. Baggy cotton trousers and jackets, which gave little indication of the female form, were combined with plain hairstyles (either plaits or 'pudding basin' haircuts) and fresh-scrubbed faces free of make-up (Fig. 6.1). Just as pervasive was the defeminising of body language, something that struck me even more than women's clothing when I lived in China in the mid-1970s (Hooper 1979).[7] The degendered appearance and behaviour of Chinese women had a strong and positive impression on some Western women visiting China during the early and mid 1970s: 'The first images that flash past the bus windows [are] simply dressed men and women free of class and sexist distinctions . . . the street scenes are drab, if dignified, largely for lack of decorative women' (Barrett 1973).

There is little doubt, however, that women's defeminised appearance and behaviour were ideologically imposed rather than universally popular, particularly amongst young women. Inside the women's dormitories at Beijing University, for example, female students discarded their outer grey or blue cotton layers to reveal brightly patterned long underwear, sweaters or shirts, often made by their mothers from materials intended for little girls' clothing. The speed with which Chinese women gave up their baggy cotton and pudding-basin hairstyles as soon as the barriers were lifted contradicted any notion that the stringencies, however much they might have impressed Western visitors, were welcomed.[8]

The post-Mao era has seen the recreation of 'femininity' in all the manifestations described by Brownmiller (1984), including the construction of distinctive female characteristics, ranging from the body, hair and clothing to voice, skin and movement.[9] This has included not just official statements about 'innate female characteristics' but, more visibly, the development in the media and especially in the consumer market of 'feminine' representations. Soon after Mao's death in late 1976, waved hair, skirts and a touch of lipstick reappeared. These were followed, from the early to the mid-1980s, by make-up, jewellery, and attention to the female form through fitted or 'revealing' clothing (Hooper 1985). The period since the mid-1980s has seen the emergence of modern (and modernised) Chinese woman, gradually drawing closer to her Taiwanese or Hong Kong counterpart. The changes can be read-

Figure 6.1 The female image: 1976

ily traced in the representation of women in popular Chinese magazines, ranging from women's and youth publications to fashion and television magazines. Apart from clothing and make-up, a striking feature of these representations is the shift in body language from being virtually asexual to obviously 'female': variously demure, coy, provocative and seductive (Fig. 6.2).

The early stage of the process can be seen as a return to the situation during less rigid periods of the communist era, what one might term 'normality' socialist-style. But over the past 15 years or so there has

Figure 6.2 The female image: 1986

been a shift towards fully fledged consumerised femininity. One of the most striking features of China's burgeoning consumerism has been the manner in which women (invariably glamorous young women) have increasingly been utilised for commercial purposes, particularly by China's fledgling advertising industry.[10] It was the complete lack of the commercial exploitation of women that so impressed some Western women in the 1970s. As visiting American actress Shirley Maclaine expressed it, there was 'no commercial exploitation of sex in order to sell soap, perfume, soft drinks, or cars' (Maclaine 1976: 159). Within less than a decade of Maclaine's statement, Chinese women were being widely featured in advertisements – on television, on street billboards and in magazines.

As in many countries, glamorous models have been used for a wide range of consumer products aimed not just at women but also at the more general market. Since the early 1980s the common Western

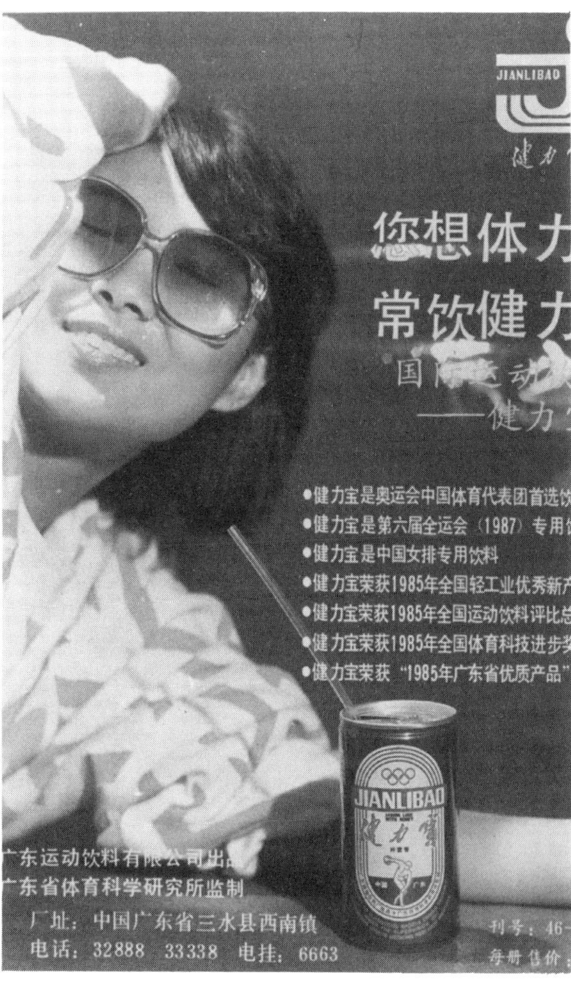

Figure 6.3 Advertising consumer products

advertisement of seductive female draped over expensive car has had its Chinese equivalent in advertisements for motorbikes as well as for the most desirable consumer goods: colour television sets, VCRs and, perhaps above all, bedroom suites. Upmarket soft drinks like *Jianlibao* and beers such as *Princess* are also associated with young glamorous women (Fig. 6.3). The 'female-specific' market is equally pervasive, with advertisements offering women almost the full international, as well as local, range of beautifying and age-defying cosmetics (Fig. 6.4).

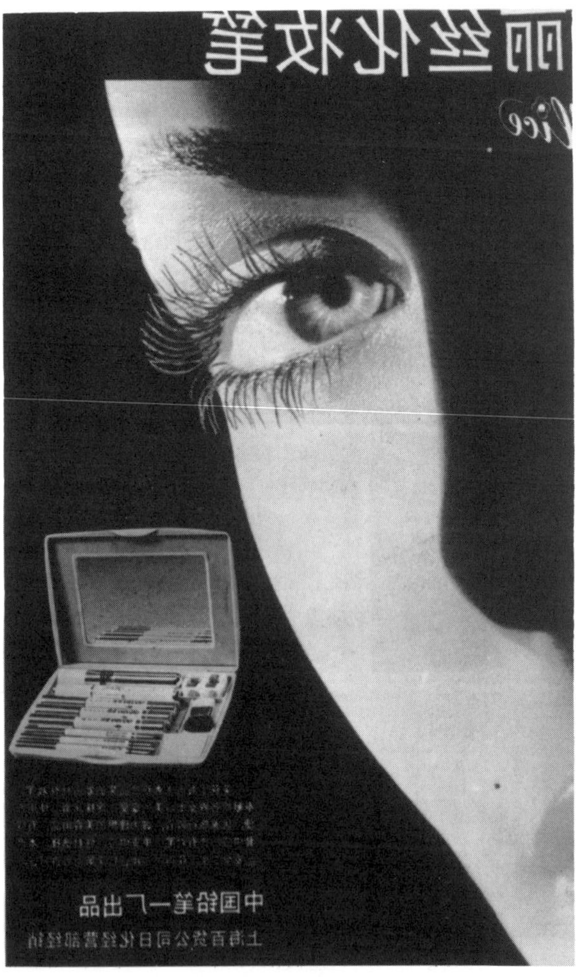

Figure 6.4 Advertising female-specific products

Since the early 1980s, female models have also been widely used as magazine cover-girls in the keen competition that has developed in China's flourishing magazine market: not just for women's and film magazines but also for general interest magazines ranging from *Culture and Life* to *Family Doctor* and – more especially – the large range of youth magazines. As early as 1982 an official survey reported that over

Figure 6.5 The Chinese cover-girl

25 per cent of a selection of popular magazines had 'pin-up girls' (something of an exaggeration at the time) on their covers (NCNA, 25 March 1982); by the mid-1980s the proportion was more like 50 per cent. Sometimes the cover-girl and the consumer product come together in an advertisement, featured as a magazine cover, for cosmetics or a domestic appliance (Fig. 6.5).

The most blatant and visible use of women for commercial purposes, however, has been for the lucrative annual calendar market. From the early 1980s attractive young women wearing Western-style fashions – still extremely conservative by Western standards – were being featured on these calendars. By the 1990s, the calendars had become much larger, glossier and more revealing, resembling Western pin-ups of the 1950s or 1960s (Fig. 6.6). With a different female for each month or two-month period and costing up to 35 *yuan* (over a day's average urban wage) the calendars came to dominate the New Year gift calendar markets, interrupted only by the occasional landscape or fluffy kitten calendar. Indeed, a glossy half-dressed calendar model 'brightens up', as one of my Chinese colleagues put it, many an otherwise very conservative academic's apartment – and even office.

It would be wrong to see Chinese women merely as passive recipients of China's expanding consumer culture. Indeed, the increasingly diverse, gendered consumer market has created substantial opportunities for women – particularly attractive young women – that simply did not exist in the Mao era. China's bevy of top models, female fashion designers and boutique owners have reaped both public recognition and financial rewards. They are the subject of articles about those 'who've made it' in glossy magazines like *Modern Life* and the Chinese edition of *Elle* where, in contrast to their spanner-waving predecessors of *China Reconstructs* 20 years ago, they are the female role models for – and symbols of – China's leap into modernity. Along with their male companions, they frequent the restaurants and bars of the Palace Hotel in Beijing (part of the Peninsula group), the Portman complex in Shanghai, and the most expensive karaoke clubs. They shop in the exclusive boutiques, buy top-brand face creams that cost more than a week's average wage, and live in a manner unimagined by their parents.

Disquiet about the new feminised glamour images – so far as it exists – has come mainly from the Women's Federation (the official women's movement), female academics and occasionally university students. Although the Federation's own magazines[11] have regularly featured glamorous cover-girls and advertisements for everything from skin-whitening cream to bust improvers, it has also argued for the

Figure 6.6 The Chinese calendar girl

monitoring of advertisements under China's new Advertising Law. A front-page article in the national economic newspaper, for example, reported on its discussions with the Bureau of Industry and Commerce and appealed for advertisers to pay respect to women. The article complained that some advertisements give publicity to feminine images of 'coquetry and gaudiness', are in poor taste and use sexy women's images for advertisements which are nothing to do with women and are discriminatory (*Jingji ribao* 22 February 1995: 1).

The glamour issue provoking the greatest opposition to date has been the holding of beauty contests. Starting off in the mid-1980s with euphemistic titles such as a 'charms of youth contest' and a 'flowers of the nation contest', the beauty contest was, by the early 1990s, 'labeled for what it was' (*China Today* February 1994: 41). Contests have meant big profits, as well as advertising opportunities, for sponsors and organisers. In one contest advertising sponsors reportedly paid 1.4 million *yuan* (over $US160,000); the organisers' profits, after paying costs, amounted to some 500,000 *yuan* (over $60,000). For young women the contests represent the most competitive face of the glamour industry, promising hoped-for fame and at least instant wealth; on some occasions the first prize has been more than an average person earns in a life time.

The holding of beauty contests, together with the large amount of money involved and the propensity for scandal and corruption, has provoked substantial criticism. 'A fever has developed for watching half-clad pretty young women pose in public,' one magazine complained in early 1994 (*China Today* February 1994: 41). Some women university students have become quite vocal in their opposition. A planned contest at Beijing University, the nation's most prestigious tertiary institution, was largely boycotted by potential entrants, attracting only thirteen students, and branded the 'epitome of sexism' by others (*China Daily* 6 May 1993: 4). Despite the use of glamour in its own magazines, the Women's Federation has stated categorically that its policy towards beauty contests is that of the 'four nots': it will not approve, not support, not organise and not participate in beauty contests (*Zhongguo funü bao* 5 July 1993: 1) .

A WOMAN'S WORLD: CREATING THE CHINESE HOUSEWIFE

> 'I have a dream: that women will return to the home'
>
> (*Xiandai huabao* June 1994: 84)

The creation of the Chinese housewife has been a major feature of changing public discourse in the post-Mao era, paralleling the revival of femininity. The housewife role, or at least women's household labour, never actually disappeared after the communist revolution, even though the official emphasis was on women's role in the public sphere in accordance with Engels' prescription for the achievement of gender equality.

While women's earning power undoubtedly improved their position within the household to some extent, any notion that their entry into the workforce would lead to changed power relations in domestic life, as some socialists anticipated, was not borne out. Post-revolutionary China fitted the pattern common to socialist states; in Catherine MacKinnon's words: 'Women become as free as men to work outside the home while men remain free from work within it' (MacKinnon 1989: 10).[12]

Although the Women's Federation and women's congresses urged men to 'help with household chores', at least until the anticipated socialisation of domestic labour eventuated, there is little evidence to suggest that even this became the actual situation. Women's entry into the paid workforce simply resulted in the 'double burden' as in the Soviet Union and other socialist societies and most capitalist countries (Molyneux 1981; MacKinnon 1989). Following her interviews in China in 1980, just four years after Mao's death, anthropologist Margery Wolf stated: 'There was a theme of constant weariness. As one woman put it, "Rush in the morning, stand in line at noon, headache in the afternoon, angry in the evening". . . . None of the men I talked with alluded to this' (Wolf 1985: 77). Women's heavy domestic burden was borne out by surveys. In the early 1980s urban Chinese women, still lacking basic labour-saving devices, spent over twice as long on average on household chores as their US and French counterparts (Wang and Li 1982).

The Chinese housewife did, however, largely disappear from public discourse, replaced by the active participant in production. Women were portrayed as workers, peasants, and less often as professionals and officials, contributing to the building of 'new China', if necessary at the expense of their personal lives. Although the gender division of labour in the workforce never completely broke down in practice (Hooper 1979; Andors 1983), 'new Chinese woman' was featured in a variety of traditionally male-dominated occupations, demonstrating the truth of the Maoist slogans that 'women hold up half of heaven' and 'whatever a man can do, a woman can do too' (Fig. 6.7).

If the Chinese housewife scarcely existed in public discourse at the end of the Mao era, within a few years she had emerged with a vengeance, albeit in 'modern' consumerised mode. Women's magazines, an important component of the expanding magazine market, began creating a culture of domesticity with a focus on cooking, home dressmaking and child care, as well as on fashion and personal life. By the late 1980s the contents of magazines differed little from the more 'traditional' mainstream women's magazines in Western countries (Ferguson 1985; Winship 1987). A rash of booklets advised women on how to prepare interesting meals, the most effective ways of doing housework and, as the range of domestic appliances increased, how best to utilise the latest labour-saving devices.

The emergence of the Chinese housewife, like that of female glamour, has been particularly visible in advertising: whether in magazines, on billboards or most strikingly in television commercials. The rapidly growing home appliance market, in particular, has linked women with the full range of activities in the domestic sphere: from cleaning and cooking to mothering (Fig. 6.8). A magazine advertisement for the *Chunhua* (Spring Flower) vacuum cleaner, for example, specifically pro-

Figure 6.7 'New Chinese Woman'

claims the product as 'the housewife's good helper'. Other advertisements feature attractive women either using, or simply admiring, refrigerators, blenders and rice cookers, as well as baby foods, talcum powder and baby oil. Advertisements such as 'I love Little Swan' (a brand of washing machine) imply a personal relationship between the housewife (invariably portrayed as young and glamorous) and the product.

Figure 6.8 Advertising domestic appliances

The domestic images of Chinese women might have been anticipated as an accompaniment to the early growth of consumerism (in particular the increasing availability of domestic appliances) and especially of advertising, paralleling developments in most industrialising Asian countries and elsewhere (Hamadan 1987; Sharma *et al.* 1987). Images may well become more diverse as incomes rise and the professional women's market is seen to warrant distinctive commercial targeting, as Krishna Sen demonstrates for Indonesia in Chapter 2. This shift has been the pattern in Western countries over the past two decades, with a 'lessening of advertising images showing women in the home or in family settings, and an increase in the number of women portrayed in work roles' (Busby and Leichty 1995; also Ferguson *et al.* 1990; c.f. Courtney and Whipple 1983). China has gone through a rather different process; the initial shift from domestic (and glamour) roles to work roles took place in accordance with the ideological prescriptions of socialist revolution; now women are being portrayed substantially in domestic (and glamour) roles to match the initial development of capitalist-style consumerism.

Just as the singular work-role images of Chinese women during the Cultural Revolution ignored women's continuing domestic roles, so too do the current domestic images largely ignore their working role: around 90 per cent of women between the ages of 20 and 40, and over 80 per cent of women between 40 and 50, are in the paid workforce.[13] The creation of female domestic stereotypes may well be reinforcing women's responsibility for domestic chores. Indeed, the double burden is one of the major sources of complaints by women and of discussion in women's magazines. In a feature entitled 'What do professional women think?' published in March 1994, the major national women's magazine reported on replies to 200 letters sent to professional women asking 'what are your greatest needs?':

> Many complain in their letters that they are under the pressure of the double burden – career and family . . . Most women say they do not get enough sleep and need understanding and support.
>
> (*Zhongguo funü* March 1994: 12)

As one senior woman official expressed it: 'I don't have any time for myself. My working hours belong to my seniors and fellow-workers. My time outside work belongs to my husband and children' (ibid.).

The domestic burden for Chinese women, even middle-class professional women, is in some ways more comparable to industrialised Western countries than to those Asian countries where huge income differentials enable most professional women to have one or more full-time maids to take care of the household chores and look after young children. Although the employment of 'nannies' (normally young women from rural areas) has increased over the past 10 years or so in China, it is still the exception rather than the rule for urban professional women.

Given the Chinese state's continuing commitment to gender equality and even its periodic reiteration that the basic road to that equality is through participation in the paid workforce, one might have expected some official criticism of the domestic representation of Chinese women. This has not been the case. Indeed, the creation of the Chinese housewife in the media and advertising has been paralleled by a changing official construction of gender by the state. Starting as early as 1978–79, women have been officially allocated a largely secondary and supportive working role in customarily 'female' occupations 'in the textile, sewing and food industries, in commercial departments and service trades as well as in professions involved with education, culture and hygiene' (*Hongqi* March 1979: 90). The official reason is their 'other responsibilities': the fact that they 'have to spend a considerable portion of their time and energy looking after children and doing housework' (ibid.; also *Women of China* July 1990: 10). Essentially, then, the post-Mao Chinese state has accepted the existence of women's 'double burden'. The promised 'socialisation of domestic labour' has not eventuated and, while men might 'help' with household chores, there is no suggestion that women's role in the paid workforce should be matched by an equivalent male role in the domestic sphere.

Since the early 1980s, the Chinese state has faced the task of reconciling its renewed emphasis on women's domestic role with the fact that most women are in the paid workforce. Those few women who *have* achieved prominent positions are held up for emulation not so much because of their professional achievements but because of their success in juggling the role of working woman and housewife; *shuang jiantiao* (carrying on both shoulders) is praiseworthy rather than a 'double burden'. A characteristic article in *Women of China* on well-known woman official Yuan Fenglan, then mayor of Guilin, stressed that despite her heavy responsibilities she had 'a very happy family. . . . Anyone familiar with her would praise her as a paragon of a wife and mother' (*Women of China* November 1992: 4–5).[14]

Why has this shift in official ideology occurred at a time when one might have expected a focus on women's professional and working role – utilising the best available talent – as part of China's overall modernisation effort? The shift fits, albeit in more extreme form, the pattern apparent throughout the post-revolutionary era: that women have been drawn into and taken out of the workforce according to the current economic situation or official strategy (Andors 1983). Although the ideology of 'full employment' in socialist societies has had some cushioning effect, this pattern is as much a feature of socialist as of the capitalist economies which have been the focus of most attention. Since the late 1970s, China's shift towards a market economy, with associated economic rationalisation and the growth of unemployment (Feng 1991; Jefferson and Rawski 1992), has been paralleled by a focus on women's domestic rather than their working role. Once again, women have been considered less 'desirable' employees than men because of their presumed gender-specific psychological makeup, and because their reproductive role means they will need maternity leave and child care facilities and, allegedly, will be less committed to their jobs than are men (Hooper 1984: 324–5; Honig and Hershatter 1988: 13–19).

The mounting unemployment problem has led to frequent suggestions, by newspaper columnists and in general conversation, that married women should 'return home'[15] to devote their time to household and family responsibilities, thereby making more jobs available to men. This suggestion, familiar in many countries experiencing unemployment, appears incongruous in a society which still officially cites Engels' formula for gender equality. The 'return home' movement has been the subject of widespread debate in China since the early 1980s.[16] From the start, strong opposition came from the Women's Federation which argued that such suggestions were contrary to basic socialist policy and anathema to the achievement of male–female equality. Perhaps its most effective argument, though, was the experience of other countries, whether socialist or capitalist, where the participation of women in the workforce reduced the birth rate. This argument was designed to appeal to economic planners wrestling with the population problem, in particular through establishing the one-child policy, as well as with unemployment (Interview Zheng Renyang 1982; also *Beijing Review* 38, 1983: 15).[17] For all the opposition, the issue re-emerged as a topic of wide-ranging debate in the early 1990s. With urban unemployment now forecast to reach 7.4 per cent by the year 2000, and the 'surplus' labour force in rural areas expected to rise to a mammoth 137 million, it is likely that the debate will become even more intense (*South China Morning Post* 13 January 1996).

A second version of the 'return home' movement has emerged with China's increasing affluence and growth of middle-class values: the idea of the 'middle-class housewife'. The non-working wife is beginning to take her place along with the other trappings of relative affluence: a 'modern' apartment with appropriate interior fittings and domestic appliances, fashionable clothing, membership of a health club, and so on. An article in *Xiandai huabao* (*Modern Magazine*), a glossy Guangzhou (Canton) publication sold in up-market hotels and shopping plazas, clearly spelled out the argument (at least in the eyes of some middle-class men) for the creation of the middle-class housewife. The division of labour, the male author stated, would enable the man to devote his full effort to his work while his wife managed the household. In the evenings both would be able to relax and enjoy each other's company. 'The man would be the ship braving the wind and waves; the woman the peaceful harbour' (*Xiandai huabao* June 1994: 84).

Given the government's continuing official adherence, even as lip service, to the socialist prescription for gender equality, the issue is a contentious one. In this case there was a note at the end of the article stating that the opinion of the author did not represent that of the magazine. The magazine's willingness to publish the article was a sign that the issue had become a matter of public discussion and that the non-working housewife was, indeed, becoming an everyday reality. As yet there is little quantitative information available on the phenomenon which is currently being researched by the Beijing Women's Studies Association as one of the social effects of China's economic development. With increasing affluence, at least on the part of some, the middle-class Chinese housewife may well become a major phenomenon by the end of the century.

THE HOMOGENISATION OF GENDERED CONSUMER CULTURE?

It would be easy to see the gendered aspects of China's consumer culture simply as catching up with, and beginning to run parallel with, developments in other countries as they become part of a heavily Western-influenced global cultural economy. How far is this global culture simply being appropriated by China's modernising society and how far is it being integrated into, and perhaps partially transformed within, an environment which currently combines a nascent market economy with some resurgence of non-Western (Confucian) cultural values?

On the one hand, Chinese women seem to be sharing with many of their counterparts elsewhere in Asia a 'bottomless appetite . . . for things Western' (Appadurai 1990: 3). The status symbols for the 'modern' Chinese woman are those of the international market; the designer label syndrome is becoming as striking in Shanghai or Beijing as it is in Singapore or Hong Kong. While not confined to the female market, it is this market that dominates the fashion scene. Chinese women are acutely conscious of the status ranking of products: from Pierre Cardin (the first big designer label to arrive in China), Gucci and Madame Rochas, available in the boutiques of the top international hotels and the new mega shopping plazas in the major cities, through Stefanel, Benetton, Shiseido and Revlon, down to the increasingly ubiquitous Oil of Ulan and Ponds dry skin cream sold in almost every small store. A Gucci handbag, Lancôme make-up kit or bottle of the incongruously named Opium perfume might each cost more than a week's average salary but, as one magazine expressed it, they are 'symbols of both social status and personal taste' (*China Today* February 1994: 13). For the moment, it seems, the status symbols of global capitalist consumerism are winning out in what Appadurai has called the 'tension between cultural homogenisation and cultural heterogenisation' (1990: 3).

But China's attitude to Western culture has long been an ambivalent one. From the beginnings of modern contact in the mid-nineteenth century, educated urban Chinese at various times both embraced and resisted Western culture. Western music, clothing and social behaviour were both adopted as an integral part of becoming 'modern', and strongly resisted in the quest to become an assertively independent nation. After almost 30 years of virtual isolation from Western culture, that love/hate attitude has re-emerged, complicated by a change in the economic power balance. While China is once again a target for Western and Japanese investment and products, the country is no longer the 'semi-colony' of the nineteenth and early twentieth centuries, but an emerging economic and political giant, both in Asia and globally. As recent trade disputes with the USA have shown, China is beginning not just to flex its economic muscles but to have a strong sense of itself as a modern independent nation, albeit one increasingly tied in with the global economy. A further twist is that many of the products for mass global consumption are now being manufactured in China.

The Chinese government and media constantly reiterate the need to 'resist' what they see as the negative features of the representation of women in Western capitalism: the 'excessive display of flesh', in everything from advertisements to movies, and 'pornography which denigrates women'. Indeed, they explicitly blame Western influences for many of the growing problems experienced by Chinese women, from domestic violence to rape, as well as for increasing sexual permissiveness and the rising divorce rate. Since the inauguration of the 'open door' policy in the late 1970s, the public has consistently been told – in language reminiscent of the Self-strengthening Movement of the late nineteenth century – to distinguish between the 'acceptable' aspects of Western culture and values, which may be integrated with Chinese culture, and the 'unacceptable' aspects which are to be rejected.[18] This has been applied even to fashion:

> Since what people wear is a reflection of both their culture and values, the task of combining traditional characteristics in Chinese dress, with the best in foreign culture, is currently an issue concerning fashion designers and couturiers, as well as ordinary people in contemporary China.
>
> (*Women of China* 11, 1991: 19)

More assertively, there has been an effort to break the perceived nexus between modernisation and Westernisation, seeking instead an amalgam of modernity and tradition. Official spokespersons have attempted to create distinctive female images from 'traditional' non-Western sources. The first image is that of 'Eastern woman' (*dongfang funü*) who, while being 'modern', retains allegedly Eastern cultural virtues: 'Eastern women have a tradition of gentleness, capacity for deep love, and dignity' (*Qingnian yidai* June 1985: 24–5). The second and more pervasive recreated image has been to draw specifically on Chinese tradition, even while continuing to condemn the treatment of women in China's pre-revolutionary 'feudal' society. In modern parlance, 'Chinese woman' integrates modernity with the best features of being Chinese, exhibiting her own 'special charm, for example exquisiteness and depth of emotions' (*Renmin ribao* 8 January 1986: 2).

The concept of Eastern or Chinese distinctiveness, as might be expected, is itself being utilised for commercial purposes as non-Western manufacturers attempt to create a market niche. For Japanese companies it is a matter of maximising East/West differences. Shiseido cosmetics, for example, are advertised as suiting 'Eastern' skins, while a shampoo advertisement states: 'please choose Huazi, the mild Eastern type'. Chinese producers, attempting to combat both Western and Japanese status symbols, make an effort to stress distinctive Chinese characteristics, harking back to – and as often reinventing – the country's long and diverse cultural traditions. Some Chinese fashion designers, for example, are praised by the media for 'turning back for their inspiration to traditional Chinese clothing' (*China Today* March 1994: 27).

Although the battle against Western status symbols is an uphill one, the high cost of most Western products has in fact made window-shopping a more common pastime than purchase for many. 'Being seen' in the upmarket shopping malls, particularly those in the Hiltons, Hyatts and other five-star Western hotels, has become a popular leisure activity. As disposable incomes rise, the consumer desires being created by the international market will no doubt increasingly be translated into consumption realities.

CONCLUSION

The 'flower vase and housewife' images of Chinese women in the 1980s and 1990s, while partially reflecting the decline of state control over people's everyday lives, have been closely linked to the shift towards a market economy and, in particular, the growth of a consumer society increasingly integrated into the global economy. Although these images and designated roles largely parallel those characteristic of countries in Asia and elsewhere undergoing the development process, they have seemed particularly dramatic in China because of the defeminised images of the Mao era and the speed with which the changes have been occurring. Indeed, post-Mao China is a striking case study not just of the development of a modern consumer society and culture but of the consequences of such developments for gender representations and practices.

Within China, debate about the changing portrayals of women, particularly in advertising, is still at an early stage, as discussed briefly in this chapter. With the sheer novelty of having access to varied fashions, cosmetics and domestic appliances wearing off, some Chinese women have begun to question the implications of recent developments. Like Western women before them, they have linked the decorative and domestic images of women to the question of role models and female aspirations. They see the premium on youthful beauty as the pathway to success, whether in public life or in the marriage stakes, as detrimental to women's educational and professional progress. As one journalist asked: 'What happens to her when she gets older and can no longer rely on her appearance alone?' (*China Today* February 1994: 42).

Since the early 1990s, commentators have also periodically questioned the implications of the combined glamour/housewife portrayals for the achievement of male–female equality. In March 1992 the national women's newspaper called on its readers to 'discuss the images of women in commercials' (*Zhongguo funü bao* 20 March 1992: 3). A lively debate ensued. While some contributors maintained that portrayals of the 'dutiful-wife-and-good-mother' simply conformed to current social reality, which itself reflected deeply rooted cultural attitudes, others argued that such images were actually promoting the gender division of labour: a situation in which 'the great part of the occupations reserved for women are of the maidservant and service type' (*Zhongguo funü bao* 27 March 1992: 3; also 3 April 1992: 3; 12 June 1992: 3). Citing, somewhat unfashionably, the Mao era slogan 'whatever men can do, women can do too', one correspondent claimed that the roles allocated to women during that period had at least 'proved to a certain extent that China's women possess unlimited capabilities' (*Zhongguo funü bao* 27 March 1992: 3).[19]

As this debate illustrated, the discussion of women's consumer-oriented images has also been linked to a wider Chinese debate about women's roles and values which is beyond the scope of this chapter. Since the early years of the post-Mao era, a growing focus on the concept of 'innate female characteristics' has underpinned widespread discussion about the 'ideal' woman: the extent to which the professional woman, in particular, is able to be a 'virtuous wife and good mother' (*xianqi liangmu*) as opposed to being the now denigrated 'strong woman' (*nüqiangren*) lacking feminine qualities (Weeks 1989; Rosen 1994). There will no doubt be a continuing debate both on this broader issue and on the more specific one of the impact of consumerism on women, as further economic growth brings higher disposable incomes, as consumer products 'trickle down' to smaller towns and the countryside, and as China becomes more closely linked to the global economy and culture.

NOTES

1 This paper is part of a broader project on *Women, Consumerism and the State in Contemporary China*, funded by the Australian Research Council. I should like to thank Wang Yi and Sharon Lim for their research assistance.

2 In text references the names of Chinese-language magazines and newspapers are cited in Chinese transliteration (for English translation see list of references); English-language magazines and newspapers are cited in English.

3 These phenomena have been analysed in Western contexts by feminist writers including Bowlby (1985), Winship (1987) and Reekie (1993).

4 The changing images of Chinese women are discussed briefly in Rosen (1993a, 1994); see also Hooper (1994).

5 For an analysis of rising incomes and personal consumption, see Chai (1992).

6 Ownership of refrigerators and colour television sets, two of the most sought-after items, increased from 0.7 per cent and 1 per cent of urban households in 1982 to over 50 per cent and 70 per cent in 1993 *(Zhongguo tongji nianjian)*. Other items with high ownership rates, compared with negligible ownership in the early 1980s include washing machines (83 per cent of urban households by 1993) and vacuum cleaners.

7 Harriet Evans, who was studying in Beijing at the same time, recently used the expression 'a kind of gender neutrality' to refer to the ' defeminisation of female appearance and its approximation to male standards of dress' (Evans, 1995: 358).

8 Western women with feminist sympathies who were impressed by the defeminised appearance of Chinese women included Sidel (1971), Rowbotham (1974), Maclaine (1976) and Broyelle (1977).
9 The concept and construction of 'femininity' have of course become a complex and controversial issue in Western feminist discourse. See for example Radner (1995).
10 For a basic account of sex stereotyping in Western advertising, see Courtney and Whipple (1983).
11 *Zhongguo funü* (*Women of China*) at the national level and a range of provincial magazines. Although the English language version of *Women of China* has the same Chinese characters as the Chinese version (*Zhongguo funü*) on the cover, it is not simply a translation of the Chinese magazine. Characteristic of China's English-language magazines, it presents a somewhat 'sanitised' version of Chinese society with less emphasis on social problems.
12 For a concise analysis of the roles of women in post-revolutionary socialist societies, see Molyneux (1981).
13 For statistics on the employment rate for both males and females, see 'The Report of the People's Republic of China on the Implementation of the Nairobi Forward-Looking Strategies for the Advancement of Women', February 1994, reprinted in *Beijing Review* (24–30 October 1994: 22).
14 This has become a very common theme in articles published in China since the early 1990s in both Chinese-language and English-language women's magazines.
15 *Hui jia qu* (return home) or *huigui guotai* (return to the kitchen).
16 See Jacka (1993); Rosen (1994:17.6–17.10). On the 'return home' debate, see media articles translated and published in Rosen (1992a) and (1992b).
17 The demand for female labour in some sectors of the economy (e.g. the electronics industry) means that the 'return home' phenomenon varies across different occupations (Jacka 1993).
18 On this dichotomy and its re-emergence after the inauguration of the post-Mao 'open door' policy, see Hooper (1986).
19 Some of the articles in this debate are translated in Rosen (1993b: 83–101).

BIBLIOGRAPHY

Andors, P. (1983) *The Unfinished Liberation of Chinese Women*, Bloomington: Indiana University Press.

Appadurai, A. (1990) 'Disjuncture and Difference in the Global Cultural Economy', *Public Culture* 2(2): 1–23.

Asiaweek.

Barrett, J. (1973), 'Women Hold Up Half the Sky', in M.B. Young (ed.) *Women in China: Studies in Social Change and Feminism*, Ann Arbor: Centre for Chinese Studies, The University of Michigan.

Beijing Review.

Bowlby, R. (1985) 'Just Looking: Consumer Culture', in Dreiser, Gissing, and Zola (eds) New York: Methuen.

Brownmiller, S. (1984) *Femininity*, New York: Simon and Schuster.

Broyelle, C. (1977) *Women's Liberation in China*, Hassocks: Harvester Press.

Busby, L. J. and Leichty, G. (1993) 'Feminism and Advertising in Traditional and Non-traditional Women's Magazines 1950s–1980s', *Journalism Quarterly* 70(2): 247–64.

Campbell, C. (1987) *The Romantic Ethic and the Spirit of Modern Consumerism*, Oxford: Blackwell.

Chai, J. C.H. (1992) 'Consumption and Living Standards in China', *The China Quarterly* 131: 721–49.

Chan, T.S. and Lin, G-.S. (1992) 'An Empirical Analysis of Consumer Decision Processes in the People's Republic of China', *Journal of International Consumer Advertising* 4(4): 33–48.

China Daily.

China Reconstructs.

China Today.

Courtney, A. E. and Whipple, T. W. (1983) *Sex Stereotyping in Advertising*, Lexington, D.C.: Heath and Co.

Evans, H. (1995) 'Defining Difference: The "Scientific" Construction of Sexuality and Gender in the People's Republic of China', *Signs* 20(2): 357–94.

Featherstone, M. (1991) *Consumer Culture and Postmodernism*, London: Sage Publications.

Feng Lanrui (1991) 'A Comparison of the Two Unemployment Peaks in China during the Last Decade', *Social Science Journal* 43(1): 191–208.

Ferguson, J., Kreshel, P. and Tinkham, S. (1990) 'In the Pages of Ms: Sex Role Portrayals of Women in Advertising', *Journal of Advertising* 19(1): 40–51.

Ferguson, M. (1985) *Forever Feminine: Women's Magazines and the Cult of Femininity*, Brookfield: Gower.

Freedman, D. S. (1972) 'Consumption Aspiration as Economic Incentives in a Developing Country – Taiwan', in B. Strumpel *et al.* (eds) *Human Behavior in Economic Affairs*, San Francisco: Jossey-Bass.

Fukutake, T. (1982) *The Japanese Social Structure: Its Evolution in the Modern Century*, Tokyo: University of Tokyo Press.

Ganglia, S. (1987) 'The Portrayal of Women in the Media', *Media Asia* 14(4): 232–5.

Hamadan, A. M. (1987) 'Women and the Media in Malaysia', *Media Asia* 14(4): 194–203.

Hongqi (Red flag).

Honig, E. and Hershatter, G. (1988) *Personal Voices: Chinese Women in the 1980s*, Stanford: Stanford University Press.

Hooper, B. (1979) *Inside Peking: A Personal Report*, London: MacDonald & Jane's.

—— (1984) 'China's Modernization: Are Young Women Going to Lose Out?', *Modern China* 10(3): 317–44.

—— (1985) *Youth in China*, Harmondsworth: Penguin.

—— (1986) *China Stands Up: Ending the Western Presence, 1948–1950*, Sydney, London, Boston: Allen & Unwin.

—— (1994) 'Women, Consumerism and the State in Contemporary China', *Asian Studies Review* 17(3): 73–84.

Interview Zheng Renyang (1982), Director, Propaganda Bureau of Department of International Relations, Chinese Women's Federation, Beijing, 18 September.

Jacka, T. (1993) 'Back to the Wok: Women and Employment in Chinese Industry in the 1980s', *Australian Journal of Chinese Affairs* 24: 1–23.
Jefferson, G. H. and Rawski, T. G. (1992) 'Unemployment, Underemployment, and Employment Policy in China's Cities', *Modern China* 18(1): 42–71.
Jingji ribao (Economic Daily).
Li Xiaojiang and Zhang Xiaodan (1994) 'Creating a Space for Women: Women's Studies in China in the 1980s', *Signs* 20(1): 137–51.
MacKinnon, C. (1989) *Towards a Feminist Theory of the State*, Harvard: Harvard University Press.
Maclaine, S. (1976) *You Can Get There From Here*, London: Corgi.
Molyneux, M. (1981) 'Women's Emancipation under Socialism: A Model for the Third World?' *World Development* 9, (9/1): 1019–37.
NCNA, 25 March (1982), in *Summary of World Broadcasts* FE 6997/B11/7-8, 6 April.
Qingnian yidai (The Youth Generation).
Radner, H. (1995) *Shopping Around: Feminine Culture and the Pursuit of Pleasure*, London: Routledge.
Reekie, G. (1993) *Temptations: Sex, Selling and the Department Store*, Sydney: Allen & Unwin.
Renmin ribao (The People's Daily).
Rosen, S. (ed.) (1992a) 'Women, Education and Employment', *Chinese Education: A Journal of Translations* 22(2).
—— (1992b) 'Women, Education and Employment (II), *Chinese Education: A Journal of Translations* 25(1).
—— (1993a) 'Women and Reform', *China News Analysis* 1477, 15 January, 7–10
—— (1993b) 'Chinese Women and Society (1)', *Chinese Education and Society: A Journal of Translations* 26 (3).
—— (1994) 'Chinese Women in the 1990s: Images and Roles in Contention', in M. Brosseau and L.C. Kin (eds) *China Review 1994*, Hong Kong: The Chinese University Press.
Rowbotham, S. (1974) *Women, Resistance and Revolution*, New York: Vintage.
Sharma, S., Weerakody, I., Panday, N., Al Muhajid, S. and Musa, A. B. M. (1987) 'Women and the Media in South Asia', *Media Asia* 14(4): 218–27.
Shenzhou xueren (China's Scholars Abroad).
Sidel, R. (1971) *Women and Child Care in China*, Harmondsworth: Penguin.
South China Morning Post.
Tse, D. K., Belk, R. W. and Zhou, N. (1989) 'Becoming a Consumer Society: A Longitudinal and Cross-Cultural Content Analysis of Print Ads from Hong Kong, the People's Republic of China, and Taiwan', *Journal of Consumer Research* 15: 457–72.
Wan, S. (1988) 'The Emergence of Women's Studies in China', *Women's Studies International Forum* 11(5): 455–64.
Wang, Y. and Li, J. (1982) 'Chengshi zhigong jiawu laodong yanjiu' (Research into urban staff and workers' housework), *Zhongguo shehui kexue* (1): 177–90.
Weeks, M. R. (1989) 'Virtuous Wives and Kind Mothers: Concepts of Women in Urban China', *Women's Studies International Forum* 12(5): 505–18.
Winship, J. (1987) *Inside Women's Magazines*, London: Pandora.

Wolf, M. (1985) *Revolution Postponed: Women in Contemporary China*, Stanford: Stanford University Press.

Women of China.

Xiandai Luabao (1994) June: 84.

Xu Bai Yi (1990) *Marketing to China: One Billion New Customers*, Lincolnwood, Illinois: NTC Business Books.

Zheng Yiping (1994) *Jiushi niandai nüxing shenghuo zhinang* (Life Wisdom for Women in the Nineties) Beijing: Overseas Chinese Publishing House.

Zhongguo funü (Women of China).

Zhongguo funü bao (Chinese Women's News).

Zhongguo qingnian (Chinese Youth).

Zhongguo tongji nianjian (Statistical Yearbook of China).

Zhu Q. (1993) 'A Brief Analysis of the Systems of Indicators of Well-Off Society and Objectives for the Year 2000', *Social Sciences in China*, Summer: 42–54.

7 Chinese cultural revivalism

Changing gender constructions in the Yangtze River delta[1]

Anne E. McLaren

In the modernising China of the 1980s and 1990s, images of Chinese women parading down the catwalk in the latest Pierre Cardin fashion have overtaken images of the revolutionary Chinese woman digging ditches in a blue 'Mao suit'. It has become customary to discuss the affluent, post-socialist Chinese woman as the target of global economic forces and Western consumerism (Hooper 1994; Ling 1994) or to decry what are seen as reversals in the socio-economic status of Chinese women working outside the home (Rai and Zhang 1994; Gao 1994; Bell 1994). Western and Chinese observers have noted the return of pre-revolutionary 'feudal' practices in kinship and marriage arrangements (Davis and Harrell 1993). Some Chinese feminists have welcomed the new space offered by economic reforms to allow women to free up a specifically female subjectivity (Li 1994), while others condemn notions of 'essential' Chinese woman as a return to discriminatory policies based on biological determinism (Woo 1994; Hom 1994; Gao 1994).

In the rush to evaluate competing cultural gender constructions in post-Mao China (after 1976), the gendered nature of the state's attempt to revive selected aspects of the Chinese pre-revolutionary heritage has been largely overlooked. Western observers of China have been quick to point to the remarkable pace of economic growth, the establishment of new economic zones open to foreign investment and the rapid transformation of Chinese cities as evidence that China has entered a post-socialist phase of development. They have failed to notice that side-by-side with the rhetoric of capitalist economic growth is another quite distinct discourse, anti-Western in implication, a discourse which is conducted in the Chinese language and targeted at the domestic population, rather than the foreign investor.

The discourse of what is termed here 'Chinese cultural revivalism' shares commonalities with other fundamentalist movements in the developing world, especially the stress on an essential national character, the importance of traditional, cultural, family and ritual issues and the demonising of the West as immoral and decadent. Post-colonial debate has demonstrated that British colonialism influenced the creation of a 'private sphere' for the Indian middle classes, one which constructed Indian women as 'moral' and 'domestic' as opposed to Western materialism and the norms of the Indian lower classes (Sangari and Vaid 1989, cited in Mohanty 1991:18-21). It is argued here that in the face of the penetration of global capital and communication technology, the Chinese state is nonetheless attempting to fashion a new ('Confucianised') woman who is 'modern' and 'Chinese' but indubitably not 'Western' in nature. The gender-marked discourse of contemporary state ideologues is in contradistinction to the revolutionary rhetoric of the Maoist past which dissolved the category of womanhood into an implicitly masculinised category of the socialist human being (Barlow 1994).

This chapter aims to outline the new gender-marked rhetoric of cultural revivalism promoted by the state, expose its operations at county level and evaluate its influence on emerging affluent groups of women in rural China. Far from being a fully constituted homogenised group awaiting inscription from state and society, this study assumes that 'women' (actual material women) must be recuperated from 'Woman', the cultural constructions of femininity (in the words of Mohanty 1991: 53). In other words 'women' must be examined in their historical specificity and as agents both complying with and resisting competing constructions of womanhood.

More specifically, this study will focus on a little-noticed but crucial aspect of the life of Chinese women: their ritual and oral genres, an aspect folklorists and anthropologists call 'expressive culture'. This 'expressive culture' will be placed within the context of the state cultural revivalist project: this carries an implicit gender code instating the 'modern', middle-class Chinese woman as one who believes in Confucian familial values and loyalty to the status quo. This implicit gender code notwithstanding, women practitioners of the folk arts and women cadres in the cultural field have welcomed and appropriated the state revivalist programme for particularistic purposes. These purposes can be both complicit with and oppositional to state attempts to reconstitute a particular kind of Chinese modernity.

CULTURAL REVIVALISM: THE UNSTATED GENDER AGENDA

The revival of religious fundamentalism and a general nostalgia for tradition is a much noted feature of modernisation in the Middle East and parts of Southeast Asia. China's particular circumstances, especially the long period of communist ideological hegemony followed by its virtual dissolution, make the emergence of Chinese cultural revivalism qualitatively different from Islamic fundamentalism and Hindu communalism, to mention two much studied movements which have had a significant influence on gender relations (Tohidi 1991; Moghadam 1994). Moghadam defines the usual view of 'fundamentalism' as 'the predominant expression of culture as an independent variable which is claimed to cut across national economies and the nation–state boundaries' (ibid.: 6). This view of fundamentalism stresses cultural, family and ritual issues and is anti-Western in nature. The West is thoroughly demonised as 'immoral' because of the 3 Ps: prostitution, pornography and promiscuity (ibid.: 6).

Chinese revivalism shares an anti-Western perspective with fundamentalist movements elsewhere, but this is tempered by the need to remain open to Western economic opportunity. Barme argues that China's rapid economic growth and its increasing recognition in world forums as a developing 'great power' have created a sense of national pride which easily converts to anti-Western xenophobia. The economic dislocation experienced by the former socialist bloc in their attempts to imitate the capitalist West and the success of other sinified economies such as Singapore, Hong Kong, Taiwan and Korea, have firmed the Chinese view that Western-style modernisation is to be abhorred (Barme 1995).[2] As I suggest here, this (notionally) Marxist/Maoist state has been very selective in choosing the elements to construct the desired 'tradition'. Victoria Bernal's view of Islamic revivalism in the Sudan 'as a facet of modernity, rather than the resurgence of tradition' applies also to Chinese revivalism (Bernal 1994: 37). It will be argued here that selective cultural revivalism is central to the statist project of 'Chinese' modernity and that an implicit 'gender agenda' is central to this project.

State-sponsored cultural revivalism, the topic of this chapter, is quite distinct from the philosophical revival of Confucianism by scholars in the USA, Hong Kong, Taiwan and, belatedly, China. This philosophical movement, known as the New Confucianism, is part of a broader pan-Chinese identity associated with Chinese communities in Southeast Asia and the West; it deals primarily with China's canonical or elite culture. One of its leading exponents, Harvard scholar Tu Wei-ming, describes the movement to 'search for one's roots' in East Asia as one which bears a 'family resemblance' to fundamentalism but is motivated by different concerns. The New Confucianism offers, he believes, a 'wholesome attitude towards the modernising process' (Marty and Scott Appleby 1991: 742).

This chapter deals with the less well-known 'state-sponsored cultural revivalism' in China. Chinese state revivalism is broader in scope and less doctrinal in nature than fundamentalism based on religious principles. For this reason 'cultural revivalism' is a more appropriate term than 'fundamentalism'.[3] The considerable efforts of the state in sponsoring and funding cultural revival to meet the new narrative of nationalism has been welcomed and appropriated by various groups for particularistic purposes, a subject treated in detail later.

China's cultural revivalism is based on an implicit gender code, but official rhetoric in fact treats the woman's issue quite gingerly. This reticence on the part of the Chinese state is due first to revolutionary fervour promoting equality of the sexes in the recent Maoist past (1949–76); and second, to a perceived need to retain a careful balance between demonising the West (for its 'immorality', naturally),[4] and encouraging those Western practices which promote economic development. Another reason for official reticence is the need to project an image of China as a rapidly modernising country with 'civilised' policies concerning women. Issues of this kind lay behind the decisions to offer to hold the UN Fourth World Conference of Women in Beijing in September 1995.

Nonetheless, beneath the official rhetoric which seeks to combine Marxist radicalism with Chinese traditionalism, an implicit gender code instates women as the major carriers of a newly reconstituted 'traditional' culture.[5] This is apparent in the editorial by literary scholar, Xu Shuofang, in the inaugural issue of the prestigious journal, *Chinese Culture: Tradition & Modernization* (1993), the main medium for state expression of the cultural revival movement. He notes approvingly the legislation concerning women and marriage in the 1980s, particularly the categorisation of women, the aged and children as groups requiring special legal protection: 'One can say this [legislation] is characteristic of Chinese socialism but it also demonstrates the positive influence of traditional culture (*chuantong wenhua*) dominated by Confucianism' (p.26). In line with the official Open Door Policy, Xu is careful to limit his critique of the West: 'The Enlightenment was a great achievement, nonetheless capitalism brought with it the evils of prostitution, drugs, violence and single-parent families' (p.27). Xu's view is worth citing in more detail as the nuanced view of a classics scholar who seeks to position a particular formulation of 'Chinese traditional culture' at the forefront of Chinese-style modernity:

> Chinese traditional culture did not stress the individual or individual freedom. Before reform began, this was its major fault. Once

> reform started [Chinese traditional culture] naturally came to play a role in resisting the negative aspects of Western culture. This is not to say that the entire set of Confucian rites and proprieties intimately associated with traditional or Confucian feudalist kinship systems should be maintained in pristine form, but to say that some principles and notions closely associated with traditional systems over the ages can still play a role in new conditions, e.g. those sayings and aphorisms found in the Confucian classics which transcend the limitations of time.

Xu refers here to a monolithic and unchanging notion of 'traditional culture', a reified domain which can be dusted off to suit contemporary needs. As a scholar who has participated in Chinese radical movements over the decades, he recognises that Confucian ideology and proprieties kept Chinese women subordinated for thousands of years and were primarily responsible for those abuses against women which twentieth-century reformers saw as the quintessential 'barbarities' of a corrupt tradition.[6] Instead of expressing his abhorrence for these notions directly, he refers to gender issues only by claiming that the socio-political changes and new legislation of recent decades will afford sufficient protection against the negative aspects of tradition:

> Because of the founding of the Republic and the thoroughness of the 'Marriage Law', and because the extended family governed by kinship protocols has now been replaced by small families of four or five people, the Three Principles and Five Constants [Confucian principles governing human relations in a gender hierarchy] can be easily reformed. . . . Traditional culture only needs some slight refurbishment, or one only needs to get rid of those elements which do not meet the needs of the times, then it can serve the interests of socialism and ensure that socialist collectivism can be full of the flavour of humanity (*renqing wei*) and can maintain its superiority in the face of lifestyles derived from overseas. This is the great contribution which only traditional culture, in which Confucianism predominates, can make to the modernization of the state.

For Xu and other members of the 'scholar-lobby', which has won the ear of a number of Chinese leaders (especially Chen Yun and Li Tieying),[7] a good dose of traditional culture can provide an antidote to the diseases brought by the West: 'We need to link Chinese culture and Marxism in order to improve the moral calibre of the population' (Li Yan in CC: 77). For leading philosopher Zhang Dainian, the central problem is that, although Confucian notions have been condemned in the current era, new moral standards have not yet been established. In his view the central Chinese spirit should remain 'collective' not individual (CC 1993:19-20). Party chief Jiang Zemin has given the seal of approval to the idea that Chinese traditional culture should be one of the main bulwarks against the flood of dysfunctional elements flooding into China from the West such as 'pluralism, national nihilism and all-out modernisation' ('Talk on the Seventieth Anniversary of the Founding of the Chinese Communist Party', 1991, CC: 94). For communist party leaders, the Chinese past is valued primarily because it is distinct from the Western-dominated present. The state-sponsored revivalist movement is not a matter of nostalgia for past triumphs, but a crucial weapon against the 'cultural' (i.e. non-material) aspects of Westernisation.

POPULAR CULTURE AND THE STATE

I have stressed the characteristic feature of the current revivalist movement in China, the strong participation of the Chinese state. The state-dominated nature of the Chinese culture enterprise marks a sharp contrast with current social movements in Southeast Asia, like the post-colonial Islamic revivalism of the Malay middle classes (see Chapters 1 and 4), or the renovated Islamic movement in Indonesia. The Chinese revivalist project is associated with the ascendancy of party chief Deng Xiaoping in 1979. What I call here 'the folk culture project' was initiated by the Ministry of Culture in 1979 and was incorporated into state plans throughout the 1980s.[8] Its major objective is the compilation of 310 volumes of particular folk genres, folk music, dance and the like for each county in the country. Up to thirty thousand folk art practitioners, culture cadres and local volunteers have been mobilised in every county and province to carry out this project, which will continue until the year 2000. Additionally, academies and universities are carrying out massive publication projects to investigate, recover and analyse remnants of Chinese folk practices and rituals.

I have discussed the aims and operations of this project elsewhere (McLaren 1994, 1997). Here I merely mention the explicit agenda, as stated in material supplied to me by the Ministry of Culture in 1994. The stated aims of the folk culture project are to promote Chinese 'traditional' culture, compile reference books on popular culture for scholars and practitioners, offer 'nourishment' for the promotion of 'socialism with Chinese characteristics', strengthen the morale of the populace and stimulate their patriotism, and facilitate the establishment of a 'material and spiritual civilisation'. The folk culture publication project, and the broader patriotic education of which it is a part (Barme 1995: 212–3) are conceived by the state as an ideological enterprise of great significance to its own legitimacy. The major task of this newly formulated 'Chinese culture' is to provide a bulwark against Western 'spiritual pollution', to provide new content for patriotic education, and to fill in the ideological vacuum left in the wake of the collapse of Maoist socialism.

A great deal is at stake here. Judging by the fervour of these official pronouncements, the very future of 'Chinese socialism' next century rests on the success of the state in incorporating 'highlights' of a (constructed) 'traditional culture' into 'socialism with Chinese characteristics'. But how is this state-conceived project received by the populace at large? Has the state succeeded in moulding the culture project to its own nationalist agenda? What happens when thirty thousand people all over China are invited to become ethnographers of their own culture? Is the enterprise shaped by the same gender roles and expectations that one finds in official pronouncements like those above? Before looking at this issue in two areas of emerging affluence within the Shanghai hinterland where I have researched, it is necessary to discuss the problematic of the gendered nature of folklore study in general.

GENDER AND GENRE

In the opening shots of one of China's most controversial recent movies, *Red Sorghum*, a girl bride is carried off in a canopied sedan chair to be the concubine of an aged leper. The half-naked carriers chant a rhythmical song hinting at the 'delights' of the girl's wedding night. On the way the party is beset by robbers. One of the sedan carriers 'rescues' the young bride and deflowers her in a field of sorghum.

The plaintive theme song of *Red Sorghum*, sung by the sedan-carriers, took China by storm, along with the indelible image of leering, taunting males carrying a young woman to an unthinkable destiny.[9] Unfortunately, as a Chinese book on sexual harassment in China has noted, the song is now commonly sung by farm labourers to young women who dare to walk on their own across the paddy fields: 'Little sister, just go bravely on, keep on going, don't turn your head . . .' (Chang Qing *et al.* 1994: 244). These poignant words, ironic within the context of the film, have become an instrument of sexual harassment and another example of how a 'traditional' folk song becomes decontextualised through mass media only to return to the folk as part of a new gender mythology.

The transmutation of genres as they cross community and gender boundaries, as they transform from folk song to pop song, and induce multiple audiences and interpretations, lies at the heart of current folklore scholarship. As Appadurai *et al.* notes, key terms in the field such as 'authenticity' and 'invention' are now problematised (Appadurai *et al.* 1991: 41). Folk genres are no longer a matter of formal properties: instead the focus is on 'ethnic genres' (Dan Ben Amos cited in Shuman 1993: 72), that is, the meaning and function of a folk genre within a particular community. The folklorist or anthropologist now adopts an 'emic' approach to the issue of folk genre and practice, which stresses what the community claims to be doing and how it understands the genre within the context of its own identity (Flueckiger 1991: 183; Appadurai *et al.* 1991: 12). According to Flueckiger, a folklore genre or practice belongs to a 'folklore region' which is 'imagined' in the same way as Benedict Anderson's posited 'imagined community' represents the nation (p. 193).

Now that genre is not seen as part of a universally applicable taxonomy, the issue of gender takes on new importance. The problem is not only to investigate folklore areas hitherto neglected by male anthropologists or folklorists but to recognise the integral relationship between a genre and its practitioners. In many communities men and women engage in separate genres and rituals which have gender-specific meanings and functions to the participants (performer and audience). In this way gender and genre are not necessarily taxonomically distinct (Appadurai *et al.* 1991: 9; Shuman 1993: 71). During the 1980s, gender-based folklore and anthropological studies made new discoveries which have fed back into culture studies in general. Wary of speaking for the 'Other' (the women under investigation), the western folklorist and anthropologist now make a 'careful attempt to discern the meanings of gender in other cultural worlds' (di Leonardo 1991: 17). For many folklorists this has led to a focus on women's oral genres as 'personal narratives' which project and construct a kind of self which is always culturally relative (Appadurai *et al.* 1991: 9). As Appadurai *et al.* note, 'finding a personal voice in male-dominated galaxies of possibilities seems to be at the centre of female-related gender issues'.

Within women's expressive culture one can find what Ramanujan calls 'counter-systems' or oppositional themes (Ramanujan 1991), but some women are complicit in male-dominated ideologies (Shuman 1993: 71). Both resistance and complicity are possible; genres thus reflect 'not consensus but debate' (Appadurai *et al.* 1991: 471). Contestation operates not only at the level of gender differences but also as a 'traditional' genre becomes a cultural commodity and an intimate audience a national public created by mass media (Appadurai *et al.* 1991: 22).

Gender, by which I mean the gender of the practitioners, their audience and the treatment of gender roles, is thus a crucial variable in the formation of 'ethnic genres', which are genres as understood by the practising community. In the two counties investigated here, Jiading and Nanhui, women have played a distinct role in the revival of folklore genres and ritual forms, participating in the formation of a new gendered narrative of Chinese modernity in collusion with, and sometimes in resistance to, the state. Following recent developments in gender and folklore scholarship, I will focus my discussion on the function of oral genres and ritual practices as constructed by communities of women within Nanhui and Jiading.

CULTURE AND COMMERCE ON THE LOWER YANGTZE DELTA

The counties of Jiading and Nanhui, which border Shanghai to the west and south respectively, are governed by Shanghai city, which in turn is under central government jurisdiction. Nanhui, a coastal county, is immediately adjacent to the Shanghai Pudong Economic Zone which is under rapid construction as China's answer to the economic and financial might of Hong Kong. The destinies of Nanhui and Jiading have been inextricably tied to the fortunes of Shanghai since the latter's rise as favoured entrepot of the western imperialists in the nineteenth century. During the reform era (post-1978), Shanghai's rate of growth was below the national average due to strict centralist controls, but after the relaxation of these controls in 1992 it is now undergoing rapid transformation in line with changes in other coastal cities in China. In 1978 the Yangtze River Economic and Development Company was founded to link Yangtze River cities with the economic dynamo of Shanghai. Every day thousands of residents of Jiading and Nanhui pour into Shanghai to become part of the city's 3 million itinerant workers toiling on roads, railways and construction sites.

The two counties are at very different levels of development, however, and represent a range of potentialities as zones for modernisation. Jiading was one of the earliest regions of China to be subject to Christian influence and played an important role in China's early modernisation. It is an ancient cultural heartland with a history of western influence dating back to the Jesuits in the seventeenth century and a proud tradition of resistance to invasion. Since the Opium Wars in the nineteenth century its destiny has been closely linked to that of nearby

Shanghai. Nanhui, which is bounded on three sides by the Eastern Sea and which until the 1990s was cut off by the Huangpu River from Shanghai, is much less advanced.

Today the two counties are rapidly becoming satellite townships of greater Shanghai. Jiading is the site of Shanghai's science park and contains a large number of research institutions in such fields as precision optics, nuclear power and computing. The county employs 4–5,000 scientific and technical personnel. Other well-educated residents of Jiading find employment in export-oriented industrial trades such as machinery, metallic products, electronics, transport and the like (People's Republic of China, 1993: 197–8). During the reform period the county had an estimated annual growth rate of 21.4 per cent (Jiading Chunqiu 1994: 9). Market commodities such as television sets, VCRs, fridges and washing machines are now found in the homes of ordinary people.

In the Yangtze delta region as a whole the economic reforms of the post-Mao period have led to higher incomes for the population, the emergence of wider avenues of employment and a new pattern of social stratification. Philip C. Huang notes the 'elaborate hierarchy of jobs' now apparent in the region. He postulates a four-level categorisation of employment in the area from most to least prestigious: state enterprises, township work units, village-level work units, and family-based farm work. Each level has a different educational requirement, ranging from high school or tertiary-trained level for state enterprise employment to low-level literacy for those who toil on the land. Status and remuneration diverge significantly at each level (Huang 1990: 290-1). The Maoist class system of values which valorises the working and peasant classes at the expense of the educated 'intellectual' class is here reversed. Aspects of socialist stratification which played a key role in social status from 1949 to the 1980s, such as class origin (*chushen*, e.g. landlord or 'revolutionary' class) and occupational role (*chengfen*, e.g. peasant, see Kuhn, 1991) have lost their importance with the declining importance of state-imposed registration by locality and birth.

Class status is thus subject to rapid and bewildering transformation. There are not only differences *between* families but also *within* families. For instance, males are much more likely to gain the education necessary to enter the higher level occupations such as industry, construction, transportation and trade. In Jiangsu province on the lower Yangtze delta, most of the men work in town enterprises and 70 per cent of the farm work is reportedly done by women (Rai and Zhang 1994: 54). In Jiangsu townships men outnumber women by 133 to 100 (Gao 1994: 94). The pressure on young women to drop out of school and work the family plot is such that state campaigns are run to encourage them to return to the classroom. However, the main aim of the rural female literacy campaign is to give these women enough skills to manage farming occupations which have been relinquished by the men for better remunerated labour elsewhere (Rai and Zhang 1994: 65-6). Young women of the poorest families pour in from rural areas to new economic zones to produce goods in sweatshop conditions (Gao 1994: 90-3; Woo 1994).

But it is not all bad news for women. The younger generation is more likely to find prestigious employment than the older (Huang 1990: 298) and the more educated daughter-in-law (usually living in her in-laws' house) is now much more able to assert her independence within the family economic unit (ibid.: 298–9). As Huang points out, 'a new value' system, one based on 'talent' or education and skill base, dominates notions of status. Furthermore, as I will argue here, notions of 'talent' have broadened to include skill at 'traditional' oral art forms and rituals which bring status and income to trained practitioners, including women. In this area of increasing affluence, a nexus is developing between a newly recreated cultural 'tradition' and commercial forces.

For Jiading residents, traditional folk culture remains in vestigial form in the memories of the elderly and in the 'archival memory' of the local Culture Bureau. Although Nanhui was settled later than Jiading its inaccessibility has ensured the preservation of more of its pre-1949 folk practices. Before 1949 Nanhui women featured prominently in Buddhist storytelling (a genre known as *xuanjuan*), still very popular in the more remote coastal areas of Nanhui (*Nanhui Culture Gazette*, 1993: 16, 148–9). These Buddhist stories are known for their strong female protagonists, Buddhist moralism, and the inclusion of women's concerns such as fertility and the birth of sons. In Jiading, on the other hand, the strongly religious content of this genre has not lent itself to easy conversion to an entertainment genre once the region became more secularised and storytelling was broadcast on radio, television and also on the Shanghai stage (Jiang 1992: 339-41, *Nanhui Culture Gazette*, 1993: 35, 40).[10] The presence of Nanhui dialect speakers in Shanghai, many of them members of the large mobile labour force which commutes to the city, has ensured the place of Nanhui genres in urban mass media. Nonetheless, these same storytelling forms have lost their specific village context with an intimate audience. They are examples of how local folk culture has merged with urban mass culture in the now familiar process of recombination of diverse elements (hybridisation) and loss of local specificity (deterritorialisation – see Rowe and Schelling 1991: 231).

An example of the cultural displacement of oral genres by modern imports was provided by Su Peizhang, a performer from Nanhui county.

Now in her fifties, she tells how the Shanghai opera known as *tanhuang* has gone from amateur ad lib performances prior to 1949 to ones scripted by the Culture Bureau for travelling troupes. At one time she could perform 114 plays but her troupe did not survive the Cultural Revolution and the era of reform. After a tentative attempt at revival, the *tanhuang* amateur troupe fell out of favour and was displaced by imported entertainments such as karaoke.[11] Another amateur troupe in Nanhui, the Yue opera troupe, was disbanded in 1989, possibly because the traditional repertoire had not adapted to meet the needs of the times (*Nanhui Culture Gazette*, 1993: 85).

The commercial challenges of the era of economic reform was a constant refrain in interviews and in material given to me by the Nanhui Culture Bureau.[12] Pressure to make cultural ventures self-supporting began in the 1980s. So-called 'Folk Art Factories' (*wenyi gongchang*) were set up by the Nanhui Culture Bureau. The 'Folk Art Factories' engage in the production of everything from plastics, electronics and printed material to cinematic equipment, lanterns and handicrafts (*Nanhui Culture Gazette*, 1993: 58). In 1987 the local Culture Bureau set up a tripartite policy for achieving economic support for the arts, namely, sideline cultural projects (*yi wen bu wen*, for example, a library leasing out photocopying and printing equipment or a temple fair leasing land for street barrows). Commercial enterprises were encouraged to sponsor cultural activities and entertainments for employees. These strategies, which aimed to minimise the burden on the state, were known popularly as 'borrowing a boat to cross a river' and 'borrowing a bird to lay an egg' (*Nanhui Culture Gazette*, 1993: 51–2).

In 1987 scholarly study of the region began in earnest as part of a nationwide project to compile encyclopedias and reference material on Chinese regional traditional culture. Jiang Bin, a famous scholar of Chinese popular culture from the Chinese Academy of Social Sciences, was in charge of the Wu dialect section of this project (McLaren 1994: 80-4). Following hard on the heels of the scholars, local cadres and entrepreneurs sought to distinguish particular areas with folk specialties for tourism purposes, e.g. a village of Shanghai opera, a village of traditional stories, villages specialising in bonsai and floriculture, and so on (*Nanhui Culture Gazette*, 1993: 32–3). In 1988 the Shanghai Municipal Culture Bureau held a meeting at Zhoupu in Nanhui to announce the new policy that 'Culture must grow economic wings' and to criticise the old view that 'those engaged in culture have nothing to do with commerce, and those tied to the soil are not concerned with wealth'. By this time, the Nanhui Culture Bureau had already established links with various local enterprises, such as the Da Tong Plastics Co., and could point to a good record of gaining industrial sponsorship and promoting various self-supporting activities (*Nanhui Culture Gazette*, 1993: 35). Shanghai papers applauded the success of Nanhui's culture in 'growing economic wings' and added the rider, 'the economy must take on the soul of culture' (a warning to enterprises to sponsor cultural activities). At the national level, the Ministry of Culture praised the Nanhui Culture Bureau as a 'Nationally Advanced Unit for Self-supported Culture' (*Nanhui Culture Gazette*, 1993: 58).

In the development of culture with 'economic wings', stereotypical images of women, based on idealised notions of Chinese womanhood, are being constructed to assist economic development. For example, the inaugural Peach Blossom Festival was held in 1991 to take advantage of the spring scene in Nanhui's extensive peach orchards. The 5,000 guests, including 39 foreigners, were welcomed by girls carrying panniers of peach blossoms and men and women in traditional costume who prepared snacks for their guests. As women performers sang songs of welcome, kites were flown and various other dances such as 'rocking the bridal boat' were performed.

'Traditions' which were once taboo to women have been restored but with a new twist. For example, the New Year Lantern Festival is enjoying a revival in Zhejiang province under the name of 'The Tourism and Trade Lantern Festival' (Jiang 1992: 614; *Nanhui Culture Gazette*, 1993: 35) but it is now denuded of its earlier ritual associations. The Lantern Festival, held on the fifteenth day of New Year, can be traced back two thousand years. Intricate lantern towers were erected in the market places and local communities came at night to watch the spectacle. The Lantern Festival was held to be a time of carnival and licentiousness. For this reason 'genteel' women were expressly forbidden to participate in the Festival in the belief that it would bring disaster on their families, although historical records indicate that a good many women did in fact come to view the spectacle. From 1949 to 1977 the custom was frowned upon as a 'feudal relic', but after Mao's death it suddenly reappeared as a signal of China's new tolerance of premodern celebrations. (As a foreign student in Shanghai in 1978 I was privileged to attend the first revival of the New Year Lantern Festival for several decades.) From 1978 onwards the ancient taboo against the participation of women in the Lantern Festival in rural areas has gradually faded. For example in Wenzhou in Zhejiang, women's associations take part in the parade of lanterns (Jiang 1992: 611–23). Lantern festivals have been revived in Nanhui too, and elaborate lanterns using electric power are constructed in Nanhui's folk-art workshops.

The local branch of the Women's Federation has been periodically active in raising the profile of women's performing arts in the region. For example, in 1987 a conference on women singers was held and local women were encouraged to perform in Shanghai in a performance shown on city television (*Nanhui Culture Gazette*, 1993: 34–50). The Women's Federation, which spent decades encouraging women to leave the home and participate in the workforce as the equals of men, is now ironically in the vanguard in promoting a new domestic role for women as guardians of 'the culture of the home' (*jiating wenhua*), specifically, those celebrations and performances which are conducted in the home. In order to win local support, the Women's Federation has set up inter-family competitions on such themes as 'Love my Nanhui, love my home' (*Nanhui Culture Gazette*, 1993: 179–80). In this case, the forces of what I term 'cultural revivalism' encourage rural women to actively develop a 'culture of the home' in order to inculcate family values and regional pride. The movement parallels and consolidates the simultaneous process of commercial advertising in urban areas and mass media, which seeks to propagate stereotypical representations of women as the focus of domestic responsibilities (see Chapter 6).

My informants at the Culture Bureau were silent on the revival of other female ritual practices such as shamanism which is still regarded as shamefully 'feudal'.[13] According to a scholarly informant who was born in Nanhui, the *wupo* or female shamans are enjoying a revival and charging high fees for their services. Jiang Bin, the leading popular culture specialist of this region, notes that *wu* performances involve dancing, chanting, singing and weeping and serve many purposes. Female shamans can take on the spirits of the dead, diagnose sickness, tell fortunes, carry out rites of exorcism and sorcery, recite curses or blessings. He too notes that shamanistic practices are still prevalent and fees are charged (Jiang 1992: 444, 604).

In some instances, 'worthy' aspects of 'traditional' culture are refined, accorded a high status and preserved artificially as 'national treasures', when they would not survive in the marketplace. Yuan Jialan of Jiading was originally taught by an older female practitioner, Wang Xiuying, whom I also interviewed. Yuan was brought up by a musical family and first appeared on the stage at the age of 13. Trained as a performer of *tanhuang* or regional opera, she could sing all sorts of folk songs including Taoist chants. Her repertoire consisted mainly of love songs, some of them performed in boy-girl pairs, but over the years political themes had intruded, such as a song about the People's Liberation Army. Yuan was highly literate and a polished singer who did not need to look at a script to perform. She had been classified as a national grade two performer of Shanghai regional opera and continually honed her skills for performances which were now solely confined to 'private occasions for the leaders'. For example, at New Year she would take part in exclusive performances of traditional opera for communist party cadres, including top party leaders in Beijing. However, her original drama troupe had disbanded during the era of reform.

In analysing the reasons for the vicissitudes of *tanhuang* in this area, it is valuable to examine the case of Yuan and her teacher, Wang Xiuying. Wang was barely educated, came from an impoverished background, and had learnt her art from her family's operatic troupe. She used skeletal scripts but composed her own songs, could perform any sort of female role and was trained in impromptu performance. The woman of the next generation, Yuan Jialan, had studied music and composition formally and had been trained to perform from scripts rather than through the usual means of oral transmission, with its intrinsic scope for improvisation. One could speculate that this scripted material, which originated from the Culture Bureau, was unable to reflect new conditions and themes in an era of great economic growth and that this has contributed to the waning popularity of this genre. In this instance, the oral art form 'lives' today only because the Chinese communist party leadership at national level (the male gerontocracy) has decided it is one of the cultural icons worthy of preservation for its own exclusive audience.

In the affluent and rapidly modernising county of Jiading, it was clear from my discussions with woman senior culture cadre, Shen Yunjuan, that women's oral arts were more a matter of documentary record than of living performances. Nonetheless, judging from the enthusiasm of the local cadres and the literate amateurs they mobilised (retired cadres, teachers, youth leaders), the project to study county culture has become a source of pride in a regional identity.[14] 'Cultural revivalism' consists for the most part of the retrieval and assembling of representative examples of regional oral arts. This is not the case in Nanhui, which is less developed economically and has retained more of its so-called 'feudal' way of life, including women's ritual practices.

WOMEN'S RITUAL REVIVALISM AT NANHUI

Many observers have noted the resurgence of popular, cultic and ritual practices in post-Mao China, after three decades of suppression.[15] An international team of scholars has been investigating Chinese ritual theatre since 1991, with funds from the Taiwanese Chiang Ching-kuo Foundation (Wang 1995). Earlier studies tended to cast the upsurge of ritual practice as an oppositional force to state hegemony. In more recent years scholars have drawn attention to the complex interrelationship or even 'complicity' between the state apparatus and religious practices at the local level, analagous to the symbiosis between the local society and the state in imperial times (Siu 1989b: 122–3; Dean 1993: 4–6, 173).

Helen Siu additionally signals the importance of consumerism and affluence to the re-emergence and reinterpretation by the populace of these 'reconstituted' rituals. For example, Fujian funerals are becoming increasingly extravagant, with expensive condolence gifts, processions, the hiring of Daoist priests and nuns to perform funeral rites and massive funeral dinners (Siu 1989b: 127). Wedding ceremonies have undergone similar inflation, with the negotiation of lavish dowries and bride prices, the hiring of elaborate costumes and wedding banquets costing several years's average salary (Siu 1989b: 127; Siu 1993: 180–8). She notes, however, that although many ancient practices have been 'revived', they do not have the same significance or function as in pre-1949 China. Practitioners often have little or no awareness of the previous significance of the ritual act. The dynamic behind the new ceremonies, according to Siu, is rather 'the new wealth and the new energies for networking'. In brief, the new rituals represent 'cultural fragments recycled under new circumstances' (Siu 1989b: 134).

The laments performed mainly by female villagers on the occasion of weddings and funerals have been enjoying a revival in Nanhui recently. These laments (*ku jia ge*) are considered in some quarters to have dangerously 'feudal' implications because they are closely associated with the exhibition of bridal dowries and lavish funeral ceremonies.[16] In this age of affluence these are seen to reach the heights of 'extravagance'. (In the Maoist era such 'extravagance' was condemned for its 'bourgeois' excess.)

This ritual revivalism is associated with two trends. One is the staging of lamentations and other examples of women's expressive culture to an audience of cadres or scholars in order to record and document ritual practices which appear to be 'dying'. This is particularly true of wedding lamentations, for reasons explained later. The other trend is the participation of women as ritual lamenters at lavish funeral ceremonies, which signal the wealth and status of the deceased in newly affluent areas.

Women's lamentations were prevalent throughout China in imperial times (Fei 1939: 76), but due to the difficulties of investigating popular rituals in Maoist China (1949–76), only laments in rural areas of Hong Kong have been thoroughly studied by anthropologists (see Johnson

1988 for summary of scholarship on Chinese laments). As with the Lantern Festival and other folk practices, women's lamentations in mainland China were largely suppressed by the state in the period 1949–78,[17] but have reappeared amongst the older generation during the 1980s and 1990s. In contemporary China very little of this tradition remains. One of my informants, Professor Chen Qinjian of the Chinese Academy of Social Sciences, believes that the tradition of lamentations at Nanhui, particularly in the isolated coastal areas, is one of the strongest and most complete surviving examples.

In Nanhui county the collection of scripts of these laments and their scholarly retrieval is largely due to the activities of one dynamic woman 'culture cadre', Pan Wenzhen, whom I interviewed in September 1994. Pan began interviewing practitioners and recording their laments in the 1960s but her material was burnt during the Cultural Revolution and it was only in the reformist era after 1978 that work could really get under way. In 1982 she recorded the performances of a foremost practitioner, Pan Cailian, when Cailian was 75 years old. At this stage she was only willing to perform marriage songs. Having lost most of her family she found the funeral songs too painful to perform. The wedding laments were duly recorded on tape and transcribed into printed scripts. By 1987 Cailian's laments were famous throughout the region. At the age of 80 she at last consented to sing funeral laments. As she began her performance of laments for one member of her family after another she became more and more impassioned with grief. Finally observers begged her to stop because she was so distressed.

Cadre Pan Wenzhen also interviewed practitioners about the cultural context in which the laments were performed. Women performers invariably came from impoverished backgrounds, were illiterate and learned their songs from each other while weeding cotton plants or drawing out cotton skeins. The songs are rich in imagery, especially that of the flora and fauna of the region and the labour associated with cotton production. Affluent women in Nanhui never learnt the laments because women from 'good' homes did not participate in the labour of the commoners (*Ceremonial Laments* 1989: 152–68) and were expected to remain completely silent with veiled faces during the marriage ceremony. Some popular texts from this same dialect region actually forbade 'good' women from participating in laments, viewing such female expressiveness as analogous to physical exposure: 'It is forbidden to expose your body, sing lamentations and weep.'[18]

Nanhui wedding laments focus on the bride's sorrow at leaving home, her concern at the possibly harsh treatment she may receive from her mother-in-law and reminders of her contribution to household management.[19] Laments provided a rare public domain for the illiterate woman, who held the floor and the attention of her family and local community throughout the period of lamentation, which could last several days. Lamentations also provided a medium for women to express a kind of culturally constructed emotion in a way denied men.[20] Chinese scholars have generally regarded women's lamentations as a form of grievance at harsh marriage practices, which saw them married off by parental arrangement to a strange man from another village. However, affluent women, also subject to arranged marriages, were allowed no such ritual expression of grievance.

In the first part of the twentieth century, Chinese radicals devalued women's expressive role as another indication of China's 'backwardness'. In his famous realist novel, *Family* (1931), Ba Jin condemned the histrionic and 'inauthentic' nature of lamentations by hired mourners at a funeral. Rey Chow notes in her discussion of this passage Ba Jin's contempt for the 'frivolous, garrulous and thus "womanly" expressiveness' of Chinese folk culture (Chow 1991: 100).[21] It is ironic that women's lamentations have only found a respectable niche in studies of Chinese folk culture with the advent of the state folk culture publication project in the 1980s and 1990s. In pre-1949 rural China, they were an important signifier of family status and female value at village level. Adept lamenters won praise as 'talented women', much as village men who attained literacy would be regarded as 'talented'.

In Nanhui the wedding laments also asserted the economic rights of the bride. This was clear in my discussion with a lamenter, Wang Xuehong, and the local cadre, Pan Wenzhen. Wang is an illiterate woman in her mid-fifties who is regarded as very capable in her labour in the cotton fields and in organising other women. She had many times won awards as an 'advanced woman' and was now a cadre in her own right. Although uneducated she was introduced to me by officials of the Nanhui Culture Bureau as 'very knowledgable' about local popular culture and an excellent ad lib performer.

Wang's ability as a lamenter was associated in the local mind with her impressive credentials as expert worker and local identity. The same association between ritual expertise and perceived competence and social status has been noted for the women of Jiangyong county in Hunan: they have a rich oral culture based on sworn sister relationships and festivals from which men are excluded. Jiangyong women who performed with large groups of 'sworn sisters' in an invented women's script also had the highest status in the community (McLaren 1996). Similarly, ability as a lamenter and ritualist gave even an illiterate woman in Nanhui a certain cachet.

Funeral laments are another important ritual function of Nanhui women. Once again these are a family event performed by women, but members of the local community form part of the audience. In Nanhui women not men have the power to prepare the deceased for the next life. The following excerpt comes from the combing ceremony, where a daughter is combing the hair of her dead mother in preparation for the laying out:

> My mother's hair is in disarray, your daughter will comb it through,
> The first comb will touch a thousand strands,
> The second comb will take it halfway through,
> The third comb will make the pathway straight,
> My mother will go straight down the path to the [Buddhist] Western Land.
>
> (Cited in Jiang, 1992: 267)

The daughter also laments when the coffin is borne out from the home. This is necessary to save the deceased from being sent to Hell. If a daughter has not mastered the art of ritual lamenting then she can hire a professional lamenter (ibid.: 269).

Wang Xuehong herself has sometimes been paid to perform on behalf of a family whose women have lost the art of lamentation. With the emergence of conspicuous consumption and lavish wedding dowry and funeral practices, practitioners such as Wang Xuehong find themselves in some demand. Wang described how neighbours, friends and even strangers would crowd around to watch a moving lamentation ceremony. An inspiring performance gave the family some local prominence. Even the culture cadre, Pan Wenzhen, finds that she is regarded as a source of advice on the 'correct' protocols of wedding and funeral ceremonies.

In Nanhui coastal areas, funeral laments, in conjunction with public processions, bands and banquets, signify the wealth and status of the deceased. The funeral laments, performed by female members of the family at key stages of the funeral process, are observed by the village community. The family's desire to demonstrate affluence, together with the relaxation of the Maoist prohibition of 'feudal excess', coincides with greater financial ability to conduct a lavish funeral. This clearly accounts for the revival of funeral lamentations in coastal Nanhui. According to my informants, however, wedding lamentations are unlikely to persist once the present generation dies out. Contemporary brides who choose their own partners find it hard to 'lament' with the necessary conviction. Young people are not learning the formulae, rhetoric and chanted melodies intrinsic to the complex art of lamenting.

Wedding lamentations belong to a very specific environment, one where illiterate women toil in the cotton fields and draw out cotton skeins, chanting as they work. In the past a good lamenter could not only win applause from her local community for her eloquence but most likely a larger dowry from her family. Women now have many avenues open to them (such as working in foreign textile ventures and factories) and have the legal right to choose their own partners. Dowries are still significant in local marriages but they are not negotiated through ritual lamentation. In this way the very specific socio-economic context which nourished wedding lamentations has all but vanished in this area. Elizabeth Johnson has noted the same phenomenon in former village areas of Hong Kong which are now part of the urban complex (1988: 138).

It appears likely that in Nanhui wedding lamentations will rapidly become part of the 'archival memory' of traditions stored in the local Culture Bureau. In the form of printed transcripts and audiotape reproductions, this oral ritual will become another item in the vast repertory of cultural artifacts which the Chinese state has culled, stored and catalogued as part of its national enterprise to construct a 'Chinese' as distinct from a Western route to modernity and wealth. Nanhui lamentations are among the oral arts which have caught the attention of Japanese scholars, whose visits and field trips to Nanhui are all carefully recorded in the local *Culture Gazette*. In this way Nanhui's cultural revivalism contributes to a reassertion of China as the home of sinitic culture and the locus of a civilisation which has had lasting influence on areas of sinitic dominance, many of which are amongst the world's most successful economies today (discussed in McLaren 1994).

CONCLUSION

The cultural revival movement in Nanhui and Jiading is the product of the complex interaction of economic liberalism, the penetration of global capital, state policy to revive aspects of 'traditional culture', and a resurgence of popular beliefs and practices. Women have long been significant bearers of Chinese oral culture (because virtually all were illiterate in pre-modern China). Now the state calls on women to act as major carriers of a reconstituted 'tradition' based on a combination of Chinese radical theory and Confucianism. Many contradictions and paradoxes have emerged as actual women have responded in a multitude of ways to the state project.

The resurgence of traditionalism in rural China does not necessarily indicate the spread of more 'fundamentalist' views of gender difference, in spite of the growing sexual division of labour in the Yangtze River delta. Rather, it would appear that cultural resurgence has thrown up once more that old favourite of the Chinese imaginary, 'the strong woman' (*nü qiang ren*), who may be a culture cadre whose amateur ethnography helps to shape the regional identity of her area, a performer of local opera who runs her own printing press, or a lamenter who wins awards for her labour in the fields and local prestige for her ability in ritual performance.

It is argued here that the effects of both globalisation and the state cultural revival movement are by no means homogeneous or unidirectional. Some 'traditional' folk genres have absorbed elements of mass consumer culture by a process of hybridisation. In other cases, new 'traditions' (such as the Peach Festival) offer an idealised depiction of 'nativised' Chinese women for the tourism industry. Former 'traditions' can be totally redefined: practices originally taboo to women, for example, now include them. Changing female subjectivities invest marriage with new meanings which preclude the re-enactment of the customary lamentation performance at the bridal home. Women's funeral lamentations, by contrast, become signifiers of wealth and status in an age of emerging affluence. As the state relaxes its controls over the private sphere, local populations engage in spontaneous participation in oral arts and entertainments, although the state, through the agency of the Women's Federation, still attempts to offer token ideological guidance. 'Superstitions' re-emerge and are tolerated by the state: female shamans set up private businesses offering fortune-telling, exorcism, healing, and so on. Certain pre-revolutionary women's oral arts are revamped and preserved artificially to provide party leaders with a purified version of an 'authentic' Chinese culture. Female 'culture cadres', under orders from the state to create a massive archival memory of past traditions, find themselves regarded at the local level as ritual experts.[22] The often illiterate women peasants whom they investigate find themselves becoming cultural icons. Rituals formerly condemned as superstition, such as funeral laments, make a reappearance as part of the conspicuous consumption of newly affluent areas.

In the cases examined here it was found that considerable scope exists for individual agency and the appropriation of state policies and institutions for particularistic purposes. In other words, the economic reforms and cultural revivalist movement offer considerable potential for the 'expressive' woman to carve out a private domain beyond the reach of the state. Future studies of the cultural construction of femininity in China will have to take into account not just the impact of the global economy and mass communications but also the influence of state cultural policies and, crucially, how these are manipulated in particular places by particular groups, as women participate in the formation of a highly gendered and sharply contested notion of how to be female, Chinese and modern, but not Western.

NOTES

1 I wish to acknowledge the support of the Australian Research Council, the Australia-China University Link Program and the La Trobe Vice-Chancellor's China Award for four field trips in the environs of Shanghai 1991–94. I am particularly grateful to Professor Chen Qinjian, folk performance specialist from East China Normal University, who accompanied me on a field trip to Nanhui and Jiading in August 1994, to Jiang Bin, veteran scholar of Chinese popular culture from the Chinese Academy of Social Sciences (Shanghai) and Zheng Tuyou, editor of the Shanghai-based journal of popular culture *Zhongguo minjian wenhua*. Two women county officials in cultural fields, Pan Wenzhen of Nanhui, and Shen Yunjian of Jiading, offered me invaluable support and information. Many women amateur folk artists shared their life experiences and allowed me to tape their performances. I express my gratitude here.

2 Scalapino notes that after the Tiananmen crisis of 1989 China's leadership increasingly denounced the West for their 'interference' in China's affairs (1993: 224). Barme gives many examples of the growth of anti-Western sentiment in the 1990s.

3 On Chinese cultural revivalism in general see the volume of essays by Lee and Syrokomla-Stefanowska (1993). On the role of the state in cultural revivalism in the Yangtze delta region, see McLaren (1994, 1997).

4 Even Chinese intellectuals who have visited the West hold views of this kind. See the words of woman writer, Wang Anyi:

> . . . the Chinese maintain a morally higher life, though sometimes that sort of life is rather inhuman. Westerners separate their emotions from sex. It's like eating, not because the food is particularly tasty, but simply because when I am hungry I will eat it. We [Chinese] only have sex when our emotions reach a high level of intensity. That seems to be a really big difference.
>
> (cited in Wang Zheng 1993: 171)

5 In my use of 'tradition' here I am indebted to Eric Hobsbawm's definition of 'invented tradition' as a 'set of practices, normally governed by overtly or tacitly accepted rules and of a ritual or symbolic nature, which seeks to inculcate certain values and norms of behaviour by repetition, which automatically implies continuity with the past (1983: 1). Smith discusses the conditions under which 'invented' traditions can flourish in global culture(s) (1990: 178). He notes that the success of any newly constituted 'tradition' depends on a shared sense of continuity, shared memories and turning points and a sense of common destiny (p. 180).

6 Ching-kiu Stephen Chan has shown how radical male writers in the early twentieth century used images of victimised Chinese womanhood as representations of male and female oppression by tradition (1993: 13–32).

7 See Li Tieying's opening address at the Third National Meeting of the Old Text Publication Plan, 25 May 1992, in CC: 7–8. Li Tieying cites previous attempts at the publication of traditional texts which were supported by the former premier, Zhou Enlai (in 1958) and by Li himself in 1981. These earlier attempts were short-lived.

8 The folk culture project is a joint project of the Ministry of Culture, the Chinese State Nationality Affairs Commission and the Chinese Folk Artists Association. For further details on the administration of this project see McLaren (1997).

9 The image of the bride is more complex than this 'victim' image in that the girl is shown as complicit with her abduction by the sedan carrier. Of course, this adds prurient interest as the woman is 'asking for it'. See Mayo (1993: 144–6).

10 Women also predominate in secular genres such as the cymbal tales (*bozishu*), gong-drum ballads (*luogu shu*) and Shanghai-style opera (*huju*).

11 Su Peizhang had not performed for 3 years and it was obvious in her performances that she relied a lot on written scripts. She is no longer associated with *tanhuang* performance and is fully engaged as manager of her own printing press.

12 The printed material I received is not available for external circulation (*neibu faxing*). The most valuable item is the *Nanhui Culture Gazette*, which offers a comprehensive survey of the role state culture practices at county level.

13 The *wupo* (shamans) are women believed to have the power to take on the spirit of a deity or the souls of the dead during cultic practice. They serve as spirit mediums, healers and fortune-tellers. Jiang details shamanistic practices in this region (1992: 442–9).

14 See the detailed report by Shen Yunjuan in *Jiading Folksongs*: *houji*.

15 See Schell (1984: 98–103), Anagnost (1989), Whyte (1988: 300–16), Siu (1989a, and 1989b), Dean (1993), Lee and Styrokomla-Stefanowska (1993).

16 On laments in the Wu dialect area see Jiang (1992: 240). The *Nanhui Culture Gazette* generally ignores cultural practices such as shamanism which run counter to the image of 'socialist spiritual civilisation'. In the case of Buddhist storytelling (*xuanjuan*), the *Gazette* notes carefully that this genre has been remodelled along 'civilised' (i.e. secular) lines. '*Xuanjuan* developed on the foundation of Suzhou *xuanjuan* to "civilised *xuanjuan*" then passed on the [more secularised] *tanhuang xuanjuan* and finally was performed in dramatic style as a *mubiaoxi*.' (*Nanhui Culture Gazette*: 149).

17 In spite of state zealotry, religious and ritual practices proved difficult to entirely eradicate. Red Guards during the height of the Cultural Revolution (1966-69) were horrified at the cultic practices they observed (for an example from one village see Chan *et al*. 1984: 87–90).

18 See a precious scroll from the nineteenth century listing the twenty prohibitions for women (Jiang 1992: 340).

19 This is true for Hong Kong laments too, see Johnson (1988: 139).

20 Grima's study of Afghan Puxtun (Muslim) women demonstrates the significance of their ritual narratives about their own personal suffering. These performed narratives of suffering (*tapos*) correlate with the male concept of

honour in that community. Excellent *tapos* practitioners win local respect, as do Nanhui practitioners of laments or Jiangyong county practitioners of *nushu*. Grima notes that *tapos* tales are highly formulaic (as in the Chinese cases above) and express a kind of emotion which is not so much spontaneous or biological as a 'learned, culturally modelled and performed behaviour' (Grima 1991: 93). The ritual significance of Nanhui lamentations is beyond the scope of this chapter.

21 Ba Jin's contempt for women's lamentations contrasts strongly with the Irish experience in the early twentieth century, where the 'keening' [ritually lamenting] woman is validated as a symbol of suffering and protest. (See the nationalistic plays of Synge discussed by Bourke 1993: 163.)

22 The Culture Bureau cadres who put enormous and largely unpaid effort into the recuperation of local folk culture have become 'ethnic spectators' retrieving a culture which otherwise would be lost to posterity. On the ambivalence of the modernised Chinese person when forced to become 'spectators' to representations of their history, see Rey Chow (1991: 28). For another example of this phenomenon, see Susan Rogers' study of G. Siregar Baumi, a school principal who has written a set of cultural texts about his home area in North Sumatra (1993).

BIBLIOGRAPHY

Anagnost, A. (1987) 'Politics and Magic in Contemporary China', *Modern China* 13(1): 41–61.

Appadurai, A., Korom, F.J. and Mills, M. (1991) 'Introduction', in A. Appadurai, F.J. Korom and M. Mills (eds) *Gender, Genre, and Power in South Asian Expressive Traditions*, Philadelphia: University of Pennsylvania Press.

Barlow, T. E. (1993) *Sex and Politics in Modern China*, London and Durham: Duke University Press.

—— (1994) 'Politics and Protocols of Fun: (Un)Making National Woman', in C.K. Gilmartin, G. Hershatter, L. Rofel and T. White (eds) *Engendering China*, Cambridge, Massachusetts: Harvard University Press.

Barme, G.R. (1995) 'To Screw Foreigners is Patriotic: China's Avant-garde Nationalists', *The China Journal* 34: 209–34.

Bell, L.S. (1994) 'For Better, For Worse: Women and the World Market in Rural China', *Modern China* 20(2): 180–210.

Bernal, V. (1994) 'Gender, Culture, and Capitalism: Women and the Remaking of Islamic "Tradition" in a Sudanese Village', *Comparative Studies in Society and History* 36(1): 36–67.

Bourke, A. (1993) 'More in Anger than in Sorrow: Irish Women's Lament Poetry', in Joan N. Radner (ed.) *Feminist Messages: Coding in Women's Folk Culture*, Urbana and Chicago: University of Illinois Press.

[CC] *Chinese Culture: Tradition and Modernization* (Chuantong wenhua yu xiandai hua) 1993:1, Zhonghua shuju.

Ceremonial Laments (*Hunsang yishi ge*) (1989) Shanghai: Shanghai Folk Arts Association Publishers.

Chan, A., Madsden, R. and Unger, J. (1984) *Chen Village: The Recent History of a Peasant Community in Mao's China*, Berkeley: University of California Press.

Chan, C.S. (1993) 'The Language of Despair: Ideological Representations of the "New Woman" by May Fourth Writers', in T. Barlow (ed.) *Sex and Politics in Modern China*, London and Durham: Duke University Press.

Chang Q., Zhu, G. and Wang, L. (1994) *Xing saorao zai Zhongguo*, Shenyang: Liaoning Renmin chubanshe.

China Statistical Yearbook (1992) Beijing: China Statistical Publishing House.

Chow, R. (1991), *Woman and Chinese Modernity: The Politics of Reading between West and East*, Minneapolis and Oxford: University of Minnesota Press.

Davis, D. and Harrell, S. (1993) 'Introduction: The Impact of Post-Mao Reforms on Family Life', in D. Davis and S. Harrell (eds) *Chinese Families in the Post-Mao Era*, Berkeley: University of California Press.

Dean, K. (1993) *Taoist Ritual and Popular Cults of Southeast China*, Princeton, NJ: Princeton University Press.

di Leonardo, M. (ed.) (1991) *Gender at the Crossroads of Knowledge*, Berkeley, Los Angeles and London: University of California Press.

Fei, H. (1939 [1980]) *Peasant Life in China: A Field Study of Country Life in the Yangtze Valley*, London: Routledge & Kegan Paul.

Flueckiger, J.B. (1991) 'Genre and Community in the Folklore System of Chhattisgarh', in A. Appadurai, F.J. Korom and M. Mills (eds) *Gender, Genre, and Power in South Asian Expressive Traditions*, Philadelphia: Pennsylvania University Press.

Gao, X. (1994) 'China's Modernization and Changes in the Social Status of Rural Women', in C.K. Gilmartin, G. Hershatter, L. Rofel and T. White (eds) *Engendering China*, Cambridge, Massachusetts: Harvard University Press.

Gilmartin, C.K. (1994) 'Gender, Political Culture, and Women's Mobilization in the Chinese Nationalist Revolution, 1924–27', in C.K. Gilmartin, G. Hershatter, L. Rofel and T. White, (eds) *Engendering China: Women, Culture, and the State*, Cambridge, Massachusetts: Harvard University Press.

Grima, B. (1991) in A. Appadurai, F.J. Korom and M. Mills (eds) *Gender, Genre, and Power in South Asian Expressive Traditions*, Philadelphia, Pennsylvania University Press.

Hobsbawm, E. (1983) 'Introduction: Inventing Traditions', in E. Hobsbawm and T. Ranger (eds) *The Invention of Tradition*, Cambridge: Cambridge University Press.

Hom, S.K. (1994) 'Engendering Chinese Legal Studies: Gatekeeping, Master Discourses, and Other Challenges', *Signs* 19(4): 1020–47.

Hooper, B. (1994) 'Women, Consumerism and the State in Contemporary China', *Asian Studies Review* 17(3): 73–84.

Huang, P.C. (1990) *The Peasant Family and Rural Development in the Yangtzi Delta, 1350–1988*, Stanford, California: Stanford University Press.

Jiading Chunqui (1992) Jiading: Jiading Publishers.

Jiading Folk Songs (*Jiading xian geyao fenjuan*) (1989) in series Zhongguo minjian wenxue jicheng Shanghai juan.

Jiang Bin (1992), *Wu Yue minjian xinyang minsu* [Folk Beliefs and Customs of the Wu Yue Areas], Shanghai: Wenyi chubanshe.

Johnson, E.L. (1988) 'Grieving for the Dead, Grieving for the Living: Funeral Laments of Hakka Women', in J.L. Watson and E.S. Rawski (eds) *Death Rituals in Late Imperial China*, Berkeley: University of California Press.

Kuhn, P.A. (1991) 'Chinese Views of Social Classification', in P.J. Corfield (ed.) *Language, History and Class*, Oxford: Basil Blackwell.

Lee, M. and Syrokomla-Stefanowska, A.D. (eds) (1993) *Modernization of the Chinese Past*, Sydney: The University of Sydney School of Asian Studies Series No.1, Wild Peony Press.

Li Xiaojiang (1994) 'Economic Reform and the Awakening of Chinese Women's Collective Unconsciousness', in C.K. Gilmartin, G. Hershatter, L. Rofel and T. White (eds) *Engendering China*, Cambridge, Massachusetts: Harvard University Press.

Ling, L.H.M. (1994) 'Democratization under Internationalization: Media Reconstructions of Gender Identity in Shanghai', paper delivered at conference on 'Sex/Cultures/ Economies', Melbourne, December 16–18.

McLaren, A.E. (1994) 'Reconquering the Chinese Heritage', *Asian Studies Review* (Asian Studies Association of Australia) 18(1): 77–88.

—— (1996) 'Women's Voices and Textuality: Chastity and Abduction in Chinese Nüshu Writing', *Modern China* 22(4): 382–416.

—— (1997) 'Reinventing "Tradition" in the Shanghai Hinterland: The New Cultural Revivalism', *New Zealand Journal of East Asian Studies* Vol. 5, 1: 67–83.

Marty, M.E. and Scott Appleby, R. (eds) (1991) *Fundamentalisms Observed*, Vol. 1, Chicago: University of Chicago Press.

Mayo, L. (1993), 'Images of "Feudal" Marriage in Recent Chinese Art Films', in M. Lee and A.D. Syrokomla-Stefanowska, *Modernization of the Chinese Past*, Sydney: Wild Peony Press.

Moghadam, V.M. (1994) 'Introduction: Woman and Identity Politics in Theoretical and Comparative Perspective', in V. Moghadam (ed.) *Identity Politics and Women: Cultural Reassertions and Feminisms in International Perspective*, Boulder: Westview Press.

Mohanty, C.T. (1991) 'Introduction', in C. T. Mohanty, A. Russo and L. Torres (eds) *Third World Women and the Politics of Feminism*, Bloomington: Indiana University Press.

Nanhui Culture Gazette (*Nanhui xian wenhua zhi*) (1993) compiled Xi Guorong.

People's Republic of China (1993) *People's Republic of China Yearbook*, Beijing: Xintua.

Rai, S.M. and Zhang Junzuo (1994) ' "Competing and Learning": Women and the State in Contemporary Rural Mainland China', *Issues and Studies*, 30(3): 51–66.

Ramanujan, A.K. (1991) 'Towards a Counter-System: Women's Tales', in A. Appadurai, F.J. Korom and M. Mills (eds) *Gender, Genre, and Power in South Asian Expressive Traditions*, Philadelphia: University of Pennsylvania Press.

Rodgers, S. (1993) 'A Batak Antiquarian Writes His Culture: Print Literacy and Social Thought in an Indonesian Society', in P. Benson (ed.) *Anthropology and Literature*, Urbana and Chicago: University of Illinois Press.

Rowe, W. and Schelling, V. (1991) *Memory and Modernity: Popular Culture in Latin America*, London and New York: Verso Books.

Sangari, K. and Vaid, S. (eds) (1989) *Recasting Women: Essays in Colonial History*, New Delhi: Kali Press.

Scalapino, R.A. (1993) 'China's Multiple Identities in East Asia: China as a Regional Force', in L. Dittmer and S.S. Kim *China's Quest for National Identity*, London and Ithaca: Cornell University Press.

Schell, O. (1984) *To Get Rich is Glorious: China in the Eighties*, New York: Pantheon Books.

Shuman, A. (1993) 'Gender and Genre', in S.T. Hollis, L. Pershing and M.J. Young (eds) *Feminist Theory and the Study of Folklore*, Urbana: University of Illinois Press.

Siu, H.F. (1989a) *Agents and Victims in South China*, New Haven and London: Yale University Press.

—— (1989b) 'Recycling Rituals: Politics and Popular Culture in Contemporary Rural China', in P. Link, R. Madsen and P.G. Pickowica (eds) *Unofficial China: Popular Culture and Thought in the People's Republic of China*, Boulder: Westview Press.

—— (1993) 'Reconstituting Dowry and Brideprice in South China', in D. Davis and S. Harrell (eds) *Chinese Families in the Post-Mao Era*, Berkeley: University of California Press.

Smith, A. (1990) 'Towards a Global Culture', in M. Featherstone (ed.) *Global Culture*, London: Sage Publications.

Smith, J. (1994) 'The Creation of the World We Know: The World-Economy and the Re-creation of Gendered Identities', in V.M. Moghadam (ed.) *Identity Politics and Women*, Boulder: Westview Press.

Tohidi, N. (1991) 'Gender and Islamic Fundamentalism: Feminist Politics in Iran', in C. Mohanty, A. Russo and L. Torres (eds) *Third World Women and the Politics of Feminism*, Bloomington: Indiana University Press.

Wang, C.K. (1995) 'Studies in Chinese Ritual and Ritual Theatre', Chinese Studies Association of Australian Fourth Biennial Conference, Macquarie University, 507.

Wang Zheng (1993), 'Three Interviews: Wang Anyi, Zhu Lin, Dai Qing', in T.E. Barlow (ed.) *Sex and Politics in Modern China*, London and Durham: Duke University Press.

Whyte, M.K. (1988) 'Death in the People's Republic of China', in J.L. Watson and E.S. Rawski (eds) *Death Ritual in Late Imperial and Modern China*, Berkeley: University of California Press.

Woo, M.Y.K. (1994) 'Chinese Women Workers: The Delicate Balance between Protection and Equality', in C.K. Gilmartin, G. Hershatter, L. Rofel and T. White (eds) *Engendering China*, Cambridge, Massachusetts: Harvard University Press.

Zhang Zhengde (1994) *Jiading Chunqiu*, Shanghai Academy of Social Sciences.

8 Vietnam's women in the renovation era

Stephanie Fahey

This chapter examines changes in the social position and cultural images of women in Vietnam from the late 1980s to the early 1990s. Most research on women in Vietnam has come out of the 'gender in development' tradition and has mainly focussed on the impact of economic transformation in areas like education, health and 'moral' issues such as the apparent increase of prostitution. Questions about women's changing social position are posed by both Vietnamese researchers as well as international agencies charged with the responsibility of 'enabling women' during the process of economic renovation. This chapter moves on from these concerns to examine changing images of women, with special attention to changing constructions of women's beauty and domesticity in modernising Vietnam.

The chapter begins with a brief account of *doi moi* (renovation) and what this means in terms of Vietnam's integration into the global economy. The varying ways in which women have been swept up in the process of globalisation have generated a complex of conflicting images of women. From observation of the emerging middle class in the urban north, it is suggested that Vietnamese women's responses to (and experience of) economic 'renovation' are mediated by the nation's history of revolutionary war and by older cultural practices that survived the war and communist legislation.

VIETNAM'S RENOVATION

The world is fascinated by the collapse of communism in the Eastern Bloc and its more gradual unravelling in China and Vietnam. In the Eastern Bloc countries, attention has focussed on the hardships produced by the transition to a market economy. Structural adjustment, retrenchment in state-owned enterprises (SOEs) and the reduced budgets for social programmes have seriously jeopardised the previous achievements in education, health, nutrition and mortality indicators (Kornai 1992; Wolf 1985; Ralph 1995). In China and Vietnam, the path to market mechanism so far has been less hampered by political and social upheaval.

For Vietnam, as well as for China and the former communist countries of Eastern Europe, media reports highlight behaviour which is symptomatic of more fundamental social change arising from economic reform. The rampant growth in consumerism and the associated emphasis on household property rather than communal, cooperative or state ownership are most obvious in the urban areas. Recent studies of former communist countries suggest that women's position in the labour force is deteriorating rapidly. This has potentially harmful effects on women's health and nutritional status, as well as their economic and social position (Paukert 1991; Sen 1990). In many of the Eastern Bloc countries women's loss of wage employment has resulted in a reduced share of household resources. By contrast, in Vietnam, the loss of employment for women has translated into increased petty trade and commodity production, a sector which women characteristically dominate in many parts of South East Asia. It will be argued that the 'old' practice of female entrepreneurship in Vietnam is a fundamental factor in preventing the widespread poverty and political instability experienced by counterparts in the Eastern Bloc.

The majority of urban and peri-urban dwellers surveyed in Vietnam in 1992–93 believe that their standard of living has improved since renovation. Those in rural areas saw somewhat lesser gains (State Planning Committee and General Statistical Office 1994). The growth of the Vietnamese economy during the late 1980s and early 1990s is certainly impressive with rates of between 5 and 8 per cent and 9.8 per cent in 1994. Inflation decreased from almost 400 per cent in 1988 to 17 per cent for 1995. Population growth has slowed from 2.2 per cent in 1990 to 2.1 per cent in 1993 (World Bank 1995). The GDP per capita has also improved to an estimated US$170 in 1993 (ibid.). According to the Human Development Report (UNDP 1994), Vietnam ranks one hundred and fiftieth of 173 countries with respect to GDP per capita but one hundred and sixteenth when the Human Development Index is considered. It is expected that the Vietnamese economy will continue to grow at between 8 and 10 per cent per annum, although the Prime Minister is aiming for an unprecedented 12 per cent. Nevertheless, under economic reform in Vietnam, inequities are increasing not only between rich and poor but between men and women and rural and urban dwellers. Public and civil institutions necessary to complement market forces are not in place and social problems are seen to have economic solutions.

Vietnam's renovation process began formally in 1986 following the Sixth Party Congress. A bevy of reforms was introduced including decollectivisation of agriculture and handicraft production, the abolition of price controls on most non-essential services, liberalisation of the exchange rate, the elimination of state monopolies in most sectors and the facilitation of foreign investment. A series of policy reforms followed: a new land law permitting the transfer of use right, rationalisation of the SOE sector, wages reform, administrative reform, and the promulgation of a new labour code. The revision of the Constitution in 1992 formalised the market mechanism and signalled the state's move away from direct intervention in business and the provision of housing and employment.

Although the changes in Vietnam are indeed impressive, I have argued elsewhere that a *de facto* market mechanism operated in Vietnam during the pre-reform period (Fahey 1993). The current growth in the economy is propelled by the unveiling of existing enterprise, formerly hidden from the view of officials. The apparent surge in private enterprise and flurry in domestic consumption evident over the past few years has a longer unofficial history. I argue that many of the successes which policy makers claim as their own were spontaneously initiated, although shrouded by necessity, long before their official formulation and belated ratification.

Interviews with government officials, researchers and business people which I conducted during 1993 and 1994 revealed that 'a hidden economy' existed in Vietnam before renovation and persists in various forms such as unregistered private enterprises, SOEs, which are shells for private enterprise, corruption, smuggling and the production of fakes. Revised official statistics suggest that from the late 1970s, 60 per cent of agricultural production took place outside the cooperative structure and was sold privately.[1]

About 90 per cent of vegetables and meat were produced and sold by women who ventured to the free urban markets or sold illegally on the streets. A 35-year-old woman in Hanoi, who is now a successful businesswoman, told me that when she was young she sold small pieces of pork on the street. When officials passed by she surreptitiously moved the pork behind her back. The interviews also revealed that many urban manufacturing enterprises which appeared to be cooperatives were in fact shells for family-run businesses. Officially, some private enterprise activity was tolerated, especially for female-headed households who used petty trade as an economic safety net. But it appears that the scope of this activity was much larger than admitted by the authorities. As fewer sanctions come to be placed on private enterprise, it is expected that the relative size of this sector will shrink.

Because the 'hidden economy' was not included in official statistics, any serious statistical economic analysis of Vietnam is problematic. Furthermore, the existence of a substantial 'hidden economy' means not only that the current level of GDP per capita is an underestimate but also that the rate of economic growth has been somewhat slower than official statistics indicate, due to a higher base line (Fahey 1993).

The existence of the 'hidden economy' is significant for the analysis of women's roles and images because women in Vietnam are the most active figures in agricultural and handicraft production and the marketplace. In fact, Dao The Tuan, former director of the Vietnam Agricultural Science Institute, attributes much of the push for economic renovation in Vietnam to rural women and the poor who insisted on conducting petty commodity trade (Dao The Tuan personal communication August 1993). According to Dao The Tuan, the authorities apparently had little success in censoring these determined women of the north.

The ambiguities of Communist Party policy in Vietnam also have implications for the position of women. Vietnam is one of the few countries in the world to have officially supported equality between men and women from as early as the 1930s. The current position of women, however, brings into question the degree to which such legal strategies can affect change. Regardless of the long list of legislative protection, equality between women and men in Vietnam has not been achieved. As in other revolutionary struggles against colonisation and capitalism, women's emancipation was subordinated to the task of national liberation. '. . . [I]f women do not participate in these struggles, never will they be able to emancipate themselves' (Mai Thi Tu and Le Thi Nham Tuyet 1978: 103–4). At the same time, party leaders believed that moves to equality must come from within the society and not from the state. 'Only women can liberate themselves,' was the initial policy of the Party (Turley 1972: 797).

RESEARCH ON GENDER IN VIETNAM

Much of the social science research to date on gender issues in Vietnam has focussed on 'gender and development', with a recent interest in the nature of the Vietnamese family. The earlier contributions to this body of research conducted mainly by Vietnamese (Mai Thi Tu and Le Thi Nham Tuyet 1978) and American scholars (Eisen 1984; Werner 1984 and White 1982) were, by and large, positive about women's progress whereas the more recent research expresses some apprehension about women's position following renovation (Le Thi and Vinh Thi 1993; Pelzer 1993; Ungar 1993; Bui Thi Kim Quy 1994).

After the reunification of Vietnam in 1976, little social science research of any sort was conducted in the country. The Communist Party's approach to social issues was prescriptive rather than analytic. It was not until the mid-1980s that social research centres were established. Most contemporary Vietnamese research on women's issues is generated through these centres including the Centre for the Family and Women's Studies (CFWS), and the Centre for Research on Gender in Hanoi and the Centre for Scientific Study of Women and the Family in Ho Chi Minh City.

The Women's Union and women's branches of organisations such as the Vietnam General Confederation of Labour have a much longer history, with the responsibility of lobbying for women's rights and conflict resolution. Although they have generated some information on women's position, more recently they have been coopted by international organisations for the administration of aid and have lost much of their lobbying role.[2]

As social science research by Vietnamese scholars emerges, there appears to be little unanimity of views. For example, research focussing on the nature of the family ranges from a stress on the dominance of the Confucian family bounded by collective interests and patriarchy (Mai Huy Bich 1991) to a view of the nuclear family as the functional unit, although the first son's responsibilities for taking care of the parents and maintaining the cult of the ancestors is emphasised (Nguyen Tu Chi 1991). For political reasons, this research largely plays down the importance of other divisions cutting across the nature of the family like class and regional differences.

Vietnamese researchers as well as those from multilateral aid agencies have concentrated on issues of female employment, access to education, prostitution and domestic violence. Other concerns with no immediate policy relevance such as the commodification of women have not been considered as yet and only those researchers who have had extensive exposure to Western academic influences consider such topics worthy of serious research. Vietnamese researchers' dismissal of questions about ideologies of beauty and the domestic begs the question of the relevance of such discourses in contemporary Vietnam.

CHANGING IMAGES OF WOMEN DURING SOCIO-ECONOMIC REFORM

Over the past 10 years, images of women in Vietnam have changed dramatically. The process of globalisation has drawn many urban Vietnamese women into the commercial sphere: women have become both consumers of products and tools to advertise products with. Multinational companies have spearheaded the large-scale promotion of fashion and beauty aids to women and use techniques developed elsewhere to harness women's sexuality in order to advertise their products. Nevertheless, it is also clear that overseas Vietnamese, of which there are several million, have identified both trading and investment opportunities in Vietnam in the creation of a domestic beauty industry.

With Vietnam's rapid transition from a command economy to market mechanism, and especially since the 1994 lifting of the US embargo, the trappings of capitalist modernity have begun to appear. It is not uncommon to be received in a home in Hanoi in air-conditioned comfort and to have conversation periodically interrupted by a mobile phone, while the children of the household, dressed in designer-ripped jeans, listen to the latest Western bands courtesy of pirated CDs from China, or watch a video of the latest Western movie. The most recent fad to hit Hanoi homes in 1995 was the microwave oven. So far McDonalds has been kept at bay but in the days following the lifting of the US trade embargo in July, the Opera House in Hanoi, once the symbol of culture for the city, was framed by giant plastic bottles of Coca Cola.

When I first visited Vietnam in 1990, very few Western products were available on the street. Electrical goods were limited to the occasional fan. Butter in the guest house bore little resemblance to butter sold in the West and milk was only of the condensed type, whereas fresh milk is now available daily. Tampons and lipstick were virtually unheard of, but by 1995 most young urban women had the choice of Max Factor or the more expensive Japanese brands of make-up.

Within this maze of rapid change, the images of Vietnamese women visible in the streets remain contradictory. Images left over from the pre-renovation period of women as war heroes appear alongside the new images of women as objects of beauty to sell 'modern' commodities. Souvenir shops in Hang Gai Street of Hanoi peddle tea towels and wall-hangings embroidered with images of female cult heroes such as the Trung sisters, who are famous for leading a short-lived rebellion against Chinese occupation in the first century. Impatiently, the storekeepers attempt to deter women with babes in arms who beg from the passing tourists. In the Women's Museum in Hanoi hang photographs of Vietnamese women war heroes, notably a petite Vietnamese woman of the revolutionary army leading a submissive American serviceman to captivity (Ungar 1993). In nearby streets, the magazine *Tien phong* (*Pioneer*) reports on forthcoming beauty contests sponsored by foreign firms such as Kodak, Singapore Airlines and Samsung.

On the poorer southern outskirts of Hanoi, remnant billboards of socialist propaganda promoting the country's progress display faded images of female farm workers standing behind a male factory worker. In the central part of Hanoi, these billboards have been replaced by portrayals of a woman as a mother caring for her family. Next to the central railway station I saw a large poster of a scantily dressed Asian woman advertising underwear. Posters in more dramatic colour, located near the universities, warn against *sida* (HIV/AIDS), while in the central city posters in support of the family planning programme feature mother, father and one child. Curiously, one picture which dominates the facade of a building overlooking Hoan Kiem Lake in the city centre depicts Ho Chi Minh holding a child. He is commemorated for his love of children rather than his role in the communist uprising. Following Maria Mies, we could view this image as a 'feminine role' of nation building rather than as a 'male role' of state building (Mies 1986: 199). The insistence of the recent billboards on the mother's nurturing role is perhaps yet another element in Vietnam's increasingly clear sexual division of labour.

From 1992 on, shops decorated by framed posters and calendars of voluptuous Asian and Western women in seductive poses have graced the streets of Hanoi. Television advertisements for health clubs and exercise equipment feature Vietnamese women in brightly coloured leotards using equipment which bears an uncomfortable resemblance to the million bicycles which grace the streets everyday. Everywhere one sees beauty parlours and hairdressers, newspapers full of advertisements for cosmetic surgery – face lift, peeling, breast augmentation – and an endless number of bridal shops.

Vietnamese women seem to be increasingly conscious of fashion and body shape. During the war and the immediate post-war period, women were cautioned by the authorities for wearing brightly coloured clothes. Concern about body shape was limited to whether a woman was too thin: this was thought to negatively affect her productive, but perhaps more importantly, her reproductive capacity. These attitudes began to change as women students and guest workers returned from Europe with the physical and ideological trappings of modernity. These women were conspicuous by their use of make-up, their display of Eastern European fashion and their personal demeanour. The first aerobics class in Hanoi was conducted in 1983 at a local state-run club and was attended only by returned migrants.

In 1989, the Vietnamese state allowed its first beauty contest. This contest for Miss *Ao Dai* (traditional dress) was held in Ho Chi Minh City and promoted by *Phu Nu* (*Woman*) newspaper. A year later the first national contest for Miss *Tien Phong* was promoted by *Tien Phong* (*Pioneer*) newspaper in Hanoi and now has become an annual event with provincial contests leading to the finals. Apart from these, smaller contests are held including those promoted by the Vietnam Confederation of Labour (*Lien Doan Lao Dong Viet Nam*) and Social Affairs Service (*So Lao Dong Thuong Binh Xa Hoi*). The spectator's entry fee of US$10 to US$30 is phenomenally high in a nation where the average worker earns about US$30 a month and university lecturers about US$50 a month.

Associated with the popularity of the beauty contests was the emergence of fashion clubs and magazines. Fashion clubs appeared in the early 1990s, with members including fashion designers, models and companies eager to establish a fashion industry. The first modelling agency CATS begun by a young overseas Vietnamese was licensed in Vietnam in 1995. Vietnam now has two locally produced fashion magazines: one for women in general (*Thoi Trang*) and the other for younger women (*Thoi Trang Tre*). Another magazine called *Thoi Trang Dien Anh* (*Movie Fashion*) reproduces sections from international fashion magazines, including French and US fashion, and appears to be more popular in the south. These magazines also have small sections for men perhaps indicating that the commercialisation of beauty is not entirely limited to women. Most newspapers now have a women's section which covers topics from how to pluck eye brows to Japanese-sponsored fashion parades.

A popular activity for middle-class women, especially those with substantial independent incomes, is attending the gym before work. Membership is about US$10 per month or 5–10 per cent of these women's monthly income. Interviews with these women reveal that they attend both for social interaction and to improve their body shape. Although these women are conscious of maintaining a shapely body and coyly admit to Vietnamese women's propensity to wear padded bras – especially with the *ao dai* (the tightly fitted traditional dress) – they inevitably refer to both inner and outer beauty when asked open-ended questions about the definition of a beautiful woman.

A parallel trend is the growth of the body-building industry for men. Street posters of body-builders, often with western faces, advertise gymnasiums; national competitions are held; and magazines are available for those who wish to know more. The body shape acquired by body-builders is significantly different from that of the majority of Vietnamese men and there appears to be no precedent for such a practice. One is tempted to assume that recently arrived foreign images contribute to the exacerbation of physical differences between women and men in Vietnam.

Although there is renewed emphasis on the physical appearance of both women and men, the fundamental difference is that beauty aids for women are expensive and fiercely marketed to the urban middle class. A straw poll conducted by *Vietnam Investment Review* found that fashion-conscious women in Vietnam spend a surprisingly high proportion of their income on clothes and cosmetics (Mandow 1995: 31–3). Sixty-eight per cent of women surveyed spend 40 to 60 per cent of their income on clothes and cosmetics. Office workers spend US$200 to US$300 per year on clothes. Not surprisingly, Vietnam's domestic fashion industry shows a strong overseas influence as Vietnamese generally seem to have lost confidence in the quality of locally produced goods and prefer imported brands. Most Vietnamese women who are resident in the rural areas, however, spend virtually nothing on clothes and cosmetics.

Legally imported cosmetics are extremely expensive in Vietnam. Duty rose from 50 to 60 per cent in 1995 and there is an additional sales tax. The cosmetics market has not been left entirely to multinationals. Early opportunities were seized by Fuji cosmetics, a firm which was established in Ho Chi Minh City by expatriate Vietnamese who returned from Japan in 1992 to produce cosmetics and who use sales tactics modelled on Avon's practice of door-to-door with follow-up service (Truong Van Khoi 1994: 51). There is also a thriving market in smuggled foreign brands.

Examination of the consumption patterns of Western products by Vietnamese women also reveals a generation gap often exacerbated by the difference in income. Young women with access to money through working for foreign firms, for Vietnamese private enterprise or in some informal sector activities such as prostitution have higher expectations than their counterparts in other fields such as government positions.

Sexuality is becoming increasingly commercialised in Vietnam. For example, in May 1995, 'Marlboro girls' wearing red sashes bearing the Marlboro name appeared in Hanoi wandering through beer gardens and coffee shops distributing sample cigarettes. They flirt with males before they move on. Dunhill also sponsors popular dance competitions. The entry fee is US$5 which includes a complimentary packet of cigarettes. In a country where the Communist Party attempted to eradicate prostitution and pornography, prostitutes are now found in almost every bar, restaurant and hotel whether private or state-owned; government research institutes are known to import pornographic magazines for resale; and government publications often feature beautiful women to advertise products such as fertiliser.

Pelzer (1993: 317–21) suggests that the beauty contests and calendars sanctioned by the state are a signal to the international business community that Vietnam is open for business.

> The new policy of displaying feminine smiles and female bodies serves as advertisement for the new Vietnam. The foreign investment law is not photogenic, and mention in an article that Vietnam now has the most favourable regulations in Asia for foreign capital investment does not produce an immediate visual impact. The beauty queens who grace the calendars given by Vietnamese ministries and trading companies to potential foreign investors have a come-hither look which projects an image of promise and availability; they can be considered Vietnam's advertisements for the foreign investment law.
>
> (Pelzer 1993: 318–19)

THE RECONSTRUCTION OF WOMEN'S IMAGE

What is commonly referred to as women's 'traditional' role in Vietnam has received much academic attention: from Western researchers during the French occupation (Huard and Durand 1954); from official histories of women (Mai Thi Tu and Le Thi Nham Tuyet 1978, the Vietnam Women's Union and the Centre for Women Studies 1989) and from more contemporary analyses by both Vietnamese (Tran Dinh Huou 1991: 27–54) and Western academics (Marr 1981: 190–251; Jamieson 1993: 1–41). Although it is not my intention to review these here, suffice to say that these reconstructions of women's 'traditional role' are driven by various research agendas. Here I consider only some aspects of women's reconstructed 'traditional role' which appear in the manufacture of contradictory contemporary images of Vietnamese women. An underlying question is whether the apparent loss of women's relative position under renovation is a result of pre-revolutionary patriarchal culture reasserting itself or a result (as seems to be the case in the former communist Europe) of the relative weakening of the state opening up more space to global market forces.

In Vietnam today women dominate petty commodity trading in the market and on the street. Even the money changers servicing smuggling across the Vietnam–Chinese border during the early 1990s were women. Furthermore, women are participants in newly emerging private enterprises, particularly in family businesses. The wives of senior politicians are often known for their business acumen. During casual conversations about corruption, Vietnamese often ridicule the wives of senior politicians for their abuse of their husbands' position of power. These women are accused of using the privileges of the state to protect their large-scale smuggling rackets while the government struggles to control corruption. Although these accusations may be a safer form of political protest than direct criticism of the government, the centrality of women in the business sector is acknowledged in such criticism.

Though highly visible, street trading in Vietnam is still viewed as unsophisticated. Female dominance of this sector is mostly uncontested, whereas formal entrepreneurial activity is more acceptable to men. Women are perceived as the guerrillas of the renovation process. They have taken the lead in unsavoury petty trading activities and have challenged long-standing values of generosity outside the nuclear family.

A famous short story, *The General Retires* by Nguyen Huy Thiep (1988), encapsulates many dimensions of the situation of contemporary middle-class women in Hanoi. The story depicts the female character as a professional woman caught in the contradiction between communist rhetoric of self-sacrifice and the reality of daily life. An excerpt from the story emphasises the moral compromises the woman has made in her quest to generate finances for the family by breeding dogs for trade.

> The Maternity Hospital where my wife worked carried out abortions. Every day, she put the aborted foetuses into a Thermos flask and brought them home. Mr Co cooked them for the dogs and pigs. I had in fact known about this, but overlooked it as something of no importance. My father led me out to the kitchen and pointed to a pot full of mash in which there were small lumps of foetus. I kept silent. My father cried. He picked up the Thermos flask and hurled it at the pack of Alsatians: 'Vile! I don't need wealth that's made of this!' The dogs barked. My father went off up to the house. My wife came in and spoke to Mr Co: 'Why didn't you put it through the meat grinder? Why did you let Father see it?' Mr Co stammered: 'I forgot, I'm sorry, Aunt.'
>
> (Nguyen Huy Thiep 1988, trans. Lockhart, 1992: 122)

In Vietnam, social status is still associated with education and position, although material possessions are also becoming components of status. A group of middle-aged academics in Hanoi joked with me recently that successful Hanoi businesswomen attempt to secure respectability in a society through marrying a husband who works for the government even though he may earn only US$50 per month while she may earn as much as US$2,000 per month – a strategy which recalls the practice of wives supporting husbands while they studied for mandarin exams in earlier times.

Images of women's courage and entrepreneurial skill are bolstered by Vietnamese folklore, female buddhas and proverbs. Vietnam has an official matriarchal heritage (Mai Thi Tu and Le Thi Nham Tuyet 1978). Women commonly occupied the rank of goddess presiding over the cultivation of rice and other food crops. Streets and districts are named after female cult heroes such as the Trung sisters and Trieu Thi Trinh who took up a similar warrior role in the third century. She is described as nine feet tall, with breasts which were three feet long and a voice like a temple bell, and as able to eat several pecks of rice and walk 500 leagues in a single day (Marr 1981:198). Vietnamese nationalists have also resurrected the poetry of Ho Xuan Huong, a female poet who was critical of gender inequality more than 50 years before French colonisation.[3]

In the 1990s another kind of women's power is being resurrected out of history and mythology. Businesswomen, especially in the north, draw on an imagery of former entrepreneurial strength. Since the late 1980s, with the relaxation of religious sanctions in Vietnam, village pagodas have undergone a frenzy of refurbishment. In a pagoda in Ninh Hiep, a village near Hanoi, a local woman pharmacist of 200 years ago is revered for the birth of the prosperous traditional craft of pharmaceutical production. Ba Chua Lieu, supposedly a princess who developed a prosperous silk industry, is featured in a temple on West Lake. Pagodas which feature female entrepreneurial deities are a hub of activity and attract patrons from long distances. The paths which lead to these pagodas are lined with anxious vendors of religious offerings of incense, foods, paper objects and imitation paper money (including US dollars from 'the bank of hell' because it is regarded as the stronger currency both economically and spiritually). Those who patronise the pagodas include the young and the prosperous who commonly implore the appropriate female deities for economic success but also, ironically, for success in producing a son. By contrast, the pagoda which honours the Trung sisters is characteristically deserted except in March when the statues of the sisters together with the 12 women generals are unveiled and washed in sacred water from the Red River.

With the demise of the communist moral code, Vietnamese are searching their past for 'traditional values' to fill the void. The 'three submissions' and the 'four virtues'[4] have been recast at various times during Vietnam's recent history in order to harness the commitment of women to the war effort and now to the renovation process. During the war the three submissions were to 'replace men and free them for combat, assume control of the family and encourage husbands and sons to enlist, and participate in combat when necessary' (Turley 1972: 800).

More recently, the director of the Centre for Women's Studies, Le Thi, argued for the reformulation of the four virtues (personal communication December 1994): if women are to work hard they need training and skills development; if they are to remain beautiful, they should have sufficient rest and fewer children; in speech they should be assertive and they should behave with dignity obtained through equality and democracy.

But younger Vietnamese women are operating in a void, rejecting both what they consider to be hollow Communist Party prescriptions for gender equality and irrelevant views of western feminists. Young women writers such as Vo Thi Xuan Ha, who recently won an encouragement award from the prestigious *Van Nghe* newspaper for her novel *A Family's Traditional Box*, challenges what she considers to be traditional Vietnamese values for women: that responsibility is more important than love and the family is more essential than passion. She writes of the indignities experienced by women as their husbands take mistresses and of women's rebellious behaviour in taking lovers themselves or seeking divorce. Questions about appropriate gender relations are one element of the moral vacuum left by the withdrawal of the Party from social engineering.

CONFUCIAN VERSUS COMMUNIST GENDER IDEOLOGY

Communism in Vietnam had its origins in France, the Soviet Union and China and as with other foreign ideologies parts were selectively absorbed. The communist ideal for women was equality with men, to be achieved through the demise of private property and women's domestic role. In Vietnam, this ideology directly confronted Confucian views of the position and role of women.

After the establishment of the Democratic Republic of Vietnam in 1945, it was necessary to mobilise all people for the reconstruction of the economy and to increase production (as in China). It is clear that the revolutionary war could not be won without women's cooperation because of the vital roles they played in the economy. Among the ten slogans of the Communist Party of Indochina on its foundation in February 1930 was the commitment to achieve equality between men and women (Ho Chi Minh 1960–62). But at the same time, equality between men and women as a primary goal was denounced as 'bourgeois ideology'. Women's struggles tended to be subordinated to the task of national liberation, following which women would receive education and then liberate themselves (Mai Thi Tu and Le Thi Nham Tuyet 1978: 103–4). The Party introduced several reforms to support equality between men and women.[5] But certain ambiguities emerged in the implementation of these reforms.[6] Nevertheless, reforms continued in pursuit of equality through legislation rather than through changes in property relations.[7]

During the war women were mobilised and entered traditionally male occupations in large numbers. Their major responsibility was to maintain agricultural production while the men went off to war. This left the cooperatives dominated by women members. The cooperative system, in which surplus was gladly relinquished to support fathers, husbands, brothers and sons at the front, proved an appropriate mechanism in war time.

Women also fought in the war, blazing trails such as the famous Ho Chi Minh Trail, carrying food and munitions to the front on their shoulders and guarding these goods, and repairing roads and bridges to ensure transportation of supplies. They were nurses, couriers, guides and propagandists, becoming 'the long-haired army'.

Because of the extraordinary demographic imbalance after the war, women continued in many of these roles. Women were actively encouraged into the workforce – into the ranks of the proletariat – which placed them at the centre of revolutionary struggle. In the north almost all women between the ages of 15 and 55 were in the workforce during the communist period and in the south this increased from 20 to 80 per cent between 1975 and the early 1980s (Eisen 1984: 141–2). Equality also meant that women were expected to engage in all forms of labour including heavy manual labour in road construction, as porters, and in heavy manufacturing. These new roles changed the views of women's capacities and loosened the authority of the family and clan. The sexual division of labour in Vietnam in the early 1980s was confronting to visitors from the West where issues of equal opportunity were being hotly debated (Mackerras 1988).

Based on Engels' view that it was women's child care responsibilities which hampered their full participation in development, a major initiative was taken by the government in 1971 to set up the Central Committee for Mother and Infant Welfare. The committee was to guide and unify the organisation of crèches. This apparently resulted in a dramatic increase in the proportion of children in crèche and kindergarten to about one-third of all children – an impressive number in a predominantly rural society. Data in Vietnam are notoriously unreliable especially during this period as the distinction between planned target and reality was often blurred. Nevertheless, it is clear from interviews that a large number of children were in crèches while an even larger number were the responsibility of grandmothers. Either way, mothers were released to enter wage employment. Support given for women to separate themselves from domestic duties was formalised in the 1980 State Constitution Article 63 which declares that the state and society ensure the development of maternity homes, crèches, kindergartens, community dining halls and other social amenities to create favourable conditions for women to produce, work, study and rest.

But the contradiction between the socialisation of the functions of the family and its importance as a nurturing unit continued. Le Duan, the leader of the Communist Party during the 1970s and early 1980s and a prolific writer and theoretician, argued for equality between men and women. Le Duan believed women should be involved in economic and state management, but at the same time carry on the noble function of mother and wife in the family. Men were asked to share household tasks, but these efforts remained at the cultural/ideological level rather than being implemented within production and reproduction. Vietnamese communists were keen to maintain the family as a social but not necessarily economic unit (Le Duan 1977: 381–2). This downgrading of the household's economic role continued until September 1979, when the Sixth Plenum of the Party's Fourth Central Committee decided to affirm the importance of small-scale production, opening the door for the family to make use of resources under-utilised by the cooperative.

The conflict between employment and domestic duties, a frequent complaint from women in Vietnam today (Bui Thi Kim Quy 1994), received little official attention during the communist period. Theoreticians, keen to get the rhetoric right, argued the necessity for both. Under communism in the urban areas, household duties were labour intensive, because services such as electricity and water were of a low standard. Women were expected to wait in line and then negotiate with corrupt officials for rations. With a goal of full employment, low work intensity was common. This allowed greater flexibility for women to meet their domestic duties during working hours. Workers were paid a subsidy to raise children and child care was more accessible during this period. If a woman was absent due to child rearing or other social responsibilities, another worker temporarily replaced her. Under the market mechanism, where the goal is profit, higher work intensity and longer hours reduce flexibility. The subsidy has been eliminated and child care is no longer a right but an expensive service. Hence, the accommodation of domestic and non-domestic roles becomes problematic.

The progressive restoration of gender inequalities after the war had a number of consequences. It is claimed that Vietnamese men resented women in their newly found leadership positions (Eisen 1984: 248–54; White 1980). Prominent women leaders were sent to the provinces and representation in the National Assembly declined. In the first National Assembly in 1946, only 3 per cent of seats were occupied by women and this ratio remained unchanged until 1960 from which point it began to increase. Beresford points out that female representation in the National Assembly began to decline immediately after the war from 27 per cent in 1976, to 22 per cent in 1981 to 18 per cent in 1987 (1988: 110). In 1992 the proportion had increased only marginally but is expected to decline as the quota which required proportional female representation of 18 per cent was eliminated before the last election (National Assembly Office, 1993). Such data suggest that the recent changes in women's position may have less to do with economic renovation as such, and more to do with restoration of certain aspects of pre-war gender practices. Some Vietnamese women have argued that the decline in representation of women in the National Assembly is irrelevant because the National Assembly is losing authority and ambitious women can use their time more productively in private enterprise (interviews with the author).

Undoubtedly, women's relative position improved under communism, with a reduction of early forced marriages, the public condemnation of wife-beating, free child care and the recognition of the economic value of housework (see Turley 1972: 799). Prostitution was to a large extent eradicated but the mistress was still common. Legislation together with women's prolonged contribution to the war effort assisted in dismantling irrevocably the absolute authority of 'the three submissions', in its traditional guise. Nevertheless, conditions in an economy drained by 30 years of war and later economic mismanagement were poor.

REFORMS AND THE DOMESTIC HOUSEHOLD

The changing social position of women is inextricably linked to the changing ideology of the domestic sphere. Renovation, the collapse of cooperatives and the new land reforms have all produced a new emphasis on the household as an economic unit. The social wages put into place under communism very quickly started to unravel. The user-pays principle has been introduced for health care and education (although primary education is supposedly still free). The state no longer guarantees employment or housing. All this has meant an increased role for the household and individuals within the household.

These changes are rapidly bringing Vietnamese women's situation into line with that of their sisters in other developing countries. The relatively high standard of infant and maternal care is now only available to those who can pay. Child care has become prohibitively expensive.

The gender balance in educational institutions is shifting in favour of male students, especially in tertiary courses suited to the new labour market. Women are losing their jobs in SOEs more quickly than men. Working conditions for women are being eroded with the reduction of paid maternity leave and the reluctance of small private firms to provide child care or meet the costs of maternity leave. Women have few new opportunities for high income earnings comparable to those of men, with the exception of prostitution, and work in restaurants, retail outlets and teaching English.

Nevertheless, the state rhetoric continues. In 1988, the Council of Ministers' Decision No. 163 gave the Women's Union the right to be consulted, informed and involved in all discussions, plans or policies relating to women and children at all levels of government. The Politburo in July 1993 made a decision on the mobilisation of women which emphasised women's role in the process of renovation with the aim of improving women's material and spiritual life. Nevertheless, membership figures indicate that the Party is losing women's support, with a drop in membership from 34 per cent women in 1960 to only 16 per cent today. Theoretically, the law in Vietnam continues to protect the rights of women, but such structures are in practice often ignored. Women's daily lives continue in accordance with unwritten laws.

During interviews conducted in late 1995, women indicated that they were feeling increasingly vulnerable in these conditions of social upheaval. Divorce is increasingly easy to obtain. Moreover, a study conducted on HIV/AIDS in 1993 found that 54 per cent of those men interviewed in places where sex is sold or where dates for sex can be made (e.g. cafes, restaurants, nightclubs, parks and the street) had had two or more sexual partners in the last two weeks (Franklin 1993: 35). Furthermore, middle-class urban women often confide during informal interviews that their husbands have a mistress or entertain several girlfriends. Women are still responsible for family finances and the welfare of the children. It seems increasingly common for women to have secret savings as a buffer against fluctuations in the economy and their husbands' indiscretions with other women, drinking and gambling.

REFORM IN THE LABOUR MARKET

An important indicator of women's changing social position is the nature of their participation in economic activity. During the war and its aftermath, women were highly represented in the labour force. According to the Vietnam Living Standards Survey (State Planning Committee and General Statistical Office 1994) in which 4,800 households across the country were interviewed in 1992–93, 91.8 per cent of the economically active female population was employed compared to 93.8 per cent for men.

Table 8.1 shows that women dominate in the industry groups of trade and restaurants, agriculture, forestry and fisheries and are highly represented in the manufacturing industry, non-productive activities (i.e. social and community services) and 'other' activities. Significantly, one fifth of those in the mining industry and one tenth of those in construction were women. These jobs include not only office jobs but heavy manual labour.[8]

Of women employed in the urban areas, the majority work in trade and restaurants (38.9 per cent), whereas 25 per cent work in manufacturing and 20 per cent in agriculture, forestry and fishery (Table 8.2). Occupations for women such as waitressing and paid domestic work have become more numerous with the expansion of the service sector and income differentials. Although maids existed during the pre-renovation period, they have become more numerous in the past few years. Maids are usually young women from the countryside who move to the city to assist their relatives in domestic care. These girls are provided food and lodgings and 'payment' when they return to their villages.

With the continued unfolding of economic reforms, women's representation in the formal labour force has declined. As SOEs have rationalised, the female workers have lost jobs faster than males. It is not unusual for women to be the first victims of unemployment.[9] According

Table 8.1 Primary job in the last 12 months of employed population by industry group and sex structure, 1992–93

	Sex structure		*Industry structure*
	Women	*Men*	
Agriculture, forestry, fisheries	51.8	48.2	71.1
Mining	22.5	77.5	0.3
Industry	49.6	50.4	9.5
Electricity industry	21.0	79.0	0.1
Construction	9.4	90.6	1.3
Trade and restaurants	76.0	24.0	9.2
Transport and communications	9.6	90.4	1.6
Finance and insurance	26.1	73.9	0.2
Non-productive	48.7	51.3	4.7
Others	47.4	52.6	1.3
Total	52.2	47.8	100

Source: State Planning Committee and General Statistics Office, *Vietnam Living Standards Survey, 1992–93*, 1994.

Table 8.2 Primary job in the last 12 months of employed population by industry group, sex structure and location, 1992–93

	Urban		*Rural*	
	Women	*Men*	*Women*	*Men*
Agriculture, forestry, fisheries	20.0	24.2	83.1	83.2
Mining	0.4	0.8	0.0	0.4
Industry	23.6	27.0	5.7	6.2
Electricity industry	0.2	0.5	0.0	0.2
Construction	1.0	6.3	0.1	1.7
Trade and restaurants	38.9	13.6	7.5	2.6
Transport and communications	0.9	9.0	0.2	1.7
Finance and insurance	0.4	0.8	0.0	0.2
Non-productive	12.0	14.2	2.6	2.9
Others	2.7	3.6	0.8	0.9
Total	100.0	100.0	100.0	100.0

Source: State Planning Committee and General Statistics Office, *Vietnam Living Standards Survey, 1992–93*, 1994.

to the Vietnam General Confederation of Labour, women made up 49 per cent of total state employment in 1989, declining to 47 per cent in 1992. Of those positions lost in SOEs, 60–70 per cent were held by women.

The reasons given by various women's groups in Vietnam for the more rapid rates of female unemployment focus on the lack of training of women, their poor health, health-related costs such as maternity benefits and absenteeism due to child care and other family responsibilities. Under communism, the state introduced regulations to protect women's rights: the free choice of spouse, the right to work, the responsibility of men to share housework and affirmative action to promote higher education for women. As the state withdraws from the provision of social services such as subsidised child care, health care and school fees, these responsibilities fall back onto women in the home. This strategy effectively reduces government expenditure and, as some women are forced to leave the labour force, it also contributes to the decline of the official unemployment levels, while forcing women to retreat into the informal sector.

Although no detailed statistics are available, it appears that women are becoming concentrated in low skill and high labour intensity occupations (Le Thi and Vinh Thi 1993). Until 'renovation', women were not disadvantaged with respect to pay because workers were paid according to their need rather than their responsibility or output. With salary reform and the creation of a labour market, the lack of skill and training for women became more obvious as unskilled women workers began to lose their jobs and concentrate at the most lowly paid end of the newly created pay scale. According to the Living Standards Survey, 1992–93 the average monthly wage for urban women was only 70 per cent of men's (State Planning Committee and General Statistics Office 1994).

The Living Standards Survey found that the mean number of years of education for women was 5.9 compared to 7.5 years for men. The difference between men and women is less than one year for those aged 18–34. The difference is exaggerated for those aged 55–64 in which mean years of education are only 2.2 compared to 5.4 years for men. Although significant gains have been made by women in terms of school enrolment and schooling levels completed over the past 30 years it appears that the gender gap has re-emerged for the younger generation with a faster decrease in the enrolments of 11 to 14 year-old girls (30 per cent) compared to boys (14 per cent).

Women are highly represented in foreign sector activities although the exact numbers are curiously unavailable. Many of the growth industries for foreign investors are those which traditionally employ women including textiles, garment production, leather products and foodstuff processing. Women workers make up 55–87 per cent of the labour force in these industries (Bui Thi Kim Quy 1994). Women also dominate in office jobs as secretaries and interpreters/translators.

At this stage it is difficult to generalise about the incorporation of Vietnamese women into global capitalist enterprises. Foreign investment is still limited within Vietnam despite the large number of approved projects and domestic private investment is still very small. Nevertheless, it appears that gender inequities are on the rise as women leave SOEs and enter foreign and private domestic firms investing in labour-intensive industries. The Institute of Social Sciences in Ho Chi Minh City recently surveyed 13 foreign-invested enterprises employing predominantly women. The survey found that the women were young (i.e. 70 per cent of women were 18–30) and usually single (i.e. 60 per cent) (ibid.). Most of these women found it difficult to maintain their family and social commitments as well as maintain full-time work in which they were expected to work overtime every two days from 7.00 a.m. to 9.00 p.m. and on weekends. Conditions in private domestic firms are no better. It is common for young women to be brought from the countryside to work in a relative's factory. Employer/employee relations mimic those of a small family business. Workers are not paid a salary; food and lodgings are provided by the factory owners in their home and other costs relating to health, transport and clothing are also provided on a perceived needs basis. Workers have flexibility to return to the village for festivals and family reasons and at this stage they may be given remuneration (Bui Thi Kim Quy personal communication November, 1995).

Women in Vietnam are still expected to take care of the domestic arrangements of shopping, cooking and cleaning as well as meeting family responsibilities for ceremonies such as at Tet (Vietnamese New Year), funerals and weddings. As a consequence, women, especially married women, are leaving paid employment within state and private enterprise and opting for the more flexible arrangements of petty trading. The Living Standards Survey found that in the urban areas, 61 per cent of employed women were self-employed compared to 48.1 per cent of men.

Self-employment opportunities for women outside the home may explain why female-headed households generally are not poor in Vietnam. According to the Living Standards Survey, 1992–93, 27 per cent (18 per cent rural, 9 per cent urban) of all households were female-headed; 41 per cent of female-heads were widowed, many due to war casualties, whereas 11 per cent were separated or divorced and another 11 per cent were married with absent husbands; 33 per cent of female household heads were married with a spouse in the household. These households were mainly in urban areas; the women were well educated and the households were highly represented in the upper income groups. In general, female-headed households were under-represented in the poorest expenditure quintile at only 23 per cent, while they were over-represented in the highest expenditure quintile at 38 per cent of households with a greater representation in the urban areas.

RECENT REFORMS TO WOMEN'S WORKING CONDITIONS

In the wide consultation which preceded the promulgation of the new Labour Code revisions, women's rights came under intense debate (*Labour Code of Vietnam* 1994, Chapter X). Some Articles in the code were uncontroversial: women retire at 55 years whereas men retire at 60 years; employers must provide assistance with the provision of child care if they employ a large number of women workers; and equal pay and conditions are required for women and men. It was clear that these benefits for women acted as a disincentive for employers. To overcome these apparent disincentives, employers are required to pay less tax if they employ women. In an economy where tax avoidance is a common practice, however, tax concessions are of limited effectiveness.

Some conditions were more controversial, viewed by women's groups as retrogressive for women. For example, paid maternity leave was reduced from '6 months' to '6–4 months'. Some textile factories, such as Minh Khai Textile Factory, which employ mainly women, have responded by drawing up schedules planning when each female worker is allowed to take maternity leave, thus forcing the women to plan their pregnancies (Quoc Vinh 1994). The Labour Code also includes a new provision for 30 minutes off every day that a woman is menstruating, which is similar to the situation in Japan, and 60 minutes when they were breast feeding. Whether these provisions are seen as improvements in conditions is debatable. Some female workers claim that such provisions are unnecessary and only contribute to discrimination, whereas others suggest that poor sanitary conditions at the workplace make these provisions necessary.

In spite of the new labour code, working conditions for women are still difficult. Women at the Cau Duong Brick factory work in 55 degree (Celsius) heat; women porters regularly carry 30–40 kilograms while those who work at ports, train stations and quarries carry 80–100 kilograms. Because of their lower pay, women often work overtime to compensate. Anecdotal evidence suggests that these poor conditions continue to affect women's reproductive capacity and weight.

In an attempt to improve women's working conditions, the Ministry of Labour, Invalids, and Social Affairs (MOLISA) prepared Circular No. 9 in 1986 which specified jobs which women were not allowed to do. The criteria for exclusion included jobs which allegedly interfered with child bearing and rearing capacity, such as cleaning steam boilers, working in contact with radioactivity, working in mines, driving heavy trucks of a carrying capacity of 2.5 metric tonnes or more, and buying and conveying buffalo. Women in these jobs were to be transferred to other positions, but many were dismissed because no new jobs existed in a state sector already in crisis. In 1994 the list was revised in a Joint Circular No. 3 of MOLISA and Ministry of Health. This list distinguished between 'women workers in general' and 'others', those who were pregnant or nursing children under 12 months, and teenagers. Previously, 106 occupations were listed, but this decreased to 49 allowed for women 'in general', who were permitted to carry 50 kilograms and 83 for 'others', who could carry 25 kilograms.

CONCLUSIONS

In the late 1980s, as the strategies of economic renovation took effect, the economy became increasingly exposed to the pressures of globalisation. Responding to the latent pressure for consumption, the government became more tolerant of the smuggling of everyday commodities such as cosmetics and clothing. This fostered the beginning of a fashion and beauty products industry. Early marketing opportunities were seized by returned overseas Vietnamese, although in more recent times, Vietnam's increased wealth has made it attractive to multinational companies.

The people of Vietnam have emerged from a drab period of their history in which beauty and colour were considered bourgeois. But with this access to fashion and glamour came the incorporation of the woman's sexualised body into the ruthless marketing of products. The discussion of the incorporation of external influences into Vietnam's beauty industry illustrates a more general point about Vietnam's contradictory dialogue with globalising processes: on the one hand, Vietnam sees itself as being nationalistic, as portrayed through its history of opposition to the Chinese, the French, the Russians and the Americans; on the other hand, however, it absorbs and adapts cultural elements from the invaders to make them uniquely Vietnamese.

I have argued that there is some evidence that women's roles are being reconstructed within the domestic sphere. During the communist period, attempts were made to socialise domestic roles such as child care in order to proletarianise all labour, including that of women. This was found to contribute to high under-employment and unemployment, high government expenditure on social services and increased cost of local production. To curb these problems, it is tempting for the state to facilitate the relocation of women into the domestic sphere with production in the informal sector, which is often compatible with domestic work. Indeed, as the current changes in work practices reduce women's flexibility to meet their conflicting responsibilities in the workplace and the home, increasing numbers of married women are moving to the informal sector. Those who have achieved high levels of education or have business acumen desperately hold onto their careers with the support of the extended family and maids from the countryside to meet their domestic responsibilities. In some cases, the family has unravelled. The current decreasing educational opportunities for girls are especially concerning. This may reduce the pool of career women in the future. In support of the retreat to the domestic and the more flexible informal sector is the media image of a 'good' wife and mother, one who produces 'bright and white' clothes from a new washing machine and who engages in voluntary community activities. This placid image is bolstered by the residual patriarchal tendencies of Confucianism which are undergoing a renewal within the elite segments of the community.

The impact of economic renovation on women's situation in Vietnam, however, is perhaps less dramatic than the changes that women in the former Eastern Bloc countries have experienced. Even though women in Vietnam have lost their positions within the formal labour force more quickly than men, a burgeoning petty trade sector which existed even during the 1970s and 1980s – but in the shadows – has provided alternative and often more lucrative income-earning opportunities for women.

With the increasing integration of Vietnam into the global market and the global media, women are being reconstructed as consumers of new products and cheap labour for multinational factories. There are resonances here with other parts of Southeast Asia in the 1970s and, closer to home, with China in the 1990s (see Chapter 6). Renovation as a formal process of opening up Vietnam to local and global market forces is not yet a decade old, so it may be a little early to predict how the new conditions will affect women's situation in public and private life. It is clear, however, that the beauty contest is replacing the revolutionary war as the battleground for defining femininities in Vietnam.

NOTES

1 Following the economic crisis in the late 1970s during which Vietnam experienced an absolute drop in GDP, a series of agricultural reforms were introduced based on the principle of subcontracting (Werner 1984: 49). Under the subcontracting system, contractors obliged the peasants to deliver a negotiated quantity of rice to the state in exchange for the state's supply of fertiliser, seeds and equipment. Furthermore, specific agricultural tasks were subcontracted to private family labour which in reality meant primarily the labour of women and children. The male tasks of ploughing, water and pest control remained part of collectivised labour with fixed labour time and wages. By contrast, family labour was not regulated, which facilitated an extension of labour time and a squeeze on returns per hour.

2 The Women's Union which is a national organisation of over 11 million members and 7,000 employees has shifted from an organisation responsible for protecting women's rights to an implementation agency for programmes of immunisation, family planning, credit and nutrition education for international funding organisations.

3 Ho Xuan Huong's father died when she was young and her mother remarried as a second wife. Ho Xuan Huong was bright and met many scholars but, because of her sex, was not permitted to enter the mandarinate or politics. She often challenged men to a battle of wits and generally held them in low esteem. She married a scholar, but as his concubine. The marriage lasted only 27 months and ended in his death. She remarried as a concubine but, following her second husband's death, she travelled to the countryside and wrote erotic poetry using double images and meanings (Woodside 1971: 46–50; My Van Tran 1994). Her lyrics expressed the experiences of women in a male-dominated world. She was critical of all forms of inequality, including inequality in sexual freedom and her poetry ranged over issues and experiences fundamental to women's inferior status.

4 According to Confucianism, a woman's position was formalised by 'the three submissions' whereby her life was divided into the stages of childhood, marriage and widowhood in which she was expected to obey successively three masters: her father, husband and eldest son. The moral code for women was guided by 'the four virtues': to work hard, remain beautiful, and to speak and behave demurely.

5 In 1931, the Women's Union for Emancipation identified women as the most persecuted element in society (Turley 1972: 796). Only a few days after the establishment of the Democratic Republic of Vietnam in September 1945 the first general conference of the Women's Association for National Salvation was convened. The Party launched the 'New Life Movement' in 1946 which extended reforms into culture: encouraged simpler dress, the elimination of lavish wedding ceremonies, the improvement of feminine hygiene and the abandonment of outmoded customs (ibid.).

6 In 1954, when the Vietnam Worker's Party secured independence of the northern part of Vietnam, ambiguities emerged in the application of principles of the 1946 Constitution. Under the Population Classification Decree which governed land reform of 1953–56, many people lost their lives due to their class position. In this situation it was significant that a woman took on the class position of her husband after a short period of marriage whereas a man's position did not alter (Turley 1972: 798). Land reform of 1953–56 also dispersed the rural concentration of wealth which removed the economic means and necessity to take second wives and concubines.

7 In December 1959 the National Assembly adopted new laws on marriage and the family which laid down equality between husbands and wives, equality between daughters and sons with respect to ownership of property and choice of occupation, freedom of marriage, monogamy, equality between the sexes and the defence of children's rights and interests. In 1986, the new Marriage and Family Law prohibited 'early' marriage of women younger than 18, of men younger than 20 and marriage without consent.

8 Results of the sample survey conducted in 1992–93 are considered more appropriate than data recorded in the 1989 census because the major impact of economic renovation took place after the census.

9 The more rapid loss of formal employment for women in Vietnam is similar to that which emerged in the Eastern Bloc countries. One of the major differences between Eastern Europe and Vietnam, however, is the position of women in trade and the informal sector. In fact, the entrepreneurship of Vietnamese women has kept many households in Vietnam above the poverty line and contributed significantly to economic reform. Furthermore, in Russia issues of equity are associated with a discredited regime (Ralph 1995).

BIBLIOGRAPHY

Allen, S. (1993) 'Women and health in Vietnam', *Development Bulletin* 26: 13–17.

Beresford, M. (1988) *Vietnam: Politics, Economics and Society*, New York: Pinter.

Bui Thi Kim Quy (1994) 'A preliminary survey on the working environment of women workers in some joint-ventures in Ho Chi Minh City', Workshop on Gender, Environment and Development, 9–11 November: 1–2.

Dao The Tuan (1993) 'The Peasant Household Economy and Social Change in Vietnam', paper presented at the Vietnam Update Conference, November: 1–12.

Eisen, A. (1984) *Women and Revolution in Vietnam*, London: Zed Books.

Fahey, S. (1993) 'The Hidden Economy of Vietnam', paper presented at the Asian Studies Association of Australia Conference, Murdoch University, Perth.

Fox, P. (trans.) (1994) *Labour Code of Vietnam*, July.

Franklin, B. (1993) *The Risk of Aids in Vietnam*, Care International in Vietnam, Monograph Series No. 1.

Ho Chi Minh (1960–1962) 'Appeal Made on the Occasion of the Founding of the Communist Party of Indochina (February 18, 1930)', *Selected Works of Ho Chi Minh*, Hanoi: Foreign Languages Publishing House.

Hoang Thi Lich (1993) 'Job Training, Generating Employment, Developing Diversified Occupations, Increasing Income, Improving the Lives of Rural Women and Families', Summing-up reports on the implementation of the project, Centre for Women's Studies and Sida.

Huard, P. and Durand, M. (1954) *Viet-Nam, Civilization and Culture*, Hanoi: Ecole Française D'Extrême-Orient.

Huynh Dinh Te (1990) *Selected Vietnamese Proverbs*, Oakland: Centre for International Communication and Development.

Jamieson, N. (1993) *Understanding Vietnam*, Berkeley: University of California Press.

Kaufman, J. and Sen, G. (1993) 'Population, Health, and Gender in Vietnam: Social Policies under Economic Reforms', in B. Ljunggren (ed.) *The Challenge of Reform in Indochina*, Cambridge: Harvard Institute for International Development, Cambridge, Massachusetts: Harvard University Press.

Kornai, J. (1985) 'Comments on Paper Prepared in the World Bank about Socialist Countries', *CDP Discussion Paper* No. 1985–10, Washington, DC: World Bank.

—— (1992) *The Socialist System: The Political Economy of Communism*, Princeton: Princeton University Press.

Le Duan (1977) 'Role and Tasks of the Vietnamese Woman in the New Revolutionary Stage', *Selected Writings*, Hanoi: Foreign Languages Publishing House.

Le Nham (1994) 'Asking for a child' Practice at An Hiep Commune', *Social Sciences* (Vietnam), 39(1): 103–9.

Le Thi (1991) 'The Development of Household Economy in Vietnamese Rural areas, Role and Living Conditions of the Female Working People', *Social Sciences* (Vietnam), 30(4): 55–62.

—— (1993)'Women, Marriage, Family and Gender Equality', *Social Sciences* (Vietnam), 36(2): 21–33.

—— (1994) 'A Participatory Approach to Gender Responsive Policy Research', Hanoi: Centre for Family and Women Studies.

Le Thi and Vinh Thi (1993) *Job Creation and Income Generation for Women*, Hanoi: Centre for Women's Studies, National Centre for Social Sciences, Social Science Publishing House.

Le Thi Quy (1994) 'Gender: The Relations between Research and Policy Making in Vietnam', Workshop on Gender Relations: Policy and Planning, 26 May–2 June, in Kuala Lumpur, Malaysia, Hanoi: Centre for Family and Women's Research.

Liljestrom, R. (1992) 'Contributions to Research on the Family in Vietnam', *Vietnamese Studies* 1: 33–46.

Liljestrom, R. and Tuong Lai (eds) (1991) *Sociological Studies on the Vietnamese Family*, Hanoi: Social Sciences Publishing House.

McIntosh, C. (1990) 'After the Long-haired Heroines', *Australian Left Review* 34–5.

Mackerras, C. (1988) 'Women in Contemporary Vietnam', in C. Mackerras, R. Cribb and A. Healy (eds) *Contemporary Vietnam: Perspectives from Australia*, North Wollongong: University of Wollongong Press.

Mai Huy Bich (1991) 'A Distinctive Feature of the Meaning of Reproduction in Confucian Family Tradition in the Red River Delta', in R. Liljestrom and Tuong Lai (eds) *Sociological Studies on the Vietnamese Family*, Hanoi: Social Sciences Publishing House.

Mai Thi Tu and Le Thi Nham Tuyet (1978) *Women in Vietnam*, Hanoi: Foreign Languages Publishing House.

Mandow, N. (1995) 'Slave to Fashion: Million-dollar Look Opens Local Purses', *Vietnam Investment Review*, 9–15 October: 31–3.

Marr, D. (1981) 'The Question of Women', in *Vietnamese Tradition on Trial, 1920–1945*, Berkeley: University of California Press.

Mies, M. (1986) *Patriarchy and Accumulation on a World Scale: Women in the International Division of Labour*, London: Zed Books.

Moghadam, V. (1993) *Gender and the Development Process in a Changing Global Environment*, Helsinki: World Institute for Development Economics Research, The United Nations University.

My Van Tran (1994) 'Vietnamese Women: Two Hundred Years of Progress', National Conference of Vietnamese Women's Association in Australia, Sydney, 13–14 May.

Nguyen Huy Thiep (1982) 'The General Retires', *The General Retires and Other Stories*, Singapore: Oxford University Press.

Nguyen Tu Chi (1991) 'Preliminary Notes on the Family of the Viet', in R. Liljestrom and Tuong Lai (eds) *Sociological Studies on the Vietnamese Family*, Hanoi: Social Sciences Publishing House.

Norland, I. (1995) 'Vietnamese Industry in Transition: Changes in the Textile Sector', in I. Norland, C. Gates and Vu Ca Dam (eds) *Vietnam in a Changing World*, Richmond, Surrey: Curzon Press.

Paukert, L. (1991) 'The Economic Status of Women in the Transition to a Market System', *International Labour Review* 130: 613–33.

Pelzer, C. (1993) 'Socio-cultural Dimensions of Renovation in Vietnam: Doi Moi as Dialogue and Transformation and Transformation in Gender Relations', in W. S. Turley and M. Seldon (eds) *Reinventing Vietnamese Socialism: Doi Moi in Comparative Perspective*, Boulder: Westview Press.

Quoc Vinh (1994) 'Women's Union Lobbies for Right of Female Workers', *Vietnam Investment Review*, 30 June–6 July: 12.

Ralph, R. E. (1995) 'Russia – Neither Jobs nor Justice: State Discrimination against Women in Russia', *Human Rights Watch Women's Rights Project*, New York and Washington, DC: Human Rights Watch, 7(5): 1–30.

Sen, A. K. (1990) 'Gender and Co-operative Conflicts', in I. Tinker (ed.) *Per-*

sistent Inequalities: Women and World Development, New York: Oxford University Press.

Standing, G. (1991) *In Search of Flexibility: The New Soviet Labour Market*, Geneva: ILO.

State Planning Committee and General Statistical Office (1994) Hanoi: *Vietnam Living Standards Survey 1992–3*.

Ta Van Tai (1984) 'Women and the Law in Traditional Vietnam', *The Vietnam Forum 3*, New Haven: Yale University Press.

Tran Dinh Huou (1991) 'Traditional Families in Vietnam and Influence of Confucianism', in R. Liljestrom and Tuong Lai (eds) *Sociological Studies on the Vietnamese Family*, Hanoi: Social Sciences Publishing House.

Truong Van Khoi (1994) 'Home Economics', *Vietnam Economic Times* December: 51.

Turley, W. S. (1972) 'Women in the Communist Revolution in Vietnam', *Asian Survey* X11(9), September: 793–805.

UNDP (1994) *Human Development Report*, New York: Oxford University Press.

Ungar, E. (1993) 'Gender, Land and Household in Vietnam', *Asian Studies Review* 17(3): 61–72.

UNICEF (1990) *Vietnam: The Situation of Children and Women*, Hanoi.

—— (1994) *Vietnam: Children and Women: A Situation Analysis*, Hanoi.

Vietnam Population Census 1989 (1992) *The Population of Vietnam*, Hanoi: Statistical Publishing House.

Vietnam Women's Union and Centre for Women Studies (eds) (1989) *Vietnamese Women in the Eighties*, Hanoi: Foreign Languages Publishing House.

Werner, J. (1984) 'Socialist Development: The Political Economy of Agrarian Reform in Vietnam', *Bulletin of Concerned Asian Scholars* 16(2): 48–55.

White, C. P. (1980) 'Women and Social Development: Reflection on the Case of Vietnam', paper presented at the PSA Conference, Exeter University, April.

—— (1982) 'Socialist Transformation of Agriculture and Gender Relations: the Vietnamese Case', *IDS Bulletin* 13(4).

Wolf, M. (1985) *Revolution Postponed*, Stanford: Stanford University Press.

Woodside, A. (1971) *Vietnam and the Chinese Model: A Comparative Study of Nguyen and Ch'ing Civil Government in the First Half of the Nineteenth Century*, Cambridge, Massachusetts: Harvard University Press.

World Bank (1995) *World Development Report,* New York: Oxford University Press.

...tiful daughters', estranged ...ers

...en in Thailand

Nerida Cook

Some of the most prominent voices in the controversies about Thai prostitution in recent decades have been those of Thailand's middle-class women. A wide variety of opinions can be heard on the sex industry in the country, from the most condemnatory to those espousing improved workers' rights for prostitutes. Medical discourse urges pragmatic considerations, while some media portray prostitutes as social victims. What are seldom heard are the voices of the prostitutes themselves (van Esterik 1992: 135). This chapter will examine the role Thailand's new middle-class women have played in these public debates and policies.

It is sometimes suggested that prostitution in Thailand has attracted a disproportionate amount of attention from both local and worldwide media and academic analysts, and it may seem that the present chapter unadvisedly adds to an already voluminous discussion not central to the role of gender within contemporary Thai affluence. It is argued here, however, that prostitution cannot be ignored in any analysis of modern Thai women's experience. A focus on prostitution, both from outside and increasingly urgently from within the country, has inevitably implicated Thai womanhood in general. It has thus significantly influenced the context within which the gender identities of the educated women of the new middle classes are discursively constructed. While many Thai women understandably wish to avoid the subject of Thai prostitution, others seek to actively engage with it, deriving both meaning and an avenue for direct social and political action from the lives of their disadvantaged sisters. In turn, the meanings attached to prostitution in Thailand have been significantly reshaped by women activists' political and discursive practices.

The prominent role of middle-class women in debates about prostitution has much to do with the ideological and historical contexts in which the new Thai middle classes have emerged. The use of the terms 'middle class' and 'elite' in this chapter adds to their generally inconsistent employment in the literature on Thai women. In general 'middle class' is used here to refer to the newly affluent middle classes which have arisen comparatively recently in Thailand. Class is a necessarily relational phenomenon, and the usage here is intended to highlight the way in which many of these women contrast themselves both with the rural majority, and with a wealthy sector of urban society associated with traditional forms of power and with a conservative world view. Elite is used in two senses. In the historical context, it refers to the small sector of Thai society associated with urban wealth, status and power, contrasted with the large rural population at the time. In the present it refers to the traditional wealthy sector against which some middle-class women distinguish their own more 'modern' position and identity.

A first important context is the overall power of Western discourses – feminist and non-feminist – in shaping the terms in which Thai women define themselves. I shall link this context to the growth of the sex trade, before exploring some of the aspects of Thai women's own history and society which women prefer to highlight, and the ways in which this history interprets recent social and economic transitions. It will be suggested that Thai activists' approach to prostitutes is constituted by the class-based nature both of their own 'modern' subjectivities, and of the gendered explanatory frameworks they have utilised. Yet their response must be understood as gender- and class-specific within a particular set of historically generated social and ideological relations.

Thailand, that 'veritable bordello of the Western erotic imaginary' (Morris 1994: 15), is an extreme case of a nation relying heavily on the commercialisation of an image of its women's sexuality: 'The bodies of Thai women have become one of the bases of growth of the Thai economy' (Boonchalaksi and Guest 1994: 1). With this Orientalist marketability, it could be expected that Thai prostitutes were to some degree benefiting from their contribution to the national economy. Indeed, not so long ago, it began to be argued that the profits to be made from the sale of sex were leading to an increased value placed on daughters in some rural Thai areas (e.g. Hantrakul 1988: 132). Now, however, the rapid spread of HIV/AIDS has rendered prostitution the focus of ever more highly critical scrutiny. Nevertheless, the current sense of crisis brought about by HIV/AIDS is simply a further stage in a long series of contests about prostitution in Thai society; contests which have only been further intensified by that industry's internationalisation.

HISTORICAL CONTEXT OF THAI PROSTITUTION

Thais have long made an association between prostitution and venereal disease. Since extremely high proportions of sexually transmitted diseases (STDs) were discovered throughout the Bangkok male population in the mid-nineteenth century, it has been argued on health grounds that the prostitution industry was against the interests of society. King Chulalongkorn's preamble to the Health Act of 1908 warned that prostitutes could 'become a great danger to mankind' (in Bamber *et al.* 1993: 149). Yet his government's new measures were not considered effective enough, generating repeated public protests. In 1922 a women's magazine launched an attack on venereal diseases, demanding either the closure of brothels or their close medical supervision. Sarit's 1960 decision to make prostitution illegal probably had much to do with 'social purification' for the benefit of local and international audiences, yet today wives' fears of contracting STDs, particularly HIV/AIDS, are very prominent in Thai women's objections to prostitution (Saengtienchai 1995).

Prostitutes are recorded in Thai history at least as far back as the start of the Ayutthayan period in the early fourteenth century, when prostitution was legal and subject to government taxation. While much prostitution has been recorded historically in urban centres, there is also evidence of rural prostitution for much of the nineteenth century (Boonchalaksi and Guest 1994: 2-3). Prostitution is now ubiquitous throughout rural and urban society. While official estimates acknowledge over 6,000 commercial sex establishments, unofficial estimates suggest Thailand has closer to 60,000 places where sex is commercially available (Sitthiraksa 1992: 97). The purchase of sexual services as a form of consumerism has pervaded Thai society to such a degree that poorer Thai farmers are offered the use of prostitutes when they hire buffalo to plough their fields (Odzer 1994: v), and cattle auctions are an unofficial venue for freelance commercial sex (Lyttleton 1994b: 274).[1]

Analyses have focussed on the nexus between Thailand's export orientation, the unequal conditions of exchange which constitute global capitalism, and the growing international demand for sex tourism (e.g. Thanh-Dam 1983; 1990).[2] The patronage of American GIs is credited with making the Thai sex industry more public, diverse and 'raunchy' (Wilson and Henley 1994; Sitthiraksa 1992: 98). Western sex tourists, following their GI predecessors, treat the prostitutes they pay for like 'girlfriends' (van Esterik 1992: 140). In all likelihood Patpong's famous sex shows are anathema to the sensibilities of the Thai women who work there, for whom nakedness in front of others would normally be unthinkable.[3] Yet from having been confined to discrete districts, Bangkok's famous night life has become 'a prominent feature of the culture of the whole city' (Phongpaichit 1982: 5).

The growth of sex tourism has been supplemented by significantly increased consumption of commercial sex services by local men over the past generation, at least until a very recent decline in the 1990s attributed to the success of HIV/AIDS campaigns (Thongthai and Guest 1995). Local patronage of prostitutes is frequently an extension of male group socialising, reinforcing the importance of venues as status markers. Accordingly, the local sex industry has expanded considerably, diversifying settings to target distinct niche markets. The spending power of Thai men, particularly those in the expanding middle class, has increased enormously as a result of the economic growth of the last few decades. It is largely among the men of the new middle classes that the association of wealth with sexual access to women and hence status has led to increased emphasis on consumption of short-term sexual services in a variety of 'enjoyable, and in many cases luxurious', settings (Boonchalaksi and Guest 1994: 12).

The social hierarchical concerns of Thai clients are also responsible for other structural aspects of the sex industry. The low esteem in which prostitutes are held in urban Thai society is exacerbated by their mostly rural origins, in turn compounded by regional ethnicity. Young women from the rural Northeast supposedly favoured by Westerners are looked down on in Bangkok as dark-skinned and 'Lao' in comparison to fair-skinned 'Chiengmai girls'. Thai consumer choice is often highly selective. Once one Northern district became particularly well known as a source of young sex workers, the prices charged for a 'genuine Dok Kham Tai girl' soared (Phongpaichit 1982: 46). Since the late 1980s, growing numbers of increasingly younger women are imported from hill tribe groups near the borders of Thailand, and even from neighbouring countries. These young women lack not only minimal language skills but also legal status. Their chief attraction for clients lies in their being thought less likely to be HIV/AIDS-infected than young women from within Thailand (Rattanapan 1993: 77). Agents and operators also find that their lack of legal standing makes them both easily manageable (Asia Watch 1993; Mahoney 1993), and more accessible than young Thai village women who are now subjected to anti-prostitution campaigns.

Although for a while Thais entertained the idea of local immunity to the AIDS virus, since the first highly publicised Thai case of HIV in Thailand in 1987 (see Cohen 1988), the association between female prostitutes and HIV/AIDS has remained the dominant focus of public concern relating to the virus (Ford and Koetsawang 1991: 406) and of government policy. The government's early attempt to assuage fears of foreign clients and maintain sex tourist numbers made its priorities clear: prostitutes were required to carry health cards but this directly threatened the women's safety, because customers saw requests for condom use as unnecessary (Cohen 1988: 484). As has been the case elsewhere, medical experts simultaneously warned the public about prostitutes' capacity to convey the virus, and also targeted prostitutes in prevention programmes as if they were the best placed to understand and insist on safe sex practices. Inevitably, lower-class sex establishments have significantly higher levels of HIV infection (Ford and Koetsawang 1991: 407), and workers in such places are reliant on receiving a disconcerting amount of their 'AIDS information' from their clients (Boonchalaksi and Guest 1994: 104).[4]

In Thai discourse, prostitution is contrasted with marriage. The HIV/AIDS threat has considerably increased local consciousness of the dangers the sex trade poses to family life. The rate of HIV infection quickly rose so high that the 'spread to middle-class women and children [became] inevitable' (van Esterik 1992: 143). Initially government campaigns promoted the use of condoms in sex establishments, but this is now extending to promotion of safe sex practices for all sexual activity, including marital relations. Since around 1990, when the HIV virus had begun to spread in significant numbers to the wives and children of prostitutes' clients, it was inevitable that there would be increasing calls for changes in Thai men's sexual behaviour and for increased power for women within marriage (e.g. Bamber *et al.* 1993: 155; Sukantarat 1995). These calls have provided a focus for the ongoing negotiation of gender relations in Thailand.

PERCEPTIONS OF THAI WOMEN

Western social scientific study of Thailand began in earnest in the 1950s. Limited and inconsistent in its depiction of Thai women, it nevertheless included them in the generalised picture of Southeast Asian women as benefiting from comparative gender equality, especially by 'Asian' standards (see Errington 1990: 3). Early on, two eminent US analysts saw Thailand as an exemplary case of 'traditional equality between the sexes' (Hanks and Hanks 1963). The sexual division of labour has been seen as reasonably flexible, with a reputation for one of the highest rates of female waged work participation in the world (in Thitsa 1980: 4); 43 per cent of Thai women are currently in the workforce (Soonthornthada 1992: 84).

This appreciation of Thai gender relations is all the more noticeable in retrospect, given the subsequent stark neglect of issues of women and gender in Thai studies. Despite calls over decades for study of central aspects of Thai women's lives, information seems scanty compared to that for other Southeast Asian women (Meyer 1988: 289). As Reynolds has recently argued (1994), there is a desperate need for the inclusion of gender as a category of analysis to inform hitherto partial and androcentric interpretations of Thai history and society (also Morris 1994: 18).

One focus of interest has been the cultural devaluation of Thai women, especially within prostitution, in spite of their active economic roles. This has been explained by the view of women within Thai Buddhism: women are supposedly seen as having inferior karma, and as having no recognised religious role. Kirsch, for example, highlighted the way in which religious views of women's spiritual inferiority could be justified by female prominence in commerce, at the same time as they enhanced men's spiritual and social superiority in both religion and politics (1975).[5] Tantiwiramanond and Pandey conclude that Western feminist generalisations applied to Thai women have resulted in unidimensional and polarised depictions of either their high visibility in the modern economic sector or their massive (presumably abject) involvement in prostitution (1987: 125–6).

Western popular depictions of Thai women moved to their increasing commodification (Manderson 1993: 12–19).[6] Many Thais find the view evident in international media of their nation as a symbol of sexual commerce highly offensive. While some high-level officials continue to blame sexual exploitation on contact with the West, vocal anti-prostitution activists are denounced by the government for giving the country a 'bad press', a castigation not extended to the sex industry itself (van Esterik 1992: 136). The international media, however, continue to make front page connections between Thailand and sex, especially now that tourist homelands are threatened by the accessibility of Thai women and girls as sexual commodities in the era of HIV/AIDS.

Accurate estimates of the number of women providing sex commercially are impossible to obtain because of the wide variety of forms of commercial sex work, high levels of turnover in the industry, and the number of ordinary working women who sell sexual services as a sideline (van Esterik 1992: 141). Moreover, there are difficulties in establishing clear boundaries between strictly commercial sexual relations and other forms of socially recognised sexual relationships in which monetary transactions could be expected (Cohen 1987; Lyttleton 1994a: 141–2).[7] These uncertainties highlight practical difficulties in designing and funding HIV/AIDS-related assistance for industry workers (Boonchalaksi and Guest 1994: 29).

It has become increasingly difficult for Thai women outside the sex industry not to be affected by its reputation. Middle-class Thai women encounter the sexual harassment and innuendo that result from the popular association of all Thai women with prostitution when they travel or study outside Thailand (e.g. Skrobanek 1990a); and the Internet has facilitated their harassment at home.[8] Thai women employ a number of strategies to emphasise their abhorrence of prostitution in constructing their own respectability. At the same time, recent rapid economic growth, bringing about significant differences in experience and outlook for urban middle-class women and poor rural women, has encouraged self-conscious explorations of this divide by educated women.

THAI MIDDLE-CLASS WOMEN'S VIEWS OF SOCIAL CHANGE

On the whole, historical representations of pre-modern urban Thai women are not especially congenial to modern educated Thai women. These representations have been replete with images of aristocratic women allowed little personal freedom within polygamous hierarchies, and of others in various kinds of slavery into which they could be sold by parents and husbands. Instead, educated women prefer to look back nostalgically to rural Thai social existence, where it is unlikely that elitist social categories held the same sway. In focussing on matrifocally based village life, they can stress women's essential economic role and secure access to land, the considerable independence implied in women's maintenance of agricultural production while men were absent for long periods of corvee labour, and women's centrality in kin-group continuity (e.g. Tantiwiramanond and Pandey 1987; Pongsapich 1988: 64–6).

Thai modernisation was elite-led, and elite women benefited from forms of modernisation introduced in the second half of the nineteenth century (Tantiwiramanond and Pandey 1991: 17). In the late nineteenth and early twentieth century, elite women agitated for their access to education, and against the practice of polygamy.[9] Significantly, their campaign in favour of monogamy partly relied on expressing concern at the number of wives forced to turn to prostitution when their polygamous husbands did not support them or their children (Pongsapich 1988: 66).

Agitation to improve women's rights in Thailand has been closely related to other political movements of the day (ibid.: 75; Tantiwiramanond and Pandey 1991: 27; Omvedt 1986). The current lobbying for significant social and cultural change in the face of AIDS is no exception. Present-day Thai feminists see the first articulate stirrings by their predecessors in elite women's attacks on polygamy and calls for rights: these surfaced amid the intellectual turmoil and questioning of tradition leading to the overthrow of the Absolute Monarchy in 1932. Although for the next three decades (led initially by Prime Minister Phibun's wife in 1943) Thai elite women organised themselves into women's groups, variously based around their statuses as wives or as professionals, they are not usually included in the history of Thai women's (liberatory) movements (e.g. Pongsapich 1988: 75) because they were (elite) status based and at best charitable towards lower-class women.[10]

'Progressive' (and 'feminist') women's organisations emerged from the thorough-going critique of Thai society by the student movement of the early 1970s (Tantiwiramanond and Pandey 1991: 103, 143; Omvedt 1986: 45–9; Pongsapich 1988: 70–6). This student movement was partly a product of the significant expansion of advanced education since the 1960s and its extension to new socio-economic levels of Thai urban and rural youth. Women's issues were rarely central to the preoccupations of the student movement of the time, despite the prominent participation of women activists. Nevertheless, it was at this time that a Marxist history containing scathing condemnation of the treatment of Thai women by elite men, written in the 1950s, was republished, and a prominent woman student activist wrote an account of Third World women, *The Fourth World*, including a Buddhist utopian vision of gender equality (see Rutnin 1978: 106–7). Such texts became accessible to an intellectual community actively reconceptualising the entire nature and trajectory of Thai history in Marxist-derived terms. Using the trope of *sakdina* feudalism (Reynolds 1985), young intellectuals created an account of long-standing exploitation by the elite of the productive peasant majority. Women activists continue to develop their own analysis through insights gained during this process, contrasting the cultural significance of the economic and social centrality of village women's role with aristocratic women's dependent subservience to husbands.

Progressive women's groups have benefited from the linked phenomena of comparative economic stability of their own middle class since the 1970s, the liberalised intellectual environment following the collapse of the Communist Party of Thailand in the early 1980s, and developing criticisms of exploitative economic growth (Tantiwiramanond and Pandey 1991: 154). In exploring the applicability of Western feminism – to which they have increased access – they develop their own views of the limitations of the older elite women's groups. These more conservative groups, with their base in an earlier era of nationalism, emphasise family roles and dependence for women (Tantiwiramanond and Pandey 1991: 153). As more privileged women, they see their role as providing welfare to alleviate immediate problems and as encouraging the development of citizenship values supportive of the status quo. They are rewarded by coveted honours bestowed by the Royal Family for sizeable donations to approved charities.

In contrast, progressive women's groups follow the contemporary intellectual leanings of their class in adopting assorted criticisms of the effects of urban crowding, rapid modernisation and patriarchy, and in their opposition to government organisations' narrow emphasis on materialist development strategies (Tantiwiramanond and Pandey 1991 162). They contrast their aims with earlier women's groups by emphasising the need to transform existing social and economic relations, and the importance of consciousness raising among both disadvantaged women and the general public. In this gendered vision of maldevelopment, young village women are seen as continuing the rural Thai woman's support of the family in declining agricultural sectors: they become 'dutiful daughters' who struggle to maintain their vital role in increasingly untenable economic circumstances; and marginalised urban groups, such as child prostitutes, become symptomatic of the 'problems, misery and violence' caused by modernisation (1991: 154).

Recent economic change in Thailand has left the comparatively large rural population badly neglected: economic growth has focused on a highly centralised urban sector; Bangkok has a per capita GDP three times that of the national average (Boonchalaksi and Guest 1994: 96). Poor infrastructural servicing in rural areas[11] has led to significant dependence on remittances from migrant labour. By 1992 a quarter of the country's children between the ages of 11 and 14 were in paid employment (Phongpaichit 1994: 9). Young women outnumber boys in the labour force between the ages of 11 to 19 (Soonthornthada 1992: 58), indicating young women's lower school participation. Female labour in particular has been credited with preventing the downward mobility of rural families who have become lower civil servants (Blanc-Szanton 1990: 85-6). Yet young migrant women, who continue to outnumber male migrants to Bangkok, are likely to be restricted to employment in the service sector (Leenothai 1991: 7-8).

Socio-economic differences are perpetuated by the selective availability of education. Rural families have little access to education beyond the elementary levels, even in comparison to urban labouring households. Professional and business households account for highly disproportionate numbers of enrolments at secondary and tertiary levels. Moreover, Thailand's low overall educational levels compared to those of its neighbours (Hussey 1993: 26) increase the unevenness of its economic growth.

Educational disparities are further accentuated along gender lines. A recent survey has confirmed that Thai parents still regard higher levels of education as being necessary for boys (Sethaput and Yoddumnern-Attig 1992: 88). Not unexpectedly, this is reflected in employment patterns, where women constitute most of the less well paid and unskilled workers. Women constitute only 20 per cent of administrative, executive and managerial levels (Pongsapich 1988: 11) and are underrepresented in economic ownership.

Despite significant class differences, however, both poor village women and urban middle-class women find the image of modernity projected by the media to be a highly feminised one. The chance to participate in a glamorous modernity is a significant attraction drawing many young village women to the city (Leenothai 1991: 24). Urban–rural differences are legitimated as 'a product of the difference between modern and traditional ways of life rather than as a result of inequitable class relations' (Mills 1992: 88). For women the image of modernity suggests links between beauty and 'active, mobile participation in urban society' even though for migrant women the actual experience of the city can be more one of material and moral vulnerability (ibid.: 83-4).

Some surveys have found that large proportions of Thai sex workers have no education (Phongpaichit 1982: 13; Apisuk 1987: 17). An uneducated and illiterate teenage girl seeking employment in Bangkok has very limited options: domestic service, factory work, labouring or prostitution. Some sex industry work is not only much the better paid option (e.g. see Hantrakul 1988: 120), in many respects it can compare favourably with conditions in other available occupations. This limited choice contrasts strongly with the case of an urban woman of the new middle class, who benefits from an extended education and, at least until recently, has had the opportunity to choose from a number of well paid prestigious jobs in comparison to her rural counterpart. She can therefore construct a very different sense of her identity. The urban middle-class woman's advantages owe more to her class position than to increased gender equality, however.[12] In Thailand recognition of women's comparative disadvantage in economic development has been somewhat belated.[13]

Tantiwiramanond and Pandey argue that all Thai women's NGOs have accepted in some form the Western idea that women's position should be upheld and promoted. They differ about which women are most appropriate to focus on, and about what status enhancement consists of (1991: 145–50).[14] Women of the new middle classes argue for forms of social change, and in many cases for the empowerment of women, not only to receive the benefits of economic change, but to have a role in the decision-making that guides it. Yet even so, they reveal their privileged position in their sometimes rather abstract analysis of women's lives (Omvedt 1986: 49), and in their insufficient attention to local women's thinking and daily needs (Tantiwiramanond and Pandey 1991: 121). Thai women's organisations fairly consistently reflect the respective values of the particular classes, times and political conditions of their origins. This leads to varied responses to central issues of concern to newer women's groups, especially prostitution and the related issue of child prostitution (Pongsapich 1988: 73).

THAI PROSTITUTION IN RELATION TO MARRIAGE

Many explanations of the demand for prostitution see some level of prostitution as inevitable, at least for single men expected to bring sexual experience to marriage. In this they draw on Thai gender conceptions in which men are thought to require outlets for their sexual urges. Over the last 30 years there appears to have been an increase in the proportion of men who had their first sexual experience with a sex worker, but this may now be starting to decline among the youngest generation (Thongthai and Guest 1995). Of course, Thai men's and women's actual sexual behaviours are more complex than statistics about prostitution suggest. Lyttleton points out that in the rural Northeast visiting prostitutes is not as socially admired in a man as reports suggest is the case elsewhere (1994a, 1994b). Such surveys may reveal very little about non-marital sexual behaviour among women; quantitative information about this aspect of women's lives has been suppressed even quite recently (Manderson 1995: 320).

There is less social acceptance, especially among women, of married men's visiting of prostitutes. At the very least married clients are expected to exercise economic restraint and take precautions against STDs if they do visit prostitutes (Pramualratana and Knodel 1995; Saengtienchai 1995). Recent surveys show that men, particularly among the middle classes, have a variety of non-commercial sexual relationships outside marriage as well as visiting prostitutes (Havanon 1994). With the fear of HIV/AIDS being associated with 'commercial' sex, non-commercial relationships are on the increase (Thongthai and Guest 1995). Men often assume that the women with whom they have such relationships do not have other sexual partners (Havanon 1994) –

in contrast to the 'sex workers' they are warned about in safe sex campaigns. Moreover, while there may have been an HIV/AIDS-related drop in patronage of sex establishments in the 1990s (Thongthai and Guest 1995), it is likely that much commercial sex is now available in less direct forms, such as that provided by restaurant waitresses and singers (Boonchalaski and Guest 1994: 43–4). These disguised forms both falsely reassure the HIV/AIDS-wary client about the women's likely health status, and make the women themselves more difficult for health workers to locate.

In the era of HIV/AIDS Thai sexual mores interact in complex ways with government information campaigns to produce an assortment of gendered sexual attitudes and behaviours. Thai girls are taught from a very early age that they must allow only one man to have access to their body (Hantrakul 1988: 116), and for some this stricture becomes reinforced by more recent inculcation. Lyttleton found a majority of Northeastern men and women sampled believed that a woman could not possibly contract HIV/AIDS if she had sex only with her husband (1994a: 142). Men associate wives with respectable domestic life and reproductive sex (Tangchonlatip 1995), and prostitutes with recreational sex. They often see the kind of sexual licence possible in a commercial context as not proper within a marital relationship. So dichotomised can these two arenas be that men resist government advice to use condoms, associated with prostitutes, when with their wives. This reluctance is compounded by the likely interpretation of men's use of condoms at home as evidence of having visited prostitutes. Since many wives react with hostility to this possibility, husbands conspire with their social companions to conceal their group brothel visits from the wives (Pramualratana and Knodel 1995).

The spread of HIV/AIDS has made Thai wives highly aware of their vulnerability to the disease, as they feel dependent on their husbands' sense of responsibility. This has created fear and anxiety in a context in which men are regarded as being accustomed to considerable sexual self-indulgence. Indeed, Thai men do not consider visiting prostitutes as being unfaithful to their wives (Havanon 1994). Aware of the health risks they may face, wives vary in their strategies to counter them according to their degree of economic dependence (Saengtienchai 1995). The practice of *de facto* polygamy in the institution of 'minor wives' causes significant concern to legal wives, who regard the possibility of their desertion as very real in such cases (Thongthew-Ratarasarn 1979; Saentienchai 1995).[15] A Hotline established in Bangkok in 1985 to help overcome women's emotional problems found that problems related to marriage and sexuality are on the rise in urban society – as is domestic violence (Tantiwiramanond and Pandey 1991: 137, 22). The Hotline estimated that 50 per cent of its clients' calls involved concern about AIDS (Batterink *et al.* 1994: 25).

Thai women's position in and views on marriage differ significantly according to class. Polygamy is mainly a feature of the upper class, where men can afford to maintain a number of households, but is also found among the poor, where a man can benefit from having several productive wives (Yoddumnern-Attig 1992a: 26). Only middle-class men have publicly opposed polygamy in favour of monogamy (Rutnin 1978: 102). Thorbek found that among the urban poor women are likely to need to be financially and socially reliant on a man (1987: 79). By contrast, education and the ability to be economically independent appear to be encouraging many urban professional women to question the desirability of marriage for themselves under current circumstances (Limanonda 1987: 12).

In contrast to the usual social separation of Thai husbands and wives, the idea of a more companionate form of marriage is growing among the urban middle class (Saengtienchai 1995), and the educated are generally adopting more egalitarian and less gender-specific ideas of husband–wife relationships (Limanonda 1987: 12; Wongsith 1994: 107). Thai middle-class women's experiences of modernity encourage exploration of the possibilities of 'a relationship of sexual and emotional equality, which is potentially explosive in its connotations for pre-existing forms of gender power' (Giddens 1992: 2). Accordingly, in the face of AIDS, social analysts are exploring the social acceptability of alternatives such as the idea that wives could offer their husbands complete sexual pleasure within marriage, thereby making the latter's recourse to prostitutes unnecessary. A majority of men and women surveyed agreed with this idea in principle, and 62 per cent of women respondents thought themselves candidates for this role. But the women's conviction was less than fully shared by their husbands, only 31 per cent of whom could conceive of their own wives in this context (Tangchonlatip 1995).

MOTIVATION IN PROSTITUTION: ECONOMICS AND MORALITY

According to some, Thai women's groups tend to decry prostitution solely in terms of the forced exploitation of young women. By focussing only on young girls and sensational cases, 'elite' women avoid direct confrontation with and criticism of the elite owners and profiteers of the wider industry, who are, in effect, of their own class

(Muecke 1992: 895). However, self-styled 'progressive' Thai women also suggest that elite women's silence about non-coerced prostitution reflects their strong disapproval of those they see as 'fallen women' (Hantrakul 1988: 132).[16] In the progressive view, elite women's groups have rarely involved themselves in the problems of prostitutes, seeing the 'problem' as personal and moral, rather than structural (Tantiwiramanond and Pandey 1991: 121). When the committee for Women's Welfare Promotion arranged a bill for the legalisation of prostitution in reaction to lack of control over the industry, a strong opponent was an elite woman representative who declared she would not countenance the further degradation of the country's reputation. Moreover, from the point of view of urban elite women, prostitutes have chosen sex work when they could have become, among other things, domestic servants of the well-to-do. In the 1970s one elite woman's idea to help prostitutes was to place them in training to fill the considerable unmet demand for domestic servants in Bangkok (Tantiwiramanond and Pandey 1991: 126). To the elite, the choice of sex work for higher income suggests the perversity of women refusing to live 'as the working peasant should' (Hantrakul 1988: 132).

In contrast to such elite views, progressive middle-class women highlight the essential economic and moral contribution young rural women make in their devotion to supporting their families, and the inequitable economic developments which have produced their unenviable role. In doing so middle-class women display their comprehension of social and economic causation, and emphasise Thai women's commitment and endurance. Middle-class women have played a significant part in arguing that young Thai women only enter prostitution out of poverty, in order to support needy parents and siblings. In this perspective daughters in the sex industry can be condoned, creating a subcategory of 'justified' prostitutes (Muecke 1992: 898). For some, the explanation of poverty in the rural sector also carries with it the *laissez-faire* assumption that as Thailand develops further such poverty will be ameliorated; the 'problem' of prostitution will solve itself when women can move to more profitable employment (van Esterik 1992: 134).

Progressive women activists have also problematised the 'choice' of young women entering the sex industry. While procurers are devising ever more elaborate disguises for the ultimate aim of their activities (Archavanitkul 1990: 19), activists point to the social pressures operating in rural communities. Young women and girls enter sex work to imitate successful village peers who bring home a substantial financial contribution. It can be very difficult to resist the requests of an older sister to join her, of a recruiting agent who is also a relative, and of teachers and village headmen who visit villager prostitutes at work to request funds for community development projects (Skrobanek 1990b: 13–14). Laws were recently introduced insisting that young women are legally required to give their 'consent' to be used in debt arrangements, yet the ability of girls to refuse such consent is severely limited under the current sociocultural imperatives for young women to honour their parents and for the poor to please their superiors. Fear of unfavourable repercussions for their parents is thought to be the most common reason for indebted girls failing to escape harsh brothel conditions (Archavanitkul 1990: 19).

Sukanya Hantrakul suggests that in the Thai code for women's sexual morality, 'the financial aspect of prostitution is not so serious a moral offence as having sexual relations with several men' (1988: 119). Since her occupation is less frowned upon in Thailand if it is undertaken for money rather than for pleasure, the ability of a sex worker – or a middle-class sympathiser – to point out that she is working for the financial upkeep of her family rather than for her own interest or enjoyment is an important source of social legitimation for prostitutes. So important is this justification that prostitutes' own emphasis on the degree to which their earnings are devoted to rural family support may exaggerate their contributions (Cohen 1993: 159). Justifying their actions by family need is not unique to Thai women and girls: such a defence of their engagement in an illegal occupation in town is common.[17] Yet to middle-class women it suggests a lack of modernity and urbanity (Hershatter 1994: 158). Rather than regarding the prostitutes as women earning a share in urban-based wealth and development, Thai activists suggest that they achieve little more than temporarily bolstering a failing agricultural sector.

The idea that Thai prostitutes are young girls dutifully sacrificing themselves for their rural families has come to be one of the widely accepted explanations for Thai prostitution among Thai middle-class and foreign commentators alike. For activists, such ideas can imply deep-seated devotion (Manderson 1995: 318), while in academic analysis they can be elaborated to suggest maintenance of social and cultural tradition. Muecke argues that there is a strong cultural continuity in Northern Thai attitudes towards daughters supporting families by prostitution, despite the disrepute attached to sex work. She suggests that prostitution is the equivalent for today's daughters of the food selling to supplement family income of their mothers' generation (1992: 891). A magazine catering to an urban educated audience recently expounded a similar view (*Sinlapa Watthanatham* 1994). In the logic of this view daughters' responsibilities to their parents are thought to have increased rather than lessened:

> Whereas mothers of lower socio-economic sector families have traditionally sold food to meet their family's subsistence needs, daughters now can sell their bodies to meet the same needs, but, the parents hope and fantasise, on a gratifyingly grander, almost grandiose, scale. Today's prostitute is upholding the same values her mother did, but constrained to seek more lucrative ways of doing so.
>
> (Muecke 1992: 897)

Yet the image of dutiful daughters is also prominent among bar/brothel clients. The image allows promoters of sex tourism to pander to the 'patriarchal and racist fantasies' (Mirkinson 1994) of non-Thai men, but without recourse to suggestions of cultural significance in the daughter's role:

> You get the feeling that taking a girl here is as easy as buying a packet of cigarettes. Many of the young women in the sex world come from the poor Northeastern region of the country or the slums of Bangkok. It has become more a habit that one of the nice looking daughters goes into the business. They have to earn money for the poor family. With this little slave you can do practically everything in the field of sex . . .
>
> (Dutch sex tour pamphlet cited in Mirkinson 1994)

The deployment of this argument among the foreign clientele can be highly articulate. In his controversial film *The Good Woman of Bangkok*, substantially structured around the white exploiter/saviour myth (Berry 1994: 48), O'Rourke records the self-justification of a young, somewhat inebriated Australian sex tourist:

> They are prostitutes and we feel sorry for them. They're very poor, but we love 'em. I feel sorry for them because they have to resort to what they do. I think that it's best we do go with them because what we give them . . . it helps them . . . if it helps them, it's not so wrong. The oldest girl comes to [Bangkok], they try to get a job and this is all they can really get because they haven't got an education. So to break a vicious cycle they send the money home to get an education for the younger ones, which is good, because eventually there won't be this, they won't need to do this.
>
> (Quoted in Manderson 1995: 318)

Berry has skilfully depicted the inevitable difficulties encountered in O'Rourke's more complex but no less compromised attempt to reconcile his own sex tourist exploitation of a Bangkok prostitute at the same time as he portrays the futility of his filmmaker's unsolicited attempts to 'save' her from her situation (1994: 48–9).

On closer examination it is difficult to assume cultural continuity in the economic support provided by rural young women. As a result of extensive land shortages and poverty many young women are no longer assured the economic support that 'rationally' justified their 'investment' in support of their families. Formerly daughters could be assured of land for their future in return for such support, but while such recompense is no longer viable, obligations apparently remain.[18] Unlike a son (who can provide merit for his parents by becoming a monk temporarily), a daughter cannot relieve her family's financial distress by seeking her own support in the local monastery (Tarr 1988: 53). She can sometimes be expected to recompense her parents for loss of her labour if she is absent from the family home earning money. Marriage does not end this obligation: a husband does not usurp parents' rights to support (Wongsith 1994: 408); and a daughter with children of her own requiring care while she works is even more indebted (Meyer 1988: 321). A daughter is expected to be a 'lifelong caretaker' for her parents in gratitude for their raising her (Tantiwiramanond and Pandey 1987: 141). Sons are expected to look after their own family after marriage. A daughter may well fear the stigma of disobedience or ingratitude to parents more than she fears the stigma of prostitution (Meyer 1988: 320).

Despite its popularity, however, it is far from clear how adequate this explanation of prostitution by reference to cultural continuity is. Despite Muecke's optimism, the support prostitutes offer suggests not the mature respected figure of the mother, the main cultural theme identified as providing respect for and appreciation of women in Thailand (Keyes 1984: 237), but rather a daughter bound by increasingly undischargeable moral and economic debts to her parents.

Evidence of the force of such expectations in rural society, however, remains elusive. Northern women who are not prostitutes can be sceptical of the degree to which parents are entitled to daughters' sacrifices. This was evident in one woman's recounting of the case of a young prostitute's journey to Japan to earn a modest fortune for her parents. When the daughter returned and presented her savings to her parents, they not only gave her none of it for her own use, but quickly squandered the lot in illegal gambling, effectively negating the moral significance of her work to support them. The daughter lost her sanity (Muecke 1992: 893–4). One survey found that most sixth-grade girls did not believe girls entered prostitution for their families of their own free will. Significantly, in the same survey only half the teachers shared the girls' views about lack of choice: 30 per cent of the teachers believed prostitution was not a problem for either rural child 'volunteers' or their 'approving' parents (Skrobanek 1990b: 14).

There seems, then, to be a significant gap between the urban middle-class construct of rural cultural continuity and the rural poor's own understandings. It is plausible to suggest that the 'family tradition' explanation favoured by clients, activists and academics alike owes much to middle-class glossing of rural social values (see Tannenbaum 1995). A further, countervailing construct of prostitute women as autonomous and self-directing has much less currency. Promoted by middle-class feminists and outside observers, this idea places prostitutes in a distinctly non-traditional category well outside ideas of cultural continuity:

> It is interesting to watch an innocent and obedient girl turn into a sophisticated and rebellious woman in such a male-dominated society where 'good' women are all subservient and respectful to male superiority beyond their question.
>
> (Hantrakul cited in van Esterik 1989: 5)

Some have noted the lure of glamour, fashion and social amusements, which may entice young women to the industry (e.g. van Esterik 1989: 4–5). It is seldom suggested, however, that the sex industry has offered women other opportunities which they have willingly grasped (e.g. Boonchalaksi and Guest 1994: 106). This is despite the numbers of observers who are impressed by women's self-determinacy once in the sex industry, irrespective of their mode of entry to it (e.g. Thitsa 1983: 37; Hantrakul 1988: 132; Lyttleton 1994b: 272).

THE EXPERIENCE OF PROSTITUTION

The need to support poor families has undoubtedly been an important motivation for women and girls to enter prostitution, but this does not obviate high personal costs. A 1986 study of young bar women in Patpong found that they lived in 'a state of submission, fear and self-loathing'. They compared themselves unfavourably with employers, agents and customers, whom they saw as implicitly deserving respect by virtue of their social advantages. They were also fearful of even minimal mobility about the city because of the stigma attached to their occupation. They were ruthlessly denied pay by employers, threatened by police, and a local abortion nurse who provided her services would deny them anaesthetic to ensure the 'female animals' suffered appropriate pain (Tantiwiramanond and Pandey 1991: 130–1).

Muecke found that the Northern sex workers she spoke to expected women to suffer more than men because of their worldly attachments. In religious terms, the suffering they experienced as prostitutes was not seen as unique: 'Typically the prostitute's choice was to stay in the suffering of a difficult family or poverty, or to live in the suffering of loneliness, alienation and personal abuse that goes with being a prostitute' (1992: 893).

Nevertheless, there are positive benefits for Thai women in sex work. The prostitutes from the North discussed by Muecke contributed substantial amounts of money to Buddhist merit-making. Indeed, local monasteries and schools can benefit from the export of village young women because of the women's desire to make religious donations. Muecke found that, while middle-class activists and officials attempt to distance Buddhism from any association with prostitution, sex workers valued themselves as good Buddhists despite their occupation because the amount of merit they are able to make can offset the demerit associated with their work (Muecke 1992: 894). It appears that in many cases Northern women may return home with some pride, and even some male admiration, if they have saved considerable amounts, and have used their earnings to support their family and to make merit (Lyttleton 1994b: 259).[19] Muecke concludes that 'the ideologies of the family and village religion, and of women's centrality in supporting both institutions, have *not* been changed by the growth of the sex trade in Thailand' (1992: 898).

Yet, in spite of the popular notion of daughters fulfilling parental expectations, in many cases prostitutes conceal how they earn their money; they fear family disapproval and sometimes maintain complex fictions to disguise their real occupation (Phongpaichit 1982: 24; Lyttleton 1994b: 275). Also many young women, like young men, migrate to urban work against the wishes or advice of their parents rather than in obedience to them (Porpora, Lim and Prommas 1989: 278). Further, as Lyttleton highlights, not all sex workers support their families in the way suggested by the stereotype. He found Northeastern sex workers could be proud of not being a burden on their family, but utilise their income only for themselves (1994b: 275-6). Many of the workers surveyed by Boonchalaksi and Guest had considerable savings, in addition to the remittances they sent home, which appeared destined to establish their own futures (1994: 92). Reasonably successful sex workers set specific goals which allow them to see this phase of their lives as a temporary one: it produces an improved economic position within a fixed period of time (Phongpaichit 1982: 24), with levels of savings sometimes as high as those in more affluent sectors. There is also a high rate of personnel turnover in the Thai sex industry (Boonchalaksi and Guest 1994: 94, 32).

In the view of some, prostitution can offer a degree of autonomy and independence which uneducated, poor women are unlikely to experience in other forms of employment: in some brothels the women workers cite being free to leave to visit home frequently as a positive aspect of their workplace (Boonchalaksi and Guest 1994: 87). Furthermore, women employ flexibility and mobility in positioning themselves in particular sectors of the industry to suit their own needs (Lyttleton 1994b: 274; Batterink *et al.* 1994: 24).

Cohen found that women operating in Bangkok coffee shops catering to foreigners frequently live together and provide important sources of informational and emotional support for each other which can become so engrossing as to affect levels of remuneration (1993: 170). DaGrossa (1989: 6) formed a similar impression of the emotional and practical support between prostitutes in cheap brothels in Chiengmai. She found that they extend their personal networks of support by inviting relatives and friends to join them from home. Cohen also argues that the more open-ended forms of prostitution, where women meet foreign men and hope to turn the encounter into a longer-term arrangement for the duration of the man's holiday/s, have produced a new subculture of prostitution (1993: 157). This gives women an opportunity to test and exercise their skill in a game of luck (ibid.: 167), where the rewards are psychologically as well as materially important.[20] He suggests that the women's behaviour represents one version of the 'culturally patterned role of the women as daring entrepreneurs'. Nevertheless the risks and uncertainties also 'call into play the contrary cultural theme of hierarchical dependency of a lower status person on a higher status person or patron' (ibid.: 164), a cultural pattern long noted as prominent in Thai social interaction. The women oscillate between the Thai cultural expectations of women's deference to men who might provide possible security, and the modern Western notion of romantic love which the men themselves play on (ibid.: 166–7). This further complicates the dynamic of intercultural misunderstanding that has so successfully fuelled the Thai–Western sex trade (Cohen 1982; Manderson 1995: 319), and that leads to the cynical resentment with which long-term expatriates (as opposed to recent tourist arrivals) approach Thai prostitutes (Cohen 1987: 231).

The phenomenon of 'open-ended' prostitution, given its parallels with minor wife status, possibly offers Thai bar workers the strongest links with a cultural and socio-economic framework with which they feel familiar, and in which they can develop a measure of self-direction. Other researchers have considered that prostitutes have been well aware of culturally recognised historical precedents for upward social mobility gained by providing sexual favours (e.g. Phongpaichit 1982: 21).

Morris (1994: 20) has pointed out that to understand Thai sexuality we need to appreciate how important it is for Thais to maintain outward form. Such an imperative allows for a variety of activities in the private domain. It may well be that these codes enable many Thai sex workers to avoid negative self-images in their work. Able to maintain their own personal standards with clients (Lyttleton 1994b), they can be indignant if greeted by clients when not 'at work' (in van Esterik 1992: 136). Some forms of sex work encourage the separation of identity based on principal occupation, such as waitress, from the sexual side of the job (Lyttleton 1994b: 273). Possibly these women do not necessarily regard the sale of their bodies as entailing the sale of themselves; indeed, like other Thais, sex workers may not necessarily invest their personal sense of identity in the work they do (Tannenbaum 1995). This would explain the ease with which women move into and out of commercial sex without feeling that they are sacrificing their personal plans for the future (Kabilsingh 1991: 75).

Lyttleton comments that it is difficult to interpret sex workers' constructed demeanour, but notes they present a 'veneer' of contentment with their lifestyles (1994b: 273). Their motivations clearly extend beyond those of submissive daughters. While some Thai women suffer considerably because of the nature of and disrepute attached to their work, others appear to find the job a suitable response to their situation, and think of themselves as doing well within their social milieu, a finding also noted elsewhere (Murray 1991: 125; Walkowitz 1980: 195).

Despite the complexities of prostitution in Thailand, middle-class attention focusses on images of prostitution as the victimisation of those who cannot know what they are getting into. Young women in prostitution are now depicted in press reports as questioning the values of parents who are deaf to their pleas for release from the humiliation, distress and inhumane treatment they have to endure. Attacks from educated women on the perceived attitudes of rural parents have become quite forceful (Muecke 1992: 898). They point out that sympathy with the women ignores the fact that the income directed home provides only temporary alleviation of poverty, but does nothing to change the circumstances under which rural dwellers are able to support themselves in the long term (Phongpaichit 1982: 69). Injustice, poverty and deprivation are transmuted into short-term greed and parental irresponsibility in these accounts. This impression is intensified by the image of young prostitute AIDS victims returning home to die, to be an economic burden on their families and a source of social stigma.

Van Esterik has noted the strikingly similar shifts in explanations of prostitution by nineteenth-century US feminists, moving from economic pressure to coercion of helpless sexual innocents:

> In their eagerness to identify the social structural forces encouraging prostitution, they denied the prostitute any role other than that of passive victim. . . . They assumed that prostitution was so degrading that no woman could freely choose it. . .
>
> (Dubois and Gordon in van Esterik 1992: 137)

The cumulative effects of foreign censure and intervention against coercion and AIDS have combined with Thai middle-class women's representations of prostitutes to further homogenise the image of prostitute-as-victim.

Thai middle-class activists urge that the moral authority with which parents are imbued in Thai society must be questioned if the inequalities and abuses it leads to are to be addressed (e.g. Hantrakul 1988: 131–2). Moreover in media coverage middle-class NGO groups now present themselves as deserving guardians for the young women 'sold' into prostitution or who have contracted HIV/AIDS.

SOLVING THE 'PROBLEM' OF PROSTITUTION

Middle-class Thai women's organised responses to the treatment of prostitutes have included requests for strengthening the law against other parties involved in prostitution, and calling for closure of government rehabilitation centres. NGOs commenced rural educational campaigns, hoping to stem the trade at its source, and provide legal support for some victims of forced prostitution. In these efforts they have been supported by the wider Thai and international NGO communities, and by the urgency characterising opposition to prostitution because of HIV/AIDS.

Activists have for some time criticised the punitive nature of the institutions established to rehabilitate girls and women arrested for prostitution (Hantrakul 1988: 125–6). The institutions have become an object of fear for prostitutes reluctant to be located there forcibly for up to a year and facing the stigmatisation such institutionalisation entails. The so-called vocational training offered is unlikely to ensure women adequate financial income. The institutions have catered to relatively few women and girls in the recent past, and arguably provide little social or educational benefit for the expense entailed (Boonchalaksi and Guest 1994: 28–9).

In March 1989 a number of mainly educated middle-class women's NGOs composed a joint statement in the form of an open letter to the government. They criticised the government's position on prostitution as inadequately recognising women's dignity, and pointed out the inconsistencies in the laws (see Asia Watch 1993: 24–8) which allow selective enforcement by police. They called for prostitution to be decriminalised; for penalties for clients and operators where underage girls were involved; and for a variety of programmes to address the causes of prostitution, including a 'public campaign to warn rural villagers that in the future they stand to be heavily punished for selling their children' (in Kabilsingh 1991: 80–1).

Despite some moves towards reform during the Anand and Chuan governments, however, there is much evidence for continuing highly amicable relations between members of the police force and brothel and massage parlour operators (Phongpaichit and Piriyarangsan 1994: 111–14; Asia Watch 1993: 28), severely limiting the chances of success of both government and NGO projects. Little action is taken against police involvement in the trade. This was even the case in the infamous 1993 murder by a policeman associated with a Songkhla brothel owner of a young prostitute attempting to escape from the brothel (Phongpaichit and Piriyarangsan 1994: 111; see Asia Watch 1993: 80–2). Police display independence from government policies and publicly counter them. High-ranking officers, for example, openly justified police tolerance of illegal immigrant prostitution on the grounds that they found the idea of Thai prostitutes catering to Burmese men 'disgraceful'; and reacted to Chuan's Prime Ministerial crackdown on prostitution (and official involvement in it) by predicting a consequent rise in sexual crime to the press (Asia Watch 1993: 14, 35). When senior police do support government policies by enforcing laws on prostitution, they find that brothel owners simply further penalise the sex workers.

In this highly charged context, middle-class women's groups seek to address the worst aspects of the prostitution industry, despite the failure of governmental organisations providing services to women to match the collaborative enthusiasm of women's NGOs (Sirisamphand and Sirisawat 1990). Two well known examples indicate the range of concerns and aspirations of these NGOs towards prostitution: an urban educational-cum-resource centre and the rural-oriented *Kamla* Project.

The Foundation for Women (FFW) started a project aimed at reducing prostitution at its source: by discouraging young women from being deceived or coerced into prostitution while at home in their villages.

The campaign focussed on providing information to prevent young women being unwittingly enticed into prostitution, and hoped to indirectly increase girls' formal education with the aim of improving their market chances for other forms of employment. The Women's Information Centre (WIC) section of the Foundation took on the challenge of conducting an educational programme through the use of various media in the mid-1980s. The campaign was first directed to rural areas in the North, especially those from which large numbers of young women were known to be recruited.

A key aspect of the campaign focussed on the writing of a children's story about a young girl named Kamla for dissemination to school children. Kamla leaves to take up prostitution to help her family out of poverty, and is killed in a brothel fire from which she is unable to escape. A rape scene illustrates what prostitution can entail. The story combined a fictional account with a dramatic ending based on an actual 1984 fire in Phuket where young women chained up in a brothel burned to death (WPCA 1991: 67). Village children were warned of the methods used to lure children into the sex industry, and were encouraged to resist such attempts.

Although the project emphasised local participation by teachers and pupils from the start, the exposure of school children to the story generated varied responses. On the whole young women became frightened of the prospect of leaving the village to work in the city, and the project's success seemed assured when subsequently no young women left for town.

The local social effects, however, were mixed. Some children maintained that the experience of another, more successful prostitute in the story was closer to their own observations, an interpretation teachers found difficult to dispel. Further, in those areas where quite a few young women were already involved in prostitution, parents forbade daughters to take any notice of the teachers. They maintained that the subject was none of the teachers' business, and even destroyed the books. Teachers reported concerns for their own safety in some of these villages, and others worried about the divisive effect the project could have on rural–urban relations. Another problem arose from the way the narrative had been constructed: the dilemma of explaining to Buddhist children familiar with teachings on karma why a girl who had performed a good deed for her parents would suffer a terrible fate (ibid.: 72–5, 94).

Another follow-up campaign was launched in 1988, targeting vulnerable young women and girls in the North, but extended to the Northeast, where increasing numbers of young women were thought likely to be recruited. The original story was felt to have less relevance in the Northeast. Young women there were usually recruited into legal jobs from which they might subsequently move into prostitution, so a new narrative was required. This time the project detailed the actual life history of a Northeastern girl, written by the girl herself while in a refuge, as the cautionary tale. Once again the process entailed negotiation between the perspectives of educationalists and audience:

> Most of the children liked the story. . . . Only a few suggested that [the protagonist] Kamkaew should have died of AIDS, whereas the others opposed this request because they wished to have a happy ending, with Kamkaew arriving in the village and finding a man to marry.
>
> (ibid.: 87)

Once again, local children failed fully to accept punishment for this choice of occupation. They maintained the agency of the protagonist, and most thought that she should be rewarded for her efforts.

Significantly, a prominent effect of the programme was heightened awareness among the teachers involved in the project. Men wanted to organise groups to change men's sexist attitudes, and women were conscientised about women's subordination in Thai society, furthering their interest in women's organisations. Study tours to a sex resort and red-light districts produced indignation that Thai women were subjected to such conditions, and strengthened participants' rejection of prostitution as 'an economic alternative for women' (ibid.: 91).

While the FFW hopes to stimulate local income-generating projects and instil a sense of regional identity and pride in rural young women, it cannot do much to provide financial alternatives. Its efforts are unlikely to prevent stigmatisation and isolation of young women already in prostitution, and may exacerbate the stigma, fears and trauma of young women who will have no other choice but to enter prostitution in the future (ibid.: 99). The project also reveals the comparative privilege of its instigators: while it recognises the economic basis of much child prostitution, and sees part of its goal as empowering young women through providing information, it nevertheless casts its education in moral terms.

It is not clear that attempts to educate the women and girls who would ordinarily become prostitutes do not risk victimising those they seek to protect. Project workers have been criticised for making judgments about the decisions by the girls' parents, given the limited nature of financial alternatives available (ibid.: 99). It has been argued too that the project is likely to be adding to the economic deprivation of the region.

There is an enormous disparity between government initiatives directed at rural areas and the remittances migrant workers send. In one year sex workers are calculated to send to rural homes eight times the amount of money spent by government on rural job creation schemes designed to stem migration (Boonchalaksi and Guest 1994: 38). In empowering Thai village young women to 'say no', moreover, the attention of agents has been encouraged further afield, to minority groups and across the borders to potential illegal immigrants (WPCA 1991: 96).[21]

A stark contrast to this preventionism is the activity of EMPOWER (Employment Means Protection of Women Engaged in Re-creation), a group of human rights activists. They work on the problems encountered by prostitutes in Bangkok's most famous red-light district for Western tourists, Patpong. Somewhat unusually, the group does not seek to question or direct the sex workers' choices, but simply to give them skills which will better equip them in their chosen situation (Tantiwiramanond and Pandey 1991: 128–32). The sex workers themselves have opted for English language training so as to better communicate with clients. To this have been added such provisions as a counselling/drop-in centre, a locally produced newspaper for free distribution to Patpong's workers, and much-needed AIDS education. Drama classes to boost personal confidence and self-esteem developed into a popular annual theatre production for which the women write and enact scripts to communicate with the public.

The EMPOWER project is unusual in its grass roots approach, whereby activists facilitate objectives identified by prostitutes themselves, providing skills training rather than ethics. EMPOWER has achieved a certain amount of public and official acceptance because of the early and effective AIDS education it provided – first to Patpong workers, and then more widely. It now has a centre in Chiengmai, and is well known internationally. The director recently supported moves to establish networks to pool resources between sex workers and support workers in Asia and the Pacific (see 'Voices Rarely Heard', *Bangkok Post* 18 September 1995). Yet, while it probably provides a supportive and non-judgmental environment for prostitutes, EMPOWER focusses on women in a comparatively lucrative sector of the industry, and does not try to address the causes of prostitution. It may be that its decision to assist those Thai women who work with foreign tourists (in bars frequently owned by foreigners) has protected it from receiving more hostility from the Thai public than it has.

As a result of its unusual perspective, EMPOWER finds itself criticised for its stance towards prostitution (in that support is taken to imply legitimisation). Other women's groups also feel distanced by EMPOWER activists' lack of involvement in the more mainstream women's movement (Tantiwiramanond and Pandey 1991: 133). International support may have helped it remain reasonably independent of such criticisms. Nevertheless it is difficult to determine how widespread the response to its promotion of prostitutes' rights has been. It would appear that the workers of EMPOWER, in dealing closely with prostitutes, and in refusing to maintain a core element of the more usual middle-class women's position of outright rejection of prostitution as a choice, have become marginalised from their own social group. Programmes for prostitutes appear more socially acceptable when oriented to assisting women to leave prostitution.

The difference between the two projects is illustrated by the way they utilise Thai prostitutes' voices. Activists were impressed at how outspoken and articulate prostitutes were about their situation when they first spoke out in the mid-1980s (Omvedt 1986: 49). In addition to using an actual biographical sketch of a 'rescued' girl, FFW invited prostitutes to share their stories with those on study tours of red-light districts (WPCA 1991: 91). Their use of prostitute narratives emphasises negative experiences in the industry. By contrast EMPOWER encourages the women they work with to communicate effectively with employers and clients for improved working conditions. An annual theatre production, scripted by the workers themselves, uses varying dramatic techniques to present their views of their human commonalities with their audience. The performance reveals the traumas and comic elements of their relations with clients, but also highlights the aims and dreams which motivate the Patpong workers, and the benefits they hope for from their situation. Significantly, the first year's audience included many Patpong 'bar girls' 'wanting to see their stories presented from their point of view for the first time' (Ekachai 1988).

Boonchalaksi and Guest have noted that proposed solutions to the prostitution 'problem' in Thailand are directed towards the prostitutes, and largely ignore men (1994: 26). As far as local clientele are concerned, this has been as true of the women's NGOs as it is of official government initiatives. After considerable international mobilisation to change international tourists' patterns of sexual consumption in Southeast Asia, workers associated with organisations such as ECPAT have only recently contended with the degree to which local Thai men also exploit children (*Australian* 29 March 1995: 7). Prostitution of adults is more difficult to combat. Nevertheless the threat of AIDS has provided a powerful opportunity for women to criticise the sexual double standard and call for men's sexual responsibility.

In the debate on gender and sexuality focussed on the prostitution 'problem', Thai middle-class women have seized the initiative in defining solutions. The 'transformation of intimacy' (Giddens 1992) that their experience of modernity entails has given them an impetus to struggle for some degree of democratisation of the private sphere, and has led to demands for a 'purer' relationship between husbands and wives, especially in their own class, and purer parent–child relations among the rural poor.

CONCLUSION

The current activism in Thailand is not the first time that middle-class women have mobilised on behalf of prostitutes facing official oppression brought on by moral panic about disease or women and girls being coerced into prostitution: nor is it the only time that feminist attempts to protect prostitutes from repressive authorities have had unfortunate political consequences – in Thailand or elsewhere (Walkowitz 1980: 247; van Esterik 1992: 136).[22] Although recent analyses of Thai prostitution have highlighted specifically 'Thai' social and cultural continuities, there are remarkable similarities between the way Thai middle-class women have approached the Thai sex industry and the recent debates about prostitution within Australian feminism (for which see Sullivan 1995). The degree to which this might be attributed to the intersection of Thai and Western feminisms, or to common class origins, or to the shared experience of modernity behind contemporary views of prostitution, is difficult to determine. Nevertheless the similarities do suggest that seemingly quite different processes of interpretation at both local and global levels can be mutually reinforcing.

While Western feminists have explored the economic continuities between prostitution and other kinds of sexual relationship such as marriage in Thailand (ibid.: 185), this has attracted little discussion. It is evident that most activists prefer to trace the origins of prostitution to historical slavery rather than break down the dichotomisation of marriage-like relationships and commercial sex. This suggests that prostitutes remain special victims of patriarchy in Thai middle-class discourse, forced to sell their bodies in ways not shared by other Thai women. By emphasising specific cultural expectations placed on daughters, these discourses primarily define Thai prostitutes not in relation to male client exploiters, but instead depict them as oppressed by parental control of their sexuality from within their own social class.

A theme marginal in some Western feminism, and all but absent from feminist discourse in Thailand, is that of prostitutes 'not as sexual slaves but as rebels and resistors of male power ... as women who are cleverly seeking to maximise their conditions and opportunities in a problematic environment' (Sullivan 1995: 190). This idea has been submerged by the growing concentration on the increasing youth of women supposedly sold or sent into sexual slavery, and the lack of autonomy which is assumed to characterise such women both within their family and their workplace. If young women's bodies are sold, there has been a strong attempt to deny that they volunteer to sell them themselves. Yet in '[c]laiming to attack the sexual slavery and the way women, according to their image, are exploited, concerned people have attacked, despised and humiliated instead the slave in slavery' (Hantrakul 1988: 117).

Anti-prostitution campaigning has assisted Thai women's resistance to the labelling of the Third World woman as 'always, already victim' (Mohanty 1991). At the same time, middle-class activists suggest that, in contrast to themselves, girls and women in prostitution are poor, ignorant and passive: they remain modernity's 'other'.

Thai middle-class women have attempted to oppose prostitution without condemning prostitutes themselves. The appeal of this strategy for Western feminists is that it holds a promise of political solidarity amongst all oppressed women (Sullivan 1995: 187). Yet in Thailand this position has set middle-class women's attitudes to prostitutes apart from historical indifference, men's exploitativeness, and conservative elite women's moral condemnation. The Thai middle-class feminist position helps forge links with sympathetic Western feminists, but does not of itself require equality between activists and prostitutes, nor is it premised on any agency among the latter. Rather, Thai middle-class women depict themselves as the prostitutes' saviours; as substitutes for the moral guardians a materialistic and venal world has failed to provide for young peasant women.

Ultimately, emphasising dominant cultural meanings in explanations of prostitution reinforces these same meanings by 'treating them as if they are fixed and given' (ibid.: 190). Middle-class opposition to Thai prostitution has largely left unchallenged the superiority of 'good women' and the inevitability of male demand. A dominant cultural meaning at the centre of the prostitution debate has therefore been the question of the (sexual) purity of Thai womanhood. By suggesting moral and cultural continuity in the face of enormous social and economic change, and by assuming homogeneity, middle-class women maintain that 'Thailand's women are no looser than any others' (Phongpaichit 1982: 75). In seeking to influence discourses about Thai female sexuality, they define the sexuality of poorer women (Hantrakul 1988:

117), but this process can easily merge into 'thinly masked coercive impulses to control' (Walkowitz 1980: 249).

There are many similarities between Thai middle-class women's views of prostitution and the interpretations of international clients and brothel owners. While no one would ascribe the same motivations or positionalities to such diverse observers as clients, brothel owners, and Thai and Western women opposed to prostitution, there currently appears to be a common preference for cultural determination overshadowing political and economic implications *and* the particular intentions of individual Thai women and men. As Lyttleton has suggested for the academic literature, middle-class feminists too consider prostitutes as 'homogeneous products of hegemonic discourses' (1994b: 276).

There is much in feminism's encounter with non-Western women which draws attention to the conflicts of interpretation arising from different intellectual frameworks and subject positions: these inevitably revolve around the 'right to speak' and the importance of contested meanings. The uncomfortable similarities among the diverse observers discerned here suggest that ostensibly different social and political agendas can also produce common ideological constructions. It may be time to further interrogate this homogenised image of Thai prostitutes and to determine what, if anything, Thai prostitutes themselves contribute to this particular construction. Meanwhile, through Thai middle-class women's vocal concern with prostitution, we might begin to understand the ways in which these women are defining their own sexuality and class identity in the context of middle-class experience and global feminist discourses.

NOTES

1 The sexual services of Thai women are also placed on offer in a wide variety of non-commercial circumstances. Just as an official hoping to impress the king in the days of the absolute monarchy could hope to further his cause by providing a pretty village girl for use in the Inner Palace (Reynolds 1977: 14), today's officials and businessmen are offered their choice of young women on visits to clients or when deals are made. AIDS-prevention officials are also reportedly accorded this status recognition.

2 Tourism continues to be a major earner of overseas exchange for Thailand, possibly generating (US) $3 billion each year (Asia Watch 1993: 15) from the six million visitors per year (*Bangkok Post Mid-Year Review 1994*) who are still disproportionately men. In personnel terms the tourist-oriented sector is a minor part of the Thai sex industry, but it maintains a disproportionate influence on political decision-making because of its significant links to the wider tourist industry. As a result, prominent politicians continue to advocate that scruples be put aside for the economic benefits that can ensue

from promotion of the sex tourist industry (Boonchalaksi and Guest 1994: 16–17), and political concern is largely restricted to child prostitution.

3 Even the cultural origins of the kinds of performances in Patpong bars are debated. Many writers suggest Americans imported the now famous go-go dancing during the GI era, although prostitutes appear to have entertained clients with Chinese opera or Thai music in the nineteenth century and Thapthong recalls Masters of Ceremony sexually handling (clothed) *ramwong* dancers in the local form of sexual entertainment to entice male clients at fairs in the 1930s (1983: 155; 63–4). Manderson queries Dawson's assertions that the more explicit sex shows which are now the Patpong trademark were only introduced in the 1980s on the grounds that some elements of such performances were depicted as if they were in existence in the 1974 film *Emmanuelle* (Manderson 1995: 312). It is possible that life imitated art in this case. Another possibility is to see Patpong as a postcolonial space, 'a space where two cultures and two histories not only collide but overlap and intermingle to form a third, hybrid, syncretic formation' (Berry 1994: 54). This possibility is explored in Manderson's interpretation of the kind of subversive reading of the sex shows according to a Thai cultural logic which suggests symbolic denigration of clients (1992: 466), but in the absence of evidence of what the women themselves think, we are left only with the impression of how severe a personal adjustment they have to make, indicated by the degree of distancing behaviour and drug abuse among women employed in this sector of the industry (van Esterik 1992: 141; Hantrakul 1988: 125).

4 Of course, estimates of HIV/AIDS cases in Thailand change constantly. Recent figures (July 1995) claim 20,000 reported AIDS cases in Thailand, and the Public Health Minister has announced an estimated 750,000 HIV carriers. Projections for the year 2000 estimate one million HIV carriers, 200,000 cases of AIDS, and an annual government HIV/AIDS expenditure of (US) $9 billion (*Bangkok Post* 25 August 1995: 1). In 1993 the ratio of infection in women as against men was 46:54, but this may be 60:40 by 2001, despite the decline in newly infected cases since 1991 (*Bangkok Post* 14 December 1994). High rates of infection in the epicentre in the North have recently been reported as being on the decline (*Bangkok Post* 25 September 1995).

5 Debate concerning the relations between Thai Buddhism and female social roles has continued (e.g. Thitsa 1980; Cook 1981; Van Esterik 1982; Keyes 1984; Kirsch 1985; Kabilsingh 1991; Kameniar 1993). Keyes argued that Buddhism offered women significant sources of social validation, and suggested that prostitution in Bangkok must be regarded as very much a recent aberrant departure from positive Buddhist roles available to Thai women (1984: 236). Kirsch (1985: 312–13) disputes the reasoning behind this assertion, and a perceptive critique of the debate has been provided by Tannenbaum (1995).

6 Manderson (1995) notes this process was accompanied by the virtual erasure of Thai men from popular representations. A number of authors have noted the effects of exclusion of Thai men, a strong theme in Western popular *and* analytic interest in Thai prostitution (Odzer 1994; Berry 1994: 29–30; Boonchalaksi and Guest 1994: 12; Lyttleton 1994b: 264). A revealing sex tourist's view of Thai men can be found in parts of O'Merry

(1990). However recent international AIDS-engendered discourse has introduced depictions of Thai men in whom 'sexual profligacy . . . [is] a national character trait' (Lyttleton 1994a: 138).

7 The supposed pervasiveness of the marketability of women's sexuality in Thailand has led estimates to be rounded off to 2,800,000, and one influential 1984 study allocated 29 per cent of the Thai female population aged 15–45 to sex work (Sitthiraksa 1992: 94–5). Boonchalaksi and Guest suggest that a figure of approximately 175,000, representing 2.1 per cent of women in the 15–29 age group, is realistic (1994: 30), allowing for 7.3 per cent of this age group in urban areas. National figures for the number of child prostitutes of both sexes ranges from 30,000 to 200,000 (see van Esterik 1992: 141 and Muecke 1992: 892 for figures). Significantly, very little attention is paid to male prostitutes, either in numerical terms, or even as an HIV risk category (Muecke 1992: 899 n 21). Skrobanek estimates that one in ten child prostitutes is male (1990b: 13).

8 As well as the explicit and detailed provision of sex tourist information on the Internet, a main Thailand-focussed newsgroup has become a forum in which foreign men try to seek Thai girlfriends. What were once bar-stool discussions about whether Thai women are capable of genuine affection as opposed to pure mercenary interest, and the best strategies for negotiating the presumed effects of Thai women's sexual upbringing, are now held in this public forum. Web homepages have been started to counteract negative national images, including one on the problem of Thai prostitution from a (Thai) women's rights perspective.

9 The noble men who had the task of responding to Western criticism of sexual self-indulgence displayed by polygamy were hampered in that they were the prime beneficiaries of the fact that an individual man's prestige was 'measured by the number of wives and women who served him' (Kulap in Reynolds 1977: 12), with the king most dependent on the hierarchy this expressed in a context in which 'gifts' of daughters also cemented political alliances. Politically, polygamy was an 'indispensable practice for the power and permanence of the kingdom' (Tantiwiramanond and Pandey 1987: 135). King Chulalongkorn (r. 1868–1910) was the last polygamous Thai king, partly as a result of Western pressure, but polygamy was only made illegal in 1935, a few years after the demise of the absolute monarchy. Unofficially it has not lost its popularity and prestige among men who can afford it.

10 An exception among the early bodies, the influential Association of Women Lawyers of Thailand continue to campaign for legal equality between men and women, an explicit principle of which was only included in the Thai Constitution during the 'democratic' period of 1973-76. Educated Thai women were reluctant to believe that their legal equality could then be revoked by the deliberate exclusion of the equality clause in the new constitution introduced by right-wing rulers in 1976 (Tantiwiramanond and Pandey 1991: 78, 107). Today, although the clause is once again part of the national constitution, laws which contradict this fundamental principle are protected and even furthered by current governments according to members of the AWLT (e.g. *Bangkok Post*, 29 July 1993: 27).

11 Thailand is geographically divided into four regions: the North, Northeast, Central and Southern regions. Of these only the Central Plains surrounding Bangkok are comparatively well served with infrastructure, including

communications, while the most populous region, the Northeast, is the least naturally well endowed. Such diversity leads to considerable inter-regional variation in per capita income, with 42 per cent of the northeastern population obtaining incomes below the poverty line compared to around 22 per cent and 24 per cent for the North and South respectively (in 1988) (Pongsapich *et al.* 1991: 4).

12 See Sen's argument in Chapter 2 for a similar argument about the case of Indonesian women.

13 Women as a category were not mentioned until the government's Third Plan (1972–76), where they featured under population control programmes which may have been partly a response to the urban sex industry (Sethaput 1992: 94), and in which they were regarded as welfare recipients. Only in 1981 were plans for women based on women's dual role in the family and the workplace (Tantiwiramanond and Pandey 1991: 35). From 1982 women were allowed to hold positions of power in local administration for the first time, but they are still legally barred from most levels of political office, allowed only local community leadership or election to parliament (Soonthornthada 1992: 78–9). After inconsistent attention to women, it is only in the seventh plan (1992–96), the first to commence after public recognition of HIV/AIDS in the Thai population in 1987, that attention is refocussed on improvement of women's participation in development, as well as research and dissemination of information on Thai women. Government response to demands by feminists and AIDS activists is apparent in this plan's egalitarian emphasis on family stability requiring shared parenting, and on sexual ethics being important for both men and women (see Sethaput 1992: 95).

14 As Stivens points out (1994: 68), we need to beware assuming an acceptance of a recently acquired Western-derived concept such as gender: this may be limited, or may have local meanings in the Thai context. Although highly educated middle-class intellectuals display increasing familiarity with and interest in the concept of gender inequality in social analysis, the extent of their influence is less clear. One of the most prominent anti-prostitution campaigners resisted gender politics prior to this involvement, and the degree of resistance to the women activists' position can be gauged by their being labelled variously 'radical', 'Western' or 'lesbian' (Tantiwiramanond and Pandey 1991: 119, 104, 110). Even for those critical of the status quo, Western feminism is often found wanting by women who feel that nonconfrontational methods are appropriate in the Thai social context (Vajrathon 1985).

15 While only monogamy is legal, men who can afford to and who wish the status enhancement will support one or more 'minor wives' and any children they may have to him. Moreover, although only one wife receives legal recognition, a man may now pass inheritance to children of a number of partnerships, in a legal move which partially acknowledges the social continuance of polygamy. At the same time men cannot be forced by law to support children of an abandoned relationship.

16 Sukanya Hantrakul appears to include middle-class activists in those influenced by this attitude.

17 See Hershatter (1994: 168) for a similar view expressed in their defence by lower-class prostitutes in Shanghai in the early twentieth century. Many of

the discursive constructions in Shanghai in this period were strikingly similar to those found in Thailand today, including explanations of kidnapping or sale by destitute parents (1994: 158).

18 See Porpora, Lim and Prommas (1989) for a discussion of this idea. Their argument is based on inheritance patterns observed in the Northeast, which differ a little from those in the more directly matrilineal North. Modernising changes in the 1920s legislated for equal inheritance for all children (Blanc-Szanton 1990: 91). Once parents would have expected to be looked after by the youngest daughter, who would stay at home after marriage for this purpose. Changes in rural areas have influenced familial relations (see Podhisita 1994). Increasing pressure on land has led to competition between sons and daughters. Where once Northern daughters could have expected to inherit land while sons were given other kinds of provisions for their future in their wife's household, many rural parents now have little or no land to offer their children. Their attempt to invest in education for their children in lieu of land is increasingly becoming necessary for girls as for boys, since their economic contribution to family survival is recognised (e.g. Blanc-Szanton 1990: 86). However, there are also pressures for daughters to enter the labour market earlier than boys, so they gain less education than their brothers, a feature exacerbated by the large sums of money young girls can temporarily make in the sex industry. The general trend to provide daughters with education has been counterbalanced by the increasing tendency to pass land on to sons instead of or as well as to daughters (Yoddumnern-Attig 1992b: 23). Despite the decreasing security daughters can be offered, parental expectations of being looked after in old age by daughters rather than sons remains strong (Pramualratana 1992: 47–8, 53; Wongsith 1994: 416).

19 Lyttleton (1994b: 276) points out that the conspicuous display of wealth often described for the North is not in evidence in the villages of sex workers in the Northeast, hence is not likely their motivation.

20 The observations upon which Cohen bases his analysis were made some years prior to the advent of HIV/AIDS in Thailand, and as he admits, would require rethinking in the light of the significantly greater health risks such 'special services' women now face.

21 Their overall approach did stir official response: the Chuan government adopted the suggestion that simple poverty was not the sole cause of rural girls' involvement in prostitution, and initiated the idea of extension of compulsory schooling for a further 3 years, while small scholarships have been provided to poorer girls to try to encourage them to improve their qualifications and thus their job prospects.

22 I am grateful to Maila Stivens for drawing my attention to the parallels in the situation discussed by Walkowitz. At the time of writing (November 1995) newer, 'tougher' laws to crack down on prostitution are in the process of being passed by Thailand's Banharn government. The legislation allows for more lenient penalties for clients of underage prostitutes and brothel operators than was introduced under the previous Chuan administration, but increases by one-third the penalties for parents who 'force or conspire to force' their children into prostitution. The bill regards enforced rehabilitation programmes as the appropriate way to treat prostitutes. Activists are now having to point out that parents are not necessarily

able to judge what jobs their children are really being recruited for. They also repeat an earlier argument: that difficulty in discouraging prostitution is not solved by stiffer penalties but by proper enforcement, an issue not helped by the new laws' granting of more arbitrary powers to police (see *Bangkok Post* 13 July 1995; Gill 1995).

BIBLIOGRAPHY

Apisuk, C. (1987) *EMPOWER 1987 Annual Report*, Bangkok: Education Means Protection of Women Engaged in Re-creation.

Archavanitkul, K. (1990) 'Girl Prostitution', *Voices of Thai Women* 4: 18–20.

Archavanitkul, K. and Havanon, N. (1990) *Situation, Opportunities and Problems Encountered by Young Girls in Thai Society*, Bangkok: Research Report funded by Terre des Hommes.

Asavaroengchai, S. (1994) 'Spelling out the Threats (AIDS)', *Bangkok Post (Outlook Section)*, September 14: 31.

Asia Watch and The Women's Rights Project (1993) *A Modern Form of Slavery: Trafficking of Burmese Women and Girls into Brothels in Thailand*, New York, Washington, Los Angeles and London: Human Rights Watch.

Bamber, S., Hewison, K. and Underwood, P.J. (1993) 'A History of Sexually Transmitted Diseases in Thailand: Policies and Politics', *Genitourinary Medicine,* 69: 148–57.

Batterink, C., de Roos, R., Wolffers, I., Intarajit, O. and Karinchai, N. (1994) *AIDS and Pregnancy. Reactions to Problems of HIV-positive Pregnant Women and their Children in Chieng Mai (Thailand)*, Amsterdam: VU University Press.

Bell, P.F. (1992) 'Gender and Economic Development in Thailand', in P. van Esterik and J. van Esterik (eds), *Gender and Development in Southeast Asia*, CSEAS XX Vol 2.

Berry, C. (1994) *A Bit on the Side: East-West Topographies of Desire*, Sydney: EMPress.

Blanc-Szanton, C. (1990) 'Gender and Inter-generational Resource Allocation Among Thai and Sino-Thai Households', in L. Dube and R. Palriwala (eds), *Structures and Strategies: Women, Work and Family*, Women and the Household in Asia Vol 3, New Delhi: Sage.

Boonchalaksi, W. and Guest, P. (1994) *Prostitution in Thailand*, IPSR Publication No 171, Institute for Population and Social Research, Nakhon Pathom: Mahidol University.

Brockett, L. and Murray, A. (1994) 'Thai Sex Workers in Sydney', in R. Perkins, P. Garrett, R. Sharp and F. Lovejoy (eds), *Sex Work and Sex Workers in Australia*, Sydney: UNSW Press.

Cohen, E. (1982) 'Thai Girls and Farang Men: The Edge of Ambiguity', *Annals of Tourism Research* 9 (3): 403–28.

—— (1987) 'Sensuality and Venality in Bangkok', *Deviant Behaviour,* 8: 223–34.

—— (1988) 'Tourism and AIDS in Thailand', *Annals of Tourism Research*, 15: 467–86.

—— (1993) 'Open-Ended Prostitution as a Skilful Game of Luck: Opportunity, Risk and Security among Tourist-Oriented Prostitutes in a Bangkok *soi*', in

M. Hitchcock, V. King and M. Parnwell (eds) *Tourism in South-East Asia*, London and New York: Routledge.

Cook, N.M. (1981) 'The Position of Nuns in Thai Buddhism', unpublished MA thesis, Department of Prehistory and Anthropology, ANU.

DaGrossa, P. (1989) 'Kamphaeng Din: A Study of Prostitution in the All-Thai Brothels of Chiang Mai City', *Crossroads* 4(2): 1–7.

Ekachai, S. (1988) 'Powerful Performance by Patpong Bargirls', *Bangkok Post (Outlook Section)*, 31 August.

—— (1990) *Behind the Smile: Voices of Thailand*, Bangkok: Post Publishing Co.

Errington, S. (1990) 'Recasting Sex, Gender and Power: A Theoretical and Regional Overview', in S. Errington and J.M. Atkinson (eds) *Power and Difference: Gender in Island Southeast Asia*, Stanford: Stanford University Press.

Ford, N. and Koetsawang, S. (1991) 'The Socio-Cultural Context of the Transmission of HIV in Thailand', *Social Science and Medicine* 33(4): 405–14.

Giddens, A. (1992) *The Transformation of Intimacy: Sexuality, Love and Eroticism in Modern Societies*, Cambridge: Polity Press in association with Blackwell Publishers.

Gill, T. (1995) 'Prostitution Law Misses Target, Say Activists', News-Scan International, Gemini News Service.

Hanks, L.M., Jr. and Hanks, J.R. (1963) 'Thailand: Equality Between the Sexes', in B.E. Ward (ed.) *Women in the New Asia*, Amsterdam: UNESCO.

Hantrakul, S. (1984) 'Dutiful Daughters on Society's Lower Rungs', *Far Eastern Economic Review*, 5 January: 39–40.

—— (1988) 'Prostitution in Thailand', in G. Chandler, N. Sullivan and J. Branson (eds), *Development and Displacement: Women in Southeast Asia*, Monash Papers on Southeast Asia 18, Centre of Southeast Asian Studies, Clayton: Monash University.

Havanon, N. (1994) 'Sexual Networking in Thai Society', *Bangkok Post (Sunday Perspective)*, 8 August.

Hershatter, G. (1994) 'Modernizing Sex, Sexing Modernity: Prostitution in Early Twentieth-Century Shanghai', in C. Gilmartin, G. Hershatter, L. Rofel and T. White (eds), *Engendering China: Women, Culture and the State*, Cambridge, Massachusetts: Harvard University Press.

Hussey, A. (1993) 'Rapid Industrialization in Thailand 1986-1991', *Geographical Review,* 83(1): 14–28.

Kabilsingh, C. (1991) *Thai Women in Buddhism*, Berkeley: Parallax Press.

Kameniar, B. (1993) 'Shifting the Focus: Self-Perceptions of a Small Group of Mae Chii in a Semi Rural wat', unpublished MA thesis, Departments of Asian Studies and Religious Studies, University of South Australia.

Keyes, C.F. (1984) 'Mother or Mistress But Never a Monk: Buddhist Notions of Female Gender in Rural Thailand', *American Anthropologist* 11(2): 223–41.

Kirsch, A.T. (1975) 'Economy, Polity and Religion in Thailand', in G. W. Skinner and A.T. Kirsch (eds) *Change and Persistence in Thai Society: Homage to Lauriston Sharp*, Ithaca: Cornell University Press: 172–96.

—— (1985) 'Text and Context: Buddhist Sex Roles/Culture of Gender Revisited', *American Ethnologist* 12: 302–30.

Leenothai, S. (1991) 'The Role of Growth Centres in Migration of Women', ANU Working Papers in Demography, Canberra: RSSS, ANU.

Limanonda, B. (1987) *Analysis of Thai Marriage: Attitudes and Behaviour. A Case Study of Women in Bangkok Metropolis*, Paper No 56, Institute of Population Studies, Bangkok: Chulalongkorn University.

Lyttleton, C. (1994a) 'Knowledge and Meaning: the AIDS Education Campaign in Rural Northeast Thailand', *Social Science and Medicine* 38(1): 135–46.

—— (1994b) 'The Good People of Isan: Commercial Sex in Northeast Thailand', *The Australian Journal of Anthropology* 5(3): 257–79.

Mahoney, C. (1993) 'Trafficking and Forced Prostitution of Chinese and Burmese Women in Thailand', in *Women Empowering Women. Proceedings of the Human Rights Conference on the Trafficking of Asian Women*, April 2–4, Quezon City, Philippines. Manila: The Coalition Against Trafficking in Women – Asia.

Manderson, L. (1992) 'Public Sex Performance in Patpong and Explorations of the Edges of Imagination', *Journal of Sex Research* 29(4): 451–75.

—— (1993) 'Intersections: Western Representations of Thailand and the Commodification of Sex and Race', paper presented to the Wenner-Gren Symposium, 'Theorising Sexuality: Evolution, Culture and Development', Cascais, Portugal, March.

—— (1995) 'The Pursuit of Pleasure and the Sale of Sex', in P. Abramson and S. Pinkerton (eds), *Sexual Nature Sexual Culture*, Chicago: University of Chicago Press.

Meyer, W. (1988) *Beyond the Mask*, Saarbrucken: Verlag Breitenbach Publishers.

Mills, M.B. (1992) 'Modernity and Gender Vulnerability: Rural Women Working in Bangkok', in P. van Esterik and J. van Esterik (eds) *Gender and Development in Southeast Asia*, CSEAS XX Vol 2.

Mirkinson, J. (1994) 'Red Light, Green Light: The Global Trafficking of Women', *Breakthrough* Spring 1994.

Mohanty, C.T. (1991) 'Under Western Eyes: Feminist Scholarship and Colonial Discourses', in C.T. Mohanty, A. Russo and L. Torres (eds) *Third World Women and the Politics of Feminism*, Bloomington and Indiana: Indiana University Press: 51–80.

Morris, R.C. (1994) 'Three Sexes and Four Sexualities: Redressing the Discourses on Gender and Sexuality in Contemporary Thailand', *Positions* 2(1): 15–43.

Muecke, M.A. (1981) 'Changes in Status Associated with Modernization in Northern Thailand', in G.B. Hainsworth (ed.) *Southeast Asia: Women, Changing Social Structure and Cultural Continuity*, Ottawa: University of Ottawa Press.

—— (1984) 'Make Money Not Babies: Changing Status Markers of Northern Thai Women', *Asian Survey*, 24(4): 459–70.

—— (1992) 'Mother Sold Food, Daughter Sells her Body: The Cultural Continuity of Prostitution', *Social Science and Medicine* 35(7): 891–901.

Murray, A.J. (1991) *No Money, No Honey: A Study of Street Traders and Prostitutes in Jakarta*, Singapore: Oxford University Press.

Odzer, C. (1994) *Patpong Sisters*, New York: Blue Moon Books and Arcade Publishing.

O' Merry, R. (1990) *My Wife in Bangkok*, Berkeley: Asia Press.

Omvedt, G. (1986) *Women in Popular Movements: India and Thailand During the Decade of Women*, Report No 86.9, Geneva: United Nations Research Institute for Social Development.

Phongpaichit, P. (1982) *From Peasant Girls to Bangkok Masseuses*: Women, Work and Development, 2. Geneva: International Labour Office.

—— (1994) '*Joa Sua, Jao Phor* and *Jao Jakkawan*: Domestic Capital and Government', paper presented at the Workshop on 'Locating Power: Democracy, Opposition and Participation in Thailand' 6–7 October, Asia Research Centre, Murdoch University.

Phongpaichit, P. and Piriyarangsan, S. (1994) *Corruption and Democracy in Thailand*, Bangkok: The Political Economy Centre, Faculty of Economics, Chulalongkorn University.

Piampiti, S. (1984) 'Female Migrants in Bangkok Metropolis', in J.T. Fawcett, Siew-Ean Khoo and P.J. Smith (eds) *Women in the Cities of Asia: Migration and Adaptation*, Boulder: Westview Press.

Podhisita, C. (1994) 'Coresidence and the Transition to Adulthood in the Rural Thai Family', in Lee-Jay Cho and Moto Yada (eds) *Tradition and Change in the Asian Family*, Honolulu: East–West Center.

Pongsapich, A. (1988) *Occasional Papers on Women in Thailand*, Bangkok: Chulalongkorn University Social Research Institute.

Pongsapich, A., Kataleeradabhan, N., Sirisawat, P. and Jarubenja, R. (1991) *Women Home-Based Workers in Thailand*, Bangkok: Women's Studies Programme, Chulalongkorn University Social Research Institute.

Porpora, D.V., Mah Lui Lim and Usanee Prommas (1989) 'The Role of Women in the International Division of Labour: The Case of Thailand', *Development and Change* 20: 269–94.

Pramualratana, A. (1992) 'The Impact of Societal Change and Role of the Old in a Rural Community in Thailand', in B. Yoddumnern-Attig, K. Richter, A Soonthornthada, C. Sethaput and A. Pramualratana (eds) *Changing Roles and Statuses of Women in Thailand*, IPSR Publication No. 161, Nakhon Pathom: Mahidol University.

Pramualratana, A. and Knodel, J. (1995) 'Social Dynamics of Condom Use in Marital Relationships in Thailand', paper presented at the International Conference on 'Gender and Sexuality in Modern Thailand', 11–12 July, ANU, Canberra.

Rattanapan, J. (1993) 'The Trafficking of Women and Girls for Prostitution', in *Women Empowering Women. Proceedings of the Human Rights Conference on the Trafficking of Asian Women*, 2–4 April 1993, Quezon City, Philippines. Manila: The Coalition Against Trafficking in Women – Asia.

Reynolds, C.J. (1977) 'A Nineteenth Century Thai Buddhist Defense of Polygamy and Some Remarks on the Social History of Women in Thailand', paper presented at the Seventh Conference of the International Association of Historians of Asia, Chulalongkorn University, Bangkok.

—— (1985) 'Feudalism as a Trope or Discourse for the Asian Past with Special Reference to Thailand', in E. Leach, S.N. Mukherjee and J. Ward (eds), *Feudalism: Comparative Studies*, Sydney Studies in Society and Culture, No 2, Sydney: Association for Studies in Society and Culture.

—— (1994) 'Predicaments of Modern Thai History', *South East Asia Research* 2(1): 64–90.

Richter, K. (1992) 'Role Strain, Deprivation and Conflict', in B. Yoddumnern-Attig, K. Richter, A. Soonthornthada, C. Sethaput and A. Pramualratana (eds) *Changing Roles and Statuses of Women in Thailand*, IPSR Publication No. 161, Nakhon Pathom: Mahidol University.

Rutnin, M. (1978) 'The Change in the Role of Women in Contemporary Thai Literature', *East Asian Cultural Studies* 17(1–4): 101–9.

Saengtienchai, C. (1995) 'Women's Views on Extramarital Sex of Thai Married Men', paper presented at the International Conference on 'Gender and Sexuality in Modern Thailand', 11–12 July, ANU, Canberra.

Sethaput, C. (1992) 'Integrating Women in Development Planning: Suggestions for the Present and Future', in B. Yoddumnern-Attig, K. Richter, A Soonthornthada, C. Sethaput and A. Pramualratana (eds) *Changing Roles and Statuses of Women in Thailand*, IPSR Publication No. 161, Nakhon Pathom: Mahidol University.

Sethaput, C. and Yoddumnern-Attig, B. (1992) 'Occupational Role Behaviours over Time', in B. Yoddumnern-Attig, K. Richter, A. Soonthornthada, C. Sethaput and A. Pramualratana (eds), *Changing Roles and Statuses of Women in Thailand*, IPSR Publication No. 161, Nakhon Pathom: Mahidol University.

Singer, L. (1993) *Erotic Welfare: Sexual Theory and Politics in the Age of Epidemic*, J. Butler and M. MacGrogan (eds), New York and London: Routledge.

Sinlapa W. (1994) *'Watthanatham thai? Luuksaaw – haa ngoen, luukchaai – chai ngoen* [Thai Culture? Daughters Earn Money, Sons Spend Money]', *Sinlapa Watthanatham,* 15(6): 76–83.

Sirisambhand, N. and Sirisawat, P. (1990) *Cooperation Between Government Agencies and NGOs in the Delivery of Social Services for Women*, Bangkok: Women's Studies Programme, Chulalongkorn University.

Sitthiraksa, S. (1992) 'Prostitution and Development in Thailand', in P. van Esterik and J. van Esterik (eds) *Gender and Development in Southeast Asia*, CSEAS XX Vol 2.

Skrobanek, S. (1990a) 'The Norwegian Women's Victory', *Voices of Thai Women* 3: 14–18.

—— (1990b) 'Child Prostitution in Thailand', *Voices of Thai Women* 4: 13–17.

Soonthornthada, A. (1992) 'Adolescent Role Behaviour, Expectations and Adaptations: Past to Present', in B. Yoddumnern-Attig, K. Richter, A. Soonthornthada, C. Sethaput and A. Pramualratana (eds), *Changing Roles and Statuses of Women in Thailand*, IPSR Publication No. 161, Nakhon Pathom: Mahidol University.

Stivens, M. (1994) 'Gender and Modernity in Malaysia', in Alberto Gomes (ed.) *Modernity and Identity: Asian Illustrations*, Bundoora: LaTrobe University Press.

Sukantarat, W. (1995) 'AIDS: A Challenge to Survival in the Twenty-First Century', paper presented at the International Conference on 'Gender and Sexuality in Modern Thailand', 11–12 July, ANU, Canberra.

Sullivan, B. (1995) 'Rethinking Prostitution', in B. Caine and R. Pringle (eds) *Transitions: New Australian Feminisms*, Sydney: Allen and Unwin.

Tangchonlatip, K. (1995) 'Sexual Expectations of Thai Married Couples,' paper presented at the International Conference on 'Gender and Sexuality in Modern Thailand', 11–12 July, ANU, Canberra.

Tannenbaum, N. (1995) 'Buddhism, Prostitution and Sex: Limits on the Academic Discourse on Gender in Thailand', paper presented at the International Conference on 'Gender and Sexuality in Modern Thailand', 11–12 July, ANU, Canberra.

Tantiwiramanond, D. and Pandey S.R. (1987) 'The Status and Role of Thai Women in the Pre-Modern Period: A Historical and Cultural Perspective', *SOJOURN* 2(1): 125–49.

—— (1991) *By Women, For Women: A Study of Women's Organizations in Thailand*, Research Notes and Discussion Paper No 72. Singapore: ISEAS.

Tarr, C.M. (1988) 'The Nature of Structural Contradictions in Peasant Communities of Northeast Thailand', *Southeast Asian Journal of Social Science* 16(1): 26–63.

Thanh-Dam, T. (1983) 'The Dynamics of Sex Tourism: The Case of Southeast Asia', *Development and Change* 14: 533–53.

—— (1990) *Sex, Money and Morality*, London: Zed Books.

Thapthong, T. (1983) *Ying Khom Khiaw* [Green Lantern Women], Bangkok: Chaophraya.

Thitsa, K. (1980) *Providence and Prostitution: Image and Reality for Women in Buddhist Thailand*, London: Change International Reports.

—— (1983) 'Nuns, Mediums and Prostitutes in Chiengmai: A Study of Some Marginal Categories of Women', *Women and Development in Southeast Asia*, Paper No 1. University of Kent at Canterbury.

Thongthai, V. and Guest, P. (1995) 'Thai Sexual Attitudes and Behaviour: Results from a Recent National Survey', paper presented at the International Conference on 'Gender and Sexuality in Modern Thailand', 11–12 July, ANU, Canberra.

Thongthew-Ratarasarn, S. (1979) *The Socio-Cultural Setting of Love Magic in Central Thailand*, Wisconsin Papers on Southeast Asia, Center for Southeast Asian Studies, University of Wisconsin-Madison.

Thorbek, S. (1987) *Voices from the City: Women of Bangkok*, London and New Jersey: Zed Books.

Vajrathon, M. (1985) 'Thailand: We Superwomen Must Allow the Men to Grow Up', in R. Morgan (ed.) *Sisterhood is Global*, Harmondsworth: Penguin.

van Esterik, P. (1982) 'Laywomen in Theravada Buddhism', in P. van Esterik (ed.) *Women in Southeast Asia*, Occasional Paper 9, Monograph Series, Center for Southeast Asian Studies, Northern Illinois University.

—— (1989) 'Deconstructing Display: Gender and Development in Thailand', Working Paper Series No 2, Thai Studies Project, Toronto: York University.

—— (1992) 'Thai Prostitution and the Medical Gaze', in P. van Esterik and J. van Esterik (eds), *Gender and Development in Southeast Asia*, CSEAS XX Vol 2.

Walkowitz, J.R. (1980) *Prostitution and Victorian Society: Women, Class and the State*, Cambridge: Cambridge University Press.

Wilson, D. and Henley, D. (1994) 'Prostitution: Facing Hard Facts', *Bangkok Post*, 25 December.

Wongsith, M. (1994) 'Attitudes towards Family Values in Rural Thailand', in L.J. Cho and M. Yada (eds) *Tradition and Change in the Asian Family*, Honolulu: East–West Center.

Workshop on the Promotion of Community Awarenesss for the Prevention of Prostitution in the ESCAP Region [WCPA] (1991) Co-operation Between Government Agencies and Non-Governmental Organizations in the Delivery of the Social Services for Women: Promotion of Community Awareness for the Prevention of Prostitution. New York: United Nations.

Yoddumnern-Attig, B. (1992a) 'Thai Family Structure and Organization: Changing Roles and Duties in Historical Perspective', in B. Yoddumnern-Attig, K. Richter, A. Soonthornthada, C. Sethaput and A. Pramualratana (eds) *Changing Roles and Statuses of Women in Thailand*, IPSR Publication No. 161, Nakhon Pathom: Mahidol University.

—— (1992b) 'Conjugal and Parental Roles: A Behavioral Look into the Past and Present', in B. Yoddumnern-Attig, K. Richter, A. Soonthornthada, C. Sethaput and A. Pramualratana (eds) *Changing Roles and Statuses of Women in Thailand*, IPSR Publication No. 161, Nakhon Pathom: Mahidol University.

Yoddumnern-Attig, B., Richter, K., Soonthornthada, A., Sethaput, C. and Pramualratana, A. (eds) (1992) *Changing Roles and Statuses of Women in Thailand: A Documentary Assessment*, IPSR Publication No 161, Nakhon Pathom: Mahidol University.

10 The gendering of post-war Philippine politics

Mina Roces

The martial law years in the Philippines (1972–1986) have often been depicted as the 'Conjugal Dictatorship of Ferdinand and Imelda Marcos' (Mijares 1976). That title points to the exercise of power by both the Marcoses, power emanating, however, from different sources: Ferdinand Marcos was the president-cum-dictator in an authoritarian regime while Imelda Marcos' power derived from both her marriage to the president and her own location within a powerful kinship network. This chapter will discuss the ways in which the dynamics of power and politics in post-war Philippines are gendered by focussing on official/unofficial power in the practice of kinship politics (defined here as the use of political power to benefit the kinship group). The main argument of this chapter suggests that an understanding of kinship politics is vital to understanding the gendering of politics and images of power. I explore the way in which women exercise power behind the scenes as wives, daughters, sisters, mothers and sometimes mistresses of male politicians, even though men have the monopoly over the official symbols of power. In other words, although men dominate Philippine politics, women are not denied access to significant sources of power and active political agency.[1]

There are many studies of women as 'victims' of the Southeast Asian development process, which look at women as workers in developing economies, women as prostitutes, or as victims of violence. But there are few studies which examine women and political power in the region (Stivens 1991, see also Sen in this volume). The Philippine literature on women's situation tends to focus on either prostitution, or mail order brides or, interestingly, a supposed decline of women's status from prehistoric times to the Spanish period, where Christianity and Spanish colonial rule are held responsible for lowering what was once a high status of women in Philippine society (Mananzan 1987; Nakpil 1963; Blanc-Szanton 1990; Neher 1982). Studies of women and politics are few and usually concentrate on women in the opposition groups, women in the bureaucracy (Tapales 1984, 1992) or on profiles of women politicians (Aguilar 1992; Tancangco 1992; National Commission on the role of Filipino Women; Ancheta and Beltran Gonzalez 1984). Because women have only rarely been visible as politicians they are not perceived to be politicial agents within this body of work unless they are either involved in the underground or in feminist movements. The idea that women without political office, without the visible symbols of power, could be political agents has not yet been explored in any detail in studies of women in the Philippines in particular and Southeast Asia more generally (but see Tapales 1992). This chapter hopes to contribute to the nascent field of women, power and politics in the region by exploring the role of women as political agents, albeit operating behind the scenes predominantly within the confines of the kinship group.

The arguments I make challenge the central perspectives of past scholars both of Southeast Asian concepts of power and of women and power. The former have assumed that power was only exercised by males (and indeed mainly over other males, see Anderson 1972 for example). Some earlier feminist critiques accepted the mainstream public/private divide as a central paradigm: they saw this division as marginalising women outside the operations of power, or as confining their power to an 'invisible', private, hidden 'domestic' domain. The idea of a fixed and essential division into private and public domains has become increasingly problematic for many feminists, however, especially in settings like the Philippines (see Chapter 1).

In arguing that a more appropriate category for analysing the relationship between women and power in the Philippine context is the concept of kinship politics, I suggest that the parameters of women's power are defined by the dynamics of kinship politics. Local Tagalog concepts of power see power as held not just by the individual politician in office but by his/her kinship group. This has critical implications for women. While on the level of formal political structures women seem to be marginalised from the exercise of power, this appearance can be deceptive. Because power is not concentrated in and confined to the one person, those close to him/her, including women, are seen to also share power, depending on the degree of closeness to the power holder. As I argue, the operation of this power is highly gendered. While male politicians hold the more prestigious official elected positions, women are assigned behind-the-scenes roles, including electioneering, fund-raising, campaigning, talking to and helping electoral constituents and involvement in civic and community work as well as kinship politics.

In contrast to those who have argued for a class analysis of power in the Philippines, I do not see an 'upper class', defined exclusively through ownership of capital, as having sole access to political power. Instead, I view the divisions in contemporary Philippine society in terms of local concepts of *malakas/mahina*: those who are *malakas* (strong/powerful) and those who are *mahina* (weak). Those who are *mahina* are those without access to political power or personal connections to those who are *malakas*. Thus, *malakas* and *mahina* are not so much based on economic class standing but on access to political power, personal connections and kinship networks.

The women discussed in this chapter are mainly from the present-day elite rather than from the new professional and other middle classes featuring in the other chapters of this book. As Pinches notes, the Philippines is regarded as being the single economic failure in a region of newly industrialising countries (NICs) (1996: 105), a failure commonly attributed in part to the plundering of the economy by the Marcos regime. But he also argues that there are in fact substantial numbers of 'new rich' in the country, 'who have to be seen in the context of a society which is highly variegated, and in which powerful elite elements continue to pursue privileges more through the accumulation of political spoils rather than through the investment of capital' (ibid.: 106).[2]

The traditional elite class in the Philippines comprised wealthy landowners, businessmen and distinguished professionals. The republican form of government introduced by the Americans created a larger professional middle class. At the same time, elections and political power via elections – power which then gave access to patronage sources and the creation of legislation that could benefit the kinship group – encouraged the creation of a new elite. Martial law produced a number of changes, including a military elite, elite status for some members of the middle and lower classes via political office, and downward mobility for some professionals. Economic problems have also created a new class of migrant workers (estimated to be up to 2 million) who may return with sufficient savings to rise to a lower middle-class level, but may also be downwardly mobile professionals like teachers becoming maids. The majority of Filipinos, however, belong to the peasant class living in rural areas (around 75 per cent), or to the urban poor.

My central premise, tied up with the dynamics of kinship politics, sees political power as the means through which a person can obtain the special privileges (tax exemptions, preferential bank loans etc.) that allow him/her to create a business empire for his/her kinship alliance group. While the wealthy in general have a much greater chance of gaining political office, because they have the resources to indulge in aggressive election campaigns or dispense patronage, other members of the society can have the opportunity to gain political power through their alliances with powerful and wealthy families. President Ferdinand Marcos did not, for instance, come from an old elite family. Similarly, his 'cronies' who became wealthy through crony capitalism (defined as the parcelling out of corporations and business interests to friends, relatives and allies of the Marcos–Romualdez alliance), were catapulted to elite status through their alliance with the Marcos–Romualdez family. On the other hand, the Lopez family lost its elite status when President Marcos destroyed their power during martial law, but since 1986 their renewed access to political power has enabled them to make an economic 'comeback'. As the swinging politico-financial fortunes of the Marcos and Lopez families suggest, one's status as *malakas* or *mahina* is never fixed.

CONCEPTS OF POWER

Southeast Asian images of power, which are inevitably male images, have generally emphasised virility and spiritual potency, harking back to pre-colonial concepts of kingship and leadership. These idealised a leader with 'soul stuff' or 'spiritual potency', a 'man of prowess' (Wolters 1982: 6, 101–4; Wolters 1988: xxiii, xxx, xxxiv, 9; Anderson 1972; Atkinson and Errington 1990: 1–58). The most satisfactory of these studies is probably Anderson's study of Java (1972), although it too assumes that power and its signs are male domains. Anthropologists who have explored the relationships between gender and power have shown how the prestige structures of some Southeast Asian societies ensure that men are more successful accumulators of spiritual power than women (Atkinson and Errington 1990: 46; cf. Ortner and Whitehead, 1981).

Studies of contemporary politics in the Philippines and elsewhere, such as Indonesia, point to the continuing links between virility and power in the representations of modern national leaders like former President Sukarno (of Indonesia) and Ferdinand Marcos whose affairs with women enhanced their prestige as men of power (Anderson 1972). These images of male power draw on and rework a number of sites of machismo: the war-hero (President Marcos), the man known to have shot someone in the past, the journalist or politician involved in fearless investigative exposés, like the late Senator Benigno Aquino, or currently Senator Ernesto Maceda, and the military man who launches a coup, like current President Fidel Ramos, Senator Juan Ponce Enrile and Senator Gregorio Honasan. Images of female power stress beauty and religiosity, tying the woman's role to that of moral guardian or *maganda*, a word which does not simply mean beautiful but also refers to behaviour that is considered socially acceptable (Mercado 1994: 88–9). To refer to someone as having *magandang loob* implies that society is pleased with that person. *Maganda* or beauty not only describes what is pleasing but also that which is virtuous. Conversely, the word for ugly (*pangit*) is used to describe behaviour that is socially unacceptable.

The Tagalog concept which invokes both power – the ruthless exercise of it – and prestige is *malakas*, literally translated as strong. In terms of political power, a person who is *malakas* is one who would use that power unscrupulously to benefit his/her kinship group. To be branded *mahina ka* (you are weak) is pejorative. The opposite – the ability to show one's *malakas* status by using one's position to bend the rules and benefit one's kinship alliance – is admired. The *malakas* concept extends not only to the one holding political office but to his/her entire network of employees and close friends as well as kin. While ultimately the person holding the symbol of power carries the most prestige, the kin group which uses its close kinship with a powerful person to influence politics or gain special privileges is also transformed into *malakas*. As members of the kinship group women therefore exercise power through their kinship ties with male politicians and as such are perceived to be *malakas*. *Malakas* women have political agency by definition.

Obviously, exercising power through kinship ties is a practice not confined to women only. The Lopez family, one of the most prominent families in the post-war years, was successful because one brother was active in politics and the other ran the family business. Politician Fernando Lopez held political power through his elective posts, but it was really businessman Don Eugenio Lopez who made the major decisions while remaining 'behind the scenes'. Filipinos were aware that although politician Fernando Lopez was the public figure, the consummate charming politician, it was Eugenio who made all critical decisions (see Roces 1990). While both men and women indulge in kinship politics behind the scenes, it is the women who excel at and dominate this indefinable 'space' outside formal institutional structures, even given the undoubted economic and political power men command within kinship circles. Images of power reflect the dynamics of kinship politics where women are assigned roles which are crucial in enhancing the political activities of their kinsmen holding political office.

While I have evoked certain specificities and continuities in the local metaphors and concepts, the dynamics of sex and power in the

Philippines is neither unique nor static and ahistorical. For instance, my argument has some parallels with Davidoff and Hall's analysis (1987: 13) of the rise of the nineteenth-century English middle class (discussed in Chapter 1). As in nineteenth-century England, so in twentieth-century Philippines men who seek success are inevitably embedded in networks of familial and female support which underpin their rise to public prominence. Also, even within fairly short periods of time we find shifts in the dominant images of women in the Philippines. For instance, while woman as moral guardian and beauty queen was the predominant image in the 1945–72 period, the martial law years transformed these representations drastically as women in the underground and opposition highlighted new images of woman as militant – the activist nun, or the woman in the communist New People's Army. Two former beauty queens, Nelia Sancho and Maita Gomez, even joined the underground movement. The post-1986 period and the return to democratic mechanisms, however, have heralded a return to reworked, pre-martial law images of women.

SEX AND POWER

Men exercise power and have a monopoly over some of its symbols through their official positions as elected politicians or appointed bureaucrats and ministers in high office. The presidents, the senators, the congressmen, the governors, the vice-governors, the mayors, vice-mayors, and councillors are predominantly men. Even the technocrats (professional, supposedly apolitical, appointees working for the nation's 'development') are men, as well as the majority of secretaries, under-secretaries and ministers. On the other hand, the organisations of the spouses of senators and congressmen are called 'Senate Ladies' (1945–72, 1986–present) and 'Congressional Ladies' (1945–72 only), reflecting the prevalence of men in elective positions and of spouses in the support organisations of these positions. Since 1987, the 'Congressional Ladies' organisation has been renamed Congressional Spouses Foundation Inc. (CFSI). However, in a major general meeting of this organisation that I attended in 1993, for example, there was not a single male present. The Senate Ladies have decided to retain their name since the male spouses of the four female senators were reluctant to participate in their activities and women senators usually send a kinswoman representative in lieu of their husbands.

Men also dominate the army, a once professional institution that became politicised after the martial law regime was imposed in 1972. The male politicians as lawmakers (senators and congressmen) accumulate cultural and tangible capital through the prestigious side of officialdom. Through the authoring and passage of bills certain businesses can be privileged or granted monopolies and likewise others disadvantaged. When democratic institutions have been in place (1945–72, 1986–present), this element has been the most tangible form of the exercise of *malakas* status.

Political speeches and exposés of the graft and corruption of other political rivals are intrinsic to the exercise of male political power. The BOMBA (defined as bombastic, loud, blatant exposés of rival politicians) expected in every campaign rally were always launched by the men. Women candidates or women speaking on behalf of kinsmen candidates refrained from these attacks in public (with the exception of Miriam Defensor Santiago, discussed below) (Zaldivar Perez 1993). In election campaign rallies men specialised in speech giving and shaking the hands of the crowds, while women were expected to entertain. Men were never expected to participate in the entertainment activities, but they were heavily involved in the wheeling and dealing, in the rituals of drinking with the other male local leaders, and in political posturing, threatening rival candidates. Women's activities in the political sphere were part of the support system for the male politician. I shall examine women's activities in three areas: in election campaigns, activities which involved civic work and communicating with electoral constituents and, finally, the practice of kinship politics – evidence of women's status as *malakas*.

The organisation, fundraising and electioneering work that go into election campaigns are largely shouldered by women, especially if the candidate is herself a woman. While the male politician focusses on speechmaking and on networking with local leaders and other male political colleagues, his kinswomen are critical in organising supporters essential for the campaign trail. Thus in the early 1950s Mrs Angelita Roces formed the 'Checkered Ladies for Congressman Roces'. In 1963, Mrs Imelda Marcos set up the Blue Ladies, groups of elite women from prominent families who, attired in their blue uniforms, accompanied her on the campaign trail all over the provinces distributing campaign literature and knick-knacks as well as gifts. Prior to the elections they also organised civic work projects like handing out free medicines or giving medical aid (Cojuangco 1993). In response to the formation of the Blue Ladies the incumbent First Lady Mrs Eva Macapagal formed her own group of women called the Lakambinis who campaigned for her husband. Mrs Consuelo Puyat-Reyes was appointed campaign manager for her brother's campaign for Councillor of Manila, forming the Yellow Belles of Lito Puyat (Puyat-Reyes 1994). Mrs Gretchen Cojuangco organised the GLAD (Gretchen Ladies Auxiliary for Danding) for her husband's presidential campaign (Cojuangco 1993). Mrs Christina Ponce Enrile founded the Pink Ladies for her husband's senatorial campaign (Ponce Enrile 1994). In the 1969 elections Minnie Osmeña, the daughter of presidential candidate Sergio Osmeña Jr., was the prominent figure of her father's campaign and named her women's support group the Osmeña Pearls. For women candidates the most outstanding group was Cory's Crusaders who campaigned for presidential candidate Corazon Aquino and the SHA women's movement for Senator Leticia Shahani (Tancangco 1992: 78–9). These women's organisations did all the legwork for the campaign, visiting the local markets in every provincial town and barrio and speaking to constituents and potential voters individually, often going on a door-to-door campaign.

There is a continuity here from the 1950s to the late 1980s, even down to the decorative titles which completely fail to acknowledge the role of the women's auxiliaries! Interestingly, the only exceptions to this rule, 'Cory's Crusaders' and SHA, whose names acknowledge their functions, were both formed to support female politicians. I shall return later to this requirement within the exercise of male power that women must both play a prominent role in the acquisition and maintenance of that power and also deny that role.

As indicated earlier, women were heavily involved in entertaining crowds at campaign rallies, an essental ingredient at elections. Wives and kinswomen of male politicians sang and sometimes danced for the crowds, hoping to woo them to vote for their male candidate. Mrs Imelda Marcos was an asset from the beginning because she could charm the voters with her singing talents. Even women who were not inclined to sing in normal social circumstances sang on stage in their desire to gain precious votes for their husbands or kinsmen. Mrs Gloria Angara sang 'The Greatest Love of All', naming that as her husband's theme song when he ran for the senate in 1992. In some cases women actually carried on the campaign for the husband who was sick or incapacitated or in one case died! Mrs Gloria Angara and her husband's sister lawyer Bellaflor Angara Castillo had to carry on a campaign when the senate candidate himself was incapacitated due to sickness (Angara 1993; Angara Castillo 1994). These women gave speeches in lieu of their husbands or male relatives. Magnolia Antonino stepped in when her husband died and was elected senator.

Once their kinsmen were successfully installed in office, women's activities did not cease. Women saw themselves as partners in politics (de Venecia 1993), believing that an intrinsic part of their supportive role was to aid their husbands in day-to-day administrative affairs. The definition of 'helping' could range from feeding visiting constituents who showed up daily, to requests for personal aid, or for solutions to local problems, to actually acting as troubleshooters and policy advisers. Of course in the end it was the woman's choice whether she wanted to become active in her husband's career or not, but the expectation was that she would actively participate at least in community service and charity work.

An examination of the duties and activities of the Senate Ladies and the Congressional Spouses indicates those required of politician's wives. During the martial law regime such wives were members of the Balikatan, which was founded by Mrs Marcos for the primary purpose of providing livelihood projects for women. First Ladies were also expected to be identified with charity work, particularly the Red Cross which has had an office in the presidential palace itself since 1954 (Aluit 1972: 578ff). The Congressional Spouses Foundation (CSFI) was inaugurated (after the 1986 ousting of Marcos) precisely for the purpose of engaging in community work and setting up livelihood projects (CSFI 1993). The Senate Ladies, an organisation parallelling the CSFI in the senate, was also involved in the Mt Pinatubo aid projects as well as in environmental projects such as cleaning the Pasig river (Angara 1993). The fact that the women of the CSFI took an oath of office for the first time (29 October 1992) in front of Philippine President Fidel Ramos highlighted their ambiguous 'political' position (*Philippine Graphic* 30 July 1993: 16). This oath-taking could be interpreted as the president's or the country's formal recognition of power behind the scenes. The activities of the foundation focussed on women's issues (they have inaugurated a centre for women and children) and fundraising for livelihood projects particularly for victims of floods, volcanic eruptions and other disasters.

Fundraising for both social and political causes is a crucial activity handled by the women. Mrs Marcos's Blue Ladies were very successful in this area because they came from wealthy families, and some women thrust into political campaigns had already had experience as successful fundraisers for charitable organisations. Mrs Consuelo Puyat-Reyes was the fundraiser for the Philippine Tuberculosis Society for 25 years (Puyat-Reyes 1994) and Mrs Edith Nakpil Rabat a fundraiser for the Philippine Red Cross (Nakpil Rabat 1994). Current president Fidel Ramos's alleged former mistress, Rosemarie 'Baby' Arenas, was a major fundraiser in the campaign that made him president, a fact that partly explained her much-remarked-upon political influence behind the scenes (Danguilan-Vitug and Gloria 1993b: 10). Prior to the campaign she was the major fundraiser (and continues to be) of her own charitable organisation the Padre Pio Lend a Helping Hand Foundation (San Diego 1992: 10–13).

But it is in the domain of kinship politics that women as kin of politicians can actively compete with men, even surpassing them. Since local concepts of power acknowledge power held by the kinship group, women are perceived to be almost as powerful as their husbands in this area. Behind the scenes, they can privilege their own families, enabling them to build business empires. Thus, in the case of the Marcoses, we can see that as a member of an extremely powerful kin group, the Romualdez family, Mrs Marcos's own access to economic and political power was highly significant. Although President Ferdinand Marcos built large business empires and conglomerates for his cronies, the Romualdez family built a larger family empire than that of the Marcoses. At the same time, Mrs Marcos's relatives, particluarly her two brothers, not only claimed the plum corporations and business monopolies but also acquired significant political and/or diplomatic positions. Although Marcos's sister Elizabeth Marcos Keon Roca was governor of Ilocos and later a diplomat, no other relative from his side of the family gained political or diplomatic positions apart from his and Imelda's children. On the other hand, Benjamin 'Kokoy' Romualdez came to be perceived as the third most powerful figure (next to the Marcos couple). He was governor of Leyte and then later ambassador to Peking and the USA. Imelda's uncle Eduardo Romualdez was also made ambassador to the USA. Kokoy Romualdez also received the choice corporations taken from the Lopez Family, the most prominent elite family before 1972, and control of the media. He gained the Manila Electric Company and the monopoly of the newspaper media, particularly *The Times Journal*, *People's Journal*, *People's Tonight*, *Taliba* and *Women's Journal* (Manapat 1991: 387–94). Imelda's other brother Alfredo 'Bejo' Romualdez was granted lucrative monopolies in the shipbuilding and ship repairing industries, stevedoring services, freight handling companies and the exclusive gambling franchise of the Philippine Amusement and Gaming Corporation (Pagcor) which controlled all gambling activities in the country including Jai Alai and the floating casinos (Manapat 1991: 394–401).

Thus, although President Marcos's family members had received special privileges allowing them to build business empires, it was Mrs Marcos's family who benefited more (see ibid.: 387–421). Many choice corporations were also granted to loyal Marcos supporters, including such well known figures as Minister of Defence Juan Ponce Enrile, Eduardo Cojuangco, Herminio Disini, Geronimo Velasco, Roberto Benedicto, Antonio Floriendo and Rudolfo Cuenca. It is crucial to note, however, that Mrs Marcos also had her own coterie of loyal allies, male and female, who likewise were rewarded with the special franchises or privileges that enabled them to enrich themselves overnight. This group of supporters owed its success to its alliance with Mrs Marcos and not the president. Among these were Bienvenido and Gliceria Tantoco, Roman Cruz, Cezar Zalamea, Cesar Virata, Jaime Laya, Carmen Guerrero Nakpil, Kerima Polotan, Ileana Maramag, Helen Benitez and Lucretia 'King' Kasilag.[3]

In the more mundane sphere of day-to-day politics or in the less powerful realm of local politics, a woman's practice of kinship politics is linked to her ability to influence her husband or male kin. These areas are much more difficult to document, but almost every female spouse I interviewed about her role as a partner in political service admitted that she would act as a conduit for those personal requests, such as requests for employment, no matter how minuscule. The important point is that wives are perceived to possess this potential power and are approached for favours. The presence of a CFSI office in the Congressional building is a clear acknowledgment of the view that wives were *malakas* or partners in politics.

The career of Mrs Imelda Marcos as First Lady reveals some of the extent of the power behind the scenes that elite women may wield. When martial law was declared she singlehandedly expanded the office of First Lady. She ordered the construction of the San Juanico bridge in 1974, built the pavilions for the 1979 UNCTAD conference (Manapat 1991: 278), the Folk Arts Theatre, several tourist hotels, the Film Centre, the Coconut Palace, the Palace in the Sky, the Philippine Heart Centre, the Lung Centre, the Kidney Centre, the Children's City and the University of Life (ibid.: 14–15). She also performed duties commensurate with the role of foreign minister though she did not have an official diplomatic position. She was sent on diplomatic missions to see US presidents Nixon, Carter and Reagan, to visit Mao Zedong in China, to negotiate with Gadaffi over his support of the southern Moro National Liberation Front in the Philippines, to the Soviet Union to meet with Premier Aleksei Kosygin and to Cuba to see Fidel Castro. She even signed a $88 million loan agreement with the World Bank and addressed the United Nations. On all her trips she was an ambiguous representative of the head of state, and she used these diplomatic visits to political advantage, particularly in the USA where she assiduously sought the audience of US presidents and State Department officials to plead for the cause of the Marcos dictatorship and to enlist US financial and moral support for the regime. It is significant that even the US officials were astute enough to recognise that she represented power and thus accorded her special treatment (Bonner 1987: 81, 83, 139, 156, 160, 201, 247, 250, 300). Clearly, Mrs Marcos in her role as the wife of a politician was a powerful political agent with a public role although she also exercised power behind the scenes. Later on she metamorphosed into a politician herself (a typical pattern for women who begin as wives of politicians and then become politicians themselves) when she became Governor of Metro-Manila and Minister for Human Settlements (1975). After the fall of Marcos she also ran successfully for congresswoman in 1995.

WOMAN AS MORAL GUARDIAN

Many men who wish to deter women from overt participation in politics argue that 'politics' is 'too dirty for women' (Puyat-Reyes 1994). Those women who have decided to enter politics directly, however, have succeeded in turning this image to their advantage by playing on the perception that women are less likely to be corrupt than men. This image is projected consciously in their political campaigns. For example, Corazon Aquino's campaign speeches stressed her difference from President Ferdinand Marcos. Her statement, 'I have to admit I have no experience in lying, cheating, stealing, or killing political opponents,' (Gonzalez-Yap 1987: 107) always received enthusiastic applause.

A look at the careers of the few women politicians from 1945 to the present shows a continuing pattern of strong ties with charity work and community organisations, education and social work. One scholar profiling Filipino women in politics points out that almost all women career politicians were active participants in civic and charity work (Aguilar 1992: 27). Such civic work was expected of male politicians' kinswomen and, especially, wives.

There were seven women senators in the 1945–72 period. All but one were active in civic or social welfare work prior to their political debuts. Senator Geronima Pecson was for 18 years a primary officer of the Associated Charities (PFP 20 September 1947: 18). Senator Tecla San Andres Ziga began her political career with an appointment as administrator of the Social Welfare Administration (usually one of the only cabinet positions given to women) but was also a member of the board of directors of the Community Chest, a member of the Central Committee of the Girl Scouts of the Philippines, and a member of the National Board of the Catholic Women's League (CWL) (Ziga n.d.). Senator Pacita Madrigal Gonzalez (later Warns), a former ballet dancer, was also head of the Social Welfare Administration before entering national politics. Senator Eva Estrada Kalaw, a well-known civic leader prior to running for office, was also an educator. For her contribution to community work in around 50 civic organisations she was awarded the Outstanding Volunteer Social Worker of the Year (Kalaw n.d.). Senator Helen Benitez, who was involved in education as president of a family-owned university (the Philippine Women's University PWU), was influential in arts and culture as well. She was founder and president of the Bayanihan Folk Arts Association and Centre (Benitez 1967). Senator Maria Kalaw Katigbak, a former Miss Philippines and newspaper columnist, was very closely associated with the Catholic Women's League; the women of the CWL (and the girl scouts) campaigned for her and were her most active supporters (Katigbak Fabella 1994, *Sunday Times Magazine* 11 February 1962, Katigbak 1967). She was executive director of the Catholic Charities of Manila, National President of the Girl Scouts of the Philippines, Governor of the Philippine National Red Cross, and President of the Quezon City Girl Scouts Council. In the martial law period Batasan Assemblywoman Edith Nakpil Rabat, another former Miss Philippines, was also a major fundraiser for the Philippines Red Cross (she even organised the Miss Philippines Red Cross beauty contest to raise money for the Red Cross, Nakpil Rabat 1994). Among the women politicians who were elected after 1986, former Congresswoman Consuelo 'Baby' Puyat-Reyes entered politics after an intense career in business and as noted, as a fundraiser and campaign chairperson of the Philippines Tuberculosis Society for 25 years (Puyat-Reyes 1994).

Two of the more prominent women politicians since 1986 have closely identified themselves with moral crusades. 1992 presidential candidate Miriam Defensor Santiago made her bureaucratic debut as commissioner of the Commission on Immigration and Deportation (CID) and subsequently built a reputation as a tough graft-buster who was determined to rid the CID of corruption. Her crusade against what she termed the 'culture of corruption' in the Philippines was not mere nationalist rhetoric. She actually severely reduced corruption in the CID through her implementation of common-sense practical solutions, actual policy changes and because of her stubborn, idealistic determination to succeed despite the odds. Her early emphasis on the persecution of 'alien' criminals involved in prostitution and paedophilia revealed an adherence to the idea of the woman's role as the guardian of morals (Defensor Santiago 1994a). She also founded the Movement for Responsible Public Service Inc. (MOVERS) in 1990 (Defensor Santiago 1994a: 147–220), an organisation dedicated to the crusade against the culture of corruption. This eventurally metamorphosed into a political party (the People's Reform Party), which nominated Defensor Santiago for presidential candidate in the 1992 elections (Defensor Santiago

1994a: 197). The MOVERS organisation published several of her manuals suggesting practical solutions to everyday graft and corruption: *How to Fight Graft and Corruption* and *How to Fight Election Fraud* were both published in 1991 (Defensor Santiago 1991a, 1991b). In her 1992 election campaign, Defensor Santiago focussed on the reform of the culture of corruption as her campaign platform/issue. She had reached the top in the poll surveys without a political machine, without extensive funds and without the backing of major political families, an unprecedented achievement in a political system where all three were necessary prerequisites for victory. In the final election count she lost, but came a very strong second to President Fidel Ramos, who not only had a massive political machine and access to campaign funds, but had the backing of the previous administration.

Another prominent woman politician who has made moral issues a central focus of her political concerns is Senator Leticia Shahani, who founded the 'Moral Recovery Program' in 1988. She began the programme with Resolution No. 10 calling for a study of the strengths and weaknesses of the Filipino culture and character which would be necessary to solve the nation's current problems (Aquino 1991: 1). Since then there has been a major seminar on moral recovery and Shahani herself has published on the subject (both in English and Tagalog), distributing the publications from her own office (Shahani 1991, 1992). The gist of Shahani's message was that through an examination of Filipino values it would be possible to isolate the ones that have been detrimental to economic progress. Programmes should be designed to encourage the development of 'positive' traits for development (Shahani 1992: 64). Her programme developed a momentum of its own after it was launched officially by President Fidel Ramos (who happens to be the brother of Senator Shahani) with the NGO Kabisig movement its official implementing arm (Shahani 1993).

BEAUTY

The links between female beauty and power are almost palpable in the highly regulated institution of the Philippine beauty pageant. It was during the US occupation that beautiful women were first officially honoured with titles, beginning with the most prestigious title of Carnival Queen (of the Manila Carnival). During the Carnival two women shared the honour of Carnival Queen, one American and one Filipina (Nuyda 1980). It is a little more difficult to determine when town fiestas began to crown their town beauties. Even without the benefits of beauty contests the towns' beautiful women (or the women from prominent families) participated as Reynas (queens) during the annual May festivities in honour of the Virgin Mary, called the Santacruzan. The Carnival Queen contest then became 'Miss Philippines' after independence in 1945.

Many beauty queen titleholders have become politically powerful subsequently. Senator Maria Kalaw Katigbak was Carnival Queen in 1931 and was introduced as such in political campaigns. Edith Nakpil Rabat, one example of a politician's wife who became a politician herself, was Miss Philippines in 1955. Both Katigbak and Rabat were introduced in political rallies as former Miss Philippines titleholders (Katigbak Fabella 1994; Nakpil Rabat 1994). Another politician's wife who made the transition to politician as Governor of Tarlac, Margarita 'Ting-Ting' Cojuangco, was a famous model and regarded as one of the country's most beautiful women (Nuyda 1980).

Among politicians' wives, the very first First Lady of the post-war republic, Trinidad de Leon, was a former Carnival Queen. Mrs Marcos herself won two minor beauty titles, the 'Rose of Tacloban' in 1946 and the 'Muse of Manila' in 1952. The wife of former Defence Minister, former senator and now Congressman Juan Ponce Enrile, Cristina Castañer, was a well known model who held the minor title of La Flor de Manila in 1956 (Nuyda 1980). President Ramos's alleged former mistress, Rosemarie 'Baby' Arenas, was also a beauty queen, the 'Pearl of the Orient' (*Mirror Weekly* 22 August 1994: 11).

These links between beauty and power are not just a question of politicians needing to have camera presence in the television age. The many 'reinventions' of the image of Miriam Defensor Santiago in post-1986 politics, for example, show clearly that woman's political power is articulated upon her body (quite literally) in a specifically gendered way that does not apply to men.

Miriam Defensor Santiago's two autobiographies, *Inventing Myself* (Quezon City: New Day, 1994) and *Cutting Edge: The Politics of Reform in the Philippines* (Metro-Manila: Woman Today Publications, 1994) elaborate this connection between women's power and beauty. In *The Politics of Reform*, she discusses her image as Commissioner of Immigration and Deportation, her first political appointment. She describes how she transformed herself into a virtual male figure which she saw as befitting her role as Commissioner.

> I could not remain a pleasant, firm-spoken young female lawyer whom the crooks would parody and ridicule behind by back. I had to instill the fear of God among the apostate . . . It became evident that I had to shed my elegant barong and put on my battle armour.

> It was war, and what was needed was not a Portia in robes, but a Patton in combat fatigue. I ordered my hair cut close to my scalp, and bought myself a cheap wardrobe of short-sleeved blouses and flowing skirts that allowed maximum mobility. And yes, I secured a permit for a handgun . . . I became not only firm but also stern, and when a crooked employee tried to remonstrate, I learned to stand up to my full height, inhale a lungful of air, and cuss him heartily up and down.
>
> (Defensor Santiago 1994a: 127)

She became famous for uttering expletives such as 'I eat death threats for breakfast!' and 'Shut up or I'll knock your teeth off!' (Defensor Santiago 1991c: 2), insulting congressmen by announcing in the congressional building: 'Beam me up Scotty, there is no intelligent life down here' (Defensor Santiago 1991c: 16), and for saying of her rival presidential candidates 'they have all the intelligence of retarded political cockroaches' (Defensor Santiago 1991c: 28). She responded to those who threatened to kill her with: '*Kung papatayin man nila ako, mumultuhin ko sila*!' ('If they kill me my spirit will haunt them!' Defensor-Santiago 1991c: 23). This image was captured in a magazine cover which featured her looking through the barrel of a gun (*Asiaweek* 4 August 1989: cover page).

Some were clearly put off by Defensor Santiago's tough image and her intelligence. In a smear campaign against her during her presidential campaign in 1992, she was dubbed 'Brenda' (brain damaged) and 'Rita' (retarded) by those threatened by her audacity, her personality and her promises to put an end to corruption in government.

Just before she ran for the presidency, the media helped in another reinvention of Miriam Defensor Santiago. A reporter wanted to do a feature on her with photographs of her swimming. Although she asked that the pictures only show her actually swimming rather than her posing in a bathing suit, in the end the published photograph exposed her legs; these eventually began to be described as her most beautiful assets:

> There I was in all my bathing-suit glory, sitting on the edge of the pool, clasping my legs, and looking straight at the camera. It was a big photo, maybe five by seven inches, and it accompanied a one-page interview in question-and-answer form . . .
>
> The photo became a *cause célèbre*. My phone kept ringing that whole day, and my friends kept reporting on the latest news. It had spread like wildfire. Office phones were tied up for hours on end, as office workers raced to give each other the hot tip. Some offices

> were deserted as early as four o'clock in the afternoon because, unable to get a copy at the news stand, the men decided to knock off early, so they could look at the notorious photograph in their copies delivered at home. One golf course became unusually busy, even though it was a working day, as golf cronies decided to practise their shots while discussing the merits and demerits of the more visible members of my anatomy. A group of business executives raised money on the spot to place an order for next year's calendars featuring my photo. Eventually, at the end of the year, one of the country's most popular political satires on TV, *Mongolian Barbecue*, flashed the famous photograph on screen, and pronounced it Picture of the Year.
>
> (ibid: 190–1)

As she goes on to point out, the furore over the 'bathing suit' photo turned out to be to her advantage:

> Now, at that time I had been a cabinet member and I would say a potential presidential candidate. If I had been a male and appeared in swim trunks, I think that might have eliminated me from the presidential race . . . it looked like a cover girl pose. I wasn't swimming. I was sitting and holding my knees, you know what beauty queens usually do (laughter) and I was sort of smiling at the camera. Now if a male had done this, what looked like an artfully contrived picture, it may have destroyed him, but not in my case. In my case, people were saying, 'She's got a great figure or she's got beautiful legs!' So I was being analysed as a female.
>
> (Interview with Miriam Defensor Santiago, Quezon City, Metro-Manila, 27 January, 1993)

The link between beauty and women's political power became even more palpable to Defensor Santiago during the presidential campaign.

> [B]ecause you know in any campaign rally I had on the average of 20,000 to 50,000 people. That's a whole lot of people! And it was like a rock concert, it got hysterical. Because when I passed people would say 'Ang ganda pala niya!' (How beautiful she is!) Now don't worry, this never distorted my own self-perception. You see, do you understand, I want to try and explain, the public had preconceived ideas about me. It's because they wanted a deliverer, a saviour, and because I was female the female had to be beautiful. It's not possible that the country can be saved by an ugly female. So they were seeing what I had invented in their mind's eye. . . .

> I had been me all my life and nobody had ever called me beautiful. But, all of a sudden, when I became a presidential candidate I became beautiful. People – the moment I stepped off my vehicle, the lower economic class, the poor in other words, would say 'Ay, ang ganda, ang ganda!' (How pretty, how pretty). Now I understand why Imelda Marcos was so dressed up every time she appeared in public. . . . So for effect I decided to dress up. So a woman must dress up.
>
> (Interview with Miriam Defensor Santiago, Quezon City, Metro-Manila, 27 January, 1993)

From the gun-wielding woman who graced the cover of *Asiaweek* nicknamed 'Top Gun' (see Figure 10.1), Defensor Santiago altered her image, deliberately wearing scarlet dresses, make-up and a hair style that looked like she had just stepped out of the beauty parlour (see Figure 10.2). With little political infrastructure and almost no patronage she came a close second to Ramos in that election.

Naomi Wolf's *The Beauty Myth*, written within a Euro-American context, has something to offer to the analysis of the workings of feminine beauty in the Philippines. Philippine beauty codes require a thin body size, a full bosom and hips, and a body decked with fashionable clothes, adorned with a perfectly made-up face and hair-do. They also require expensive clothing, perfume, jewellery, high heeled shoes, manicured nails and coordinated accessories. But Wolf's main argument – captured in the book's subtitle 'How Images of Beauty are Used Against Women' – is too simplistic, at least for the Philippine context. Wolf sees the trappings of female beauty as mainly efforts to keep women feeling insecure, arguing that the professional beauty qualification (PBQ) undermines the seriousness of women's work:

> The message was finalised: the most emblematic working women in the West could be visible if they were 'beautiful,' even if they were bad at their work; they could be good at their work and 'unbeautiful' and therefore invisible, so their merit did them no good. In the last resort, they could be as good and as beautiful as you please – for too long; upon which, aging, they disappeared.
>
> (Wolf 1990: 35)

Although the outward trappings of this beauty (make-up, manicured nails, fashionable dresses, trim figure, neat, fashionable hairstyle, high heels and jewellery, etc.) that may be required of a Philippine woman are measured within the globalised standards epitomised by beauty contests and fashion magazines, my research suggests that female beauty

Figure 10.1 Miriam Defensor Santiago as 'Top Gun' on the cover of *Asiaweek*, 4 August 1989 (photograph of magazine cover by Doug Steley)

Figure 10.2 Miriam Defensor Santiago's image change as shown on the cover of the *Sunday Inquirer*, 8 September 1991 (photograph of magazine cover by Doug Steley)

can and frequently is mobilised by women in the Philippines in quite different, culturally specific ways. Moreover, the relation between power and beauty is dialectical, in the sense that beauty can be a source of power, but similarly closeness to power is also a source of beauty. A woman who abides by certain codes of appearance and behaviour can be perceived as beautiful, whatever her physical attributes, as long as she is associated with political power, Mrs Marcos was clearly wrong in denying any possibility that the widow in yellow, 'an un-made-up and un-manicured non-beauty' (*Mr and Ms* 1986: 1–2), would have a chance to defeat her husband in the 1986 snap elections. In the Philippine context, 'beauty' and power can be translated into each other, as in the case of a beauty queen who becomes a powerful politician or *malakas* woman, and the powerful woman is almost inevitably constructed as a beautiful woman. Corazon Aquino herself was never redefined as beautiful. But she came to power at precisely the moment when all that was associated with Mrs Marcos was under challenge – Cory Aquino was elected precisely because she was the antithesis of everything Mrs Marcos stood for, including the power–beauty articulation within her public identity. It is worth pointing out too that Mrs Aquino remained comparatively powerless throughout her reign despite the institutional symbols of her office.

SOME THOUGHTS ON GENDER, POWER AND MODERNITY

As mentioned earlier, the 'models' of female/male power and female/male images of power briefly presented here[4] are not fixed but fluid and shifting. In this final section I want to look at some of the tensions and accommodations between persistent Filipino cultural paradigms (particularly the *malakas/mahina* concept) discussed above, and globally circulating concepts of modernity, nationalism and globalisation. Abu-Lughod's work (1990), in a very different context, suggests that the woman's body is often at the centre of tensions between ideologies and paradigms struggling for dominance in a society. Similarly, Chapter 4 shows that ideas about femininity are central to the struggles over national self-definition. In line with such ideas, I would argue that, in the Philippines, the tensions between local and global paradigms of power and legitimacy are best observed in the discourses about women, as individuals and as a social category.

I have argued elsewhere (Roces 1990) that the colonial period introduced a new dynamic into Philippine politics: the modernist 'nationalist' idea that loyalty to the nation–state should be esteemed above the family produces conflict with the supposed primordialism of kinship politics. Western ideas of democracy, nationalism, the predominance of the nation-state over the family and the frowning on corruption and nepotism even triumphed over kinship politics at critical moments in Philippine history, like the 1986 revolution. This conflict between two sets of values in the post-war Philippines explains the cycles of administrations where one kinship group claims power, is overthrown because of charges of graft and corruption, only to be replaced by another regime riddled with the same culpabilities. Filipino politicians who use the clearly modernist rhetoric of loyalty to the nation-state to criticise others for graft and corruption might seem eminently 'modern', and indeed, exposing graft and corruption has been a characteristic trademark of politicians since 1945. Their behaviour once elected, however, suggests an ambivalent engagement with 'modernity'.

Women's power is one of the most significant sites where this contradiction is played out. Women's behind-the-scenes political power becomes one of the easiest targets of democratic rhetoric. The 'scandal' involving 'Baby' Arenas is a recent case in point. At the heart of the dispute was the contradiction between the practice of *malakas* and the Western democratic model of public behaviour.

In October 1993 the Centre for Investigative Journalism accused Mrs Rosemarie 'Baby' Arenas of using her past intimate relationship with President Ramos to exercise influence on government and to acquire concessions for friends, and of hosting a 'Wednesday Club' gathering at her home with officials close to the president to plot Malacanang strategy. The Wednesday Club was a group formed for the presidential campaign of Ramos in the 1992 elections, but it still continued to meet in the Arenas house even after his electoral victory in 1992. The journalists argued that Arenas' power was 'both real and perceived' and that her defence, that she was merely 'helping' and not 'meddling', betrayed her interference in political matters. In Arenas' mind, lobbying for the interests or requests of those who had helped or contributed in the campaign was to fulfil obligations. When asked in an interview if she would go to the presidential office to lobby for those who asked her for favours she replied: 'I really wished I have nothing to do with the campaign, [so that] the people will not come to me. For since I asked favours from them, now they come to me.' (Interview with Rosemarie 'Baby' Arenas, Makati, Metro-Manila, 16 February 1993).

Some time before the scandal broke, when asked whether women used 'unofficial power' because they did not have official power, she had said candidly: 'Yes, I think some, and one of them is me already. I'm always hiding, and yet I get attacked, pa.' (Interview with Rosemarie 'Baby' Arenas, Makati, Metro-Manila, 16 February 1993).

The problem with Arenas was not merely that she had exercised power in contravention of democratic institutions, but, more importantly, that she had refused to do so discreetly, as required in local practice. As one journalist, Rigoberto Tiglao observed, Mrs Arenas had broken one major rule in the etiquette for mistresses in Philippine culture – she had refused to remain silent in the background:

> And then, deliberately or not, Arenas has drawn even more attention to herself because of the high profile she maintains. She's been on the cover of four local magazines since 1992, and the guests at her charity fundraisers include the luminaries of Manila's elite.
>
> Arenas' critics, however, say that in being outspoken, she is breaking an unwritten rule in macho Philippine culture that calls for a mistress to remain silent. Her response: 'Not even the president can tell me what to do. Why should those people in Makati [the country's corporate centre] tell me to shut up?
>
> (Tiglao, *Far Eastern Economic Review* 24 March 1994: 66)

At the other end of the equation, female politicians' frequent involvement in exposés and crusades against graft and corruption is doubly legitimised through both the 'modern' discursive prioritising of the nation-state and in women's traditional gendered roles as moral guardians. Thus, Miriam Defensor Santiago, the most avid female campaigner against graft and corruption, can be seen as simultaneously a modern 'nationalist' 'gun-wielding' feminist and a woman performing the role ascribed to her gender.

Indeed, the Filipino political scene may be witnessing a peculiar negotiation between democracy as a global modernist ideology and what we might think of as a Filipino traditional practice, 'kinship politics'. Clearly there are scores of women's organisations in the Philippines today agitating for globalised ideas such as women's empowerment and increased representation, but it is the intersection of the democratic constitution of 1986 with 'kinship politics' that is opening up political offices for women. The new constitution of 1986 limits the term of office in the senate to two consecutive terms of 6 years each, and in the congress and local government to three terms of 3 years each. If a congressman can only serve for three terms (9 years) consecutively, but he wishes to retain the family's political privileges, he will clearly have to consider asking his wife (who, next to the congressman is usually the best known figure amongst the electorate) to run! Ironically, then, in the democratic Philippines, women will enter representational politics not through the influence of globalised ideas of various kinds of feminisms, nor through pressure for equal opportunity for women, but through the adjustments of kinship politics to constitutional rule.

We have argued throughout this book that inserting the figure of the woman into questions about modernity inevitably unsettles the category of 'modernity' itself. As my reading of contemporary Philippines suggests, women's engagement with the modern political system may best be promoted along 'old', reinvented trajectories of sex and power embedded in languages, metaphors and practices of the country.

NOTES

1 The discussion here derives from work on newspapers, periodicals and magazines, personal papers, campaign literature, speeches, autobiographies, written essays by *malakas* ('strong') women, interviews and field work. See Roces (1990).
2 See Pinches (1996) for one interpretation of the place of the rising middle classes in the Philippines.
3 Bienvenido Tantoco was made Ambassador to the Vatican, Gliceria Tantoco owned the Rustan's department store, Roman Cruz was a journalist, Cesar Zalamea and Jaime Laya were technocrats, Cesar Virata was also a technocrat who became Prime Minister to legitimise the martial law regime to the IMF and the World Bank, Carmen Guerrero Nakpil, Kerima Polotan and Ileana Maramag were all writers or journalists, Helen Benitez was a senator and President of the Philippine Women's University and Lucretia 'King' Kasilag was an ethnomusicologist and composer.
4 This chapter is part of a forthcoming monograph entitled *Women, Power and Kinship Politics in Post-war Philippines* (Connecticut: Praeger, 1998).

BIBLIOGRAPHY

Abu-Lughed, L. (1990) 'The Romance of Resistance: Tracing Transformations of Power Through Bedouin Women', *American Ethnologist* 17: 41–55.

Aguilar, C. (1992) 'Filipino Women in Electoral Politics', in Proserpina Domingo Tapales (ed.) *Filipino Women and Public Policy*, Manila: Kalikasan Press.

Aluit, A.J. (1972) *The Conscience of the Nation: A History of the Red Cross in the Philippines 1896–1972*, Manila: Philippine National Red Cross Silver Jubilee Edition.

Ancheta, H.M. and Beltran-Gonzalez, M. (eds) (1984) *Filipino Women in Nation-Building*, Quezon City: Phoenix Publishing House.

Anderson, B. (1972) 'The Idea of Power in Javanese Culture', in C. Holt (ed.) *Culture and Politics in Indonesia*, Ithaca: Cornell University Press.

Angara, G. (1993) interview with author, Manila.

Angara Castillo, B. (1994) interview with author, Manila.

Aquino, B. (ed.) (1991) *Moral Recovery and Philippine Development*, Metro-Manila: Raintree Trading and Publishing Inc.

Arenas, R. (1993) interview with author, Manila.

Asiaweek, 4 August, 1989, cover.

Atkinson, J. and Errington, S. (eds) (1990) *Power and Difference: Gender in Island Southeast Asia*, Stanford: Stanford University Press.

Benitez, H. (1967) File from the *Manila Times* Morgue, Lopez Memorial Museum, Manila.

Blanc-Szanton, C. (1990) 'Collision of Cultures: Historical Reformulations of Gender in the Lowland Iisayas, Philippines', in J. Atkinson and S. Errington (eds) *Power and Difference: Gender in Island Southeast Asia*, Stanford: Stanford University Press.

Bonner, R. (1987) *Waltzing with a Dictator: The Marcoses and the Making of American Foreign Policy*, New York: Random House.

CFSI (1993) 'What is the Congressional Spouses Foundation All About?', manuscript given to the author by Mrs Gina de Venecia, 29 January, Manila.

Cojuangco, G. (1993) interview with author, Manila.

Danguilan-Vitug, M. and Gloria, G. (1993) 'Past Relationship Impinges on Present Affairs of State', *Philippine Daily Inquirer*, 11 October: 1, 12–13.

Davidoff, L. and Hall, C. (1987) *Family Fortunes: Men and Women of the English Middle Class 1780–1850*, London: Hutchinson.

De Venecia, G. (1993) interview with author, Manila.

Defensor Santiago, M. (1991a) *How to Fight Graft and Corruption*, Metro-Manila: MOVERS.

—— (1991b) *How to Fight Election Fraud*, Metro-Manila: MOVERS.

—— (1991c) *The Miriam Defensor-Santiago Dictionary*, Makati: MOVERS Youth.

—— (1994a) *Cutting Edge: The Politics of Reform in the Philippines*, Metro-Manila: Woman Today Publications.

—— (1994b) *Inventing Myself*, Quezon City: New Day.

Esplanada, J. (1993) 'Baby A: Involved But Not Meddling', *Philippine Daily Inquirer*, 29 October: 1 and 10.

Far Eastern Economic Review, 24 March 1994: 66.

Far Eastern Economic Review, 10 November 1994: 12.

Gonzalez-Yap, M. (1987) *The Making of Cory*, Quezon City: New Day Publishers.

Guerrero Napkil, C. (1963) *Women Enough and Other Essays*, Quezan City: Vibol Publishing.

Hooper, B. (1994) 'Women, Consumerism and the State in Post-Mao China', *Asian Studies Review* 17(3): 73–83.

Jurado, E. (1993) 'The Backlash Favours Baby', *The Manila Standard*, 14 October: 10.

Kalaw, E. (n.d.) Kalaw File, Lopez Memorial Museum, Manila.

Katigbak, M. (1967) Katigbak File, Lopez Memorial Museum, Manila.

Katigbak Fabella, M. (1994) interview with author, Manila.

Lowe, V. (1994) 'Women in Arms: Representations of Vietnamese Women at War 1965–1975', paper presented at the Workshop on Southeast Asian Women, Monash University.

Macbeth, J. (1989) 'Time for Toughness', *Far Eastern Economic Review* 21 December: 11.

Mananzan, M.J. (1987) 'The Filipino Woman: Before and After the Spanish Conquest of the Philippines', in M.J. Mananzan (ed.) *Essays on Women*, Manila: Women's Studies Program, St. Scholastica's College.

Manapat, R. (1991) *Some Are Smarter Than Others: The History of Marcos' Crony Capitalism*, New York: Aletheia Publications.

Mercado, L.N. (1994) *The Filipino Mind*, Washington, DC: The Council for Research in Values and Philosophy and Divine Word Publications, Manila.

Mijares, P. (1976) *The Conjugal Dictatorship of Ferdinand and Imelda Marcos*, San Francisco: Union Square Publications.

Mirror Weekly, 22 August 1994: 11.

Nakpil-Rabat, E. (1994) interview with author, Manila.

Neher, C. (1982) 'Ambiguous Cebuana', in P. van Esterik (ed.) *Women of Southeast Asia*, DeKalb: Northern Illinois University Centre for Southeast Asian Studies, Occasional Paper No 9.

Nuyda, D. (1980) T*he Beauty Book: A History of Philippine Beauty from 1908–1980*, Manila: Mr and Ms. Publishing Company.

Ortner, S. and Whitehead H. (eds) (1981) *Sexual Meanings: The Cultural Construction of Gender and Sexuality*, Cambridge: Cambridge University Press.

Philippine Daily Inquirer, 30 October, 1993: 6.

Philippine Free Press, 20 September, 1947: 18.

Philippine Graphic, 30 July, 1993: 16.

Pinches, M. (1996) 'The Philippines New Rich: Capitalist Transformation Amidst Economic Gloom', in R. Robison and D. S. G. Goodman (eds) *The New Rich in Asia: Mobile Phones, McDonalds and Middle-class Revolution*, London: Routledge.

Ponce Enrile, C. (1994) interview with author, Manila.

Puyat Reyes, C. (1994) interview with author, Manila.

Rigoberto T. (1994) 'Controversial Woman: Profile of Rose Marie Jimenez de Arenas', *Far Eastern Economic Review*, 24 March: 66.

Roces, A. (1968) 'Faulty Yardstick', *The Manila Times*, 25 January: 4A.

Roces, A. and Roces, G. (1985) *Culture Shock Philippines*, Singapore: Times Books International.

Roces, M. (1990) 'Kinship Politics in Post-War Philippines: The Lopez Family, 1945–1989', Phd dissertation, University of Michigan.

—— (1991) 'Cultural Conflict as a Framework for Interpreting Philippine Post-War History', *Asian Studies Review* 15(2): 94–102.

—— (1994) 'Can Women Hold Power Outside the Symbols of Power?', *Asian Studies Review* 17(3): 14–23.

Rosaldo, M.Z. (1980) *Knowledge and Passion: Ilongot Notions of Self and Social Life*, Cambridge: Cambridge University Press.

Rosaldo, M.Z. and Atkinson J.M. (1975) 'Man the Hunter and Woman: Metaphors for the Sexes in Ilongot Magical Spells', in R. Willis (ed.) *The Interpretation of Symbolism*, London: Malaby Press.

Rosaldo, M.Z. and Lamphere, L. (eds) (1974) *Woman, Culture and Society*, Stanford: Stanford University Press.

San Diego, B. S. Jr (1992) 'The Importance of Being Baby Arenas', *Philippine Graphic*, 4 October: 10–13.

Shahani, L. (1991) 'Building a Filipino Nation', *The Power of Human Values*, np.

—— (1992) *Filipino Values and National Development Readings on the Moral Recovery Program*, Metro-Manila: Economic Development Foundation.

—— (1993) interview with author, Manila.

—— (n.d.) *Paghubog sa Mamamayan, Katatagan ng Bayan*, Metro-Manila: Senado ng Kongreso ng Pilipinas.

Stivens, M. (ed.) (1991) *Why Gender Matters in Southeast Asian Politics*, Melbourne: Monash Papers on Southeast Asia No. 23, Centre of Southeast Asian Studies, Monash University.

Sunday Inquirer Magazine, 8 September 1991, cover.

Sunday Times Magazine, 11 February 1962, Lopez Museum File on Maria Kalaw Katigbak.

Tancangco L.G. (1992) 'Voters, Candidates and Organizers: Women and Politics in Contemporary Philippines', in P.D. Tapales (ed.) *Filipino Women and Public Policy*, Manila: Kalikasan Press.

Tapales, P.D. (1984) 'Women in the Philippine Bureaucracy: Toward an Alternative Approach to the Study of Political Participation', PhD dissertation, Northern Illinois University.

—— (1992) 'Filipino Women in Politics and Public Affairs: Activism in the Patriarchal System', in P.D. Tapales (ed.) *Filipino Women and Public Policy*, Manila: Kalikasan Press.

Ungar, E. (1994) 'Gender, Land and Household in Vietnam', *Asian Studies Review*, 17(3): 61–72.

Weekly Graphic, 12 May 1965: 6–7.

Wolf, N. (1990) *The Beauty Myth*, London: Vintage.

Wolters, O. (1982) *History, Culture and Region in Southeast Asian Perspectives*, Singapore: Institute of Southeast Asian Studies.

—— (1988) *Dai-Viet in the Fourteenth Century*, New Haven: Yale University Southeast Asian Studies.

Zaldivar Perez, S. (1993) interview with author, Manila.

Ziga, T. (n.d.) Ziga File, Lopez Memorial Museum, Manila.

Index

Note: Page numbers in **bold** type refer to figures. Page numbers in *italic* type refer to tables. Page numbers followed by N refer to notes e.g. 119N.